AMERICAN ANTIFA

Since the election of President Trump and the rise in racist and white supremacist activity, the militant antifascist movement known as antifa has become increasingly active and high profile in the United States. This book analyzes the tactics, culture, and practices of the movement through a combination of social movement studies and critical criminological perspectives.

Based on extensive fieldwork and interviews with activists, this book is the first scholarly sociological analysis of contemporary antifascist activism in the United States. Drawing on social movement studies, subculture studies, and critical criminology, it explains antifa's membership, their ideology, strategy, tactics, and use of culture as a weapon against the far right. It provides the most detailed account of this movement and also cuts through much of the mythology and common misunderstandings about it.

This book will be of interest to scholars and students in sociology, political science, anthropology, criminology, and history; however, a general audience would also be interested in the explanation of what drives antifa tactics and strategy in light of the high-profile conflicts between fascists and anti fascists.

Stanislav Vysotsky is a sociologist whose research focuses on fascist and antifascist movements. Dr. Vysotsky's research on the militant antifascist movement and the relationship between threat, space, subculture, and social movement activism has been published in journals such as *Interface: A Journal for and about Social Movements* and *Critical Criminology*. He has also published research on fascist and supremacist movements in the *Journal of Political and Military Sociology*, the *Journal of Crime and Justice*, the *Journal of Hate Studies*, as well as several edited volumes.

ROUTLEDGE STUDIES IN FASCISM AND THE FAR RIGHT

Series editors
Nigel Copsey, Teesside University, UK and Graham Macklin, Center for Research on Extremism (C-REX), University of Oslo, Norway.

This new book series focuses upon fascist, far right and right-wing politics primarily within a historical context but also drawing on insights from other disciplinary perspectives. Its scope also includes radical-right populism, cultural manifestations of the far right and points of convergence and exchange with the mainstream and traditional right.

Titles include:

Researching the Far Right
Theory, Method and Practice
Edited by Stephen D. Ashe, Joel Busher, Graham Macklin and Aaron Winter

The Rise of the Dutch New Right
An Intellectual History of the Rightward Shift in Dutch Politics
Merijn Oudenampsen

Anti-fascism in a Global Perspective
Transnational Networks, Exile Communities and Radical Internationalism
Edited by Kasper Braskén, Nigel Copsey and David Featherstone

British Fascism After the Holocaust
From the Birth of Denial to the Notting Hill Riots 1939–1958
Joe Mulhall

American Antifa
The Tactics, Culture, and Practice of Militant Antifascism
Stanislav Vysotsky

For more information about this series, please visit: www.routledge.com/Routledge-Studies-in-Fascism-and-the-Far-Right/book-series/FFR

AMERICAN ANTIFA

The Tactics, Culture, and Practice of Militant Antifascism

Stanislav Vysotsky

Routledge
Taylor & Francis Group

LONDON AND NEW YORK

First published 2021
by Routledge
2 Park Square, Milton Park, Abingdon, Oxon OX14 4RN

and by Routledge
52 Vanderbilt Avenue, New York, NY 10017

Routledge is an imprint of the Taylor & Francis Group, an informa business

British Library Cataloguing-in-Publication Data
A catalogue record for this book is available from the British Library

Library of Congress Cataloging-in-Publication Data
Names: Vysotsky, Stanislav, 1973- author.
Title: American antifa : the tactics, culture, and practice of militant anti-fascism / Stanislav Vysotsky.
Description: Abingdon, Oxon ; New York, NY : Routledge, 2020. |
Series: Fascism and the far right | Includes bibliographical references and index.
Identifiers: LCCN 2020004588 (print) | LCCN 2020004589 (ebook) |
ISBN 9780367210571 (hardback) | ISBN 9780429265174 (ebook)
Subjects: LCSH: Antifa (Organisation) | Radicalism--United States. |
Anti-fascist movements--United States.
Classification: LCC HN90.R3 V87 2020 (print) | LCC HN90.R3 (ebook) |
DDC 303.48/4--dc23
LC record available at https://lccn.loc.gov/2020004588
LC ebook record available at https://lccn.loc.gov/2020004589

ISBN: 978-0-367-21057-1 (hbk)
ISBN: 978-0-367-21060-1 (pbk)
ISBN: 978-0-429-26517-4 (ebk)

Typeset in Bembo
by Taylor & Francis Books

CONTENTS

1 Introduction   1

2 Fascists and antifascists: A countermovement overview   26

3 Fascist and antifascist tactics   71

4 "Sometimes anti-social, always antifascist": Antifa culture   105

5 Fascist threat and antifascist action   128

6 The anarchy police (revisited): A critical criminology of antifa   146

7 Antifa unmasked: A sociological and criminological
   understanding   168

Appendix – Against Methodology: Ethnography, Autoethnography,
and the Intimately Familiar   *175*
Bibliography   *186*
Index   *206*

1

INTRODUCTION

It was the punch memed around the world. On January 20, 2017, as Donald Trump was ascending to the presidency of the United States and protests raged in the streets of Washington, DC, Richard Spencer, the media gadfly who coined the term "alt-right," was filmed being punched in the face by a masked, black clad protester. The image became an instant social media sensation generating endless memes, debates about the utility and ethics of punching fascists, and public awareness of a social movement that had largely operated underground – the militant antifascist movement, or antifa. In many ways, 2017 would become the year of antifa as supremacists, emboldened by the president and his administration, began mobilizing, so did counter-protesters who sought to oppose or prevent such mobilizations. High profile clashes between "alt-right" protesters and antifa counter-protesters occurred in Berkeley, CA, Portland, OR, and, most notably, Charlottesville, VA. Here militant antifascists defended pacifist protesters from fascist violence and successfully routed a supremacist rally, only to suffer violent reprisals in the form of targeted attacks on individuals and the intentional ramming of a crowd, resulting in the death of one person and the injury of 19 more. Charlottesville left many people asking questions about antifa activism and speculating about its strategies and methods.

Antifascism is simultaneously a complex and simple political phenomenon. At its core is a basic notion, the opposition to fascism. This generates a series of more complex debates about both what constitutes fascism as well as opposition to it. In the broadest sense, antifascism can be understood as "a thought, an attitude or feeling of hostility toward fascist ideology and its propagators which may or may not be acted upon" (Copsey 2000, 4). Such a definition takes an extremely broad view that antifascism is both an "active and passive" form of opposition that can incorporate a range from individual activists and collective groups to mass media and the state. An alternative framework views antifascism through the lens of activism distinguishing between non-fascists, that is individuals and groups that simply oppose fascism from an ideological or practical consideration and/or are not open fascists, and antifascists who actively organize to oppose fascist activity and mobilizations (Renton 1998). Antifa activism lends itself much more to the latter framework than the former; however, it may be useful to make an additional distinction between non-militant and militant antifascism. While both forms of antifascism involve some type of action in response to fascist movements, militants are defined by their willingness to use confrontational means, including violence, as part of their tactical repertoire (Vysotsky 2013). The sociological analysis of militant antifascists in this book reflects a synthesis of these three perspectives. Antifa can best be understood as activists who organize direct, confrontational opposition to fascism out of a distinct ideological and/or emotional response. The dynamics of militant antifascism are therefore driven by a series of ideological, emotional, and cultural processes that explain both movement formation and tactical preferences.

Additionally, an understanding of antifa must distinguish between formal and informal militant antifascism. Informal antifascism involves ad hoc and spontaneous activities that confront immediate threats posed by fascists. Much of this activism takes place outside of the public eye in subcultures and the underground spaces that they inhabit. Formal forms of antifascism consist of the activities of groups and organizations that distinctly focus on opposition to fascist organizing. These groups have clear membership structures and guidelines and work to strategically undermine fascist organizing. These two forms of antifascist activism are not mutually exclusive. As we shall see, there is significant overlap between formal and informal antifascism in the work of antifa activists. Individuals often come to formal antifascism through informal activity, and informal forms of activism are often driven by the active proliferation of antifascist politics within subcultural spheres.

Classical analyses of social movements often focus on the way in which movements engage with state and economic actors in an attempt to influence policy changes (Fitzgerald and Rodgers 2000; Jasper 2010). The "grand theories" of social movement activity have similarly looked at the way in which such changes are driven by macro forces such as political process and access to resources. Increasingly, social movement theory focuses on micro processes such as the role of emotion, interactions, and culture in movement dynamics (Jasper 2010). However, all such theories consistently analyze movements that are petitioning state or economic actors for change. Even the literature on countermovements or, more commonly, opposing movements, often looks at movements that operate on two sides of a policy domain rather than as movements developed in direct opposition to one another (Meyer and Staggenborg 1996; Zald and Useem 1987). In this respect, analysis of antifa activism is fundamentally unique in its examination of social movement activity. Unlike most opposing movements, antifascists are exclusively oriented in opposition to another social movement, or what could be more broadly described as an ideology. In many respects, this means that antifa activism represents an almost ideal-typical version of a countermovement. Militant antifascists are focused on opposing the movement activities of fascists rather than on working to develop state policies that address such movements. Their strategies and tactics are singularly focused on subverting the activity of fascists in any form. As such they are at best skeptical of state intervention, and more often outright hostile to it. Unlike most social movements, even other radical ones, militant antifascists "do not rely on cops or courts" and "go where they go" in their resistance to fascists. This dynamic of movement resistance often takes the form of (sub)cultural work and the active policing of cultural boundaries.

The primary question regarding antifa activism in popular discourse is one of tactical choice. Why do these antifascists purposely include violent and confrontational tactics in their movement repertoire? What dynamics drive militant antifascist tactical choices? What are the purposes of this use of confrontational and violent tactics in opposing fascist organizing and mobilizations? By framing antifascism as both a subcultural and social movement phenomenon, this book seeks to expand the framework of social movement studies by analyzing its intersections with the fields of subculture studies as well as cultural and critical criminology. In order to understand these dynamics, we must first address the historical processes that led to the contemporary incarnation of American antifascism.

Antifascism in the United States: a history and overview

Historical fascism and antifascism are often viewed as a European phenomenon. The term fascism is, after all, an Italian one coined by Benito Mussolini for his nationalist movement in 1919. As fascist movements developed in Italy, Germany, and throughout Europe, anarchist, communist, and socialist activists mobilized against them (Bray 2017; Testa 2015). Leftists often understood the struggle against fascism as an existential one, and they turned to militancy as a distinct model for opposing fascist organizing. Wherever fascist movements developed, they were often met with direct confrontation and even violence as a means of destabilizing them and demobilizing their supporters (Bray 2017; Copsey 2000; Renton 2001; Testa 2015).

The history of American fascism and antifascism is much murkier than its European counterparts. The United States, like Great Britain, has not experienced a period of formal fascist government, but traditions of authoritarianism, right-wing populism, and white supremacy run deep in American history and political life (Berlet and Lyons 2000; Burley 2017; Ross 2017). Militant antifascism in the United States draws on a history unique to the American experience including radical abolitionism, resistance to the Ku Klux Klan, African American self-defense, and the growth of domestic fascist movements, as well as the experience of their European counterparts.

The historical role of slavery in the formation of white supremacy and the "racialized social system" of contemporary American society (Omi and Winant 2014; Bonilla-Silva 2018) informs part of the contemporary framework of antifascism. The abolitionist movement represents in many respects a proto-antifascist movement because it is viewed, at least in part, as opposing white supremacy through its advocacy of the end of slavery and the rights of people of African descent in the antebellum era. Because of its advocacy of moral enlightenment and legal reform, in addition to its stalwart pacifism, the abolitionist movement may be understood as an early form of "liberal" or even "state" antifascism (Bray 2017; Burley 2017; Copsey 2000). Militant antifascists look to abolitionists' most radical factions for inspiration and especially venerate the actions of John Brown whose activism against slavery culminated in the raid of a federal armory in Harper's Ferry, Virginia (now West Virginia) with the objective of arming and fomenting a mass rebellion against slavery. Brown symbolizes the willingness to wage "war against slavery, working closely with black people and the hope that [white anti-racists] can step outside of their color and take part in building a new human community" (Garvey et al. 1999, 1). This type of bold action to oppose white supremacy is understood by many contemporary militant antifascists as a historical antecedent to their fight against white supremacists at the core of the contemporary fascist movement.

In the wake of the Civil War, the formation of the Ku Klux Klan and other organizations of white supremacist reaction to reconstruction serve as the historical originators of organized American fascist organizations (Berlet and Lyons 2000; Bray 2017; Burley 2017; Ridgeway 1995; Ross 2017). Formed as a fraternal organization by Confederate veterans shortly after the end of the war, the Klan spread quickly throughout the South as a means of terrorizing African Americans and their allies in Reconstruction and laid the groundwork for a culture of lynching and racial violence that would in part define the Jim Crow era and nearly a century of American history. Klan activity consisted of a series of mobilizations and demobilizations that can roughly be referred to as unique eras each with its own structure, tactics, and ideology: the first Klan (1867 to early 1870s), the second Klan (1915 to mid-1920s), the third Klan (1950s–1960s), and the fourth Klan (1970s–present). The first three eras of the Klan could not be accurately described as explicitly fascist, in part because the term itself would only be coined during the group's second era; however, the form of nationalist white supremacy that they advocated ideologically aligned with more explicitly fascist movements in Europe and the United States. The first two eras of the Klan could be described as proto-fascist, whereas the third era represents a transition phase, and contemporary fourth era formations explicitly embrace fascist and Nazi ideology and imagery (Belew 2018; Berlet and Lyons 2000; Burley 2017; Ridgeway 1995; Ross 2017). Opposition to the Klan, therefore, is a crucial pillar of American antifascist history.

Resistance to each manifestation of the Klan involved a diverse range of tactical approaches ranging from campaigns to criminalize the organization and the practice of lynching more broadly to armed self-defense by African Americans. In response to violence and intimidation by Southern whites, black self-defense organizations developed as early as the reconstruction era. Many of these organizations were based on the Union Leagues, black fraternal organizations that "became the voice and instrument of newly freed slaves" (Cobb 2014, 41), which often included armed defense of meetings and community events from racist attacks. This tradition of African American self-defense carried over into the Civil Rights movement where individuals (including Martin Luther King, Jr.) and organizations such as the Deacons for Defense and autonomous chapters of the NAACP asserted their right to armed self-defense against white racist terror (Cobb 2014; Hill 2004; R. F. Williams 1998). It is specifically this tradition of self-defense that inspired the Black Panther Party (BPP) to demonstrate publicly asserting their right to openly carry firearms in protest against police violence against the African American community and the systemic racism of American society. The BPP identified the actions of police and the white supremacist system specifically as fascism, explicitly defining their activity as a form of antifascism (Burley 2017).

While the Klan represents the most persistent fascist movement in American history, European-style fascism also made in-roads into the United States generating a vigorous antifascist response. In 1933, the Friends of New Germany was founded as an official organ of Nazi Germany in the United States. The organization operated for several years with strong support in New York and Chicago. This group formally disbanded in 1936 and its members were incorporated into the German American Bund led by Fritz Kuhn, a German immigrant who had been naturalized as a US citizen. The activities of the Bund quickly attracted the attention of antifascist activists primarily from communist and socialist parties as well as Jewish communities in the cities in which it organized. Meetings of the Bund in New York, Newark, Chicago, and Milwaukee were routinely stormed by socialist and communist opposition who violently attacked attendees (Berninger 1988; Bernstein 2014). Among the most militant opposition to the Bund were notorious Jewish gangsters like Meyer Lansky, Abner Zwillman, Benjamin "Bugsy" Siegel, and Meyer "Mickey" Cohen who recruited their toughest and often most brutal compatriots into antifascist action against the Bund in order to protect their communities (Bernstein 2014). These men ruthlessly smashed fascist meetings and attendees in acts of intimidation designed to demobilize the American Nazi movement. The peak of the Bund, and ironically its antifascist opposition, came in 1939 when 20,000 people attended a mass meeting in Madison Square Garden in order to ostensibly celebrate George Washington's birthday. This event featured speeches by Kuhn and his deputies on a stage decorated in red, white, and blue, an image of Washington, and banners that declared him to be America's first fascist. While the fascists rallied inside, 100,000 protesters massed outside engaging in skirmishes with police and Bund supporters. As Kuhn delivered his address, Isadore Greenbaum stormed the stage and attacked him in an act of futile antifascist defiance. Bund guards rushed to defend their leader and began pummeling Greenbaum, "It was an uncanny replication of Nazi street thuggery, a pack of uniformed men blasting away with fists and boots on a lone Jewish victim" (Bernstein 2014, 189). Police intervened and took Greenbaum into custody, but he fought against them in what contemporary militant antifascists would term a "three-way fight" (Bray 2017; Burley 2017) against both fascists and the state. The Bund collapsed shortly after this rally when Kuhn was imprisoned after being charged with embezzlement from the organization by the state of New York and membership declined with the entry of the United States into the Second World War. The public reaction to the German American Bund demonstrated the mass appeal of antifascism and the possibility of mobilizing militant opposition.

Post-war antifascism in the United States largely manifested in the Civil Rights movement. Its most militant forms were led by African American mobilizations for armed self-defense discussed above. The largely white student movement of the New Left took inspiration from the pacifist mobilizations of the Civil Rights movement and engaged in classroom and administrative building occupations as a form of protest against racism and the Vietnam War. As students experienced repression through arrest and dead ends in negotiations with college and university administrations, they took on more militant protest tactics engaging in conflicts with police. Informed by a countercultural anti-authoritarianism and Maoist anti-imperialism, the New Left often shared an analysis of fascism that extended well beyond American populist white supremacists to condemnation of all aspects of American capitalism. For these student protesters, the entire capitalist system built on racism and imperialism represented a kind of fascism (Varon 2004). It is during this era of radical protest in the 1960s and 1970s that fascism became diluted in the American popular conception to refer to any form of illiberalism or authoritarianism. Opposition to fascism essentially came to mean a kind of generic and symbolic anti-authoritarianism, an issue that plagues the antifascist movement to this day (Burley 2017).

The Workers Viewpoint Organization, which ultimately came to be known as the Communist Workers' Party (CWP), developed out of the experience of New Left activists of the 1960s and 1970s; but unlike their compatriots who turned to underground terrorism or academic pursuits and campus organizing, these activists focused on organizing workers within their workplaces (Waller 2002). In Greensboro, North Carolina, organizers had been making in-roads in the textile mills and building anti-racist coalitions of black and white workers. In July 1979 CWP members disrupted a Klan rally and the screening of the notorious racist film *Birth of a Nation*. Building on this success, they organized a rally and march against racism under the banner of "Death to the Klan" on November 3 of that year. Local Klansmen and members of the American Nazi Party organized a "United Racist Front" to take on the demonstrators. As the antifascist marchers gathered, several vehicles full of armed fascists approached the rally and opened fire. A handful of antifascists armed with pistols attempted to defend themselves, but when the smoke cleared five protesters had been murdered by fascists and another ten had been injured (Bray 2017; Burley 2017; Waller 2002). The "Greensboro Massacre" represents a low-point for American antifascism and an important lesson carried to this day. There is speculation that the lack of law enforcement intervention that day may have been driven by a strategic desire on the part of the state to repress the organizing activity of the CWP. Although local and federal law enforcement were working with informants in the Klan and were aware of their plans, they did little to intervene and may have encouraged the actions of the Klan (Waller 2002). For antifascists, the tragedy at Greensboro indicated both the potential collusion between fascists and the state and the limitations of small-scale and non-violent opposition to fascist movements.

The John Brown Anti-Klan Committee (JBAKC) took the lessons of the Greensboro Massacre to heart and represents the transition point between historical and contemporary American antifascism. Formed in 1978 by former Weather Underground and other Maoist and far-left organizations, the JBAKC "took the lesson that a community self-defense project and mass organizing model needed to be combined, where white antiracists needed to step up in support of black neighbors securing their neighborhood [from supremacist threat]" (Bray 2017; Burley 2017, 208). The decision to name the organization after John Brown was a conscious move designed to demonstrate the willingness of its members to engage in confrontational tactics in opposition to white supremacy.[1] The organization built its support base through the publication of a newspaper initially titled *Death to the Klan*, which was later renamed *No KKK – No Fascist USA* (a lyric from the Punk band MDC that is an antifascist rallying cry to this day) in order to appeal to the growing subcultural antifascism of the 1980s. Yet, the JBAKC was in most respects a militant organization that encouraged the direct, even violent mass confrontation of supremacists, "In 1983, they helped organize a counterdemonstration of 1,200 people who confronted the KKK amid a hail of rocks" (Bray 2017, 68). In cities such as Chicago, they consistently "overwhelm[ed] Klan and skinhead gangs like Romantic Violence at public appearances despite the racists showing up with wooden shields lined with razor blades" (Burley 2017, 208–209). Their relative success throughout the 1980s made the JBAKC a model for future antifascist organizations in the United States that would ally with them and learn from their organizing experience.

The origins of the contemporary antifascist movement in the United States are rooted in the subcultural underground of the 1980s and 1990s. This section has outlined the long history of opposition to supremacist movements in America, but a direct lineage can be drawn to today's antifa activists from the efforts to combat racist involvement in punk, skinhead, and metal subcultures in those decades (Bray 2017; Burley 2017). The earliest forms of this resistance were often informal sentiments and mobilizations. As American punks adopted the imagery of their European counterparts, some took to incorporating the politics of fascism along with the swastika symbol. Punk antifascism was famously enshrined in the Dead Kennedys' now classic anthem "Nazi Punks Fuck Off," which came packaged with an armband that featured a crossed-out swastika and the song title. The sentiment would be repeated by numerous bands and individual punks across the nation throughout the 1980s in a relatively disorganized manner.

The first organized antifascist activism in the American punk and skinhead subculture would appear in the mid to late 1980s. An informal multi-ethnic group of skinheads in New York formed an official group under the name Skinheads Against Racial Prejudice (SHARP) in 1987 partially in response to the media moral panic regarding racist Skinheads. Members of SHARP wanted to present a history of the skinheads as a multi-racial, working-class subculture with roots in

Jamaican Rude Boy style and ska music. The group also vigorously opposed racist skinhead organizing within punk and skinhead subcultures utilizing violence when necessary. As skinheads who were opposed to racism and fascism learned of the organization through fanzines and music, it developed into a global phenomenon that exists to this day (Bray 2017; E. Wood 2017). Part of the strength of SHARP was its informal organizational structure. While the original founders maintained a post office box in New York in the late 1980s and early 1990s, there was no formal criteria for membership. Individuals and groups can identify as SHARP simply if they are affiliated with skinhead subculture and oppose the racist factions within it. This allows SHARP to proliferate without formal organization or coordination, which has significant implications for the broader antifascist movement in terms of a recruitment and a support base predisposed to opposition to fascist subcultural organizing.

American antifascism would be formalized in the Anti-Racist Action network (ARA), which also had its roots in anti-racist skinhead subculture. Beginning in late 1987, a multi-ethnic skinhead crew from Minneapolis, known as the Baldies, built a small regional network with like-minded skinheads in Milwaukee, Chicago, and throughout the Midwest. The network was modeled on the European Antifascist Action groups that had developed throughout the 1980s, but chose to call itself Anti-Racist Action because the term fascism did not resonate in the American political climate of the time (Bray 2017). Because of its diffuse network model, ARA was able to expand rapidly by incorporating like-minded individuals and groups within the punk subculture and ideologically similar militants from anarchist and Marxist organizations. In order to affiliate with ARA, a group or individual simply needed to adhere to a set of core "Points of Unity":

> 1. We go where they go. Whenever fascists are organizing or active in public, we're there. We don't believe in ignoring them or staying away from them. Never let the Nazis have the street!
> 2. We don't rely on the cops or courts to do our work for us. This doesn't mean we never go to court, but the cops uphold white supremacy and the status quo. They attack us and everyone who resists oppression. We must rely on ourselves to protect ourselves and stop the fascists.
> 3. Non-sectarian defense of other anti-fascists. In ARA, we have a lot of different groups and individuals. We don't agree about everything and we have a right to differ openly. But in this movement an attack on one is an attack on us all. We stand behind each other.
> 4. We support abortion rights and reproductive freedom. ARA intends to do the hard work necessary to build a broad, strong movement against racism, sexism, anti-Semitism, homophobia, discrimination against the disabled, the oldest, the youngest and the most oppressed people. We want a classless, free society. We intend to win!

(Burley 2017, 198)

Using these basic principles as a basis for organizing and mobilization, ARA was able to build a militant resistance to fascist organizing that included dozens of formally organized chapters and thousands of individuals. The network could readily mobilize to confront some of the largest and most active fascist organizations in the 1990s including the World Church of the Creator (currently known as the Creativity movement) and the National Alliance. The ARA network would serve as the backbone of the contemporary militant antifascist movement in the United States.

The first American group to formally use the antifascist label was Northeast Antifascists based out of Boston and founded in 2002. While they were officially part of the ARA network, the group chose not to use the anti-racist label because several founding members came from European antifa traditions and as a conscious response to a critique of ARA that it did not focus on institutional forms of racism in favor of populist supremacist mobilizations. Northeast Antifa, as it was called by its members and allies, addressed this critique by reframing the terms of its activism. In this case, the group formally oriented its mission toward opposition to fascist movement organizing while its members often addressed issues of structural racism in other organizations and networks.

Inspired by the nominal shift of this Boston group and a similar European antifascist influence, Portland based activists were the first to adopt the shortened version of antifascist in naming their group Rose City Antifa (RCA). RCA affiliated with the ARA network at a time when the American antifascist movement was at a lull, in part because of its own success in confronting fascists (Bray 2017). Portland, despite its reputation as a hub of liberal creativity, had retained a vibrant underground fascist movement that RCA confronted with campaigns of public shaming and protest that were often controversial. Gradually, groups in the ARA network made similar name shifts as new groups using the antifa name affiliated with the network, and existing groups adopted the label in their names. Driven in part by an ideological shift, and in part by a reorganization effort by American antifascists, a number of former ARA network groups formed the Torch Antifa network in 2013. As the direct descendent of ARA, Torch Antifa retained much of its spirit in its points of unity:

1. We disrupt fascist and far right organizing and activity.
2. We don't rely on the cops or courts to do our work for us. This doesn't mean we never go to court, but the cops uphold white supremacy and the status quo. They attack us and everyone who resists oppression. We must rely on ourselves to protect ourselves and stop the fascists.
3. We oppose all forms of oppression and exploitation. We intend to do the hard work necessary to build a broad, strong movement of oppressed people centered on the working class against racism, sexism, nativism, anti-Semitism, Islamophobia, homophobia, transphobia, and discrimination against the disabled, the oldest, the youngest, and the most oppressed people. We support abortion rights and reproductive freedom. We want a classless, free society. We intend to win!

4. We hold ourselves accountable personally and collectively to live up to our ideals and values.
5. We not only support each other within the network, but we also support people outside the network who we believe have similar aims or principles. An attack on one is an attack on all.

As fascist mobilizations increased throughout the 2016 presidential campaign and into the first year of the Trump presidency, so too did antifascist mobilizations. The Torch network grew as new chapters joined in a climate of emboldened fascism, and informal antifascist mobilizations have been bolstered by the experience and activism of seasoned antifa activists. Yet, in order to understand militant antifascism, one cannot simply look to the past as a prologue. Contemporary antifascist activism is best viewed through the prism of the sociological dynamics that animate the militancy of activists who take up the antifa banner. Antifa activism may be understood as social movement, subculture, and force of protection.

Thinking about antifa: social movements, subcultures, and criminology

As a sociological phenomenon, antifa activism defies simple categorization. It's basic mission, to confront fascist organizing and mobilization efforts, would classify it as a social movement. Yet, the context of a great deal of antifascist activity is situated within subcultures and involves a large portion of cultural work to challenge fascism. To complicate the analysis even further, militant antifascism is criminalized and stigmatized by a range of people precisely because it is subcultural, radical, and confrontational. Finally, antifa activism often serves as a means of self-defense against the threats and violence of fascist activists. In order to understand the complex dynamics of antifascism discussed in this book, it is necessary to move beyond the boundaries of traditional sub-fields of sociology. The analysis of antifa in subsequent chapters is informed by, and ultimately synthesizes, concepts from social movement studies, subculture studies, and critical criminology. A holistic analysis of militant antifascism is achieved by incorporating these disparate fields of analysis.

Social movements

At the core of this analysis of antifa activism is an understanding that it is a social movement. In order to accurately assess militant antifascism, it must be understood first and foremost as a radical social movement that operates in a manner that is outside of the bounds of normative social movement processes. This leads to a unique dynamic between antifascists and their fascist opposition that represents an almost ideal-typical movement-countermovement interaction because it exists outside of the realm of policy or state appeals. As a radical countermovement, militant antifascists deploy a series of tactics that reflect their ideological position as well as practical strategic concerns. These tactics are consistent with sociological analyses of new social movements (NSMs) and the deployment of culture and emotion in social movement activity.

Radical social movements

The structure, actions, and culture of militant antifascism are best understood in an analytical framework which recognizes that it is a radical social movement. Much of the social scientific scholarship on social movements has traditionally been biased toward the activity of reform oriented social movement organizations (SMOs). Kathleen Fitzgerald and Diane Rodgers (2000, 577) indicate that radical social movement organizations (RSMOs) are distinguished from other more moderate social movement organizations by their unique forms of "structure, ideology, tactics, communication, and definitions of success." As a radical social movement, militant antifascism isn't easily categorized by existing models developed in the social movements canon.

RSMOs often avoid the hierarchical, bureaucratic structure of more moderate social movements in favor of a more decentralized model where power is distributed horizontally. This is often an intentional practice that centers individual participation and where "indigenous" leadership is developed through experience and action (Fitzgerald and Rodgers 2000, 578). As we shall see in Chapter 2, such a model is reflected in the organizational structure of antifascist groups and serves to explain in part the ability of militant antifascism to rapidly mobilize in response to public fascist mobilizations.

The ideology of moderate SMOs is based on enacting reforms to the existing economic, political, and/or social system. As a result, they will engage in non-violent, legal action. On the other hand, RSMOs have an agenda that emphasizes structural change. Rather than relying on existing structures, RSMOs seek to form solidarity networks and rely on building global consciousness and connections to replace structures that they see as fundamentally flawed. As such, RSMOs are critical of, if not outright hostile to, the state and the use of state power to resolve contentious issues. Because they do not rely upon the state, RSMOs engage in non-legalistic, direct action to affect change. They are also more likely to innovate their tactical repertoire because RSMOs possess "the freedom of being not constrained by moderate financial supporters" (Fitzgerald and Rodgers 2000, 584) or a desire to not alienate the state and other potential allies within the system. Because of this dynamic, the tactics of RSMOs are sometimes intentionally designed to bring attention to the group and the specific grievances that it has. While moderate SMOs have direct access to and are able to rely on mainstream forms of communication, RSMOs are often ignored and/or misrepresented by the mainstream media. Therefore, RSMOs rely on alternative forms of communication that are often both part of their tactical repertoire and the culture of the organization – music, street theater, pamphlets, newsletters, and the internet serve as means of communication for such movements (Fitzgerald and Rodgers 2000). Militant antifascists frequently rely on unconventional tactics and cultural work in order to effectively oppose fascist mobilization and organization consistent with the model of radical social movements. This activism often reflects a radical orientation as well as the subcultural framework discussed later in this chapter.

Countermovements

Since militant antifascists organize specifically in opposition to fascist social movement activity, they represent an ideal-typical example of a countermovement. Perhaps the most thorough outline of the concept of countermovements was developed by Meyer Zald and Bert Useem (1987), which delves into the complexity of movement-countermovement dynamics by situating them in a theoretical framework, analyzing their patterns of mobilization, and explaining their tactical choices through a framework of strategic goals.

In order to understand militant antifascist activity, we can apply the countermovement model of mobilization and demobilization. Countermovement activity is designed to achieve three distinct strategies: damage or destruction of the other group, preemption or dissuasion of group mobilization, and recruitment of the other group's members. Damage or destruction is used primarily to "try to raise the cost of mobilization for the other group" (Zald and Useem 1987, 260). These actions include, but are not limited to, gathering information, limiting the flow of resources, portraying the movement in a negative light, and direct attacks against the movement. Preemptive strategies are developed "in ways that undercut the moral and political basis of a mobilization or counter mobilization" (Zald and Useem 1987, 264). Such strategies are designed to put opponents on the defensive and force them to act in response to the mobilizing movement's actions potentially placing them in the undesirable position of being an immoral or inappropriate actor. Finally, persuasion and recruitment involve attempts by social movements to convince members of opposing movements to disengage from their commitments to a movement and actively work for the opposition. While this tactic is difficult in the short term, it is useful in a long-term struggle and aids in the effectiveness of the other tactics discussed. By focusing on subverting fascist activity, much of the work of militant antifascists may be classified as guided by these strategic goals.

Rather than analyzing movements as countermovements, scholars have shifted to an "opposing movements" model that sees them as operating in a similar political sphere on a common issue that affects them (Meyer and Staggenborg 1996). The dynamic between antifascists and fascists is a clear indication of this opposing movements concept. Both movements developed on opposite sides of political and social debates around a number of economic, political, and social issues. The most obvious of these issues often being the fight for racial, ethnic, religious, gender, and sexual equality. However, fascists and antifascists also operate on a political and social terrain that seeks to resolve crises of economic inequality, deindustrialization, globalization, foreign military intervention, and even environmental destruction. What makes this dynamic unique is the distinct focus on antifascism as an oppositional movement against fascist movements and ideology. In this sense, antifascism always finds itself in the role of countermovement because the initiating factor in this dynamic is fascist mobilization. While the dynamics between the two movements represent those of opposing movements, antifa activists generally represent a countermovement in their motivations and activities.

New social movements

In the context of the broader theoretical framework of social movements, new social movements (NSM) theory and the "cultural" turn in social movement analysis are clearly applicable to the analysis of militant antifascism. The (sub)cultural activism of antifa focuses on identity, operates outside of traditional left-right political dichotomies, and engages in cultural activity as political activity (Johnston, Laraña, and Gusfield 1994).

Unlike their historical predecessors, NSMs place a high priority on the development of collective and personal identity, as well as social activism, as fundamental to individual lifestyle. NSMs traditionally cluster around broad identities such as age cohort (youth), gender, or sexual orientation or develop broad based concerns like nuclear disarmament or environmental protection (Johnston, Laraña, and Gusfield 1994). Because of this potentially broad support base and constituency, NSMs have developed belief systems that do not follow traditional ideological boundaries of left and right in favor of more autonomist or even anarchist ideologies. NSM activists propose practical solutions and greater democracy in political and economic decision-making processes (J. L. Cohen 1985; Johnston, Laraña, and Gusfield 1994; Melucci 1985; Offe 1985). Rather than engaging in mass social protest, social movement membership is seen as an action in and of itself. This process transforms everyday experiences into political activities. To paraphrase a cliché, for NSMs the personal becomes the political. As a result, NSMs tend to reject traditional, mass-based political parties, labor unions, and SMOs because they view them as centralized and bureaucratic. Instead, they advocate for organization in decentralized, diffuse, and segmented groups (Johnston, Laraña, and Gusfield 1994). The preferred model of organization within NSMs is a network of local "affinity groups" that have ties to one another, but no direct organizational structure. This allows them to maintain their individual autonomy while still creating the possibility of mass action around common issues (Jasper 1997). In addition, NSM groups tend to prefer direct democratic or consensus-based decision-making models to representative, hierarchical models (Jasper 1997; Johnston, Laraña, and Gusfield 1994).

The targets of demands have also changed drastically as NSMs turn away from the state to other social institutions to make demands for change (Jasper 1997; Offe 1985). As an alternative, NSMs often choose to engage in largely symbolic forms of protest such as civil disobedience. These disruptions demonstrate both the willingness of participants to actively intervene against what they feel must be changed in a society and the possibility of new forms of social interaction embodied in the social movement (Johnston, Laraña, and Gusfield 1994). The form of organization and choice of tactics of new social movements demonstrates their desire to construct alternative social systems within existing ones.

NSM activity is particularly useful for understanding the structure and tactics of antifa activism. The tactical choices of organizations and activists within the militant antifascist movement are most appropriately contextualized through an understanding of NSM activity. Specifically, the focus of militant antifascists on subcultural activity and the importance of subculture to the political conflict between supremacists and antifa activists reflects the kind of cultural work typical of NSMs. This conflict is in part the result of the opposing groups engaging in similar forms of NSM activity within the bounds of distinct subcultures. As subsequent chapters will illustrate, the ideological positions of antifa activists and the threat that they face from supremacists is a result of both opposing movements operating in a manner typical of NSMs. It is therefore useful to understand the conflict between fascists and antifascists as one that is in many respects defined by each movement's classification as an NSM.

Subculture, resistance, and social movements

Much of what constitutes militant antifascist action in recent American history has been performed "underground" within a series of subcultures that are the targets of fascist recruitment and the contested spaces where ideological struggles play out (Berlet and Vysotsky 2006; Blazak 2001; Burley 2017; Simi and Futrell 2010; Vysotsky 2013). In order to truly develop an understanding of the organizational processes and tactical choices of militant antifascism, one must situate it in an understanding of subculture. While often operating as its own field of inquiry, subculture studies provide a unique perspective on social movement concepts of resistance and notions of authenticity that drive participation.

Subcultural resistance

Since the 1950s, scholars of subculture have identified the activities of "delinquent" youth as a form of resistance to the strain of normative society through the creation of an alternative culture with its own status and activity requirements (A. K. Cohen 1955). By the 1960s and 1970s, subcultural activity was conceived as a form of political resistance that proposed an alternative form of social organization (K. A. Roberts 1978; Yinger 1960). Yet, much of the work that constructs subculture as a form of active resistance to economic, political, and social structures is embedded in the NSM research and theory discussed above (J. P. Williams 2011). The dominant frameworks in subculture theory largely conceive of resistance as either purely symbolic (Hall and Jefferson 1976; Hebdige 1979) or irrelevant in relation to the expressive and hedonistic aspects of subcultural practice and presentation (Muggleton 2000; Muggleton and Weinzierl 2003). American subculture theorists J. Patrick Williams (2011) and Ross Haenfler (2014) systematically critique these "grand theories" of subculture embodied in the Center for Contemporary Cultural Studies (CCCS) (developed at the CCCS at the University of Birmingham) and post-subculture perspectives on resistance; and, more importantly, develop frameworks for understanding the ways in which subcultures engage in acts of opposition. This dynamic of subcultural resistance is particularly useful in understanding the conflicts between fascists and militant antifascists as both movements often engage within distinct subcultural spaces and produce distinct subcultures of their own.

For J. P. Williams (2011), subcultural resistance may be understood as involving actors, defined as participants in subcultures, and observers. Resistance may be a conscious or unconscious effort on the part of the individual involved in a subculture regardless of the form that the actions take. These subcultural acts of resistance may also be focused against peers or immediate authority figures (parents, teachers, bosses, etc.), serve as a means for reinforcing values of rebellion among subculturalists, or distinct acts of insubordination against cultural, economic, or political norms. Finally, the forms of subcultural resistance may be explicit or implicit in their manifestations. Subcultures may actively engage in acts of protest or alternative lifestyle practices, or they may involve subtle markers of resistance that can only be understood by fellow travelers.

Haenfler (2014) builds on these concepts and indicates how subcultures engage in distinct forms of social movement activity. Subcultural participation may serve as a form of resistance in and of itself when it is framed as a "lifestyle movement" that seeks change through individual-level behaviors and practices (Haenfler, Johnson, and Jones 2012). Subcultures may also serve as "free spaces" where participants engage in "prefigurative practices" that model a future society in everyday activity (Futrell and Simi 2004; Haenfler 2014). These practices and spaces also can function as "abeyance structures" that allow social movement ideologies and practices to thrive in periods when they lack mass appeal or support (Haenfler 2014; Taylor 1989). By providing these essential social movement functions, subcultures provide a unique manifestation of resistance.

These concepts of resistance may be applied to the (sub)culture of militant antifascism as individuals negotiate subcultural spaces and assert a broader antifascist culture. As distinct movement actors, both fascists and antifascists engage with subcultures to perform many of the functions described above. As Chapters 3 and 4 will discuss, subcultures serve as sites of recruitment, resource development, and prefigurative and abeyance structures for both fascist and antifascist movements.

Subcultural authenticity

The question of authenticity has been central to subcultural theory at least since the work of the CCCS in the 1970s (Hall and Jefferson 1976; Hebdige 1979). This work framed the symbolic resistance of subcultural practice as easily commodified and stripped of its authenticity by mass marketing in a capitalist system. In this framework, the only authentic representation of a subculture exists in its original incarnation, and all subsequent iterations lose their resistant quality as a result of capitalist reproduction. An alternative framework based on a postmodern interpretation of subculture, the post-subculture paradigm, developed by asserting that identity and authenticity are fluid concepts (Bennett 1999; Muggleton 2000; Muggleton and Weinzierl 2003). Rather than presenting subcultures as distinct forms with their own style or ideology, this perspective instead conceives of a diverse field of "neo-tribes" or local and/or temporary "scenes." In the post-subculture framework, authenticity is constructed as an ideal type by subcultural participants rather than as an achievable outcome of participation (Muggleton 2000). Individuals involved in subculture often accumulate "subcultural capital" in relation to others through the acquisition of knowledge, artifacts, and stylistic representations (Thornton 2013). This perspective, therefore, views authenticity as a consistently shifting set of standards that vary from scene to scene and era to era.

Yet, analyses of certain subcultures, particularly punk and skinhead where conflicts between fascists and antifascists have occurred, presents a model of subcultural authenticity that challenges both the CCCS and post-subculture frameworks. Katherine Fox's (1987) groundbreaking work on this subculture revealed not only a status hierarchy, but also a set of standards and expectations for authentic expression of subcultural values. Punk and skinhead subcultures put great value on authentic performance of identity. This is the product of these subcultures' relationship to mass media and marketing. Each subculture has experienced diffusion through the spread of the style and identity beyond original adherents and defusion through the moderation of subcultural values as it gains mass appeal. In response to these processes, many subcultures assert an authentic, often underground, expression that serves to resist processes of commodification (Daschuk 2011; Force 2011; Spracklen and Spracklen 2014; J. P. Williams 2006). Punk, in particular, developed in a dialectical relationship to mainstream commodification and representation by constructing an underground network of bands, music distribution systems, and promoters outside of corporate and normative structures (Clark 2003; Daschuk 2011; Force 2011). The process of maintaining authenticity serves as a means of defining and maintaining subcultural boundaries (Force 2011; J. P. Williams 2006; J. P. Williams and Copes 2011). Antifascism is often a core component of authentic subcultural identity for punks and skinheads who view fascist ideology and elements as interlopers in what are defined as politicized, prefigurative, or simply working-class spaces (Goodyer 2003; Marshall 1994; M. J. Roberts and Moore 2009; Travis and Hardy 2012; R. T. Wood 1999). The contest over subcultural authenticity drives a great deal of antifascist militancy ranging from cultural signifiers (Chapter 4) and conflicts over space (Chapter 5) to the boundaries of subcultural participation and safety (Chapters 5 and 6).

Criminology and militant antifascism

To identify as antifa is to be criminalized and deviant. It is to operate in a subterranean world of subculture and RSMOS away from the official control of the forces that seek to maintain social order. It is to engage in a series of tactics that, even in their most benign forms of surveillance and information gathering, are criminalized. It is to challenge the monopoly on the use of force asserted by police and the state when confronting fascist mobilizations and acts of public intimidation. Naturally, to analyze this pattern of criminalization, one must turn to the field of criminology. As a diverse and interdisciplinary field, criminology provides a variety of possible points of analysis; however, in order to understand a social movement that operates in subcultural spaces and outside of the normative order to political engagement, it is best to employ the perspective of critical criminology, which challenges dominant notions about crime and criminality. Critical criminology encompasses a number of differing and unique theoretical perspectives. In this book, the sub-fields of cultural and anarchist criminology are applied to understand militant antifascism's interplay of culture and militant action.

Cultural criminology

The concept of cultural criminology arose in the late 1990s as both a synthesis of theoretical tendencies and a challenge to the dominance of positivist and rational choice theories in understanding crime and deviance. By incorporating concepts from cultural studies, sociological symbolic interactionist theory, postmodernism, anarchism, and other critical approaches, this perspective seeks to explore the "meaning of crime" (Ferrell, Hayward, and Young 2008, 2). As a critical perspective, it seeks to understand the subjective, often emotional, perspective of people who experience crime – as perpetrators, victims, or simply criminalized people – as well as the dynamics of power that operate in the constructions of crime and criminality by governments, corporations, and their agents. Cultural criminology, therefore, is as much a methodological orientation as it is a theoretical one. It stresses the importance of "thick description" that results from ethnographic research, the experience of "edgework," and interpretive content analysis (Ferrell and Hamm 1998a; Ferrell, Hayward, and Young 2008; Geertz 1973). As such, it forms an ideal theoretical and methodological framework for this book.

The synthesis of social movement analysis and subcultural studies discussed earlier in this chapter requires an understanding of the subjective meaning of militant antifascism for participants in the movement. Much of what constitutes informal antifascist action is the product of constructing and understanding the meaning of signs of fascism by an increasingly broad set of actors. Interactive dynamics and meaning construction are crucial in short- and long-term tactical decision-making for antifascists, especially when decisions regarding the use of force are made (see Chapters 3 and 6). Antifascists must also negotiate a complex world where even potential sympathizers may be alienated as a result of misinterpretations of signifiers and meanings of certain actions, and contributing to further stigmatization and criminalization (see Chapters 4, 5, and 6). By utilizing the analytical tools and theoretical perspective of cultural criminology, it is possible to achieve a greater depth of understanding of antifascist militancy.

Anarchist criminology

For many readers, the very notion of an anarchist criminology will seem like an oxymoron. After all, aren't anarchists opposed to government; and, therefore, basically criminals? Wouldn't an anarchist criminologist simply justify crime? Given the pejorative association of anarchism with nihilistic violence and lawlessness, this type of reaction is understandable. Yet, anarchism is a political and social philosophy that stresses a critique of all forms of domination and power. Anarchist criminology, first and foremost, criticizes the legitimacy of the state and its attempts to engage in maintaining social order and control. These critiques can be summarized into three key areas: 1) the idea that the state has legitimate power over individual lives; 2) the production and reproduction of criminality through the construction and repression of criminal identities and acts; and 3) the actions of the state in relation to criminal justice reproduce its legitimacy while not actually preventing anti-social crime. In response to these failures of the state, anarchists propose alternative forms of justice consistent with the non-hierarchical principles of the philosophy.

Max Weber ([1910] 1998) asserted that the legitimacy of the state was based on its ability to maintain a monopoly on the use of force. Anarchist theory would on some level agree with this assertion; although from a critical standpoint. Larry Tifft (1979) in his groundbreaking summary of anarchist criminology indicates that the state has exclusive power to "appropriate" the property or life of any individual that it has jurisdiction over, up to and including imprisonment or death for violators of the law. This serves to legitimize the actions of the state; and ultimately, its power. Anarchist criminology challenges the very notion of criminality and the processes of defining who is and isn't criminal. As Jeff Ferrell (1998, 10) asserts, "the confinement of people and groups within state-administered categories of criminality, and within state-administered systems of punishment and retribution, promotes … a downward spiral of crime, criminalization, and inhumanity." When the state does intervene, it is not very effective or efficient in its crime control. Rather than putting an end to crime, the state merely builds a bureaucracy to control it with increasing rates of criminal justice careers, institutions such as courts and prisons, and people under the control of the criminal justice system (Pepinsky 1978). This system is ultimately contradictory and self-defeating because the state cannot achieve its goals of crime prevention and control. "The rule of criminal law," as enacted by the state, requires "swiftness, sureness, and severity" (Pepinsky 1978, 317). If the state acts to ensure one or more of these principles, it will violate another.

Consistent with anarchist principles of "direct action," this school of criminological theory proposes alternative systems of justice that can serve as prefigurative models for a non-hierarchical society (Ferrell 2001; 2011; Niman 2011; Pepinsky 1978; Pepinsky and Quinney 1991; Sullivan and Tifft 2010; L. Tifft and Sullivan 1980). The formative theoretical work in this area has focused on practices of restorative justice, which rejects punitive and retributive systems of justice in favor of a process that humanizes both victims and perpetrators in an effort to address the harms caused by criminal activity (Pepinsky and Quinney 1991; Sullivan and Tifft 2010). This approach provides a prefigurative model for addressing the outcomes of crime, but not the attempts at intervention or prevention. When anarchist criminologists have theorized more proactive approaches to social control, these have been rooted in a pacifist approach (Ferrell 2011; Niman 2011). These actions are distinctly anarchist because they are marked by spontaneity and a lack of institutionalized power.

The practices of militant antifascism present a unique model of anarchist response to threats of violence and disruption of social order. As Chapter 6 discusses in detail, antifa practices form a kind of non-hierarchical "policing" practice based on anarchist principles. Antifascists engage in many of the activities of a formal police force – investigation, surveillance, assertion of force to contain violence or potential violence – without the monopoly power or authority rendered to police in contemporary society. Antifascist actions are often spontaneous, always directly democratic, and ultimately responsible to a community within which they are situated. Because of these characteristics, antifa serves as a threat to the claims of monopoly on the use of force by the state; and therefore, the legitimacy of not only the state, but the political system as a whole.

A way forward

In order to understand the tactics, culture, and actions of militant antifascism, we must move beyond a one-dimensional view of the movement. Antifa is simultaneously a social movement, a subculture, a stigmatized and criminalized phenomenon, a challenge to existing norms of political engagement and social control, as well as a means of protection and social control. Such a complex undertaking requires breaking down the silos of sociological research in order to develop a holistic understanding. The subsequent chapters will provide an analysis that synthesizes concepts from the often divergent, yet complimentary, fields of social movement studies, subculture studies, and criminology. In doing so, this book breaks new theoretical ground by highlighting the relationships between these fields. By centering the importance of culture, emotion, and prefigurative practice, it contributes to recent theoretical developments in all three theoretical fields while charting new territory in the understanding of the fluidity of social movement participation, identity, and lifestyle.

Accessing antifa

The primary challenge of conducting research on militant antifascism is access. Unlike many other social movements, even militant ones, antifa activists do not have official or unofficial spokespeople who can serve as contacts for media, the general public, or potential researchers. Each militant antifascist group makes an individual decision regarding its method of public communication. As historian Mark Bray (2017, xxi) indicates, this is primarily driven by a need to protect the identities of antifa activists from "fascist and police backlash." Chapter 4 will discuss in detail the types of threats faced by antifascists from their fascist opposition. Such circumstances create a climate where communication with anyone outside of the antifascist and radical milieu is extremely guarded. Needless to say, conducting formal research on antifa activism requires a great deal of trust.

Orthodox sociological methodology constructs the study of any group in the society as a process where an outsider enters an unfamiliar setting and represents its structures and practices. The insistence on such a process is designed to maintain objectivity and avoid criticism from manuscript reviewers and, more importantly, academics outside of the discipline who view our methods as "soft science" and question the validity of our findings. Employing such a method would render any study of militant antifascism impossible. In order to ensure their safety, antifa activists would never open up to an outsider without serious restrictions on reporting. Unlike the ideal-typical model presented above, I had a clear advantage that allowed me unprecedented access to the world of militant antifascism: I had been involved in formal and informal antifascist activism since the early 1990s.

The research presented in this book is, therefore, a product of a variety of sociological methods that combine formal interviews, ethnographic data gathered from observation of antifascist activity, autoethnographic reflection, evidence from public statements made by formal militant antifascist groups and activists, and journalism on contemporary antifascist activism and related issues. The formal component of data collection occurred between 2007 and 2010. During that period, I interviewed 15 individuals who were active in militant antifascism at that time. These individuals played key roles in the movement and represented a variety of formal militant antifascist groups from all regions of the United States. During this period, I also participated in a number of formal and informal antifa events including, but not limited to, two national conferences, confrontational and non-confrontational protests, and a variety of social events such as Punk, Oi!, and Hardcore shows, DJ nights, film screenings, house parties, and informal gatherings in bars and other social spaces associated with punk and skinhead subculture. The data collected during this period is supplemented with auto-ethnographic reflection on personal experiences of formal and informal antifascist activity. These reflect informal antifascism as part of the punk subculture as well as formal participation in antifascist groups that includes many of the activities described above. Finally, in order to validate and generalize the data to the current antifascist movement, this book relies on public statements made by antifa activists through blog and social media communication as well as media coverage of the movement. Details of the methodological approach of this book are discussed in the appendix, "Against methodology: ethnography, autoethnography, and the intimately familiar."

In order to protect the identities of the individuals involved in militant antifascist activism, the data presented in this book will at times be intentionally vague. This is a product of not only conventions of sociological research that require the protection of the confidentiality of participants, but also out of a desire to protect the individuals from being identified by fascists. To that end, each formal interview participant, as well as others quoted in this book, has been assigned a pseudonym. Details about specific individuals are intentionally withheld unless they are necessary to the analysis. Ethnographic data similarly avoids identifying locations and specific groups. However, for purposes of clarity, organizations that I participated in for data collection and autoethnographic reflection are referred to by pseudonyms as well. The group observed in the 2007–2010 research period will be identified as New City Antifa. Additionally, I participated in a formal antifascist group from 2002–2005 that will be referred to as Old City Antifa. Unlike statements by interview participants and details of observation and reflection, public statements made by militant antifascist groups will be credited to those sources. Antifascists often take great pains to protect the identities of their membership, so public statements already have anonymity consistent with sociological conventions.

Structure of the book

This book seeks to understand the strategy and tactics of militant antifascism through a synthesis of sociological and criminological analyses. Chapter 2 provides a profile of both fascist and militant antifascist activists and organizations. It begins with an overview of the fascist movement with a discussion of its key forms and dynamics. An overview of antifa is presented through demographics of antifascist organizations with a discussion of gender, race, and ethnicity, sexual orientation, age, and other identities of antifa activists observed and interviewed in the research process. The ideological position of individual antifascists as well as militant antifascist groups is discussed in order to situate militancy in relation to political processes. The ideological position of antifa activists serves to frame their activism beyond opposition to fascist organizing and mobilizations. The chapter concludes with a discussion of the alliances between antifascist groups and other social movement organizations in order to situate activism in a broader social movement sector.

The dynamics of tactical choices of both fascists and militant antifascists are discussed in detail in Chapter 3, which presents an overview of the breadth of fascist and antifa tactics in order to place the spectacular confrontations between movements in a broader context of a diverse tactical repertoire (Tilly 2006; Tilly and Tarrow 2006). The relationship between history, culture, and antifa tactics is addressed with a focus on the diffusion of repertoires across time and space. The primary focus of the chapter, however, is on the way in which dynamics between movements and countermovements inform the tactical choices of militant antifascists. Tactical choices are placed in the context of the ideological position of antifa in relation to normative social movement processes. Finally, militant tactics are framed as part of a larger strategy of social movement demobilization with a focus on the effectiveness of militancy in achieving antifascist goals.

Chapter 4 continues the discussion of antifascist tactics with a specific focus on the way in which the movement develops and deploys culture. It begins with an overview of antifascist activity within subcultures that fascists target as spaces for recruitment. This serves as the basis for a discussion of antifa as a distinct subculture that operates across subcultural categories. Of particular interest in regard to antifascist culture is the visual culture that is produced to unite and motivate activists to action. The depictions of violence in this culture are further situated in a cultural criminological framework. The chapter concludes with a discussion of militant antifascist culture in the public sphere through the public distribution of style and culture.

The tactical choices and cultural work of militant antifascists is framed in relation to the threat posed by fascist presence and organizing experienced by individuals involved in the movement in Chapter 5. A distinct feature of antifa activists is the immediacy of threat that they face from fascist movements. This threat is conceptualized as occurring within and across three distinct categories: physical, political, and spatial. Physical threat involves the direct threat of violence faced by individuals by virtue of possessing an identity targeted by fascists for violent intimidation or elimination. Political threat operates at the ideological level as antifascist activists struggle with fascists to organize a similar base in similar populations. Finally, spatial threat discusses the direct proximity of militant antifascists to fascist violence with particular focus on the everyday violence of fascist tendencies in subcultural spaces.

Chapter 6 synthesizes social movement, subculture, and criminological analyses with a discussion of antifascist militancy as community self-defense. Specifically, antifascism is framed as a form of subcultural and radical policing activity that serves as a potential framework for reconsidering how social order may be secured in a direct democratic and non-hierarchical manner. By asserting a right to the use of force, militant antifascism challenges the state's monopoly on violence, which leads to its criminalization.

The book concludes by demonstrating how synthesizing the diverse perspectives of social movement studies, subcultural studies, and critical criminology produces a holistic understanding of radical social movements. By calling for interdisciplinary analysis, this work provides a way forward for social scientific research of movements, subcultures, deviance, and radical prefigurative action beyond the silos of existing fields in the disciplines of sociology and criminology.

Note

1 The decision to name the organization after John Brown also indicates a clear link between contemporary antifascist movements and the historical legacy that they see in resistance to slavery and white supremacy. The name reflects a uniquely American history of resistance that antifa activists identify with to this day. In this sense, the JBAKC not only represents the transition to the modern era of militant antifascism, but also links contemporary antifascism to a historical legacy of American activism.

Works cited

Belew, Kathleen. 2018. *Bring the War Home: The White Power Movement and Paramilitary America*. Cambridge, MA: Harvard University Press.

Bennett, Andy. 1999. "Subcultures or Neo-Tribes? Rethinking the Relationship between Youth, Style and Musical Taste." *Sociology* 33 (3): 599–617. doi:10.1177/S0038038599000371.

Berlet, Chip, and Mathew N. Lyons. 2000. *Right-Wing Populism in America: Too Close for Comfort*. New York, NY: Guilford Press.

Berlet, Chip, and Stanislav Vysotsky. 2006. "Overview of US White Supremacist Groups." *Journal of Political and Military Sociology* 34 (1): 11.

Berninger, Dieter George. 1988. "Milwaukee's German-American Community and the Nazi Challenge of the 1930's." *Wisconsin Magazine of History* 71 (2): 118–142.

Bernstein, Arnie. 2014. *Swastika Nation: Fritz Kuhn and the Rise and Fall of the German-American Bund*. New York, NY: Picador.

Blazak, Randy. 2001. "White Boys to Terrorist Men: Target Recruitment of Nazi Skinheads." *American Behavioral Scientist* 44 (6): 982–1000.

Bonilla-Silva, Eduardo. 2018. *Racism without Racists: Color-Blind Racism and the Persistence of Racial Inequality in America*. Lanham, MD: Rowman & Littlefield.

Bray, Mark. 2017. *Antifa: The Antifascist Handbook*. Brooklyn, NY: Melville House Publishing.

Burley, Shane. 2017. *Fascism Today – What It Is and How to End It*. Chico, CA: AK Press.

Clark, Dylan. 2003. "The Death and Life of Punk, the Last Subculture." In *The Post Subcultures Reader*, edited by David Muggleton and Rupert Weinzierl, 233–238. New York, NY: Berg.

Cobb, Charles E. 2014. *This Nonviolent Stuff'll Get You Killed: How Guns Made the Civil Rights Movement Possible*. New York, NY: Basic Books.

Cohen, Albert K. 1955. *Delinquent Boys: The Culture of the Gang*. Glencoe, IL: The Free Press.

Cohen, Jean L. 1985. "Strategy or Identity: New Theoretical Paradigms and Contemporary Social Movements." *Social Research* 52 (4): 663–716.

Copsey, Nigel. 2000. *Anti-Fascism in Britain*. New York, NY: St. Martin's Press.

Daschuk, Mitch Douglas. 2011. "The Significance of Artistic Criticism in the Production of Punk Subcultural Authenticity: The Case Study of Against Me!" *Journal of Youth Studies* 14 (5): 605–626. doi:10.1080/13676261.2011.559215.

Ferrell, Jeff. 1998. "Against the Law: Anarchist Criminology." *Social Anarchism* 24: 5–15.

Ferrell, Jeff. 2001. *Tearing Down the Streets: Adventures in Urban Anarchy*. New York, NY: Palgrave.

Ferrell, Jeff. 2011. "Corking as Community Policing." *Contemporary Justice Review* 14 (1): 95–98. doi:10.1080/10282580.2011.541079.

Ferrell, Jeff, and Mark S. Hamm, eds. 1998a. *Ethnography at the Edge: Crime, Deviance, and Field Research*. Boston: Northeastern University Press.

Ferrell, Jeff, Keith J. Hayward, and Jock Young. 2008. *Cultural Criminology: An Invitation*. Thousand Oaks, CA: Sage Publications.

Fitzgerald, Kathleen J., and Diane M. Rodgers. 2000. "Radical Social Movement Organizations: A Theoretical Model." *Sociological Quarterly* 41 (4): 573–592.

Force, William Ryan. 2011. "Consumption Styles and the Fluid Complexity of Punk Authenticity." *Symbolic Interaction* 32 (4): 289–309. doi:10.1525/si.2009.32.4.289.

Fox, Kathryn J. 1987. "Real Punks and Pretenders: The Social Organization of a Counterculture." *Journal of Contemporary Ethnography* 16 (3): 344–370. doi:10.1177/0891241687163006.

Futrell, Robert, and Pete Simi. 2004. "Free Spaces, Collective Identity, and the Persistence of U.S. White Power Activism." *Social Problems* 51 (1): 16–42.

Garvey, John, Beth Henson, Noel Ignatiev, Adam Sabra, Russell Banks, Derrick Bell, John Bracey, et al. 1999. "Renew the Legacy of John Brown." *Race Traitor* 10: 1–2.

Geertz, Clifford. 1973. *The Interpretation of Cultures: Selected Essays*. New York, NY: Basic Books.

Goodyer, Ian. 2003. "Rock against Racism: Multiculturalism and Political Mobilization, 1976–81." *Immigrants & Minorities* 22 (1).

Haenfler, Ross. 2014. *Subcultures the Basics*. New York, NY: Routledge.

Haenfler, Ross, Brett Johnson, and Ellis Jones. 2012. "Lifestyle Movements: Exploring the Intersection of Lifestyle and Social Movements." *Social Movement Studies* 11 (1): 1–20.

Hall, Stuart, and Tony Jefferson. 1976. *Resistance through Rituals: Youth Subcultures in Post-War Britain*. Abingdon: Routledge.

Hebdige, Dick. 1979. *Subculture: The Meaning of Style*. New York, NY: Routledge.

Hill, Lance. 2004. *The Deacons for Defense: Armed Resistance and the Civil Rights Movement*. Chapel Hill, NC: University of North Carolina Press.

Jasper, James M. 1997. *The Art of Moral Protest: Culture, Biography, and Creativity in Social Movements*. Chicago, IL: University of Chicago Press.

Jasper, James M. 2010. "Social Movement Theory Today: Toward a Theory of Action?" *Sociology Compass* 4 (11): 965–976. doi:10.1111/j.1751-9020.2010.00329.x.

Johnston, Hank, Enrique Laraña, and Joseph R. Gusfield. 1994. "Identities, Grievances, and New Social Movements." In *New Social Movements: From Ideology to Identity*, edited by Enrique Laraña, Hank Johnston, and Joseph R. Gusfield, 3–35. Philadelphia, PA: Temple University Press.

Marshall, George. 1994. *Spirit of '69: A Skinhead Bible*. Dunoon, Scotland: S.T. Publishing.

Melucci, Alberto. 1985. "The Symbolic Challenge of Contemporary Movements." *Social Research* 52 (4): 789–816.

Meyer, David S., and Suzanne Staggenborg. 1996. "Movements, Countermovements, and the Structure of Political Opportunity." *American Journal of Sociology* 101 (6): 1628–1660.

Muggleton, David. 2000. *Inside Subculture the Postmodern Meaning of Style*. New York, NY: Berg.

Muggleton, David, and Rupert Weinzierl. 2003. *The Post-Subcultures Reader*. New York, NY: Berg.

Niman, Michael I. 2011. "The Shanti Sena 'Peace Center' and the Non-Policing of an Anarchist Temporary Autonomous Zone: Rainbow Family Peacekeeping Strategies." *Contemporary Justice Review* 14 (1): 65–76. doi:10.1080/10282580.2011.541077.

Offe, Claus. 1985. "New Social Movements: Challenging the Boundaries of Institutional Politics." *Social Research* 52 (4): 817–868.

Omi, Michael, and Howard Winant. 2014. *Racial Formation in the United States*. New York, NY: Routledge.

Pepinsky, Harold E. 1978. "Communist Anarchism as an Alternative to the Rule of Criminal Law." *Contemporary Crises* 2 (3): 315–334. doi:10.1007/BF02741899.Pepinsky, Harold E., and Richard Quinney. 1991. *Criminology as Peacemaking*. Bloomington, IN: Indiana University Press.

Renton, Dave. 1998. "*The Attempted Revival of British Fascism: Fascism and Anti-Fascism 1945–51.*" Sheffield, UK: University of Sheffield.

Renton, Dave. 2001. *This Rough Game: Fascism and Anti-Fascism*. Stroud: Sutton.

Ridgeway, James. 1995. *Blood in the Face: The Ku Klux Klan, Aryan Nations, Nazi Skinheads and the Rise of a New White Culture*. New York, NY: Thunder's Mouth Press.

Roberts, Keith A. 1978. "Toward a Generic Concept of Counter-Culture." *Sociological Focus* 11 (2): 111–126.

Roberts, Michael James, and Ryan Moore. 2009. "Peace Punks and Punks Against Racism: Resource Mobilization and Frame Construction in the Punk Movement." *Music and Arts in Action* 2 (1): 21–36.

Ross, Alexander Reid. 2017. *Against the Fascist Creep*. Chico, CA: AK Press.

Simi, Pete, and Robert Futrell. 2010. *American Swastika: Inside the White Power Movement's Hidden Spaces of Hate*. Lanham, MD: Rowman & Littlefield Publishers.

Spracklen, Karl, and Beverley Spracklen. 2014. "The Strange and Spooky Battle over Bats and Black Dresses: The Commodification of Whitby Goth Weekend and the Loss of a Subculture." *Tourist Studies* 14 (1): 86–102. doi:10.1177/1468797613511688.

Sullivan, Dennis, and Larry Tifft. 2010. *Restorative Justice: Healing the Foundations of Our Everyday Lives*. Boulder, CO: Lynne Rienner Publishers.

Taylor, Verta. 1989. "Social Movement Continuity: The Women's Movement in Abeyance." *American Sociological Review* 54 (5): 761. doi:10.2307/2117752.

Testa, M. 2015. *Militant Anti-Fascism: A Hundred Years of Resistance*. Oakland, CA: AK Press.

Thornton, Sarah. 2013. *Club Cultures: Music, Media and Subcultural Capital*. Cambridge: Polity Press.

Tifft, Larry L. 1979. "The Coming Redefinitions of Crime: An Anarchist Perspective." *Social Problems* 26 (4): 392–402. doi:10.2307/800503.

Tifft, Larry, and Dennis Sullivan. 1980. *The Struggle to Be Human: Crime, Criminology, and Anarchism*. Sanday: Cienfuegos Press.

Tilly, Charles. 2006. *Regimes and Repertoires*. Chicago, IL: University of Chicago Press.

Tilly, Charles, and Sidney G. Tarrow. 2006. *Contentious Politics*. Boulder, CO: Paradigm Publishers.

Travis, Tiffini A., and Perry Hardy. 2012. *Skinheads: A Guide to an American Subculture*. Santa Barbara, CA: Greenwood.

Varon, Jeremy. 2004. *Bringing the War Home: The Weather Underground, the Red Army Faction, and Revolutionary Violence in the Sixties and Seventies*. Berkeley, CA: University of California Press.

Vysotsky, Stanislav. 2013. "The Influence of Threat on Tactical Choices of Militant Anti-Fascist Activists." *Interface: A Journal for and about Social Movements* 5 (2): 263–294.

Waller, Signe. 2002. *Love and Revolution: A Political Memoir*. Lanham, MD: Rowman & Littlefield.

Weber, Max. [1910] 1998. "Politics as a Vocation." In *From Max Weber: Essays in Sociology*, translated by H.H. Gerth and C. Wright Mills, 77–128. New York, NY: Routledge.

Williams, J. Patrick. 2006. "Authentic Identities: Straightedge Subculture, Music, and the Internet." *Journal of Contemporary Ethnography* 35 (2): 173–200. doi:10.1177/0891241605285100.

Williams, J. Patrick. 2011. *Subcultural Theory: Traditions & Concepts*. Chichester: Polity Press.

Williams, J. Patrick, and Heith Copes. 2011. "'How Edge Are You?' Constructing Authentic Identities and Subcultural Boundaries in a Straightedge Internet Forum." *Symbolic Interaction* 28 (1): 67–89. doi:10.1525/si.2005.28.1.67.

Williams, Robert F. 1998. *Negroes with Guns*. Detroit, MI: Wayne State University Press.

Wood, Evan. 2017. "Marcus Pacheco and the Birth of Skinheads Against Racial Prejudice." *Frank151*. https://web.archive.org/web/20170501185813/http://frank151.com/marcus-pacheco-sharp.

Wood, Robert T. 1999. "The Indigenous, Nonracist Origins of the American Skinhead Subculture." *Youth & Society* 31 (2): 131–151. doi:10.1177/0044118X99031002001.

Yinger, J. Milton. 1960. "Contraculture and Subculture." *American Sociological Review* 25 (5): 625–635.

Zald, Meyer N., and Bert Useem. 1987. "Movement and Countermovement Interaction: Mobilization, Tactics and State Involvement." In *Social Movements in an Organizational Society: Collected Essays*, edited by Meyer N. Zald and John D. McCarthy. New Brunswick, NJ: Transaction Books.

2

FASCISTS AND ANTIFASCISTS

A countermovement overview

It is a scene that has become all too familiar: masked, black clad antifa activists facing off against fascists wearing helmets and body armor. To the casual observer, the opposing movements look so similar that it seems impossible to distinguish one group from the other in the clashes that have become associated with antifascism. This distinction becomes even more blurred as one descends into the subcultures where fascist and antifascist punks, skinheads, and metalheads share a similar style that can only be distinguished by a close reading of their aesthetic. To further complicate this issue, proponents of "horseshoe" or "fishhook" theory assert that the far-right and far-left have greater similarity than difference (Burley 2017). Such pronouncements and perceptions reflect a superficial examination of both antifascist and fascist movements, often devoid of in-depth understanding and analysis of either movement's ideology or structure.

Antifa activism is exclusively focused on opposition to fascist social movement activity. In this respect, militant antifascism represents an almost ideal-typical countermovement because it exists exclusively to oppose the fascist movement. Fascist and antifascist movements, therefore, serve as negations of one another. Social science studies of countermovements focus almost exclusively on the relationship between such movements and structures of government or social policy. Even when such research looks the dynamics of movements opposed to one another, it is generally focused on the political process of their mobilization and interaction (Gale 1986; Meyer and Staggenborg 1996; Peleg 2000).

By contrast, this chapter will concentrate on the internal workings of fascist and antifascist movements in order to develop a framework for analyzing the countermovement dynamics between them. To understand the tactics, culture, and motivations of antifa activists, one must have a sense of the movement that they organize to oppose. The fascist movement in the United States is distinguished by a distinct ideology that is rooted in white supremacy and patriarchy, and follows a clear organizational structure and strategies that unify disparate tendencies into a cohesive movement. Distinctions within the movement reflect alignment with at least one of five sectors – political, religious, intellectual, subcultural, and criminal – that are determined by their relationship to fascist ideology and their tactical repertoire (Berlet and Vysotsky 2006). Categorizing the movement as consisting of these sectors provides a more holistic understanding of its internal differences.

Antifascism, of course, represents the polar opposite of the fascist movement. The demographic profile of formal, militant antifascist groups reflects the diversity of identities targeted for fascist violence: women, LGBTQ people, people of color, and religious minorities. Just as they have been historically, contemporary militant antifascists identify as leftists and primarily adhere to anarchist and anti-authoritarian ideologies that seek to challenge the types of formal hierarchy and inequality that fascists advocate. Militant antifascists are often active in other forms of social movement activity that address issues of social justice and often come to antifa activism as a reflection or extension of that activism. Because of their activism, militants are able to build alliances within the broader leftist milieu and across ideological boundaries. Militant antifascism, therefore, represents a diverse opposition to fascism activism.

The fascist movement

Fascism is often an extremely murky concept in and of itself. In the American context, the term has been diluted to such a degree that it is used as a generic epithet at worst or a stand-in for authoritarianism at best. For many on the left, the term was used generically to describe everything from the white supremacist legacy of state policy to the authoritarian, reactionary, and neoliberal policies of contemporary conservatism (Burley 2017). Conversely, there is a tendency among scholars of fascism to reduce it solely to a movement that existed in the interwar period in Europe or a static and specific ideology (Renton 2001). These approaches treat fascism as an ideal type, often limited to a specific geographic location and historical moment, against which contemporary far-right tendencies can be compared and found lacking sufficient conditions to qualify as fascist.

Definitions of fascism are similarly variable. In his formative work, Robert Paxton (2004, 218) defines fascism as,

> a form of political behavior marked by obsessive preoccupation with community decline, humiliation, or victimhood and by compensatory cults of unity, energy, and purity, in which a mass-based party of committed nationalist militants, working in uneasy but effective collaboration with traditional elites, abandons democratic liberties and pursues with redemptive violence and without ethical or legal restraints goals of internal cleansing and external expansion.

Based on these criteria, fascism is manifested in five stages: the formation of social movements, their participation in the political system, their ascendency to power, the application of power, and "the long duration, during which the fascist regime chooses either radicalization or entropy" (Paxton 2004, 23). This definition has some limitations when analyzing contemporary fascist movements. In particular, modern American fascism intentionally avoids the building of a mass party, often positioning itself in opposition to party politics and the state, in favor of a "leaderless resistance" organizational model and insurrection against the state rather than its seizure. Using an explicitly antifascist perspective, Shane Burley (2017, 50–55) proposes that fascism is "inequality through mythological and essentialized identity" that advocates for inequality, mobilizes populism, constructs identity, foments revolution, encourages elitism, establishes a cult of tradition, colonizes leftist issue sets, and venerates violence and authority.

Understanding fascism may be less an issue of definition than of diagnosis. The necessity of precision in definitions fundamentally constricts analysis of fascist movements because it reduces the scope of what constitutes fascism, significantly limiting the possibility of identifying contemporary movements as such. Rather than comparing contemporary manifestations of fascism to an ideal-typical definition or specific historical party, scholars of fascism as a movement generally outline distinct features that are shared across time and place (Berlet 1992; Burley 2017; Eco 1995; Paxton 2004). By establishing a set of criteria, contemporary movements may be linked to their historical predecessors while maintaining unique ideologies, organizational structures, and action repertoires that are specific to their historical and national context. By focusing on criteria, movements may have shared features without exact replication. This allows for contemporary movements to be assessed as fascist regardless of their self-identification and framing (Eco 1995; Paxton 2004).

An analysis of fascism as a social movement avoids the pitfalls of over-generalization and the limitations of specificity (Renton 2001). Sociological study of fascist movements provides a broad framework for understanding its key ideas and the ways in which it operates. The turn in social movement theory from grand theories concerned with the allocation of resources and dynamics of conventional political process to concerns of culture, identity, and post-materialist issues (Goodwin and Jasper 2004; Jasper 2010) provides a structure for discussing the form of contemporary fascism. Outlining the framing processes through which supremacist movements construct messages and meaning indicates key elements of fascist ideology. Contextualizing contemporary fascist movements in a "new social movements" (NSMs) analysis reveals the ways in which it engages with current social issues and movement dynamics. Contemporary American fascist movements are defined by a commitment to inequality and strict social hierarchy, populism that is translated through a distinct series of social movement frames, and a decentralized organizational structure. The operationalization of ideology and tactical repertoires of contemporary fascists are further organized into distinct movement sectors that encompass the variety of organizations and actors that make up the movement.

Framing fascism

All social movements practice a continuous pattern of message and meaning construction. The process of "framing" facilitates social movements constructing strong statements regarding issues that they view as crucial. In the framing perspective, messages are not simply a resource or a product of a leader's ideological control they are actively constructed by social movement members through a variety of social interactions. The messages and meanings of social movements are carefully crafted for movement members, their opponents, and others who have not committed to a position on the issue at hand (Benford and Snow 2000). Framing processes take on three distinct forms: "diagnostic framing," the process of identifying and attributing the cause of a problem; "prognostic framing," the process of defining how a social movement seeks to solve the problem; and "motivational framing," the process of developing a rationale for action (Benford and Snow 2000). The framing process is an active one where participants engage in a constant discourse within the movement and between movement members and opponents, as well as the unaffiliated public. For fascist and far-right movements, these processes are evident in a series of metaframes, or "master frames" (Benford and Snow 2000; Carroll and Ratner 1996; Mooney and Hunt 1996; Snow and Benford 1992) that reflect movement ideology: dualism, conspiracism, apocalypticism, populism, and authoritarianism/domination (Berlet 2004a; Berlet and Vysotsky 2006). Fascist movements also use "ethnic claims-making" and "intellectualization" frames in order to reduce the social stigma of their ideology and introduce it into public discourse (Berbrier 1998; Berbrier 1999; Burley 2017).

Dualism

Dualism consists of the notion that the world is divided into the forces of good and evil with no middle ground. According to Chip Berlet (2004a, 24), this frame is defined by a lack of "acknowledgement of complexity, nuance, or ambiguity in debates, and hostility is expressed toward those who suggest coexistence, toleration, pragmatism, compromise, or mediation." Processes of "radical dualism" serve to demonize perceived enemies (Wessinger 2000), which is reflected in fascist scapegoating of people of color, religious minorities, and LGBTQ people (Berlet and Vysotsky 2006; Burley 2017). Supremacist framing constructs a world where heroic warriors – white, heterosexual men and women of faith – are in conflict with degenerate "others" seeking to subvert their way of life. The image of the warrior in the dualism frame not only aligns with classical fascist notions of violence and war as moral and spiritual superiority (Berlet 1992; Griffin 1993; Paxton 2004), but also serves to undergird the conspiracism and apocalypticism frames.

Conspiracism

The conspiracism frame claims that most major historic events have been shaped by massive, long-term, secret conspiracies that benefit elite groups and individuals. This framing process constructs a narrative of scapegoating where "demonized enemies [are] part of a vast insidious plot against the common good, while it valorizes the scapegoater as a hero for sounding the alarm" (Berlet 2004a, 24). Anti-Semitism is at the core of fascist conspiracism that lays blame on Jewish plots for virtually all economic, political, and social problems, and links fascist conspiracism to 19th century anti-Semitism (Burley 2017; A. R. Ross 2017; Ward 2017). A central theme in contemporary fascist rhetoric is a belief that the state is under the control of Jewish interests in the form of a Zionist Occupation/Occupied Government (ZOG) that is imposing multicultural and socialist policies on the white American majority (Barkun 1997; Barkun 2013; Dobratz and Shanks-Meile 1997; Ridgeway 1995). Contemporary theories of the "great replacement" or "white genocide" of the United States assert that non-white immigration is the result of a Jewish plot to eliminate the country's white population as well as its cultural heritage and character (Burley 2017; Wendling 2018). Fascist conspiracism manages to play both sides of the economic fence by asserting that capitalism and communism are plots of Jewish bankers and intellectuals, respectively (Berlet and Vysotsky 2006; Burley 2017). The conspiracism frame is intrinsically dualistic in its view of conspirators and those who are subject to conspiracy. Similarly, those who have knowledge of the conspiracy are given a kind of power in their knowledge and opposition to it. Individuals who uncover conspiracies and spread information about them can achieve status within fascist movements because of the "stigmatized knowledge" that they possess (Barkun 2013; Berlet 2004a). The combination of the dualist and conspiracist frames ultimately leads to apocalypticism because of the belief in an inevitable clash between the forces of evil (conspirators) and the forces of good (those who oppose the conspiracy).

Apocalypticism

The conspiracism and dualism frames combine together to construct a world where nefarious people are actively working to harm the righteous. If, as both frames indicate, the forces of good must act in order to oppose the evil conspirators, then the conflict between these groups becomes inevitable. The concept of apocalypticism is based on the idea that there is an approaching confrontation that will change the nature of the world, during which important hidden truths will be revealed. This is the essence of this frame – that a war between the forces of virtue and the forces of villainy is inevitable, and that the virtuous will triumph in this ultimate battle. The apocalyptic vision of many fascists involves some form of conflict between the races, which is articulated in both religious and secular sectors of the movement described later in the chapter (Barkun 1997; Berlet 2004b; Dobratz and Shanks-Meile 1997; Ellwood 2000; Gardell 2003; Tenold 2018). This frame contributes to the ideological imperative toward violence embedded in fascist ideology because it constructs war as a preordained fulfillment of the historic mission of the movement (Berlet 1992; Griffin 1993; Eco 1995; Paxton 2004). The appeal of the apocalypticism frame is driven by the promise of victory for fascists against their enemies.

Populism

Populism seeks to mobilize "the people" in service of political or social change. Utilizing the conspiracist frame, right-wing populism heralds a call for popular action to eliminate "illegitimate elites" – the politicians, bankers, academics, and journalists who are seen as secretly controlled by powerful sinister forces.[1] This is typically accompanied by dualistic and apocalyptic attacks against "parasitic" subordinate groups that assert that immigrants, people of color, religious minorities, and/or LGBTQ people are out to destroy the country from within (Berlet 2004a; Berlet and Lyons 2000; Stock 1997). This form of populism is driven by producerism narratives that "portray a noble middle class of hardworking producers being squeezed by ... parasitic elites [from] above and lazy, sinful, and subversive parasites [from] below" (Berlet 2004a, 25). Right-wing populism is driven by periods of cultural, economic, or political change that serve to energize a cross-class segment of the population that perceives itself as being alienated by such shifts (Berlet 2004a; Berlet and Lyons 2000). This often takes the form of issue sets and arguments that have been the traditional provenance of the left (Berlet and Vysotsky 2006; Burley 2017; A. R. Ross 2017), which will be discussed in more detail later in this chapter. The ultimate goal of the populist frame is to build broad appeal and a mass movement in the service of a fascist agenda.

Authoritarianism/Domination

Authoritarianism is typically understood to be a core component of fascism with its classical form being characterized by a strict bureaucratic hierarchy where ultimate power rests in an autocratic, charismatic leader. Fascist authoritarianism, however, is not reduced simply to the characteristics of the leadership, but also requires individual subordination, acquiescence, and compliance to the directives of their superiors and the dictates of the state (Berlet 1992; Eco 1995; Griffin 1993; Paxton 2004). Contemporary American fascist movements and their associated ideologies do not reflect this version of authoritarianism. The era of the hierarchical fascist party under the sway of a charismatic leader died with the old-guard of supremacist leadership in the 1990s and early 2000s (Berlet and Vysotsky 2006; Burley 2017; Gattinara and Pirro 2018; Griffin 2003; Vysotsky and Dentice 2008). This does not mean that contemporary fascists reject authoritarianism altogether, it simply means that the form of authoritarianism has changed. Rather than seeking the ascent of a leader or party, fascist movements active in the United States seek to assert a strict hierarchy and build a world of fundamental inequality. In response to increasing movements for economic, political, and social justice by historically marginalized people, fascists assert an intrinsic inequality between people that is justified as either biological or cultural, or usually both, in origin (Berlet 2004a; Burley 2017; Neiwert 2017; Simi and Futrell 2010; Tenold 2018; Wendling 2018). The core principle for contemporary fascists is domination and subordination of "others" (Berlet 2004a; Berlet and Vysotsky 2006). To the extent that it is individualized, it is done so on the basis of the identity of individual movement members. The authoritarianism of contemporary American fascists is marked by an individual sense of superiority and expectations of structural entitlement as well as deference and submission from people whom they deem to be fundamentally inferior.

Ethnic claims-making

The concept of ethnic claims-making consists of an "effort to portray white supremacist ideology as representing that of an ethnic group, arguing ... that if, according to the values of 'cultural pluralism' and 'diversity,' ethnic or racial pride is legitimate for (other) ethnic or racial minority groups ..., then it is also legitimate for whites" (Berbrier 1998, 498–499). At the core of this framing process are two fundamental assumptions: that culture is biologically determined and that the actions of non-white ethnic groups are driven by a sense of intrinsic superiority. Concepts such as "ethno-differentialism" assert that ethnic groups require their own distinct national culture. The unspoken assumption in the contemporary fascist ethnic claims-making process is that the process of ethnic identity construction results in segregation and separatism. "[Fascists] want people of African descent to 'realize their African history,' to think of themselves as black people and to return to the African continent to live in racially homogeneous communities defined by ethnocentric cultural standards" (Burley 2017, 100). Contemporary fascist movements, therefore, focus much of their organizing and rhetoric on issues of immigration and notions of national identity. For fascist "identitarians," white ethnic identity, nationalist sentiment, and spirituality blend into a movement that links intellectual theorists with populist movements that reject traditional structures of party politics and left-right distinctions (Burley 2017). So, while fascists engage in ethnic claims-making in an attempt to frame their movement as an advocacy group in a pluralist, multicultural society, the reality of their vision is ultimately a white supremacist one (Berbrier 1998; Vysotsky and McCarthy 2017).

Intellectualization

Mitch Berbrier (1999, 411) conceived of intellectualization as a "stigma management" strategy designed to reduce the negative perceptions of the supremacist movement as "boorish" or "violent." Instead, fascist movements seek to present themselves as driven by scholarly pursuit and empirical knowledge. As an ideological framework, this process manifests itself as "race realism" or the scientific validation of racial difference and hierarchy. At its base, this scientific racism asserts that races are distinct biological categories that possess discrete differences between them that can be ranked in a hierarchical order. According to this frame, the most common demonstration of difference can be found in IQ test results that are purported to be objective measures of intelligence. Intelligence is, therefore, considered a heritable trait that is not only passed from one generation to another, but also cannot and should not be modified through any form of social intervention. The racialized hierarchy of intelligence articulated by the race realist frame has been described as follows: "Asians and Ashkenazi Jews are at the top, non-Jewish whites just slightly below them, Arabs way below, and blacks at the bottom" (Wendling 2018, 85). The implication of this argument is that racial equality and interracial relationships between white and brown or black people degrade the "superior" white race and Jewish people manipulate whites into subservience. Intelligence is largely symbolic of a broader set of beliefs about racialized genetic difference with some scholars such as the late J. Philippe Rushton (1997) arguing for genetic differences between racial groups in everything from stature to size of sex organs to criminal activity. Contemporary proponents of "human biological diversity" serve to revitalize "old racial science arguments to suggest that recent evolution presents dramatic human differences, like arguing that people of African descent have different brain structures [from white Europeans] that make them unable to survive well in European cultures" (Burley 2017, 73). The not-so-subtle implication of these frameworks is one of not just fundamental biological difference between races and the inherent superiority of the white race, but also of the policies of racial separation and subordination that are at the core of fascist ideology. Intellectualization, therefore, serves as a means of legitimating the basest and crudest forms of fascist racism.

Contemporary fascist movements, like all social movements, engage in processes of messaging and meaning-making that constitute the process of framing (Benford and Snow 2000; Berlet 2004a; Berlet and Vysotsky 2006; Snow and Benford 1992). At the core of supremacist framing processes are a series of master frames – dualism, conspiracism, apocalypticism, populism, and authoritarianism/domination – that reflect movement ideology in assigning blame for social problems, propose solutions, and motivate participation (Benford and Snow 2000). Processes of ethnic claims-making and intellectualization are not only designed to reduce the stigma associated with the fascist movement, but also serve as rationalizations for an ideology of domination.

Fascism as a new social movement

The fascist movement cannot by any means be referred to as a literal NSM. Its ideological bases potentially stretch back hundreds of years and its organized component in the United States is over 150 years old.[2] However, the movement as it exists today bears very little resemblance to its historical predecessors and may, in fact, lend itself to analysis via the NSM perspective (Vysotsky and Dentice 2008). The modern supremacist movement may adhere to reactionary ideologies, wear the symbols and uniforms of its historical antecedents, and engage in the rituals of its namesakes, but it has also developed a style and analysis that is unique to contemporary social conditions.

In recent decades, analyses of NSMs have prioritized a qualitative shift in movement activity to analyze the way in which movements focus on identity, operate outside of traditional left-right political dichotomies, and engage in cultural activity as political activity (Johnston, Laraña, and Gusfield 1994). Unlike previous social movements, NSMs place a high priority on the development of collective and personal identity and social activism as intrinsic to individual lifestyle. These movements consist of individuals who, unlike movement members of the past, do not have a clear relationship between their structural role and movement participation. Movement members tend to be members of the "new middle class" (individuals with high levels of education, economic stability, and jobs in service occupations of the "knowledge industry), "decommodified or peripheral groups" (groups that are not part of the labor market by virtue of their social status), and aggrieved members of the "old middle class" (Offe 1985). Such movements cluster around broad identities like age cohort (youth), gender, or sexual orientation or develop broad based concerns like nuclear disarmament or environmental protection (Jasper 1997; Johnston, Laraña, and Gusfield 1994). As a result of this broad support base and potential constituency, NSMs have developed belief systems that do not adhere to traditional ideological boundaries of left and right. They have instead constructed systems that contain a plurality of ideas and propose practical solutions and greater democracy in political and economic decision-making processes (Cohen 1985; Johnston, Laraña, and Gusfield 1994; Melucci 1985; Offe 1985). Rather than engaging in mass social action, social movement membership is seen as an action in and of itself, which transforms everyday experiences into political activities. NSMs tend to reject traditional mass-based political parties, labor unions, and social movement organizations because they view them as centralized and bureaucratic; and in their place, posit decentralized, diffuse, and segmented groups (Johnston, Laraña, and Gusfield 1994).

Contemporary fascist movements are clearly evolving in their ideology and activity in order to address the concerns of this historical moment. This movement orientation aligns the supremacist movement with other types of social movements in American society, including their antifascist opposition in terms of their form (Meyer and Staggenborg 1996; Peleg 2000; Zald and Useem 1987). Today's fascist movement shares a number of characteristics that fall under the NSMs category: 1) a focus on collective and personal identity, 2) a cross-class social base defined by post-materialist demands and "global" issues, 3) a rejection of the left-right political dichotomy, 4) decentralized, diffuse forms of organization, 5) political activity through cultural construction, and 6) the construction of a future society within movement activity (Johnston, Laraña, and Gusfield 1994; Vysotsky and Dentice 2008).

Collective and personal identity

Identity is at the core of contemporary fascist movements; in particular white racial identity. Pete Simi and Robert Futrell (2010, 2) summarize this position as a belief "that the white race is genetically and culturally superior to all nonwhite races and deserves to rule over them." Burley (2017, 57) similarly indicates that "no matter how fascists self-define, their ideology is still rooted in feelings of supremacy and the historic legacy of white colonialism." By racializing every social interaction and structure, fascists construct a world where collective racial identity becomes the ultimate marker of individual identity. Using the "dualism" and "ethnic claims-making" frames discussed earlier, they construct collective identities both for themselves and for groups that they view as "the other" (Burley 2017; Daniels 1997; Dobratz and Shanks-Meile 1997; Ferber 1999; Neiwert 2017; Tenold 2018; Wendling 2018). As discussed earlier in this chapter, the fascist worldview is one that essentializes all aspects of the human condition and provides a clear framework of expectations based on one's racial categorization. In this sense, it is not only engaging in a consistent process of identity construction, but also in the most egregious form of "identity politics" (Burley 2017).

Cross-class base and post-materialist concerns

Because race is the primary issue around which the fascist movement organizes, materialist concerns such as class are viewed as secondary to the organization of the social movement. Contemporary movement membership in the United States consists of individuals who could be identified as part of "decommodified or peripheral" economic groups employed in service or trades occupations or members of the "old middle class" with a college education in mid-level knowledge and tech industry jobs who feel threatened by advances made by minority groups and women (Blazak 2001; Blee 2003; Simi and Futrell 2010; Tenold 2018; Wendling 2018). Individuals who are recruited into the movement tend to view themselves as having few options for social mobility and turn to the movement as a means to achieve self-empowerment. Recruits to the fascist movement come from the same social structural locations as many newcomers to NSMs (Berlet and Vysotsky 2006; Blazak 2001; Blee 2003; Ezekiel 1995; Simi and Futrell 2010). Finally, many of the issues of primary concern to supremacists are post-materialist in nature – environmental protection, economic and political globalization, government surveillance and repression, etc. – and reflect the conspiracist and populist frames discussed earlier. These issues overlap significantly with the concerns of left-oriented traditional NSMs and represent a "fascist creep" into the political terrain of such movements (Berlet and Vysotsky 2006; Burley 2017; A. R. Ross 2017; Vysotsky and Dentice 2008).

Rejection of the left-right political dichotomy

Despite their positioning on the right of the classical political spectrum, the positions of many contemporary fascists reflect their opposition to post-industrial social and economic relations. Many modern fascist groups and individual adherents reject pathways to state power because they view democratic states as intrinsically liberal and interventionist in individual's lives. In response to this critique, they frequently make libertarian arguments for their reactionary positions on race, gender, religion, and sexuality (Berlet and Vysotsky 2006; Burley 2017; A. R. Ross 2017; Sunshine 2008; Sunshine 2014; Vysotsky and Dentice 2008). Contemporary fascists routinely reject capitalist economic structures, yet they do not support socialist and communist alternatives. Instead, they argue for a "third position" that "rejects both capitalism and communism" as the product of a conspiracy created by Jewish bankers and academics respectively and calls for organic, localized, cooperative economic systems based on what they believe to be traditional Aryan lifestyles (Berlet and Vysotsky 2006; Burley 2017; Gardell 2003; A. R. Ross 2017; Sunshine 2008; Vysotsky and Dentice 2008). While the fascist movement still holds characteristics of reactionary movements due to its views on the subordinate social status of historically marginalized people and the idealization of "old" social hierarchies, in recent years its ideologues have argued for a rejection of the left-right dichotomy in favor of the politics of "third position," national anarchism, national Bolshevism, or pagan tribalism. The popularity of this philosophy has led to acceptance of this ideology, in part or in whole, by much of the fascist movement.

Decentralized, diffuse forms of organization

Historically, as discussed earlier in this chapter, fascist movements have been hierarchical in their organization and ideology (Berlet 1992; Eco 1995; Griffin 1993; Paxton 2004). The authoritarian ideologies and patriarchal structures of these movements placed great importance on leaders, creating both strong organizations and, conversely, a great deal of factionalism and internal conflict. Since the late 1980s, the American fascist movement has shifted its organizational strategy to a "leaderless resistance" model that urges a series of individual acts of violence against the state and racially, religiously, ethnically, and sexually subordinate groups that will trigger a larger apocalyptic war and bring about the supremacist society that they envision (Belew 2018; Berlet and Vysotsky 2006; Burley 2017; Gardell 2003; A. R. Ross 2017; Vysotsky and Dentice 2008). First articulated by Klansman Louis Beam, this strategy encourages small cells and lone actors to engage in acts of violence in service of a supremacist agenda (Belew 2018; Berlet and Vysotsky 2006; Burley 2017; Dobratz and Waldner 2012; Gardell 2003; Michael 2012). The leaderless resistance approach constructs a movement structure that combines elements of "all-channel" and "market" organizational models because it consists of distinct organizations with clear leadership, thought leaders with little organizational control, and individuals or cells with no organizational affiliation (Kilberg 2012). The contemporary fascist movement is organized around a core set of ideas that link a variety of actors and organizations in service of a common goal.

The leaderless resistance strategy is greatly facilitated by access to and use of the internet. Supremacists were early adopters of online communication beginning in the era of dial up bulletin boards where members could communicate, download propaganda materials, and identify movement enemies and potential targets of violence (Belew 2018; Daniels 2009; Levin 2002). While these early forums were operated by distinct organizations, with the advent of the modern internet consisting of discrete, yet networked sites accessible simultaneously by multiple users, the fascist movement became fundamentally decentralized (Burris, Smith, and Strahm 2000; Daniels 2009; Futrell and Simi 2004; Gerstenfeld, Grant, and Chiang 2003; Simi and Futrell 2010). Today, a vast network of forums, blogs, and social media, both movement specific and mainstream-oriented, link individual fascists, formal organizations, and potential recruits.

Subcultures, which will be discussed in more detail later in this chapter, also serve to facilitate the diffuse structure of the contemporary fascist movement. The basis of most fascist subcultural groups is small groupings of friends who share similar tastes in music, aesthetics, and socio-political ideology – in this case, variations on white supremacy. These groups generally do not belong to a formal organization and may have no formal membership besides that which is decided by group members' preferences. Yet their commitment to fascist ideology often goes beyond merely toying with symbols in order to offend authority figures or peers (Berlet and Vysotsky 2006; Burghart 1999; Futrell and Simi 2004; Hamm 1993; Simi and Futrell 2010). The contemporary fascist movement can best be understood as a network of organizations, members of youth subcultures, and individual sympathizers.

Cultural construction

Contemporary fascist movements constitute a counterculture to what they perceive as normative, (neo)liberal, multicultural society (Nagle 2017; Neiwert 2017; Wendling 2018). Such countercultural movements produce alternative belief systems that manifest in distinct cultural forms such as language, music, and style (Kriesi et al. 1995; Haenfler 2014; Miller-Idriss 2018; Roberts 1978; Simi and Futrell 2010; J. P. Williams 2011; Yinger 1960). Fascist movement members developed a complex language of symbols, codes, and signs to discern sympathizers and organization members from non-members. A partial result of the "dualism" frame that requires the movement to make clear distinctions between good and evil, ally and enemy, this system of symbols, etc. is also an adaptation to social standards that may make overt expressions of supremacy unacceptable. There is a series of numeric codes and iconographic symbols used specifically by movement members to demonstrate sympathy with white supremacist ideology and organizational membership (Burley 2017; Simi and Futrell 2010). In the decentralized, highly mediated fascist movement of today, memes represent the core of movement culture by spreading supremacist ideological themes and providing a form of "ironic" and iconic entertainment for committed members (Burley 2017; Nagle 2017; Neiwert 2017; Wendling 2018). The subcultural sector discussed below contributes two additional forms of culture: music and style. The ties between subcultures and fascist ideologues produce a vast array of music for internal consumption and recruitment purposes. This music conveys the core ideological messages of the movement that appeals to young people and new recruits (Burley

2017; Corte and Edwards 2008; Futrell, Simi, and Gottschalk 2006; Pieslak 2015; Shekhovtsov 2009). Style as manifested in clothing also serves as a cultural marker of fascist affiliation. The presentation of fascist style occurs in overt and covert forms ranging from "fashy" haircuts to ideological message and supremacist band t-shirts to implicitly symbolic subcultural or street style (Burley 2017; Hesse and Zak 2016; Miller-Idriss 2018; Simi and Futrell 2009; Simi and Futrell 2010). Through the construction of cultural symbols, the contemporary fascist movement reinforces collective identity and also projects a carefully framed image to the general public.

Prefigurative practice

Like many of its progressive counterparts in NSMs, the contemporary fascist movement turns to the construction of "prefigurative" practices and spaces as a means of social change. This strategy involves the creation of the world that a movement envisions through everyday practices and within distinct movement spaces (Breines 1989; Polletta 1999). Because of the stigma associated with overt expressions of bigotry inherent in fascist ideology in mainstream culture, much of the prefigurative practice of the contemporary movement occurs in "free spaces" that are outside of the purview of normative society and free from official sanctions (Futrell and Simi 2004). These spaces allow fascists to express their ideology without fear of reprimand or consequence for their bigotry and model the ideal fascist society in terms of racial and gender dynamics. Futrell and Simi (2004; 2010) identify two forms of prefigurative spaces: indigenous and transmovement. Indigenous spaces "are small, locally-bound, interpersonal networks where members engage in political socialization, boundary marking, and other cultural practices which create prefigurative Aryan relationships" (Futrell and Simi 2004, 17). These spaces are often unknown to people outside of the movement and involve relatively ordinary actions such as family activities, Bible study groups, and parties. Spaces may also become indigenous if they are frequented by fascists or temporarily used for events, which brings bars, restaurants, and even tattoo shops not explicitly owned by movement members into this category. Finally, there are indigenous spaces controlled by supremacists such as their homes or tattoo, music, and clothing stores owned by movement members. Transmovement spaces tie "otherwise unconnected local networks into broader webs of white power culture and identity" (Futrell and Simi 2004, 17) and take the form of conferences, festivals, intentional communities, and online activities. Through the construction of prefigurative spaces, fascists are able to develop a movement that is already living out many of its ideals. This allows members to feel secure in their belief systems and facilitates further activity outside of the confines of movement constructed spaces.

The gender question

The essentialist framework of the fascist movement extends beyond race to incorporate all aspects of a person's identity with a particular concern toward issues of gender and sexuality. Contemporary fascist ideology is driven by two complimentary and at times contradictory patriarchal perspectives on gender: paternalism and misogyny. Among supremacists, paternalism serves as a framework for defining both men's and women's roles in the movement and future society. It constructs an ideal-typical image of women that simultaneously constricts their social roles and generates opportunities for activism. Paternalism also serves as a means of male control through its obsession with sexuality, particularly interracial sex and homosexuality. While paternalism operates as a means of control, misogyny serves as a means of exclusion and alienation through patterns of degradation and harassment of women. Differing factions of the movement exhibit each of these perspectives. For example, neo-Nazi and militia movements tend toward more patriarchal orientations while the more amorphous alt-right tends toward misogyny. In both cases, the core ideology of the movement is fundamentally patriarchal.

Paternalism

Contemporary fascist movements are inherently patriarchal. By essentializing all aspects of individual identity, they define strict social roles for men and women that ultimately align with their racist worldview. The paternalistic perspective of fascist ideology defines a clear set of expectations for men involved in the movement. Jesse Daniels (1997, 39) summarizes this perspective, "[the] highest duty and honor of a White man, according to white supremacist discourse, is to preserve the white family and with it the hierarchy of race, gender, and sexuality." Movement propaganda consistently stresses that white men are hard workers, warriors, and protectors of white women's sexual purity (Arena and Arrigo 2000; Daniels 1997; Dobratz and Shanks-Meile 1997; Ferber 1999). This constructs an identity for men within the movement as warriors for their race and gender. In order to justify the white man's identity as a racial warrior, he must be given an enemy. For the fascist movement, the enemy becomes a social system that is pitted against the white male. In propaganda and discourse, fascists frame themselves as "victims of racial discrimination, of class oppression, and as the special victims of race, gender, and class oppression at the hands of the racial state" (Daniels 1997, 37). The intelligent man, therefore, not only stays in a fascist movement because it is his role to be a warrior for his race and a protector of his family and heritage, but because the movement protects him in a world that is hostile toward him and his material and emotional interests.

The fascist movement presents a fundamentally different view of gender identity for women. In most cases, women's roles are traditionally defined by their relationships to the men in their lives. This is consistent with movement propaganda that espouses traditional, patriarchal relationships between men and women based on their "natural" sex differences. Women in the movement are consistently encouraged to have children as a duty to the movement (Blee 2003; Daniels 1997; Ferber 1999). In addition, the maternal identity of women is also applied to their relationship with men in the movement. They are encouraged to nurture men in the movement, to provide for their daily well-being, to nurse them back to health when they are hurt in racial attacks, and to support them when they are imprisoned (Blee 2003; Daniels 1997). Thus, the identity of women within the fascist movement is reduced to being an object of male sexual desire, the mother of future white children, and the nurturer of male warriors. For women who have a personal desire to maintain an extremely traditional, patriarchal relationship with men, the fascist movement serves as a location to both find the type of man who will fulfill this role, and maintain their own understanding of "proper" roles for women. Therefore, it is only logical that women who hold such traditional values regarding their gender identity would find a place within this movement.

The place of women in paternalistically oriented organizations and formations within fascist movements is driven by a series of contradictory expectations that are reconciled as essential to fulfilling their ideological mission. Kathleen Blee (2003) identifies three key forms of activism defined for women involved in supremacist movements: familial, social, and operative. Activism through familial roles is the operationalization of the maternalism described above: bearing and caring for children, socializing them and others into movement ideology, and supporting activist partners and spouses. Social roles facilitate the cultural and social aspects of the movement which are crucial for movement success. In fascist movements, women's work consists of the "background" labor necessary for events to function such as preparation and cleaning of event spaces and cooking meals for gatherings. As social facilitators, women also serve as confidants and develop support networks for members of the movement regardless of their gender. In a final social role, women create links between the movement and mainstream society because they present a "normalized" image of fascists that contradicts negative perceptions, deliberately seek out roles in conventional society that can be used to recruit sympathetic individuals, and facilitate personal contacts that can serve as bridges for new recruits into the movement. Despite the public rhetoric regarding women's submission articulated by members and propaganda, they also engage in operative roles as movement activists. In a highly gendered division of labor, women often engage in crucial clerical roles and serve as core organizers for movement events. Yet, women's operative roles are not solely supportive as they partake in forms of public activism ranging from attending demonstrations to acts of fascist violence (Blee 2003; Ezekiel 1995; Hamm 1993). The type of role that women engage in within fascist movements is often distinctly tied to the organization or sector of the movement with which they are affiliated, with women in racist skinhead or neo-Nazi groups more likely to engage in operative roles whereas those who are affiliated with Klan or other Christian Identity groups primarily take on familial and social roles (Blee 2003; Castle 2012; Castle and Chevalier 2011; Ezekiel 1995; Hamm 1993).

Misogyny

The corollary to the paternalistic model of patriarchy described above is a fascist tendency toward misogyny. Kate Manne (2018, 13) describes the concept of misogyny as "uphold[ing] patriarchal order ... by visiting hostile or adverse social consequences on a certain ... class of girls and women to enforce and police social norms that are gendered either in theory ... or in practice." If paternalism is defined by a protective sense of gender dynamics that opens a space for women within fascist movements, misogyny represents violence toward and virulent hatred of women. Fascist misogyny is most clearly evident among organizations and individuals associated with the alt-right. The misogynist patriarchal faction of the contemporary fascist movement gained prominence during the Gamergate controversy in which women in the video game industry, journalists, cultural critics, and even gamers were viciously harassed for critiquing the gender dynamics in video games (Burley 2017; Lyons 2017; Neiwert 2017; Wendling 2018). This event brought together the various strains of misogynists operating under the guise of the "manosphere" – so-called men's rights activists, supposed pick up artists, incels, and a faction of internet trolls – with sectors of the white supremacist movement often under the banner of the alt-right or its more mainstream variant known as the alt-light. This misogynist fascist tendency is marked by its violent orientation toward women, "[the] Gamergate campaign took the pervasive, systematic pattern of threats and abuse that has been long used to silence women on the internet, and sharpened it into a focused weapon of attack" (Lyons 2017, 9). The punitive violence advocated by misogynists takes the form of rape and death threats backed by doxing campaigns that make such threats especially visceral and immediate (Manne 2018). While the paternalist tendency in the fascist movement provides a space for women's participation, the misogynist tendency presents the movement as fundamentally hostile toward women, severely limiting the possibilities for recruitment and participation.[3]

Sectors of the fascist movement

The notion of a unitary, mass based fascist movement is a relic of history. While popular consciousness of fascism is defined by the "mass society" vision of an authoritarian party marching lock-step behind a charismatic leader (Kornhauser 1959; Paxton 2004) and the American historical legacy of THE Klan as a singular terrorist organization looms large, the reality is far from cohesive. As this chapter has already discussed in some detail, the organizational structure of the contemporary fascist movement represents a leaderless resistance model consisting of networks of individuals and organizations (Belew 2018; Berlet and Vysotsky 2006; Burley 2017; Kilberg 2012; Michael 2012). The contradiction between popular conceptions of fascist movements and the reality of their multiplicity presents problems of classification for scholars and watch-dog organizations.

Categories of far-right and supremacist movements vary greatly depending on the source and have little consistency both internally and between sources. These often conflate ideologies, subcultures, and organizations, as well as increasingly broad tendencies such as the alt-right. The Southern Poverty Law Center (SPLC), whose criteria is ostensibly based on ideology consists of a dozen categories ranging from "anti-immigrant" to "neo-Nazi," but also lists "hate music," which has great ideological variability, and a catch-all category of "general hate."[4] In their groundbreaking ethnography of racist skinheads, Pete Simi and Robert Futrell (2010) similarly classify the "Aryan" movement into five categories: Ku Klux Klan, Christian Identity and neo-paganism, neo-Nazis, and racist skinheads. Again, the categories engage in both parsing and lumping of fascist ideological tendencies, specific organizational formations, and subcultural tendencies. As I will indicate later in this chapter, most Klan groups adhere to a Christian Identity ideology, which would be a more accurate classification; whereas, racist skinheads represent just one subcultural tendency within an increasingly varied set of supremacist countercultures.

To rectify these issues, I developed a broad typology designed to capture the variability of organizations and individual orientations within supremacist movements (Berlet and Vysotsky 2006; Vysotsky 2004). By focusing on ideological distinctions within the fascist movement and differences in the action repertoires of organizations and individuals,[5] I identified three sectors: political, religious, and subcultural. Two additional sectors – intellectual[6] and criminal – expand the original typology in order to incorporate scholarly development in the study of supremacists and more completely categorize the breadth of the movement.

Political sector

The political sector represents what are commonly understood to be social movement organizations that are presented as "instrumental" by addressing economic, political, and/or social concerns (Kriesi et al. 1995). Organizations and individuals in the political sector most clearly reflect the platforms and philosophies of fascist ideology with some openly identifying as fascist or neo-Nazi (Berlet and Vysotsky 2006). Others rely on more populist framing strategies preferring to identify as nationalist or identitarian (Burley 2017). While some individuals in this sector advocate for participation in the American electoral system, a number of organizations and individuals advocate for building supremacist communities and alternative structures or outright insurrection (Belew 2018; Burley 2017; Dobratz and Waldner 2012; Lyons 2017; Sunshine 2008; Tenold 2018).

The political sector represents the reactionary pole on a number of key contemporary issues. Groups and individuals in the political sector openly advocate for white nationalist or white supremacist positions on questions of race, promoting racial separation at best and genocide at worst as the stated policy goal should they achieve power (Burley 2017; Lyons 2017; Neiwert 2017; Tenold 2018). Their positions on other issues reflect a critique of neoliberal hegemony that appear as a fun house mirror of far-left positions in a kind of "fascist creep" into the process of political dissent often under the guise of a third position or "neither left nor right" stance (Berlet and Vysotsky 2006; Burley 2017; A. R. Ross 2017). The political sector is openly critical of capitalism from a distinct white supremacist, conspiracist perspective that Jewish people are responsible for its origins and persistence as discussed earlier in this chapter. While most fascists in this sector are also critical of communism from a similarly conspiratorial framework, a variety of national socialists, national Bolsheviks, and national anarchists advocate for non-capitalist economic alternatives (Berlet and Vysotsky 2006; Burley 2017; A. R. Ross 2017; Sunshine 2008, 2014). Environmental protection has long been a fundamental aspect of fascist ideology and the political sector continues the tradition of "ecofascism" (Berlet and Vysotsky 2006; Biehl and Staudenmaier 1995; Burley 2017; A. R. Ross 2017). After all, if fascists are to "ensure a future for white children," then there must be a planet for those white children to inherit. Conspiracist and populist framing also drives opposition to foreign intervention, war, and economic globalization as processes driven by "globalist" (read: Jewish) forces (Burley 2017; A. R. Ross 2017). For virtually any issue of economic, political, or social import, there is a policy position articulated from a fascist ideological position in this sector.

Organizations within the political sector engage in activities that are typical of marginal political parties in a liberal democracy. They hold protests and rallies, print propaganda flyers and pamphlets, attract membership through debate and sloganeering, and maintain websites with their political platform and analysis of current events (Berlet and Vysotsky 2006; Burley 2017; Lyons 2017). Because they are relatively marginalized, fascists in the political sector actively work to engage their perspective on issues into legitimate and mainstream political debate through a strategy of "meta-politics" (Burley 2017; Lyons 2017; Wendling 2018). The actions of the political sector are designed to shift the public conversation to engage with fascist ideology, even if it is in derision and critique because this results in exposure and serves as a form of legitimation. For fascists, practicing meta-politics effectively translates to the old adage that there is no such thing as bad press.

Other, more extremist, actors within this sector reject forms of "conventional" political activity in favor of more drastic or insurrectionary measures. Certain factions within the political sector of the fascist movement advocate the type of prefigurative practices described above. These groups and individuals argue for the creation of intentional communities that can serve as the bases for a future fascist society defined by white supremacy, patriarchy, and heteronormativity (Burley 2017; Lyons 2017; Simi and Futrell 2010). The most extremist elements of the political sector advocate for full-scale insurrection against what they view as the "Zionist Occupation/Occupied Government." These groups and individuals engage in paramilitary training and advocate acts of terrorist violence against civilian and government targets (Belew 2018; Burley 2017; Dobratz and Waldner 2012; Neiwert 2017; Wendling 2018). Whether through conventional political activity, meta-politics, or insurrection and terrorism, the political sector of the fascist movement ultimately takes a revolutionary stance against the existing system.

Religious sector

The religious sector aligns fascist ideology with some form of spirituality. Although classical fascism, and many of the old guard political organizations of the 1970s to the early 2000s, possessed elements of spirituality and mobilized it in service of the movement, individuals and organizations in this sector present religious belief as the source of their fascist ideology (Berlet and Vysotsky 2006). In this sector, core religious texts serve as the justification for inequality that is central to fascist ideology and spiritual practice is designed to reaffirm supremacist beliefs, norms, and values. "Members of groups that fit into the religious category structure their lives to include religious services, meetings dedicated to the study of sacred texts, and special rituals and ceremonies limited to loyal adherents" (Berlet and Vysotsky 2006, 27; see also Futrell and Simi 2004). Group leaders in this sector may also use religious titles such as the reverends of Christian Identity and Creativity. Finally, many of the tendencies within the religious sector combine dualistic and apocalyptic framing in visions of a "holy war" that will purge their "unholy enemies" – people of color, religious minorities (especially Jewish people), LGBTQ people, feminists, and their leftist allies – and usher in a paradise for the "righteous" supremacists (Berlet and Vysotsky 2006). Betty Dobratz (2002) identified three distinct religious tendencies within the supremacist movement: Christian Identity, Creativity, and neo-paganism (Odinism/Wotanism/Ásatrú). More recently, fascists have also developed a presence within the non-belief systems of Satanism (Burley 2017; Gardell 2003; A. R. Ross 2017) and the new atheist movement (Arel 2017; Gardell 2003; Torres 2017).

Christian Identity represents the oldest religious tendency within the fascist movement and predates Nazism with its core ideas being articulated in the late 19th century, and formal organization occurring in the 1920s and growing throughout the mid-20th century (Barkun 1997; Berlet and Vysotsky 2006; Gardell 2003). This belief system is associated with the Aryan Nations, but is also central to the ideology of many Ku Klux Klan factions operating today (Belew 2018; Berlet and Vysotsky 2006). Its core beliefs, rooted in evangelical Christianity, identify white Christians as the true children of Israel of the Bible, whereas Jewish people are believed to be the children of Satan and people of color are regarded as not fully human. Because adherents to this religion interpret the Bible through a racist lens, they construe the Armageddon predicted in the book of Revelation as "a final apocalyptic struggle between good and evil with Aryans battling a Jewish conspiracy to try to save the world" (Dobratz 2002, 289; see also Barkun 1997; Gardell 2003). While still maintaining adherents, this religious tendency has lost some of its influence in the fascist movement in part due to the relative collapse of the Aryan Nations and its convoluted reinterpretation of Christianity.

Creativity, formerly known as the World Church of the Creator (WCOTC), which was founded in 1973 by Ben Klassen, and propagated by Matthew Hale after Klassen's death, presented neo-Nazi ideology with a spiritual veneer. It rejected Christianity as a "Jewish" religion and instead elevated the supposed biological superiority of white people as a spiritual mission (Dobratz 2002). Klassen was openly hostile toward competing religious tendencies such as Christian Identity and racist paganism, ridiculing them as absurd superstitions, and presented his belief system as a spiritual manifestation of secular beliefs (Gardell 2003). For "creators," the term for adherents, their race was their religion (Berlet and Vysotsky 2006;

Dobratz 2002; Gardell 2003). An essential component of Creativity is the belief that white people are singularly responsible for the creation of civilization and destined to dominate the world through the elimination of their racial enemies in a "racial holy war" (RaHoWa) (Berlet and Vysotsky 2006; Gardell 2003). This tendency came to prominence in the 1990s in part as a result of its association with the racist skinhead subculture. It fell into disarray as its most prominent spokespeople were effectively neutralized. First, its single greatest subcultural proponent George Burdi, owner of the music label Resistance Records, publisher of *Resistance* magazine, and vocalist for the band Rahowa, was twice incarcerated and subsequently left the movement. Then, Hale lost the right to the WCOTC name in a civil lawsuit which was followed by his arrest and incarceration as a result of a foiled assassination attempt on the judge who ruled against his group in 2003. While the tendency has some adherents, it is a faint shadow of its former glory.

The relative decline of Christian Identity and Creativity is accompanied by a rise in supremacist religious activity within neo-pagan practices associated with Odinism, Wotanism, and Ásatrú,[7] a worship of the Norse Gods. While Ásatrú is a diverse practice that has many inclusive adherents, including most official and established practices, it has become a home for many fascists who see the worship of Nordic gods as the true religion of white people (Burley 2017; Gardell 2003). Part of the appeal of Ásatrú is the rejection of the normative religious practices of Christianity and opposition to Abrahamic religions that originated in the Middle East and are therefore non-white. Ásatrú provides a potent spiritually based critique of modernity, positing a return to small-scale, tribal societies as an alternative, which are conceived of as ethnically homogenous for its racist practitioners (Burley 2017; Gardell 2003). The decentralized structure of Ásatrú and its iconography also lend themselves to fascist appropriation and overlap with subcultural elements within the movement (Berlet and Vysotsky 2006; Burley 2017; Gardell 2003). At present, it may be argued that this is the dominant religious tendency within the contemporary American fascist movement.

Fascist participation within Satanism reflects a similar pattern to neo-pagan practices. Contrary to popular belief, Satanism is generally not the literal worship of Satan as a deity; rather it is a view that identifies Satan as an allegory for individualism and egoism. The religion's core tenets, as outlined by Anton Szandor LaVey in the Satanic Bible and practiced by the Church of Satan, venerates independence and hedonism. This creates a blind spot in the religion for fascist involvement because its themes of social Darwinism often align with aspects of supremacist ideology. This connection is most evident in "several passages in the *Satanic Bible* that [are] plagiarized verbatim from *Might is Right*, an iconoclastic anti-Christian Social Darwinist book published in 1896" that serves as an influence for fascist activists to this day (Gardell 2003, 289). Satanism also serves as a useful theme for many subcultural supremacists, especially those involved in Black Metal, Goth, Noise, and neo-folk scenes (Burley 2017; Gardell 2003; A. R. Ross 2017).

The new atheist movement represents a trend within atheism of extreme opposition to religion not just in the public sphere, but in its very existence. New atheists are often more aggressive in their beliefs and advocate developing a culture that extols the virtue of reason and positivism through aggressive denigration of religion. Islam is of particular focus for new atheists because it is viewed as especially "incompatible" with Western, liberal, secular values and culture (Arel 2017; A. R. Ross 2017; Torres 2017). Overall mockery of religion in the movement also takes on an anti-Semitic tone when it involves Judaism, particularly in memes that trade on anti-Semitic tropes and stereotypes. The veneration of rational thought and scientific positivism among new atheists results in certain prominent adherents espousing essentialist notions about race and gender that align with "alt-right" ideological positions (Arel 2017; A. R. Ross 2017; Torres 2017). This tendency also significantly overlaps with the Intellectual and Political sectors of the fascist movement because prominent new atheists have offered a platform to supremacist intellectuals and political activists under the guise of providing a space for free speech and expression. Because of this pattern of platforming, the new atheist tendency is viewed as a major recruiting ground and pathway into fascist movements.

Intellectual sector

The intellectual sector serves as the incubator of fascist ideology as well as the space where ideas are rationalized through empirical evidence consistent with the intellectualization frame discussed earlier in this chapter (Berbrier 1999; Vysotsky and McCarthy 2017). Many individuals in this sector, like Bruce Gilley, Richard Lynn, and Kevin McDonald, hold legitimate scholarly credentials and have established roles in academic institutions (Burley 2017, 2018). Others, like Richard Spencer and Jared Taylor are affiliated with distinctly white supremacist think tanks such as the National Policy Institute and the New Century Foundation (Burley 2018). The primary activities of individuals and organizations in this sector mirror those of legitimate academics and scholarly associations, only with a fascist twist, such as conducting empirical research, publishing their work in research reports and scholarly journals, critiquing existing scholarship, as well as attending and hosting academic conferences. The annual conferences hosted by the National Policy Institute and *American Renaissance* journal have managed to fill ballrooms with attendees and facilitate interaction between like-minded supremacist scholars as well as members of the political sector. Individuals associated with this sector are often the most public face of contemporary fascism because they present the most respectable version of the movement's ideologies and are the most accessible to journalists as a result of their academic affiliations and profiles.

Subcultural sector

The subcultural sector is likely the most diverse and decentralized of the fascist movement. As a result, it is also the hardest to formally track by mainstream watchdog groups and law enforcement. This sector aligns fascist ideology to subcultural values and norms of behavior. Members of this sector often express their supremacist beliefs through cultural production and expression in personal style, music, fanzines, and websites (Berlet and Vysotsky 2006; Burley 2017; Simi and Futrell 2010).[8] Fascists actively seek out participation in subcultures because they provide access to young people who are experiencing strain (Blazak 2001; Corte and Edwards 2008; Hamm 1993; Simi and Futrell 2010). In this sector, subcultural activity becomes a form of fascist activism consistent with notions of prefigurative practice and lifestyle activism (Haenfler, Johnson, and Jones 2012; Simi and Futrell 2010).

The first, and likely most iconic, fascist subculture is racist skinheads who began to appear in the mid-to-late 1970s and became affiliated with the punk scene. Racist skinheads began to participate in punk subculture in the UK because of its use of fascist iconography, specifically the swastika, and nihilism (Berlet and Vysotsky 2006; Burley 2017; Hamm 1993). The National Front and British National Parties sought to capitalize on this youth phenomenon and worked to recruit skinhead youth into the fascist movement. The Oi! sub-genre of punk – discernible for its mid-tempo melodies, repetitive choruses based on soccer chants and drinking songs, and working-class themes – was associated with skinheads and quickly became the focus of fascists (Corte and Edwards 2008; Futrell, Simi, and Gottschalk 2006; Pieslak 2015). Using the "do-it-yourself" (DIY) ethos and networks of punk subculture, the racist tendency spread beyond the UK to mainland Europe, the United States, and around the world through the distribution of music and fanzines (Lefkowith 1999; Travis and Hardy 2012). In the United States, the racist skinhead subculture was amplified due to a moral panic that featured fascist youth on daytime television talk shows. After a clash between racist and anti-racist skinheads on the Geraldo Rivera Show, the subculture became a regular feature for programs looking to increase ratings and build an audience. Prominent fascists such as Tom Metzger of White Aryan Resistance actively recruited racist skinheads and trained them to be violent, culminating in a deadly attack on Ethiopian immigrant Mulugeta Seraw in Portland, OR (Langer 2003), and skinheads became a regular feature at the Aryan Nations World Congress and similar events (Belew 2018; Simi and Futrell 2010). By the late 1980s, racist skinheads became the embodiment of the fascist movement in the popular American imagination. However, because punk subculture has a very strong left-wing ideological orientation, racist skinheads were actively resisted in many places where they organized (Bray 2017; Burley 2017; Sarabia and Shriver 2004; Vysotsky 2013, 2015; Wood 1999). This resulted in supremacists essentially building their own punk and skinhead subculture that exists parallel to the majority of these scenes.

As punk and skinhead resistance to white supremacy was reaching its peak in the 1990s, fascists found refuge in other subcultural genres that were less overtly ideological. One of the most prominent was the black metal scene, which values individualism, rejection of external authority, and opposition to organized religion. Some of the founding members of this music scene were aligned with white supremacy; however, a distinct genre, National Socialist Black Metal (NSBM), overtly expresses neo-Nazi and fascist views (Berlet and Vysotsky 2006; Gardell 2003; Olson 2012). Many of the adherents to this subculture view themselves as intellectuals and consume the material produced by that sector as "stigmatized knowledge" consistent with their subcultural identity (Gardell 2003). This subculture also uses many of the symbols associated with Ásatrú or are active practitioners of the racist version of the religion. Similarly, there are fascist tendencies in goth, industrial, noise, and neo-folk subcultures (Burghart 1999; Burley 2017).

Recently, a phenomenon of white supremacist hipsters, or nipsters (a portmanteau of Nazi hipster), has flourished that utilizes mainstream hipster irony, appropriation, and aesthetics to spread fascist and neo-Nazi ideas (Burley 2017; Rogers 2014; Smith IV 2018). This category of the subcultural fascist sector avoids many of the overt symbolic presentations of supremacist affiliation in favor of a bricolage of subcultural imagery with subtle markers of the movement combined with street style and even mainstream aesthetics. Similarly, unlike the subcultures described above, this new form often lacks a distinctive association with a single musical genre with adherents consuming a variety of musical styles that include fascist and non-political versions of the subcultures described above as well as electronic music and even hip hop (Rivers 2018; Rogers 2014; Smith IV 2018). The true irony of this tendency is manifested in the postmodernist subcultural approach to fascism that it embodies by employing a "supermarket of style" and fluidity (Bennett 1999; Polhemus 1997) to the expression of their fascist affiliations. The most apparent version of this subculture is the Proud Boys, a quasi-fraternal social club meets activist group started by former Vice Media founder Gavin McInnes. This group brands itself as a "Western chauvinist" formation utilizing a combination of ethnic claims-making and intellectualization stigma management frames discussed above coupled with hipster irony to point to and away from its white supremacy. Members have been known to attend overtly fascist mobilizations and other extremist events. Similar to the hipster subculture, an online culture of trolls and gamers engage in overt white supremacy and misogyny typical of contemporary fascists under the guise of irony and "lulz," a process of pranking that is often designed to attack viewer/player sensitivity. Websites such as 4chan and 8chan[9] are gathering places for people who spread racist, anti-Semitic, and misogynist memes and images purportedly for humor purposes, and an entire network of video streamers and podcasters provide fascist content on a number of public and private platforms (Burley 2017; Lyons 2017; Nagle 2017; Wendling 2018). The deployment of supposed irony by both fascist hipsters and trolls is designed to simultaneously allow them to express bigotry and deny its impacts.

Criminal sector

The criminal sector consists of groups and individuals who are adherents to fascist ideology, but primarily are oriented toward "profit-oriented criminal activity" (Simi, Smith, and Reeser 2008, 754). This sector consists of racist prison gangs like the Aryan Brotherhood, biker gangs, and street gangs. While members of this sector hold fascist beliefs of racial supremacy, these may be modified in order to achieve short- and long-term criminal goals. Historically, the criminal sector was essential to the political and religious sectors of the movement because it provided financial and material resources, often in the form of illegal weapons, to supremacist groups and would-be insurgents. Its importance and strength of association has waned as subcultural commodities generated larger profits for the movement than criminal activity (Burghart 1999). There is, however, some overlap between the criminal sector and the subcultural and religious sectors. Racist skinheads may organize into criminal gangs or join established prison gangs if they become incarcerated, and the religious sector often provides a cover for fascist organizing inside correctional institutions under the guise of spiritual practice.

The movement model described above is meant to serve as an ideal type (Weber 1949) with each category representing a distinct tendency in the broader fascist movement. When applied to individuals and organizations within the movement, the categories often overlap forming a Venn diagram of sector classifications. For example, groups such as the American Guard and Keystone United present as ostensibly actors in the political sector, but have membership that largely consists of racist skinheads from the subcultural sector (Anti-Defamation League 2017; Vysotsky and Madfis 2014). Similarly, alt-right progenitor Richard Spencer is rooted in the intellectual sector as a result of his role at the National Policy Institute, but has engaged in distinct political activity, most notably attending the infamous "Unite the Right" rally in Charlottesville, VA with a contingent of supporters (Lough 2018). Rather than viewing the sectors described as exhaustive categories, they are better understood as tendencies within which fascist movement members and organizations primarily operate that influence their approaches to ideology, framing, and activity.

The antifascist movement

For most people antifa is a mystery wrapped in an enigma wearing a black mask. As a movement wherein most members strategically guard their identities, antifascists rarely provide interviews or even commentary to mass media, or social scientists for that matter, and engage in very specific forms of outreach and movement building outside of the public eye. This translates into a series of strange caricatures of the movement. For many on the right, antifa activists are hyper-violent terrorists working to suppress the free speech of conservatives. For moderates and some liberal observers, they are undemocratic criminals who unilaterally use violence to achieve their goals and ignore the rule of law, as well as the norms of debate and protest in liberal democratic society (Beinart 2017). For some on the far left, they are heroes who bravely put their bodies on the line to defend protesters as well as protect communities and society more broadly, from the violence of the far-right. All of these visions of antifa activism are simultaneously true and false. The organizational structure of the antifascist movement provides a framework for a wide range of participants who can engage in countermovement activities in a variety of forms beyond confrontational street protests. Despite, or possibly in spite of, the caricatures and propaganda, beneath the masks, antifa activists are in many respects ordinary individuals who participate in a movement with a distinct ideology, organizational structure, strategy, and tactics. Most people outside of the movement would be surprised at the ordinariness of antifascists; and placed into a context of sociological study of social movements, militant antifascist practices reflect many of the dynamics identified by scholars.

The organization of antifascism

Contrary to the claims of far-right media, there is no centralized antifa organization; however, this does not mean that militant antifascism is a disorganizing movement. Antifascism as a movement, regardless of its type, is defined by a specific orientation in opposition to fascist movement mobilization (Bray 2017; Burley 2017; Copsey 2000, 2018; Renton 2001). This results in a diversity of approaches in opposition to fascism. The structure of antifascism broadly involves complex interplay of informal and formal activists and activities.

Informal antifascism

Since antifascism is simply opposition to fascist mobilization and activity, becoming an antifascist activist does not require people to join a group or even attend a formal antifascist event. This type of informal, or "everyday," antifascism requires nothing more than some type of public expression of opposition to fascist ideology or activity (Bray 2017; Burley 2017). It can take a variety of forms ranging from expressions of sympathy for targets of fascist degradation and violence to verbal or physical confrontation with fascists. Informal antifascism is always spontaneous because it happens when an opportunity arises. The people involved in informal activism may have a range of commitment to antifascism as a principle. At the most basic level, a person may be an informal antifascist because fascism offends their core sensibilities and they feel compelled to express their beliefs and/or act. In its more advanced forms, informal antifascism can take on distinct efforts of opposition to fascist presence in subcultures.[10] One of the most common forms of informal antifascism is cultural expression of opposition to fascism, which will be discussed in detail in Chapter 4. Wearing an item of clothing or accessory such as a pin displaying an antifascist symbol does not require an individual to become involved with a formally constituted antifascist group, but does send a message that the individual is sympathetic to antifascism. Because informal antifascism is relatively spontaneous and takes the form of everyday activities, it is rarely acknowledged or recorded in any formal manner. A person or group acts to defy fascist ideology or activity successfully, then go on with the rest of their day and their life. This form of antifascism is, therefore, also largely inaccessible to researchers except through the recollections of formal antifascist activists and those acts that achieve attention in mass or social media.

Formal antifascism

To the extent that formal organization requires a hierarchical structure with clearly defined criteria for membership, there is no such thing as an antifa organization. However, this does not mean that militant antifascism consists exclusively of informal activities. There are, of course, formal groups operating explicitly as militant antifascists, often with antifa or antifascists in their names.[11] These groups are not chapters of a formal organization; however, they are affinity groups operating to achieve the goal of opposing fascist mobilization. Noel Sturgeon (1995, 38–39) describes the structure of affinity groups as:

> small groups of people … that serve as the primary organizational structure of the movement. Affinity groups autonomously decide the nature and extent of their participation in a direct action. They also provide material, emotional, and sometimes legal support for themselves, resulting in the creation of a relatively self-sufficient unit.

Like other networks of affinity groups, the formal antifascist movement consists of a decentralized network based on common political goals that is unencumbered by bureaucracy or formal leadership – antifa has no leaders or central offices. Formal antifa groups may be formed by individuals with a common ideological commitment to opposing fascism or coalesce from consistent informal antifascist activity, replicating a general pattern for affinity groups (Jasper 1997; Sturgeon 1995). The affinity groups that make up the structure of formal antifascism may affiliate with one another such as the former Anti-Racist Action or the contemporary Torch Antifa networks; but in an era of social media and decentralized mass communication antifascist affinity groups need not affiliate with a formal network. Formal affinity groups represent the most public manifestation of antifascist activism. Because they are able to pool skills and resources, affinity groups are capable of taking on the fascist movement in a coordinated manner using the tactics described in the following chapter. Since they operate in a more structured manner than cases of informal antifascism, formal antifascist groups provide a framework for analysis of the movement as a whole.

Antifa: a profile

The public perception of militant antifascism is often colored by a series of essentialist assumptions that feed into critiques of its actions as ineffectual and elitist. The descriptions of antifa levied by a range of commentators, ranging from the far right to center left, are based on assumptions that militant antifascists represent a series of privileged demographics. The black clad street fighter is presumed to be a white, heterosexual, cisgender man whose radical politics are a product of some form of social alienation. While this may apply to some extent to the informal antifascists within subcultures, it is much less the case with formal antifascist groups. The demographic reality of antifa challenges many of the assumptions about and criticisms of militant antifascism. In a statement responding to the attempted criminalization of antifascist activism, Rose City Antifa (2019) described movement participants in the following manner:

> Anti-fascists are your neighbors. Some anti-fascists are people fighting for our lives and dignity, because we are people of color, queer, trans, of a targeted ethnicity or religion. Some anti-fascists are people who are cashing in on our privileges to protect those who are more vulnerable. Anti-fascists are regular people: moms, teachers, carpenters, servers, healthcare workers, and veterans.

The gender, sexual orientation, race, age, and even occupational demographics of the members of formal militant antifascist groups that I observed, as well as the broader movement, validate this assertion and reflect a greater diversity than critics, and the general public, often assume.

Gender

Militant antifascism is often critiqued for its perceived hypermasculinity because its most public manifestations involve confrontational and at times violent clashes with fascists (Bray 2017). The internal structure of antifascist groups paints a very different picture of the gender of participants and internal gender dynamics. Both Old City Antifa and New City Antifa had gender parity in their membership because each group had at least 50 percent representation of women within the groups. In both cases, this was as much a product of a conscientious desire to address issues of hypermasculinity as it was recruitment strategy and membership base. The gender composition of each group was a product of organic development and a distinct desire on the part of group members to reflect a feminist plank represented by the antifascist position. The following case example demonstrates the conscientious approach that militant antifascists take to addressing gender dynamics in their activism:

> I am sitting at an early meeting of New City Antifa in the home of one of the members. We are engaging in conversation before the start of the formal meeting and group business when Ruby, one of the founding members noted the gender demographics of the group as an off-hand remark. The group had organically developed a gender balance in its membership, but the observation was taken as a mark of pride for the dynamics of the group. This spontaneous observation generated a pointed discussion among the group members of the benefits of maintaining gender parity or even a minority of cisgender men, and how it can inform group recruitment. As the group sought to expand its membership, careful attention was paid to the gender of potential recruits and how it would impact the dynamics of the New City Antifa's activism.

The gender distribution of both Old City and New City Antifa is reflective of an ideological commitment to gender equality within antifascist activism. Both the Anti-Racist Action network, of which both antifa groups observed were members, and the current Torch Antifa network decidedly included a plank in their "Points of Unity" that specifically addresses the need to maintain an intersectional approach to antifascist struggle. These specifically address network commitments to fight for "abortion rights and reproductive freedom" as well as against sexism, homophobia, and transphobia. Both groups saw the active recruitment of members who would reflect a gender balance as an important check on the hypermasculine tendencies that exist within militant antifascist activism.

Sexual orientation

As Chapter 5 will discuss, a key factor in antifascist militancy is the sense of threat perceived by individuals who are targeted by fascists for violence. This threat is extremely salient for people who identify as LGBTQ. Indeed, individuals who identify as Queer are highly represented in formal and informal antifa activity.

In my formal interviews with militant antifascists, exactly half of the sample identified as Lesbian, Gay, or Bisexual. During my time observing New City Antifa, roughly one-third of members identified as Queer with representation growing to one half shortly after the end of the formal ethnographic research period. The group also built strong ties to the LGBTQ community in New City with a number of supporters and members often participating in events with the community. During the formal research period, specifically Queer oriented militant groups such as Bash Back, which provide protection to Queer communities facing violence, received solidarity from formal antifa groups and at times worked in solidarity with one another on actions against fascists who threatened LGBTQ communities in parts of the United States.

Race

The antifascists groups with which I was involved were collectives made up of primarily white members. Both Old City Antifa and New City Antifa had a majority of members who identified as white. Interview participants in the formal research I conducted were also exclusively white. The whiteness of Old City Antifa was tempered by a dynamic where a number of members identified as Jewish. While Jewish people are incorporated into white identity in the United States, their status is often considered one of "conditional whiteness" because it may be revoked if the majority of white people decide to racialize Jewishness as an "other," as history has often demonstrated. Jewish people are often drawn to antifascist activity for reasons similar to members of other historically marginalized groups – because they are targets of supremacist violence. For Jewish people this is both a personal and historical fact as well as one embedded in the knowledge that anti-Semitism is essential to the conspiracism and ideology of fascist movements (Berlet and Vysotsky 2006; Ward 2017).

This racial dynamic of majority white membership cannot be expanded to all antifascist groups in the United States because membership and recruitment bases vary greatly based on local populations and recruitment strategies. Locations with greater racial diversity, particularly larger cities, often have much greater racial diversity than the groups observed and the individuals whom I interviewed. National conferences of formal antifascist groups represent the full diversity of membership and have distinct caucuses of people of color in attendance.

Age

Militant antifascism is often perceived as a young person's game. After all, street confrontations with fascists require a certain strength and stamina assumed of the young. My experiences with antifa activists indicate that, like so many other demographic categories discussed so far, there is much greater diversity in the movement than would be assumed. In formal interviews, the majority of respondents identified as being in an age range of 26–35.[12] New City Antifa was composed of individuals almost entirely in their mid-20s to early 30s, and approximately half of Old City Antifa members also would be classified in a 25–30 age range. As antifa activists age, some do not age out of the movement. Many of the individuals involved in New City Antifa during the formal research period continue to engage in antifascist activity to this day as they have aged into their late 30s and 40s. The most prominent public figure in the militant antifascist movement, Daryle Lamont Jenkins of One People's Project, is now officially in his fifties. He is joined by lifelong antifa activists and committed leftist activists who are mobilizing in response to an emboldened supremacist movement in the Trump era. These include baby boomers who are 60 or over and have been referred to as "Grantifa" based on their age.

What drives the range in the age of militant antifascists is not just the timeline of activism in the United States – since antifascist activism formalized in the 1990s, many seasoned activists came of age in the movement – but also the diversity in forms of activism within the movement. As Chapter 3 will discuss, street confrontations are the most spectacular tip of the iceberg of antifascist activism. While street fights might be best left to the youth, seasoned activists often have the skills and capacity to engage in the information gathering and dissemination that is the day-to-day of antifa activism.

Employment and class

Militant antifascism has historically been a working-class phenomenon, and the contemporary movement in the United States shares a similar class orientation. The antifascists whom I interviewed were employed in construction, nursing, social work, teaching, and other working-class professions. The members of New City Antifa had similar employment with a handful of college students who balanced education with employment in working-class occupations. The interviewees and militant antifascists with whom I interacted generally indicated that they were raised in working- or middle-class environments, which largely reflects their current class location.[13]

Anti-authoritarianism and antifascism: the ideology of antifa

Antifascism has always been an explicitly leftist position. After all, if fascism is the most extreme right-wing ideology, then it would follow that the movement to oppose it would be organized by its ideological opponents on the left. Historically, socialists, communists, and anarchists engaged in militant opposition to nascent fascist street movements and parties. The contemporary antifascist movement follows in the footsteps of its historical predecessors. In the United States, Marxists such as the Communist Worker's Party and John Brown Anti-Klan Committee took militant stances against populist fascist organizing in the late 1970s and 1980s. The latter found support from the growing punk scene, which was experiencing infiltration of fascist ideology (Bray 2017). The punk influence on American antifascism aligned its ideological orientation toward anti-authoritarianism and anarchism. Although organizations such as Anti-Racist Action (ARA) and the Torch Antifa Network are dedicated to a non-sectarian approach to antifascist activism, both operated along anarchist and anti-authoritarian lines, which drew greater participation from individuals with such orientations. My own research indicates that formal militant antifascism within groups that identify as antifa in the United States is a largely anarchist phenomenon.

Anarchism is an often misunderstood or misinterpreted ideology that is believed to advocate chaos, disorder, and absolute violence. Such depictions rarely come from anarchists themselves and are often developed to delegitimize anarchist beliefs and actions (Goldman 1969; Kropotkin 1904). Anarchist ideology consists of a set of core principles rooted in a radical socialist tradition: opposition to all forms of formal authority, especially as they manifest themselves in state power; resistance to capitalism and the free market system; and advocacy for democratic self-management and organization of all aspects of social life (Guérin 1970). Anarchist activism takes the form of building alternative structures based on the aforementioned principles within the framework of existing society and engaging in direct action against the state and other forms of authority (Graeber 2002; Guérin 1970). Much of anarchist practice is therefore fundamentally prefigurative because it serves to model anarchist forms of social structure and interaction (Graeber 2002; Leach 2013; Shantz 2011; Springer 2014; D. M. Williams 2018; Yates 2015). These guiding principles drive much of the activism that militant antifascists engage in.

One of the clearest indicators of the anarchist affiliation of antifa activists is in the iconography of the movement. The overlapping flags and three arrows pointing left, originally designed in red to symbolize the democratic socialist inspired German "Iron Front," have been modified into the iconic black of contemporary anarchism. The flags are alternately presented as red and black to symbolize anarchist communism. Antifa groups consistently rely on red and black color schemes to signify their anarchist and anti-authoritarian orientation.

The anarchist position of militant antifascists is not simply symbolic. Individuals who I interviewed often either directly identified as anarchists or made statements that reflected elements of anarchist ideology such as opposition to the state and existing hierarchical structures and values. Kam's statement, "I'm an anarchist" was echoed by most interviewees. Others, like Helena, viewed antifascism as integral to developing a proper anarchist analysis, "a lot of the anarchist endeavors ultimately should have defeating white supremacy as a main keystone." In addition to such statements, all of the members of both Old City Antifa and New City Antifa identified as anarchists or were members of anarchist groups. Contemporary militant antifascism is marked by anarchist participation whether it is the individual members of antifascist groups or organizations such as New York's Metropolitan Anarchist Coordinating Council or the local General Defense Committees (GDCs) of the Industrial Workers of the World.

Understanding the ideology of militant antifascists is crucial to contextualizing the tactics that they employ. Sociologists studying social movements rarely focus their analyses on the beliefs of movement participants or ideologies espoused by organizations; instead focusing on movement dynamics and processes. Mayer Zald (2000) proposed that social movement scholarship as a whole should place more emphasis on the role of ideology in understanding movement activity; ultimately arguing that it should be understood as "ideologically structured action." Ideology serves as a framework for actions taken by movement participants and constructs the boundaries of acceptable and effective tactics (Fitzgerald and Rodgers 2000; Jasper 1997; Oliver and Johnston 2000; Tilly 2006; Zald 2000). The anarchist ideology of militant antifascists is manifested in the culture and tactics deployed by the movement. In those respects, antifa activism serves as a key component of radical movement activity in the United States.

Beyond antifascism: activism outside of antifa

The radical orientation of militant antifascists points to a broader activist sensibility than the focus on confronting fascism. As with other radical activists, militant antifascists are involved in a broad variety of social movement activity with a wide array of organizations reflecting an orientation toward social justice (Bray 2017; Fitzgerald and Rodgers 2000; Jasper 1997). While antifascism was a major focus for the activists I observed and interviewed, it was not the sole concern. For many, antifa activity reflected existing anarchist activism; while others viewed it as a necessary adjunct to other forms of leftist engagement.

The path to militant antifascist activism often comes through a variety of leftist activities and organizations. The direct-action orientation of the movement against corporate globalization drew Brock to antifa:

> I started out with anti-globalization activism, and I did that for probably about a year and started doing antifascist stuff because it was a point in my life where I was actually looking for a lot of stuff to do and anti-globalization stuff was

like once every year and a half that something actually happened …, and that was at a time … when there actually was quite a bit of activity by white supremacists and by neo-Nazis and so it really was at the point where I was just like "I have this interest in doing stuff regularly" and I found out about antifascist work and there was something to do like every few days. Really, like it was pretty intense for a long time, and so I did it.

This activism continued as Brock participated in anti-globalization protest by traveling and protesting with the antifa group that he had become involved in. In a similar vein, the direct-action orientation of militant antifascism led Mark to become involved in this type of activism:

I joined an organization that was organizing around [racial justice], where we used direct methods such as Copwatch and also street demonstrations as a tool of preventing police brutality and that organization had a history of … having opposed overt racist organizations and later as being a member of the organization there were instances where that presented itself again.

Mark's work on issues of police violence and racial inequality drew him to antifascist activism because of the ideological and tactical overlaps between such work. As a participant in such movements, he gravitated toward militant opposition to fascist mobilization. These narratives speak to the overlaps between forms of leftist activism and militant antifascism. Antifa activists do not trade their desire to address one set of issues for antifascism, but incorporate it into their existing activist work.

Other militant antifascists maintained memberships in broader organizations such as anarchist groups and federations. Old City Antifa probably demonstrated the strongest overlap between antifascist and anarchist political activism. The group was formed by members of an anarchist organization as part of a commitment to engage in confrontational protest against fascist mobilizations. Over time, its membership expanded to include individuals who weren't members of the anarchist organization, but the majority and core membership still maintained an organizational overlap. Most antifa groups do not hold such strong organizational ties and member overlaps. While all of the members of New City Antifa identified as anarchists, they did not share exact ideological orientations within the movement and came from a variety of organizational backgrounds. This is more typical of militant antifascists who have greater individual autonomy of activist affiliation. Individuals who I interviewed similarly identified as being members of groups that work toward greater economic, gender, racial, and sexual orientation justice in a variety of capacities. Contemporary antifa activists continue to maintain engagement with issues of social justice in conjunction with antifascism. Singer-songwriter and community organizer Tae Phoenix (2019) described the antifascists who came to their defense after experiencing threats after performing at an anti-racist community event as follows:

One Antifa activist I know has become adept at navigating the local social services system and is fighting to make sure that families experiencing homelessness do not lose their shelter beds due to technicalities beyond their control.

Another focuses on making sure that people living in poverty are able to afford their prescription medications and is raising money to help a local trans activist purchase a new motorized wheelchair.

Another provides rides to prisons around the region, to make sure that people who cannot afford a car do not lose touch with loved ones who are incarcerated.

For militant antifascists, opposition to fascist mobilization is just one aspect of a broader engagement with activism. Many activists come to antifa activity from work on issues that are related or have similar tactical approaches. For others, antifascism is one aspect of a broader set of social movement activities. In all cases, militant antifascism is viewed as complementary to other forms of activity.

A popular front: coalitions between antifa and other activists

Virtually all social movements consist of a series of allied groups working together in order to achieve relatively similar goals. Sociologists have documented the way in which groups coalesce to engage in planning and action on a variety of issues (Barkan 1979; Fantasia and Voss 2004; Ferree and Hess 2000; McAdam 1999; Polletta 2007; Rochon and Meyer 1997; Van Dyke 2003; Van Dyke and Amos 2017). Researchers also identified coalitions across social movements in focused campaigns against specific targets (Beamish and Luebbers 2009; Obach 2004; Staggenborg 2015). Antifascism is, of course, no different. Opposition to fascist mobilization and organizing involves broad coalitions of activists employing a diverse range of tactics. Militant antifascism similarly requires building alliances with a variety of groups and organizations that differ from antifa groups in terms of ideology, organizational form, and tactics.

Ideological coalitions are most common between formal antifa groups and other leftists. As discussed above, the anarchist and anti-authoritarian ideological position of many militant antifascist groups facilitates coalition work with other anarchist organizations and individual, unaffiliated anarchists. Old City Antifa often leveraged its overlap with a larger anarchist organization to mobilize in public actions. In its early stages, New City Antifa worked in coalition with the local affiliate of a nationwide anarchist organization despite the antifa group's members' lack of ideological agreement with the specifics of that organization's analysis. Because New City Antifa operated independently of any formal anarchist organization, it was also able to mobilize individual anarchists from a variety of interpretive traditions. Such mobilizations are typical of antifa contingents in protest scenarios. Contemporary militant antifascist blocs at protests have been buttressed by members of local GDCs and affiliates of John Brown Gun Clubs as well as independent affinity groups of anarchist sympathizers.

Yet, participation in militant antifascism is not exclusively an anarchist or anti-authoritarian endeavor. Militant antifascist blocs in public protests often consist of a diverse grouping of left-oriented activists motivated to confront fascist mobilizations. Like the historical antecedents to contemporary militant antifascist movement discussed earlier in this chapter, Marxist organizations are keen to mobilize in opposition to fascists for many of the same reasons as anarchists or other leftists. In the 1990s, the Anti-Racist Action network consisted of a breadth of ideological tendencies including Marxists and socialists. Militant antifascist blocs that Old City Antifa participated in also often included a contingent from a local chapter of a Marxist-Leninist organization with a history of aggressive confrontations with overt racists dating back to the 1970s.

The fascist mobilizations inspired and emboldened by the candidacy and election of Donald Trump inspired a renewed focus on supremacist activity and antifascist counter-mobilizations. This diversified the ideological orientations of militant antifascist activity. A variety of leftists mobilize alongside anarchist oriented antifa activists and groups. Socialists are organizing through the work of individual chapters of Democratic Socialists of America, which mobilize members to protest against fascist events. Marxists are often represented in militant confrontations with supremacists at public demonstrations. On June 26, 2016, a coalition of antifascist groups and activists sought to disrupt a neo-Nazi rally on the California State House steps in Sacramento. Among the militant antifascist protesters, which included a regional affiliate of the Torch Antifa network, were members of By Any Means Necessary, who were famously captured on news cameras in clashes with fascists and gave interviews to reporters. The militant coalition of antifascist activists in the Pacific Northwest includes members of the Freedom Socialist Party, the Party for Socialism and Liberation, and International Socialist Organization. While there are often vast ideological differences within militant blocs, the immediacy of threat posed by fascist mobilization allows for unity in confrontational protest.

Antifascist coalitions do not simply rely on far-left blocs bent on confrontation. As the following chapter will discuss, successful antifascism requires a broad set of tactics. It also requires a broad association of movements and organizations. Militant antifascists work with a variety of organizations that actively oppose fascist movements including community groups, unions, and religious organizations. This is driven by the importance of building strategic solidarity between militant and non-militant groups against a common opposition regardless of tactical differences. In a formal interview, Damon explained that the militant antifascist group with which he was involved was able to successfully build ties with civil rights activists in his city. This included a number of veteran activists who were deeply committed to nonviolence as a tactic. Although they differed in tactics, the militant antifascists were given legitimacy through their ties with non-violent activists with strong community reputations. The militant antifascists were also able to serve as a protective force when pacifist activists in the coalition were threatened by fascists.

A similar coalition is necessary for successful opposition to public fascist mobilizations. When the far-right group, Patriot Prayer, whose rallies are ostensibly in support of free speech and Donald Trump often draw overtly white supremacist attendees, planned a rally in Portland, OR on June 4, 2017, Rose City Antifa organized an opposition rally. The call for opposition demonstrates both the ideological alliances discussed above and coalitions with more moderate progressive groups such as the Portland State University Student Union and the Portland chapter of Showing Up for Racial Justice (SURJ) (Rose City Antifa 2018a). A subsequent statement from the group encouraged a non-confrontational rally in order to maintain the coalition and draw mass opposition (Rose City Antifa 2018b). Momentum for the opposition rally increased as local unions and progressive groups committed to the rally in the wake of an attack that killed two men and wounded one who defended two young women of color from harassment by Jeremy Christian, an attendee at earlier Patriot Prayer rallies. The June 4 rally drew several thousand counter-protesters from a variety of ideological positions and tactical approaches who actively opposed the fascist mobilization. This strategy has been fruitful since, with similar events in Portland drawing a wide range of antifascist opposition,

> the majority of the opposing crowd was comprised of socialists from a local labor organization and anti-racists. They were locals who were there to protest peacefully, but who said they also came prepared to defend themselves and other people who might be attacked.
>
> *(Neiwert 2018a)*

This strategy of mass opposition and coalition work between formal, militant antifascist organizations and a diverse range of allies is the model for protests large and small in the Trump era from Pikeville, KY to New Orleans, LA to Charlottesville, VA to Boston, MA and Berkeley, CA; anywhere fascists rally militant antifascists are sure to mobilize in opposition as part of a broad coalition.

Fascists versus antifascists

The contemporary fascist movement distinctly adapts central ideological tenets of inequality, militarism, and authoritarianism to a modern, technologically advanced, globalized world. Its core beliefs are transmitted through five master frames: dualism, conspiracism, apocalypticism, populism, and authoritarianism (Berlet 2004a). These principles are made palatable to the wider society through processes of ethnic claims-making and intellectualization (Berbrier 1998; 1999). Eschewing the authoritarian model of charismatic leadership typical of classical fascism, contemporary movements instead advocate a decentralized, leaderless resistance model of organization that facilitates movement recruitment and activity in an age of mass internet and social media access (Berlet and Vysotsky 2006; Michael 2012; Simi and Futrell 2010). As fascists have adapted to the material and cultural changes in

American society, the movement demonstrates many of the elements of NSMs associated with the left – activism around identity, a cross-class social base and post-materialist concerns, rejection of the left-right political dichotomy, diffuse, decentralized structure, and activism through prefigurative and cultural practice (Johnston, Laraña, and Gusfield 1994). This framework presents a movement that is much more varied than the unitary, hierarchical model established in interwar Europe. The contemporary fascist movement can be classified into five sectors – political, religious, intellectual, subcultural, and criminal – based on the way in which they interpret fascist ideology and the activities that they engage in (Berlet and Vysotsky 2006). Identifying contemporary fascism as a culturally based movement with a variety of sectors that represent distinct tendencies serves to inform potential opposition.

The antifascist movement stands in stark contrast to the fascist movement that it opposes. As a result of the variety of forms of fascist ideology and activism, antifascist activism must be highly adaptive to any manifestation of fascism. The antifascist movement, therefore, is extremely decentralized in its structure consisting of informal and formal forms of activism. Informal antifascism consists of relatively spontaneous "everyday" (Bray 2017; Burley 2017) forms of opposition by individuals who are not affiliated with formal antifascist groups. Formal antifascism consists of affinity groups of activists who coalesce around activity in opposition to fascism. These groups may coordinate with one another in formal antifascist networks or operate independently in the service of the common countermovement goal. The individuals involved in antifascist struggle reflect a broad cross-section of the population; but also, as Chapter 5 will discuss in detail, demonstrate the breadth of people targeted by the fascist movement. Antifascist groups, and militant antifa activists in particular, demonstrate a diversity of gender identities, sexual orientations, as well as racial, ethnic, and religious identities. While antifascism is a cross-class movement, formal antifascist groups tend to consist of working-class activists.

Because antifa activists oppose fascist veneration of inequality and authoritarian domination, they frequently articulate an anti-authoritarian or anarchist ideology (Bray 2017; Burley 2017). These activists often come to antifascism as a result of their leftist ideological position or activism. Antifa activists regularly participate in social movement activity beyond antifascism in support of greater economic, political, and social justice. This activism creates ties between militant antifascists and other social movements that are crucial for movement success. Antifascist mobilizations reflect these ties through broad alliance networks that draw participants who range from non-militant community-based organizations to labor unions to leftist radicals. The alliances formed between antifascists and other activists facilitate the types of mass mobilizations and activity necessary for successful opposition to fascist movements (Bray 2017; Burley 2017; Copsey 2000; Renton 2001). The antifascist movement, therefore, is defined by diversity of membership, activism, alliances, and, ultimately, tactics.

Notes

1 The populist anti-elitist frame is rooted in the anti-Semitism of the conspiracist frame. The elites critiqued by fascists are ultimately viewed as either directly or indirectly controlled by Jewish interests. The populist critiques levied by fascists are therefore ultimately anti-Semitic dog-whistles designed to put forth a message of racial supremacy (Dobratz and Shanks-Meile 1997; Ezekiel 1995; Ward 2017).

2 Although the term, fascism, was coined in reference to Benito Mussolini's ultra-nationalist political movement formed in 1919, the core ideological framework predates this manifestation (Berlet and Lyons 2000; Burley 2017; Ross 2017).

3 In her philosophical treatment of misogyny, Kate Manne (2018) indicates that misogynists do not have a blanket hostility toward women. For misogynists, a space is created for women who fulfill men's needs and desires in a manner that is consistent with their patriarchal expectations. Women who are willing to accept a subservient position or advocate for misogyny are spared some aspects of misogynist hostility. This dynamic explains why women may not be completely alienated from the contemporary fascist movement, especially those organizations and spaces associated with the alt-right.

4 Another critique of the SPLC's categorization typology is the inclusion of "black nationalist" as well as other groups of historically marginalized people who espouse anti-Semitic, Islamophobic, or homophobic ideologies. This inclusion serves to draw a false equivalence between the actions of a minority within a minority in the United States to movements whose potential recruitment base represents the white majority and advocates for a reaffirmation of white supremacy. Robert Paxton (2004, 203) explains the futility of categorizing groups organized by historically marginalized people who convey prejudice and authoritarianism in the United States as fascist and equivalent to the white supremacist movement:

> such a movement within a historically excluded minority would have so little opportunity to wield genuine power that, in the last analysis, any comparison to authentic fascisms seems far-fetched. A subjugated minority may employ rhetoric that resembles early fascism, but it can hardly embark on its own program of internal dictatorship and purification and territorial expansionism.

5 Social movement analysis acknowledges the role of ideology in a movement's formation, mobilization, and activity. In the study of social movements, ideology may be understood as a "focus on systems of ideas which couple understandings of how the world works with ethical, moral, and normative principles that guide personal and collective action" (Oliver and Johnston 2000, 44). Ideologies, therefore, serve as a means of interpreting the world and defining what actions need to be taken in order to change it. Meyer Zald (2000) argues in favor of interpreting all social movement activity as "ideologically structured action." In this framework, social movements engage in "ideologically structured behavior," which is "behavior which is guided and shaped by ideological concerns – belief systems defending and attacking current social relations and the social system" (Zald 2000, 3–4). The role of ideology is ultimately to shape and guide social movement activity. The specific tendencies of contemporary fascist ideology inform the internal dynamics of the movement as well as the action repertoires of individuals and organizations of which it comprises.

6 The original research contained a significant proportion of sites that were dedicated to Holocaust denial (read: revisionist) content (~10 percent, n=25), which were not coded because they were not associated with a specific organization (Vysotsky 2004). The content and framing of these sites would inform my thinking regarding the intellectual sector and should have been coded as such in the original study. The intellectual sector is defined by a scholarly engagement in the service of the fascist movement, which includes analysis of the historical subject of the Holocaust. Much of the work in the area of Holocaust denial has been performed by renegade scholars seeking to minimize the impact of genocide committed by Nazis and their allies during the Second World War and reduce the stigma for

contemporary fascists. As a result, evidence of the intellectual sector may be traced to the original research despite its lack of inclusion.

7 Although Odinism, Wotanism and Ásatrú are distinct neo-pagan religious tendencies, for ease of discussion, this book will refer to Ásatrú as representative of fascist neo-pagan beliefs and practices because it is identified as the primary form practiced by American supremacists (Burley 2017; Gardell 2003).

8 It is crucial to note that the subcultures discussed generally are constructed by members as inclusive spaces with often progressive values; therefore, fascist participation is often a contested issue for many adherents (Sarabia and Shriver 2004; Vysotsky 2013; 2015; Wood 1999). Chapters 4, 5, and 6 will discuss the conflicts that occur within subcultural spaces and the role that antifascists play in maintaining values of openness and diversity within subcultures as well as the safety of participants.

9 As of the writing of this book, 8chan was offline after its implication in the mass shooting targeting Latinx shoppers at a Walmart in El Paso, Texas on August 3, 2019, which killed 22 people. The alleged shooter posted a statement to the forum expressing white nationalist views on immigration and environmental destruction. The forum had become a go to for fascist terrorists to post manifestos after Brenton Tarrant, the alleged mass shooter who attacked two mosques in Christchurch, New Zealand earlier that year, posted a lengthy statement explaining the rationale behind his attack. Other users of the forum encouraged mass violence with discussions about beating previous shooter's "high scores." The increased public pressure on the site led security platform Cloudflare to stop working with them, which left 8chan vulnerable to attacks and forced it to be removed (Sherr and Van Boom 2019).

10 The defense of subcultures from fascist infiltration and recruitment often takes the form of informal antifascism because it is driven by the spontaneous activity of individuals who believe that such activity is anathema to subcultural authenticity. These acts of spontaneity are performed by people who may not have any affiliation with formal antifascist groups and are organized in an organic manner by antifascist-oriented participants. This can be juxtaposed against formal antifascist activism in subcultures by formations such as Skinheads Against Racial Prejudice, Red and Anarchist Skinheads, or subculturalists who are affiliated with formal antifascist groups and represent them at subcultural events.

11 Some contemporary antifa groups also operate using variations on the Anti-Racist Action name despite the dissolution of that network as a distinct reference to its history and legacy of militant antifascism in the United States (Bray 2017; Burley 2017).

12 Interviewees were asked to identify their age in a range rather than specify their age in part to protect their identities.

13 Two members of New City Antifa were raised in upper-class environments, but had assumed a déclassé lifestyle consistent with subcultural affiliation and/or an anarchist political ideology.

Works cited

Anti-Defamation League. 2017. "Behind the American Guard: Hardcore White Supremacists." *Anti-Defamation League.* https://www.adl.org/blog/behind-the-american-guard-hardcore-white-supremacists.

Arel, Dan. 2017. "New Atheism's Move from Islamophobia to White Nationalism." *The New Arab.* https://www.alaraby.co.uk/english/comment/2017/7/12/new-atheisms-move-from-islamophobia-to-white-nationalism.

Arena, Michael P., and Bruce A. Arrigo. 2000. "White Supremacist Behavior: Toward an Integrated Social Psychological Model." *Deviant Behavior* 21 (3): 213–244. doi:10.1080/016396200266243.

Barkan, Steven E. 1979. "Strategic, Tactical and Organizational Dilemmas of the Protest Movement Against Nuclear Power." *Social Problems* 27 (1): 19–37. doi:10.2307/800014.

Barkun, Michael. 1997. *Religion and the Racist Right: The Origins of the Christian Identity Movement*. Chapel Hill, NC: University of North Carolina Press.

Barkun, Michael. 2013. *A Culture of Conspiracy Apocalyptic Visions in Contemporary America*. Berkeley, CA: University of California Press.

Beamish, Thomas D., and Amy J. Luebbers. 2009. "Alliance Building across Social Movements: Bridging Difference in a Peace and Justice Coalition." *Social Problems* 56 (4): 647–676. doi:10.1525/sp.2009.56.4.647.

Beinart, Peter. 2017. "The Rise of the Violent Left." *The Atlantic*, September. https://www.theatlantic.com/magazine/archive/2017/09/the-rise-of-the-violent-left/534192/.

Belew, Kathleen. 2018. *Bring the War Home: The White Power Movement and Paramilitary America*. Cambridge, MA: Harvard University Press.

Benford, Robert D., and David A. Snow. 2000. "Framing Processes and Social Movements: An Overview and Assessment." *Annual Review of Sociology* 26 (1): 611–639.

Bennett, Andy. 1999. "Subcultures or Neo-Tribes? Rethinking the Relationship between Youth, Style and Musical Taste." *Sociology* 33 (3): 599–617. doi:10.1177/S0038038599000371.

Berbrier, Mitch. 1998. "White Supremacists and the (Pan)-Ethnic Imperative: On 'European-Americans' and 'White Student Unions.'" *Sociological Inquiry* 68 (4): 498–516.

Berbrier, Mitch. 1999. "Impression Management for the Thinking Racist: A Case Study of Intellectualization as Stigma Transformation in Contemporary White Supremacist Discourse." *The Sociological Quarterly* 40 (3): 411–433.

Berlet, Chip. 1992. "Fascism!" *Political Research Associates*. https://www.politicalresearch.org/1992/09/28/fascism.

Berlet, Chip. 2004a. "Mapping the Political Right: Gender and Race Oppression in Right-Wing Movements." In *Home-Grown Hate: Gender and Organized Racism*, edited by Abby L. Ferber, 19–48. New York: Routledge.

Berlet, Chip. 2004b. "Christian Identity: The Apocalyptic Style, Political Religion, Palingenesis and Neo-Fascism." *Totalitarian Movements & Political Religions* 5 (3): 469–506. doi:10.1080/1469076042000312221.

Berlet, Chip, and Mathew N. Lyons. 2000. *Right-Wing Populism in America: Too Close for Comfort*. New York, NY: Guilford Press.

Berlet, Chip, and Stanislav Vysotsky. 2006. "Overview of US White Supremacist Groups." *Journal of Political and Military Sociology* 34 (1): 11.

Biehl, Janet, and Peter Staudenmaier. 1995. *Ecofascism: Lessons from the German Experience*. Edinburgh: AK Press.

Blazak, Randy. 2001. "White Boys to Terrorist Men: Target Recruitment of Nazi Skinheads." *American Behavioral Scientist* 44 (6): 982–1000.

Blee, Kathleen M. 2003. *Inside Organized Racism: Women in the Hate Movement*. Berkeley, CA: University of California Press.

Bray, Mark. 2017. *Antifa: The Antifascist Handbook*. Brooklyn, NY: Melville House Publishing.

Breines, Wini. 1989. *Community and Organization in the New Left, 1962–1968: The Great Refusal*. New Brunswick, NJ: Rutgers University Press.

Burghart, Devin. 1999. *Soundtracks to the White Revolution: White Supremacist Assaults on Youth Subcultures*. Chicago, IL: Center for New Community.

Burley, Shane. 2017. *Fascism Today – What It Is and How to End It*. Chico, CA: AK Press.

Burley, Shane. 2018. "How White Nationalists Hide in Academia." *Truthout*. www.truth-out.org/news/item/43117-how-white-nationalists-hide-in-academia.

Burris, Val, Emery Smith, and Ann Strahm. 2000. "White Supremacist Networks on the Internet." *Sociological Focus* 33 (2): 215–235.

Carroll, William K., and Robert S. Ratner. 1996. "Master Frames and Counter-Hegemony: Political Sensibilities in Contemporary Social Movements." *Canadian Review of Sociology & Anthropology* 33 (4): 407.

Castle, Tammy. 2012. "Morrigan Rising: Exploring Female-Targeted Propaganda on Hate Group Websites." *European Journal of Cultural Studies* 15 (6): 679–694. doi:10.1177/1367549412450636.

Castle, Tammy, and Meagan Chevalier. 2011. "The Women of Stormfront: An Examination of White Nationalist Discussion Threads on the Internet." *The Internet Journal of Criminology*, 1–14.

Cohen, Jean L. 1985. "Strategy or Identity: New Theoretical Paradigms and Contemporary Social Movements." *Social Research* 52 (4): 663–716.

Copsey, Nigel. 2000. *Anti-Fascism in Britain*. New York, NY: St. Martin's Press.

Copsey, Nigel. 2018. "Militant Antifascism: An Alternative (Historical) Reading." *Society* 55 (3): 243–247. doi:10.1007/s12115-018-0245-y.

Corte, Ugo, and Bob Edwards. 2008. "White Power Music and the Mobilization of Racist Social Movements." *Music and Arts in Action* 1 (1): 4–20.

Daniels, Jessie. 1997. *White Lies: Race, Class, Gender, and Sexuality in White Supremacist Discourse*. New York, NY: Routledge.

Daniels, Jessie. 2009. *Cyber Racism: White Supremacy Online and the New Attack on Civil Rights*. Lanham, MD: Rowman & Littlefield.

Dobratz, Betty A. 2002. "The Role of Religion in the Collective Identity of the White Racialist Movement." *Journal for the Scientific Study of Religion* 40 (2): 287–302. doi:10.1111/0021-8294.00056.

Dobratz, Betty A., and Stephanie L. Shanks-Meile. 1997. *White Power, White Pride!: The White Separatist Movement in the United States*. New York, NY: Prentice Hall.

Dobratz, Betty A., and Lisa Waldner. 2012. "Repertoires of Contention: White Separatist Views on the Use of Violence and Leaderless Resistance." *Mobilization: An International Quarterly* 17 (1): 49–66. doi:10.17813/maiq.17.1.3282448743272632.

Eco, Umberto. 1995. "Ur-Fascism." *The New York Review of Books*, June 22. https://www.nybooks.com/articles/1995/06/22/ur-fascism/.

Ellwood, Robert. 2000. "Nazism as a Millennialist Movement." In *Millennialism, Persecution, and Violence: Historical Cases*, edited by Catherine Lowman Wessinger, 241–260. Syracuse, NY: Syracuse University Press.

Ezekiel, Raphael S. 1995. *The Racist Mind: Portraits of American Neo-Nazis and Klansmen*. New York, NY: Viking.

Fantasia, Rick, and Kim Voss. 2004. *Hard Work: Remaking the American Labour Movement*. Berkeley, CA: University of California Press.

Ferber, Abby L. 1999. *White Man Falling: Race, Gender, and White Supremacy*. Lanham, MD: Rowman & Littlefield.

Ferree, Myra Marx, and Beth B. Hess. 2000. *Controversy and Coalition: The New Feminist Movement across Three Decades of Change*. New York, NY: Routledge.

Fitzgerald, Kathleen J., and Diane M Rodgers. 2000. "Radical Social Movement Organizations: A Theoretical Model." *Sociological Quarterly* 41 (4): 573–592.

Futrell, Robert, and Pete Simi. 2004. "Free Spaces, Collective Identity, and the Persistence of U.S. White Power Activism." *Social Problems* 51 (1): 16–42.

Futrell, Robert, Pete Simi, and Simon Gottschalk. 2006. "Understanding Music in Movements: The White Power Music Scene." *Sociological Quarterly* 47 (2): 275–304.

Gale, Richard P. 1986. "Social Movements and the State: The Environmental Movement, Countermovement, and Government Agencies." *Sociological Perspectives* 29 (2): 202–240. doi:10.2307/1388959.

Gardell, Mattias. 2003. *Gods of the Blood: The Pagan Revival and White Separatism.* Durham, NC: Duke University Press.

Gattinara, Pietro Castelli, and Andrea L.P Pirro. 2018. "The Far Right as Social Movement." *European Societies* 21 (4): 447–462. doi:10.1080/14616696.2018.1494301.

Gerstenfeld, Phyllis B., Diana R. Grant, and Chau-Pu Chiang. 2003. "Hate Online: A Content Analysis of Extremist Internet Sites." *Analyses of Social Issues and Public Policy* 3 (1): 29–44. doi:10.1111/j.1530-2415.2003.00013.x.

Goldman, Emma. 1969. *Anarchism and Other Essays Emma Goldman.* New York, NY: Dover Publications.

Goodwin, Jeff, and James M. Jasper. 2004. "Trouble in Paradigms." In *Rethinking Social Movements,* edited by Jeff Goodwin and James M. Jasper, 75–93. New York, NY: Rowman & Littlefield.

Graeber, David. 2002. "The New Anarchists." *New Left Review* 13: 61–73.

Griffin, Roger. 1993. *The Nature of Fascism.* New York, NY: Routledge.

Griffin, Roger. 2003. "From Slime Mould to Rhizome: An Introduction to the Groupuscular Right." *Patterns of Prejudice* 37 (1): 27. doi:10.1080/0031322022000054321.

Guérin, Daniel. 1970. *Anarchism: From Theory to Practice.* New York, NY: Monthly Review Press.

Haenfler, Ross. 2014. *Subcultures the Basics.* New York, NY: Routledge.

Haenfler, Ross, Brett Johnson, and Ellis Jones. 2012. "Lifestyle Movements: Exploring the Intersection of Lifestyle and Social Movements." *Social Movement Studies* 11 (1): 1–20.

Hamm, Mark S. 1993. *American Skinheads: The Criminology and Control of Hate Crime.* Westport, CT: Praeger.

Hesse, Monica, and Dan Zak. 2016. "Does This Haircut Make Me Look Like a Nazi?" *Washington Post,* November 30, sec. Arts and Entertainment. https://www.washingtonpost.com/news/arts-and-entertainment/wp/2016/11/30/does-this-haircut-make-me-look-like-a-nazi/.

Jasper, James M. 1997. *The Art of Moral Protest: Culture, Biography, and Creativity in Social Movements.* Chicago, IL: University of Chicago Press.

Jasper, James M. 2010. "Social Movement Theory Today: Toward a Theory of Action?" *Sociology Compass* 4 (11): 965–976. doi:10.1111/j.1751-9020.2010.00329.x.

Johnston, Hank, Enrique Laraña, and Joseph R. Gusfield. 1994. "Identities, Grievances, and New Social Movements." In *New Social Movements: From Ideology to Identity,* edited by Enrique Laraña, Hank Johnston, and Joseph R. Gusfield, 3–35. Philadelphia, PA: Temple University Press.

Kilberg, Joshua. 2012. "A Basic Model Explaining Terrorist Group Organizational Structure." *Studies in Conflict & Terrorism* 35 (11): 810–830. doi:10.1080/1057610X.2012.720240.

Kornhauser, William. 1959. *The Politics of Mass Society.* New Brunswick, NJ: Transaction.

Kriesi, Hanspeter, Ruud Koopmans, Jan Willem Duyvendak, and Marco G. Guigni. 1995. *New Social Movements in Western Europe: A Comparative Analysis.* Minneapolis, MN: University of Minnesota Press.

Kropotkin, Peter. 1904. *Anarchism: Its Philosophy and Ideal.* London, UK: Freedom Press.

Langer, Elinor. 2003. *A Hundred Little Hitlers: The Death of a Black Man, the Trial of a White Racist, and the Rise of the American Neo-Nazi Movement in America.* New York, NY: Metropolitan Books.

Leach, Darcy K. 2013. "Culture and the Structure of Tyrannylessness." *Sociological Quarterly* 54 (2): 181–191. doi:10.1111/tsq.12014.

Lefkowith, Michele. 1999. "A Brief History of Skinheads." In *Soundtracks to the White Revolution: White Supremacist Assaults on Youth Subcultures,* edited by Devin Burghart, 41–42. Chicago, IL: Center for New Community.

Levin, Brian. 2002. "Cyberhate: A Legal and Historical Analysis of Extremists' Use of Computer Networks in America." *American Behavioral Scientist* 45 (6): 958–988. doi:10.1177/0002764202045006004.

Lough, Adam Bhala. 2018. *Alt-Right: Age of Rage*. DVD. El Segundo, CA: Gravitas Ventures.

Lyons, Matthew N. 2017. *Ctrl-Alt-Delete: The Origins and Ideology of the Alternative Right*. Somerville, MA: Political Research Associates. https://www.politicalresearch.org/2017/01/20/ctrl-alt-delete-report-on-the-alternative-right/.

Manne, Kate. 2018. *Down Girl: The Logic of Misogyny*. Oxford: Oxford University Press.

McAdam, Doug. 1999. *Political Process and the Development of Black Insurgency, 1930–1970*. Chicago, IL: University of Chicago Press.

Melucci, Alaberto. 1985. "The Symbolic Challenge of Contemporary Movements." *Social Research* 52 (4): 789–816.

Meyer, David S, and Suzanne Staggenborg. 1996. "Movements, Countermovements, and the Structure of Political Opportunity." *American Journal of Sociology* 101 (6): 1628–1660.

Michael, George. 2012. *Lone Wolf Terror and the Rise of Leaderless Resistance*. Nashville, TN: Vanderbilt University Press.

Miller-Idriss, Cynthia. 2018. *The Extreme Gone Mainstream: Commercialization and Far Right Youth Culture in Germany*. Princeton, NJ: Princeton University Press.

Mooney, Patrick H., and Scott A. Hunt. 1996. "A Repertoire of Interpretations: Master Frames and Ideological Continuity in U.S. Agrarian Mobilization." *The Sociological Quarterly* 37 (1): 177–197.

Nagle, Angela. 2017. *Kill All Normies: The Online Culture Wars from Tumblr and 4chan to the Alt-Right and Trump*. Washington, DC: Zero Books.

Neiwert, David. 2017. *Alt-America: The Rise of the Radical Right in the Age of Trump*. New York, NY: Verso.

Neiwert, David. 2018a. "Freedom to Bash Heads." *The Baffler*. https://thebaffler.com/latest/freedom-to-bash-heads-niewert.

Obach, Brian K. 2004. *Labor and the Environmental Movement: The Quest for Common Ground*. Cambridge, MA: MIT Press.

Offe, Claus. 1985. "New Social Movements: Challenging the Boundaries of Institutional Politics." *Social Research* 52 (4): 817–868.

Oliver, Pamela E., and Hank Johnston. 2000. "What a Good Idea! Ideologies and Frames in Social Movement Research." *Mobilization* 5 (1): 37–54.

Olson, Benjamin Hedge. 2012. "Voice of Our Blood: National Socialist Discourses in Black Metal." *Popular Music History* 6 (1): 135–149. doi:10.1558/pomh.v6i1/2.135.

Paxton, Robert O. 2004. *The Anatomy of Fascism*. New York, NY: Alfred A. Knopf.

Peleg, Samuel. 2000. "Peace Now or Later?: Movement–Countermovement Dynamics and the Israeli Political Cleavage." *Studies in Conflict and Terrorism* 23 (4): 235–254.

Phoenix, Tae. 2019. "Ban Antifa? I've Met Golden Retrievers Who Scared Me More." *Newsweek*. https://www.newsweek.com/ban-antifa-cruz-cassidy-golden-retrievers-1451271.

Pieslak, Jonathan R. 2015. *Radicalism and Music: An Introduction to the Music Cultures of Al-Qa'ida, Racist Skinheads, Christian-Affiliated Radicals, and Eco-Animal Rights Militants*. Middletown, CT: Wesleyan Uniwersity Press.

Polhemus, Ted. 1997. "In the Supermarket of Style." In *The Clubcultures Reader*, edited by Steve Redhead, Derek Wynne, and Justin O'Connor, 130–133. Malden, MA: Blackwell.

Polletta, Francesca. 1999. "'Free Spaces' in Collective Action." *Theory & Society* 28 (1): 1.

Polletta, Francesca. 2007. *Freedom Is an Endless Meeting: Democracy in American Social Movements*. Chicago, IL: University of Chicago Press.

Renton, Dave. 2001. *This Rough Game: Fascism and Anti-Fascism*. Stroud: Sutton.

Ridgeway, James. 1995. *Blood in the Face: The Ku Klux Klan, Aryan Nations, Nazi Skinheads and the Rise of a New White Culture*. New York, NY: Thunder's Mouth Press.

Rivers, Damian J. 2018. "Where Is the Love? White Nationalist Discourse on Hip-Hop." In *The Sociolinguistics of Hip-Hop as Critical Conscience: Dissatisfaction and Dissent*, edited by Andrew S. Ross and Damian J. Rivers, 101–129. Cham, Switzerland: Springer International Publishing. doi:10.1007/978-3-319-59244-2_5.

Roberts, Keith A. 1978. "Toward a Generic Concept of Counter-Culture." *Sociological Focus* 11 (2): 111–126.

Rochon, Thomas R., and David S. Meyer. 1997. *Coalitions & Political Movements: The Lessons of the Nuclear Freeze*. Boulder, CO: Lynne Rienner.

Rogers, Thomas. 2014. "Nipsters: The German Neo-Nazis Trying to Put a Hipper Face on Hate." *Rolling Stone*. https://www.rollingstone.com/culture/news/heil-hipster-the-young-neo-nazis-trying-to-put-a-stylish-face-on-hate-20140623.

Rose City Antifa. 2018a. "Portland Stands United Against Fascism." https://rosecityantifa.org/articles/call-out-to-oppose-warriors-for-freedom-llc/.

Rose City Antifa. 2018b. "Statement on Strategy and Tactics for June 4th Rally." https://rosecityantifa.org/articles/statment-on-strategy-and-tactics-for-june-4th-rally/.

Rose City Antifa. 2019. "Statement on the Far-Right's Attempt to Criminalize Protest of Concentration Camp Deaths and Hate Groups." http://rosecityantifa.org/articles/statement-against-criminalizing-protest/.

Ross, Alexander Reid. 2017. *Against the Fascist Creep*. Chico, CA: AK Press.

Rushton, J. Philippe. 1997. *Race, Evolution and Behavior: A Life History Perspective*. New Brunswick, NJ: Transaction Publishers.

Sarabia, Daniel, and Thomas E. Shriver. 2004. "Maintaining Collective Identity in a Hostile Environment: Confronting Negative Public Perception and Factional Divisions Within the Skinhead Subculture." *Sociological Spectrum* 24 (3): 267–294. doi:10.1080/02732170390258614.

Shantz, Jeff. 2011. *Active Anarchy: Political Practice in Contemporary Movements*. Lanham, MD: Lexington Books.

Shekhovtsov, Anton. 2009. "Apoliteic Music: Neo-Folk, Martial Industrial and 'Metapolitical Fascism.'" *Patterns of Prejudice* 43 (5): 431–457.

Sherr, Ian, and Daniel Van Boom. 2019. "8chan Is Struggling to Stay Online in Wake of El Paso Massacre." *CNET*. https://www.cnet.com/news/8chan-is-struggling-to-stay-online-in-wake-of-el-paso-massacre/.

Simi, Pete, and Robert Futrell. 2009. "Negotiating White Power Activist Stigma." *Social Problems* 56 (1): 89–110.

Simi, Pete, and Robert Futrell. 2010. *American Swastika: Inside the White Power Movement's Hidden Spaces of Hate*. Lanham, MD: Rowman & Littlefield.

Simi, Pete, Lowell Smith, and Ann M.S. Reeser. 2008. "From Punk Kids to Public Enemy Number One." *Deviant Behavior* 29 (8): 753–774. doi:10.1080/01639620701873905.

SmithIV, Jack. 2018. "This Is Fashwave, the Suicidal Retro-Futurist Art of the Alt-Right." *Mic*. https://mic.com/articles/187379/this-is-fashwave-the-suicidal-retro-futurist-art-of-the-alt-right#.VIpHlKt84.

Snow, David A., and Robert D. Benford. 1992. "Master Frames and Cycles of Protest." In *Frontiers in Social Movement Theory*, edited by Aldon D. Morris and Carol McClurg Mueller. New Haven, CT: Yale University Press.

Springer, Simon. 2014. "Human Geography without Hierarchy." *Progress in Human Geography* 38 (3): 402–419. doi:10.1177/0309132513508208.

Staggenborg, Suzanne. 2015. "Event Coalitions in the Pittsburgh G20 Protests." *Sociological Quarterly* 56 (2): 386–411. doi:10.1111/tsq.12090.

Stock, Catherine MacNicol. 1997. *Rural Radicals from Bacon's Rebellion to the Oklahoma City Bombing*. New York, NY: Penguin Books.

Sturgeon, Noel. 1995. "Theorizing Movements: Direct Action and Direct Theory." In *Cultural Politics and Social Movements*, edited by Marc Darnovsky, Barbara L. Epstein, and Richard Flacks, 35–51. Philadelphia, PA: Temple University Press.

Sunshine, Spencer. 2008. "Rebranding Fascism: National-Anarchists." *The Public Eye*, January 28. https://www.politicalresearch.org/2008/01/28/rebranding-fascism-national-anarchists.

Sunshine, Spencer. 2014. "The Right Hand of Occupy Wall Street." *The Public Eye*, February 24. https://www.politicalresearch.org/2014/02/23/the-right-hand-of-occupy-wall-street-from-libertarians-to-nazis-the-fact-and-fiction-of-right-wing-involvement.

Tenold, Vegas. 2018. *Everything You Love Will Burn: Inside the Rebirth of White Nationalism in America*. New York, NY: Nation Books.

Tilly, Charles. 2006. *Regimes and Repertoires*. Chicago, IL: University of Chicago Press.

Torres, Phil. 2017. "How Did 'New Atheism' Slide so Far Toward the Alt-Right?" *Salon*. https://www.salon.com/2017/07/29/from-the-enlightenment-to-the-dark-ages-how-new-atheism-slid-into-the-alt-right/.

Travis, Tiffini A., and Perry Hardy. 2012. *Skinheads: A Guide to an American Subculture*. Santa Barbara, CA: Greenwood.

Van Dyke, Nella. 2003. "Crossing Movement Boundaries: Factors that Facilitate Coalition Protest by American College Students, 1930–1990." *Social Problems* 50 (2): 226–250. doi:10.1525/sp.2003.50.2.226.

Van Dyke, Nella, and Bryan Amos. 2017. "Social Movement Coalitions: Formation, Longevity, and Success." *Sociology Compass* 11 (7). doi:10.1111/soc4.12489.

Vysotsky, Stanislav. 2004. "*Understanding the Racist Right in the Twenty First Century: A Typology of Modern White Supremacist Organizations*." American Sociological Association Annual Meeting. San Francisco, CA.

Vysotsky, Stanislav. 2013. "The Influence of Threat on Tactical Choices of Militant Anti-Fascist Activists." *Interface: A Journal for and about Social Movements* 5 (2): 263–294.

Vysotsky, Stanislav. 2015. "The Anarchy Police: Militant Anti-Fascism as Alternative Policing Practice." *Critical Criminology* 23 (3): 235–253.

Vysotsky, Stanislav, and Dianne Dentice. 2008. "The Continuing Evolution of the White Supremacist Movement: A New Social Movement." In *Social Movements: Contemporary Perspectives*, edited by Dianne Dentice and James L. Williams, 86–97. Newcastle upon Tyne, UK: Cambridge Scholars Publishing.

Vysotsky, Stanislav, and Eric Madfis. 2014. "Uniting the Right: Anti-Immigration, Organizing, and the Legitimation of Extreme Racist Organizations." *Journal of Hate Studies* 12 (1): 129. doi:10.33972/jhs.106.

Vysotsky, Stanislav, and Adrienne L. McCarthy. 2017. "Normalizing Cyberracism: A Neutralization Theory Analysis." *Journal of Crime and Justice* 40 (4): 446–461. doi:10.1080/0735648X.2015.1133314.

Ward, Eric K. 2017. "Skin in the Game: How Antisemitism Animates White Nationalism." *Public Eye*, June 29. https://www.politicalresearch.org/2017/06/29/skin-in-the-game-how-antisemitism-animates-white-nationalism/.

Weber, Max. 1949. "'Objectivity' in Social Science and Social Policy." In *Max Weber on the Methodology of the Social Sciences*, translated by Edward Albert Shils and Henry A. Finch. Glencoe, IL: Free Press.

Wendling, Mark. 2018. *Alt-Right: From 4chan to the White House*. London: Pluto Press.

Wessinger, Catherine Lowman. 2000. "Introduction." In *Millennialism, Persecution, and Violence: Historical Cases*, edited by Catherine Lowman Wessinger, 3–39. Syracuse, NY: Syracuse University Press.

Williams, Dana M. 2018. "Contemporary Anarchist and Anarchistic Movements." *Sociology Compass* 12 (6): 1–17.

Williams, J. Patrick. 2011. *Subcultural Theory: Traditions & Concepts*. Chichester: Polity Press.

Wood, Robert T. 1999. "The Indigenous, Nonracist Origins of the American Skinhead Subculture." *Youth & Society* 31 (2): 131–151. doi:10.1177/0044118X99031002001.

Yates, Luke. 2015. "Everyday Politics, Social Practices and Movement Networks: Daily Life in Barcelona's Social Centres." *British Journal of Sociology* 66 (2): 236–258. doi:10.1111/1468-4446.12101.

Yinger, J. Milton. 1960. "Contraculture and Subculture." *American Sociological Review* 25 (5): 625–635.

Zald, Mayer N. 2000. "Ideologically Structured Action: An Enlarged Agenda for Social Movement Research." *Mobilization* 5 (1): 1–16.

Zald, Meyer N., and Bert Useem. 1987. "Movement and Countermovement Interaction: Mobilization, Tactics and State Involvement." In *Social Movements in an Organizational Society: Collected Essays*, edited by Meyer N. Zald and John D. McCarthy. New Brunswick, NJ: Transaction Books.

3

FASCIST AND ANTIFASCIST TACTICS

The general understanding of antifa tactics is relatively one-dimensional – antifascism is essentially about physically fighting people. Let us, for a moment, return to where we began with the punching of Richard Spencer. The act itself is lauded to this day as a daring act of antifascism, but there is also no way of knowing whether this was a planned action by a formally constituted antifa group or a spontaneous, informal act of antifascism taken in the heat of a broader protest – a punch of opportunity as it were. The punch itself serves as a reinforcement of the narrative that the core of antifa action is violence. Since then, the discourse around antifascist tactics largely centers around the use of violence. Yet, like any other social movement, militant antifascism incorporates a wide variety of tactics in order to achieve its goals. Most of these tactics, however, do not draw the kind of controversy that physical confrontations do; and therefore, are largely ignored by the general public and media.

Militant antifascist tactics serve as a countermovement maneuver to fascist mobilization and organization efforts. In effect, antifa tactics are approaches designed to counteract fascist tactical moves. Contemporary fascist movements deploy a distinct set of tactics designed to establish a membership and support base, disseminate supremacist frames into public discourse, and produce and reproduce movement structures. In order to juxtapose antifascist tactics, this chapter will begin with a brief overview of fascist tactics and place them in the context of broader social movement analysis.

The core of this chapter addresses the breadth and diversity of antifascist tactics. Sociological analysis of social movement tactics allows us to understand the processes by which movements make decisions to deploy certain types of tactics. Antifa activism is, first and foremost, a radical response to fascist activity, which both constrains and facilitates certain types of tactics. The new social movement form of antifa activism, particularly its countercultural orientation further explains the breadth of tactics employed. Ultimately, the range of tactics utilized by militant antifascists reflects the countermovement orientation of the movement. Antifa activism is, of course, designed to stop fascist movements, which drive the movement's tactical choices and repertoire.

Social movement tactics

In theory, social movements have an infinite number of tactics that they can deploy in order to achieve their goals. In reality, of course, social movements are constrained by a variety of factors such as culture, history, and opportunity. Charles Tilly (2006; Tilly and Tarrow 2006) referred to the scope of tactics used by a movement as its "repertoire." Although tactical repertoires are limited in their scope by culture, history, and precedent, they are also intentionally flexible. That is to say that repertoires are never as fixed as they may seem to either movement participants or outsiders. The perception of choice in terms of repertoires is influenced by the awareness people have of a repertoire and available tactics, their inclination toward a specific repertoire or tactic, the likelihood of innovation, and changes in the circumstances in which a repertoire or tactic is deployed. This notion of tactics as simultaneously unlimited and limited provides the foundation for understanding the actions of all social movements, including antifascism.

Movement tactical choices may be more than simply choosing from an à la carte menu of available actions. A movement's "taste in tactics" (Jasper 1997, 229) also reflects dynamics of identity and ideology. James Jasper's (1997) research into the tactical differences and choices of militant and non-militant activists against nuclear power plants points to dynamics similar to those found in the antifascist movement. Unlike Tilly's work which answers the question of how movements make tactical choices, Jasper was far more interested in the question of why. In this framework, "Tactics are rarely, if ever, neutral means about which protestors do not care. Tactics represent important routines, emotionally and morally salient in [activists'] lives" (Jasper 1997, 237). Tactics, therefore, take on a life of their own as they become core signifiers of identity and belief. Although social movement participants may frame tactics as chosen because of their effectiveness, they may just as easily be chosen because they perceive such tactics to be effective. These perceptions are often the products of the interplay of culture and structure. Non-militant activists choose legitimate means of action because they are structurally positioned to have access to power and because their life experience indicates that such access may be successful, even when it isn't. Militant activists make similar choices based on their countercultural identity and sense of moral righteousness. Tactics, therefore, may be chosen as much for their external messaging and influence as they are for internal consumption by movement members. For movement participants, tactical choice can be as much the product of ideology as identity, with certain tactics reflecting beliefs about the world around them and the individual activist's sense of self. In this conception of tactical repertoires, culture, identity, and ideology serve as much to influence tactical choice as structural availability of means.

While some of these dynamics will be addressed later in this chapter, Chapters 5 and 6 will detail the cultural, emotional, and identity dynamics of militant antifascist tactical choices, particularly the use of force in response to fascists.

Ideology and identity as markers of tactical preferences for militant antifascists reflect their radical and countercultural social movement orientation (Fitzgerald and Rodgers 2000; Kriesi et al. 1995). The anarchist and anti-authoritarian ideology of many antifa activists, as discussed in Chapter 2, manifests in tactical choices that are understood as radical. Radical social movements, including antifa, do not need to limit their tactical repertoires for fear of losing financial or allied support from mainstream activists and organizations (Fitzgerald and Rodgers 2000). This lack of restrictions allows radical social movements to engage in much more innovative tactical approaches than mainstream movements. Although radicals may "share with some moderate [social movement organizations] a non-violent orientation, they also are invested in confrontation tactics through direct action" (Fitzgerald and Rodgers 2000, 583). Such tactics can take a variety of forms ranging from the symbolic to directly violent (Kriesi et al. 1995). While mainstream social movements often rely on methods that appeal to those in power, radical social movements frequently have a countercultural orientation that is at odds with power. Among contemporary social movements, countercultural movements that are built around a radical identity are more likely to deploy confrontational and militant tactics, including the use of violence (Fitzgerald and Rodgers 2000; Jasper 1997; Kriesi et al. 1995). Finally, radical tactics are often oriented toward putting movement ideology into practice. In this sense, social movement tactical choices reflect as much the kind of society activists wish to build as the strategic concerns of the moment. This can equally manifest itself in a determined commitment to non-violence as well as a commitment to use violence against certain opponents. This is not to say that militant antifascists envision a world of mass violence, but that violence is an acceptable approach as a defensive response to fascist mobilization and violence. Such a response is part of the movement-countermovement dynamic at the core of antifa practice.

The tactics deployed by movements that mobilize in opposition to other movements are strategically different from those used by social movements interested in achieving policy or cultural change. Countermovements operate to intervene against the activity of another social movement. In many cases these "opposing movements" are not only acting in conflict with one another, but also in support of broader economic, political, or social change (Meyer and Staggenborg 1996; Peleg 2000). While the individuals involved in antifa activities also advocate for broader transformation, their work as antifascists is focused specifically on opposing fascist activity as a social movement. In this sense, antifa represents an almost ideal typical countermovement. The tactics adopted by militant antifascists can, therefore, be understood as part of a movement-countermovement strategy.

Meyer Zald and Bert Useem (1987) identified three categories of tactics used by countermovements: damage or destruction of the other group, preemption or dissuasion of group mobilization, and recruitment of the other group's members.

When a movement engages in damage or destruction of another movement, it seeks to "try to raise the cost of mobilization for the other group" (Zald and Useem 1987, 260). This may be achieved through tactics such as information gathering, restriction of resources, negative representations of the movement, and direct attacks against it. Gathering information on a movement is designed to discredit the leadership or the entire movement, which undercuts its ability to function successfully. When movement resources are restricted, its ability to operate and mobilize becomes severely diminished. Movements that are portrayed in a negative light are discredited in the arena of public opinion and struggle to recruit new members or mobilize existing membership. Direct attacks against a movement increases the cost of participation to such a degree that individuals begin to question the utility of involvement with it. Tactics designed to preempt or dissuade mobilization are designed to "undercut the moral and political basis of a mobilization or counter mobilization" (Zald and Useem 1987, 264). This forces a movement to act defensively and engage in activities that may be perceived as inappropriate or immoral further eroding public support and increasing internal conflict as well as demobilization. The last strategy of persuading or recruiting opposing movement members results in a set of tactics that are designed to convert members and encourage them to mobilize in opposition to their former movement. Militant antifascists engage in tactics that represent each of these strategic approaches to some degree.

The tactical repertoire of militant antifascists represents a broad scale of approaches to counter fascist movements. As a radical social movement, antifa groups employ a variety of tactics ranging from relatively uncontroversial, non-militant activities to the confrontations that give them notoriety. Because they are unburdened by the necessity to appeal to mainstream movements or sentiments, militant antifascists are able to innovate their approaches in order to respond to the maneuvers of the fascists they oppose. This signals the countermovement strategy of militant antifascism where tactics are deployed in order to ensure successful opposition.

Fascist tactical repertoire

The fascist movement engages in a wide variety of tactics in order to build movement support and achieve its ideological goals. Movement activity serves to construct not just an activist identity typical of most social movements, but also a distinct racial and gender identity. Yet, the identity work that occurs in fascist movements also serves a strategic ideological goal. Fascist movements practice an identity politics of inequality and domination that distinctly influences their tactical repertoire. The activity of groups and individuals affiliated with this movement, therefore, ultimately serve the movement's ideological goals. This contemporary fascist tactical repertoire effectively consists of four key forms of activism: propaganda campaigns, internet online activity, cultural activity, and violence.

Propaganda campaigns

The public face of the fascist movement consists of propaganda campaigns designed to promulgate movement ideology and goals as well as mobilize movement participants. Rallies and protest events, literature distribution, and mass media exposure serve to represent the core positions of the movement and energize individual adherents to engage in further activity. These types of activity ultimately serve to promote fascist meta-politics by injecting movement ideas into public discourse (Burley 2017; Lyons 2017). Movement members and sympathizers take inspiration from such public displays to mobilize or engage in other forms of activism. Additionally, propaganda campaigns serve as a means of targeting historically marginalized communities and populations for intimidation.

Fascist literature campaigns are designed to spread the ideology and positions of the movement. Traditionally, these campaigns involved the distribution of flyers, pamphlets, as well newspapers and magazines; but in the internet era, the primary form of literature distribution consists of flyering campaigns. In suburban communities or those with numerous single-family homes, fascists will leave flyers on front lawns in weighted plastic bags. However, the most common contemporary tactic is posting leaflets, posters, or stickers on utility poles, walls, or other public spaces in urban areas and college campuses (Anti-Defamation League 2019b; Hatewatch 2017). The content of this material combines populist claims regarding current economic, political, or social issues with overt and covert fascist symbolism and provides contact information for the organization or source of the propaganda (Berlet and Lyons 2000; Daniels 1997; Dobratz and Shanks-Meile 1997; Ferber 1999). This form of activity serves as a means of spreading movement information and recruitment, but also as a message to opponents and targeted groups. Fascist flyering campaigns signify that movement members are active in a community and specifically in a neighborhood or college campus. By posting flyers, posters, or stickers in a community, fascists indicate to their opponents that they are claiming that space as territory that they are at minimum active in, and potentially control. This material also sends a message of intimidation to people of color, religious minorities, LGBTQ people, and leftist activists that fascists are active in that community, which, as Chapter 5 will discuss constitutes a form of intimidation and threat.

Public protests and rallies organized by fascists serve as a form of "demonstrative" social movement activity (Kriesi et al. 1995). These events are ostensibly designed to demonstrate opposition to any number of social issues utilizing the populist framing of supremacist discourse (Berlet 2004a; Berlet and Lyons 2000; Berlet and Vysotsky 2006). Historically, such rallies have been organized under the guise of reaction to economic concerns such as free trade and deindustrialization, the perceived changes to the cultural, economic, and political landscape posed by immigration, and foreign intervention such as US support for Israel as well as the wars in Iraq and Afghanistan. Consistent with the conspiracism frame, the fascist position is that any social problem is ultimately the product of the biological and cultural inferiority of people of color and secret plots connived by Jewish people (Berlet and Vysotsky 2006; Daniels 1997; Dobratz and Shanks-Meile 1997; Ezekiel 1995; Ferber 1999; Tenold 2018). These events were intentionally scheduled in "defended neighborhoods" where demographic changes create the perception that recent immigrants or integrating racial groups represent a threat to the status of white residents (Green, Strolovitch, and Wong 1998). While American fascists still engage in this strategy for choosing protest and rally locations, a new pattern has emerged in the Trump era. Reflecting a shift in the style of fascist activism inspired by the alt-right and trolling subculture, the most high-profile fascist rallies increasingly occurred in cities with extremely liberal reputations such as Berkeley, Portland, and even Charlottesville. These rallies are held under the guise of support for President Trump, opposition to immigration, and even freedom of speech, but ultimately are designed to instigate conflict between fascist participants and antifascist counter-protesters. Portland has become the epicenter of fascist demonstrations because of its branding as a liberal city and its history of strong antifascist activism. A conglomeration of far-right activists routinely rally and march in the city as a means of attacking leftists and antifascists (Burley 2019; Neiwert 2018a). While clashes between fascist and antifascists at rallies are not new, the strategy of fascists organizing rallies specifically to provoke an antifascist response and potentially violent clashes is an innovation. From the fascist perspective, these clashes serve to demonstrate their willingness to engage in violence in support of their ideals and build sympathy across the political right and even in mainstream media by framing antifascists as aggressors (Gupta 2019). For fascists, attendance at public rallies provides more than just an opportunity to "trigger" their opposition and engage in acts of violence. Ultimately, such activity demonstrates commitment to the movement and serves as a means for members to bond with one another and build ties between different factions and sectors of the movement (Berlet and Vysotsky 2006; Ezekiel 1995).

Mass media appearances by fascist organization leaders, spokespeople, and intellectuals serve as a major avenue for supremacists to advance their ideological position and movement agenda. Although the intent of mainstream media anchors and producers may be to present fascists honestly in order to discredit them and expose them to public stigma, these appearances still serve as a means of transmitting movement ideology. In mass media appearances, fascists rely on a combination of ethnic claims-making and intellectualization processes (Berbrier 1998; Berbrier 1999) in order to present their ideology as a legitimate position in a broader marketplace of ideas. Such presentations serve as exposure for fascist leaders and facilitate recruitment by profiling specific organizations.

Fascist propaganda campaigns serve as a means of propagating core movement ideas into mainstream discourse. These efforts are part of a wider movement strategy of engaging in meta-political activity that "gradually transform the political and intellectual culture as a precursor to transforming institutions and systems" (Lyons 2017, 3). Fascists seek to shift the Overton window of acceptable political debate to include the overtly racist and misogynist elements of their ideology (Burley 2017;

Vysotsky and Madfis 2014). Visual campaigns of flyers, posters, and stickers introduce fascist talking points and imagery into communities. Public rallies and protests
focus attention on the fascists as legitimate claims-makers and stakeholders. Finally,
mass media exposure facilitates broad fascist messaging to a wider audience of
potential members and sympathizers.

Online activity

To say that the internet has been a boon to the fascist movement is an under-
statement. Online activity is at the core of the contemporary movement. Fascists
are early adopters of internet technology with supremacists setting up dial up bulletin board systems in the 1980s, numerous websites in the mid-to-late 1990s, and
aggressive use of social media to this day (Belew 2018; Burris, Smith, and Strahm
2000; Gerstenfeld, Grant, and Chiang 2003; B. Levin 2002; Daniels 2009). Fascist
internet activity serves internal and external movement functions. Internally, fascist
online activity serves as a transmovement space where like-minded individuals can
come together to discuss ideology, find solace and community, and even provide
personal and movement resources (Futrell and Simi 2004; Simi and Futrell 2010).
External activity continues the pattern of meta-political activity by spreading
ideology beyond adherents and facilitating recruitment into the movement.

Internal activity

At the core of fascist online activity are a series of platforms for internal communication between movement members. These range from blogs whose intended audience
is movement members to private forums limited to members to secret chat groups for
members of fascist groups. Whereas blog sites such as VDare or Radix Journal are
seemingly available to the general public, their audience is clearly ideologically sympathetic white nationalists. Similarly, an open discussion forum like Stormfront may be
accessible to any internet user, which has been instrumental in its pivotal role in the
fascist movement, but its discussions are clearly designed for movement insiders with
ideological opponents steered specifically to a forum titled "Opposing Views." In the
wake of the deadly "Unite the Right" rally in Charlottesville in 2017, the Daily
Stormer moved much of its operation to the "dark web," and use of a TOR compa-
tible browser is required to access its discussion forum. This move further limited
access to the site forcing it to become further restricted to committed movement
members. Even supposedly public forums such as 4chan's "politically incorrect" board
and the social media site Gab are dominated by fascist users, making them de facto
supremacist movement organs. Some forms of online activity require communication
exclusively with movement compatriots in relatively private forums, so fascists turn to
publicly available communication applications like Discord or Telegram to create
private, and in some cases public, group chats where fascist group members can coordinate forms of in-person action. Finally, supremacist podcasts, audio streams, and
videos proliferate online bringing fascist analysis directly to movement members.

This internal online world constructs a vibrant "transmovement" space that performs a number of key movement functions (Futrell and Simi 2004; Simi and Futrell 2010). First and foremost, transmovement spaces link together disparate sectors of the movement in order to share ideas and strategies for activism. Fascist activists provide one another with ideological reinforcement as well as strategies for overcoming ideological and rhetorical challenges from opponents. Additionally, the discourse on supremacist forums serves to construct and reinforce justifications for eliminationist violence (Vysotsky and McCarthy 2017). A similar dynamic occurs within smaller scale private chats among supremacists who utilize them to plan and coordinate potential acts of violence (Hayden 2019; Schiano 2019; Unicorn Riot 2017). Online transmovement spaces also provide an infrastructure for a decentralized movement by providing access to reading, video, and propaganda material (Daniels 2009; B. Levin 2002). The latter becomes crucial for activists who wish to transition from maintaining an online persona to real world action. In an ideal example of the leaderless resistance model, an individual with loose ties to any formal organization can access its propaganda material and take it upon themselves to print and distribute it as described earlier in this chapter. The final major function of the online world of contemporary fascists is the accrual of resources, particularly financial resources, necessary for the success of social movements (Jenkins 1983; McCarthy and Zald 1977). Fascist websites provide a simple means of acquiring revenue for movement and personal enrichment. Movement organizations and individual participants routinely sell everything from codified and branded clothing to classical and contemporary reading material to music catering for a variety of tastes and subcultures, and even racist and anti-Semitic first-person shooter video games (Burghart 1999; Corte and Edwards 2008; B. Levin 2002; Miller-Idriss 2019; Simi and Futrell 2010). The purchase of merchandise links individuals to the broader movement, while the revenue generated is used to sustain movement activity creating what Simi and Futrell (2010, 149) label a "coop effect" where "organizations were sustained by members' participation and resources with the most successful becoming enduring indigenous institutions and lending a strong sense of efficacy to members' efforts." This internal form of online activity provides a cultural feedback loop where individuals consume movement-oriented products, which not only demonstrates commitment to the movement, but also serves to fund movement activity that encourages further participation and consumption.

External activity

Fascist online activity is, of course, not limited to movement-oriented platforms. Supremacists engage in a clear strategy of engagement with popular, mainstream online spaces. Activists participate covertly and overtly in a variety of internet activities. One of most peculiar forms of this dynamic are cloaked websites developed by fascists, which Jesse Daniels (2009, 118) describes as "those published by individuals or groups who conceal authorship or intention in order to deliberately disguise a hidden political agenda." Such sites avoid overt references to fascist ideology and symbolism in favor of a presentation that appears non-ideological and as a neutral source on the topic presented. One of the most notorious examples of this model is the Stormfront affiliated site Martin Luther King: A True Historical Examination (martinlutherking.org), which at first glance appears to be a resource for students interested in information regarding the life of the civil rights leader. The racist intent of the site becomes clear upon closer, critical examination. Such sites are designed less as points of recruitment to the movement than as points where the ideas of the movement may be introduced into the culture and to naïve or vulnerable readers (Borgeson and Valeri 2004; Daniels 2009; Lee and Leets 2002; Valeri and Borgeson 2005). Unlike these cloaked sites, fascists openly engage with social media distinctly as supremacist voices in the digital marketplace of ideas. Popular social media sites like Facebook, Reddit, Twitter, and YouTube are extremely valuable forums for fascist users and provide a means for organizations to communicate with supporters and the broader public. Despite efforts by each of these platforms to reign in the spread of hate speech and fascist activism by enacting policies that result in deletion of supremacist user accounts, there is a significant fascist presence that includes high-profile figures and groups (Anti-Defamation League 2019c; Cox and Koebler 2019; Hern 2019; Lytvynenko, Silverman, and Boutilier 2019; O'Brien 2019; Ward 2019).[1] In addition to a number of explicitly fascist users, there is a network of users that may be categorized as belonging to the alt-lite or the "intellectual dark web"[2] as well as nominally apolitical or centrist users who espouse positions that mirror those of fascist ideology regarding racial and gender inequality. These individuals are often linked to distinctly fascist social media accounts and frequently serve as the gateway into the fascist movement (Lewis 2018). The scale of fascist presence facilitates recruitment, contributes to the movement's meta-political strategy, and enables targeted harassment campaigns.

Fascist online activity is specifically designed to sway individuals to the ideological positions of the movement; and, ultimately, to recruit members and encourage activism. Whether internal or external, covert or overt, fascist online messaging involves "the use of narrative to persuade or convince" known as persuasive storytelling (Lee and Leets 2002, 929). These narratives are most successful when they employ a "soft sell" approach that avoids the most egregious expressions of prejudice (Borgeson and Valeri 2004; Daniels 2009; Lee and Leets 2002). This points to the difference in the style of internally and externally oriented activity, with internal spaces often defined by overtly bigoted imagery and statements whereas external activity tends to be more coded and uses ethnic claims-making and intellectual frames (Berbrier 1998; 1999). Rather than engaging in direct recruitment, this external online activity serves to reinforce the meta-political strategy of shifting discourse to include fascist positions (Burley 2017; Lyons 2017). Such a strategy undermines "the value of racial equality by challenging the epistemological basis of hard-won political truths about the civil rights era, about the Holocaust, and about the end of slavery, [and argues] that the cultural values about race, racism, and racial inequality that many consider to be settled … are, in fact, open for debate once again as white supremacy online offers alternative ways of presenting, publishing, and debating ideas that take issue with these cultural values" (Daniels 2009, 119). This externally oriented online strategy ultimately serves to legitimize the fascist movement and encourages real world activity.

Cultural activity

In the previous chapter, I argued that the fascist movement should be analyzed using a new social movement framework in part because of the primacy of cultural work in movement activism. Contemporary fascist movements construct a complex culture of language, signs, and symbols as well as music and art that serves to develop both a distinct fascist culture and an ideological cultural pole in oppositional subcultures.

Since overt expressions of fascism and white supremacy are generally socially stigmatized, movement participants develop a complex series of ways to indicate their affiliation (Berlet and Vysotsky 2006; Blee 2003; Simi and Futrell 2009). An ever-shifting and ever-expanding vocabulary of terms is used by movement members to signify the racism, anti-Semitism, and misogyny at the core of the movement. The language of the movement incorporates a great deal of slang available exclusively to insiders who are able to consistently engage with online discourse among compatriots. While some terms like "14 words"[3] are movement staples that have existed for decades, others like "Jewish question," often abbreviated as JQ, simultaneously evoke classical Nazism and serve as contemporary slang in typical alt-right style that simultaneously points to and away from its bigoted meaning (Burley 2017; Wendling 2018). The visual culture of the movement invokes similar overt and covert meanings. While swastikas are common among the most ardent of fascists, Nordic Runes and other iconography are a staple of contemporary fascists, especially those in the subcultural and religious sectors discussed in the previous chapter (Gardell 2003). Fascist memes consistently appropriate popular culture imagery like Pepe the frog and Moon Man[4] to serve as avatars and movement signifiers (Caffier 2017). Even the choice of colors in movement propaganda, memes and infographics, and clothing can signify fascist ideology and movement membership. The combination of black and yellow are used by identitarians, Proud Boys, and national anarchists to name just a few of the fascist tendencies that may be identified with such color coding. These codes function as a means of signaling membership to ideological compatriots eliciting levels of trust among supporters of a stigmatized movement (Hegghammer 2017). The approach to fascist signifiers, especially by the highly online alt-right, is to confound outsiders and signal to insiders using what they term as irony; although, it is more realistically deniability. Images are deployed by fascists who then claim victimization by, and lack of sense of humor from, their detractors (Burley 2017; Wendling 2018). The claim of victimization is intrinsic to fascist ideology that constructs white people as targets of oppression and exclusion by leftist activists and

Jewish conspiracies (Berbrier 2000). This strategy is clearly evident in the use of the OK sign by fascist and far-right activists. Because of its innocuous use in the wider culture, its intentional use in far-right contexts can be denied as a hate symbol; yet its users routinely demonstrate fascist affiliations and are deliberately deploying it to signal their ideological position, ultimately serving as a movement signifier (Neiwert 2018b). The complex vocabulary of terms, symbols, and signifiers allows movement members to identify one another while avoiding social stigma or potential repercussions (Blee 2003; Simi and Futrell 2009).

The language and symbolism of the fascist movement represents one aspect of a unique movement subculture. As Futrell and Simi (2004) indicate, the indigenous spaces of the movement facilitate a distinct culture that movement members adhere to and have in common. This "lifestyle fascism" (Burley 2017, 133) links together disparate practices in a shared form defined by ideological overlap. By engaging in online banter using fascist language or memes or presenting subtle movement signifiers, individuals can participate in the movement without committing to more high-risk, overt forms of activism such as attending a rally or acts of violence discussed later in this chapter. Ross Haenfler, Brett Johnson, and Ellis Jones (2012, 2) developed the category of "lifestyle movements" for collections of people who engage in activities that "consciously and actively promote a lifestyle, or way of life, as their primary means to foster social change." For many members of the fascist movement, activism may be as simple as engaging in everyday activities in the service of their ideology. Indigenous prefigurative practices such as homeschooling or bible study become crucial movement activities when they are framed through a supremacist lens (Futrell and Simi 2004; Simi and Futrell 2010). Lifestyle movements are particularly suited to the subcultural and religious sectors of the movement where social and spiritual practice become synonymous with activism (Berlet and Vysotsky 2006). Maintaining an identity in and of itself becomes a sign of effective movement participation where "[success] means personal, moral integrity, often regardless of collective impact" (Haenfler, Johnson, and Jones 2012, 9). Consistent with the meta-political strategy of fascist movements that seeks to impact cultural norms rather than political systems, individual subcultural identity serves to undermine what fascists perceive as a multicultural hegemony. Producing and consuming fascist subcultural products becomes the means by which resistance is enacted (Berlet and Vysotsky 2006; Haenfler 2014; Simi and Futrell 2010; J. P. Williams 2011). Cultural construction and production, therefore, becomes the means through which certain activists within the movement contribute to the greater cause.

Violence

The fascist movement is unique in that it is rooted in an ideological imperative to violence. Classical fascism centered violence as a necessary component of foreign and domestic policy as well as individual, spiritual superiority. For fascists, violence is not just a means to an end, it is an end in itself that demonstrates the superiority of the movement and its adherents through their ability to impose domination (Berlet 1992; Eco 1995; Paxton 2004). Despite spokespeople like Richard Spencer advocating for "peaceful ethnic cleansing" (Southern Poverty Law Center 2019), the goal of racial separatism or supremacy advocated by fascists cannot be achieved without force or acts of genocide. Notwithstanding attempts by leaders to paint it as non-violent, mainstream ethnic advocacy, movement propaganda, rhetoric, and individual beliefs advocate violence (Belew 2018; Dobratz and Waldner 2012; Perry 2000). Violence is, therefore, an essential component of fascist activism.

Targeted harassment and doxing

In the age of social media, campaigns of targeted harassment and doxing have become an activist norm. Whereas many movements, including antifascist movements discussed later in this chapter, employ this tactic to leverage public shaming and stigma to encourage opponents' disengagement, fascist doxing campaigns represent a form of violence. Public shaming is dependent on the subject engaging in an activity that is stigmatized. The subjects of fascist targeted harassment campaigns – academics, journalists, and antifascist as well as other leftist activists – simply do not possess the social stigma that is currently associated with virulent bigotry. Fascist campaigns of targeted harassment are designed to denigrate and threaten the subject. This strategy that was perfected by the "manosphere" during the Gamergate campaign where women involved in game design, journalism, and cultural criticism were subjected to mass campaigns of internet harassment including rape and death threats as well as doxing that revealed their home addresses. In the most extreme cases, the subjects of these threats were forced to cancel public events and leave their homes for fear of violence (Allaway 2014; Nagle 2017; Wendling 2018). These online campaigns were not new to fascists, after all "anti-antifa" blogs that attempted to dox militant antifascists were online in the early 2010s, but Gamergate transformed the scale of harassment by weaponizing it in a particularly aggressive manner. For the alt-right and other fascists who participated in or observed the phenomenon, this new approach to levying threats against their opponents was a tactical innovation (Burley 2017; Lyons 2017).

The violence of targeted online harassment and doxing campaigns lies not just in the assault, rape, and death threats levied, but in the possibility that they might be carried out. When fascists publish the home address of someone they've labeled an opponent, they are specifically targeting that individual, and often their family, housemates, and neighbors, for potential violence by movement members. The threats rely on the decentralized, leaderless resistance model to inspire a movement member to "take action," which is where their real power lies. As Chapter 5 will discuss in some detail, for the subjects of fascist threats, the threat is amplified by the knowledge that they may become a target of violence. As stated earlier, this is because violence is both the means and the end of fascist ideology. Fascist threats carry weight because of the possibility that they may be realized.

Bias crime and terrorism

Scholars of bias crime have found that it is hard to estimate the total number of incidents in any given year, let alone those perpetrated by individuals affiliated to the supremacist movement. Official bias crime data collected by the FBI is prone to under-reporting, and it is estimated that there may be an average of 250,000 bias crimes annually in the United States (Langton and Masucci 2017; McDevitt et al. 2003). Of the bias crimes that do occur, the majority are acts of "thrill-seeking" committed by individuals who do not have a strong ideological commitment driving them. "Hatemongers," individuals who are deeply committed to prejudice and are most likely to be affiliated with the fascist movement, are typically associated with the least common form of "mission" bias crimes that are designed to eliminate the targeted group of people and are, therefore, often the most violent (J. Levin and McDevitt 2002; J. Levin and Nolan 2017). These acts of violence specifically target vulnerable, historically marginalized groups based on an immutable, ascribed characteristic – race, ethnicity, religion, gender identity, or sexual orientation – that also is meant to signal to others who share that characteristic that they are vulnerable to attack. It is, therefore, arguable that bias crimes operate as a form of terrorism regardless of the depth of ideological commitment of the perpetrator (Iganski 2001; Perry and Alvi 2012). However, the ideological component of violent incidents committed by fascists firmly places many of them in the category of terrorism as understood by the general public and law enforcement.

The contemporary pattern of supremacist terrorism has its origins in the campaigns of organized violence associated with affiliates of Christian Identity, the National Alliance, and other supremacist organizations in the 1980s (Belew 2018). With the shift to a leaderless resistance strategy and growth in the subculture of racist skinheads, these acts of terror became more limited in scope to resemble the interpersonal violence of bias crimes. Yet, distinct acts of fascist terrorism persist. The Anti-Defamation League (2019a, 16) reported that "right wing extremists were responsible for the vast majority of extremist-related murder" in the United States since 2009, with every incident in 2018 linked in some manner to far-right activists. Late 2018 and 2019 are marked by an increase in mass shooting attacks by individuals affiliated to the fascist movement; including, but not limited to, the murders at the Tree of Life Synagogue in Pittsburgh, the Al Noor Mosque and Linwood Islamic Center in Christchurch, and Walmart in El Paso (Cai et al. 2019). In most cases, the individuals responsible are engaging in copy-cat actions drawing inspiration from past perpetrators and replicating their activity including the publication of manifestos with direct references to similar ideological concerns and the use of similar weaponry. These incidents are cheered on by movement adherents in the internal online world described above, urging one another to beat a previous shooter's "high score" in numbers of people killed (Schiano 2019; Sherr and Van Boom 2019). Compounded with the daily violence of bias crime, such acts of terrorism construct a climate where fascist violence becomes routine.

violence of bias crimes and acts of terrorism, fascism encourages
bcultures. This phenomenon has been most thoroughly studied
inhead subculture, which has a reputation for extreme acts of vio-
1; Bowen 2008; Hamm 1993; Simi and Futrell 2010). Racist skinheads frequently utilize violence within subcultures as a recruitment tactic by
presenting themselves as heroic, masculine champions of the underdog. Additionally,
violence serves the utilitarian ideological purpose of asserting hegemonic control over
the subculture through attacks on individuals who identify as anti-racist, those who are
perceived to be outsiders, people who are identified as a racial or ethnic other, or
participants who openly identify as queer or gender non-conforming (Blazak 2001;
Bowen 2008; Simi and Futrell 2010). "The goal was that the skinheads would be seen
as 'kicking ass' and doing something about the problem of threats to [their] ascribed
status" (Blazak 2001, 991). The effect of this level of violence is ideological control of
the subculture by fascists. In doing so, fascist subculturalists are able to construct the
type of prefigurative space that is crucial for movements to survive decline, recruit new
members, and provide material resources (Simi and Futrell 2010).

Protest violence

The fascist rallies discussed earlier in this chapter are frequently sites of contestation
between event participants and antifascist counter-protesters. Fascists have at various
times and to various degrees organized demonstrations preparing for, or seeking out,
violence. Unlike previous protests that brought fascist violence to "defended neighborhoods" (Green, Strolovitch, and Wong 1998) or contested spaces, the Trump era is
marked by far-right rallies that intentionally instigate violence. These fascist events are
deliberately organized in locations that will draw a vigorous and militant antifascist
response, and event organizers often explicitly goad antifascists into confrontation by
bragging about their strength and making threats against antifa activists on social
media. Such rallies increasingly draw attendees from across the country who are
energized by fascist leaders to clash with antifa activists and other perceived movement
enemies. That violence is the primary purpose of these events is evident in the
appearance of fascists who come in body armor and armed with various blunt objects
as well as cans of mace or pepper spray, and on occasion even firearms in open-carry
states. The cartoonish presentation of certain high-profile activists who have been
derided as LARPers[5] belies the seriousness of their intent. While such activists may
appear absurd to the uninitiated, their armor and weaponry indicate an explicit desire
to engage in violence. This violence is encouraged by movement leaders and event
organizers as they incite participants to attack their opposition with violent rhetoric
shouted through megaphones (Burley 2019; Neiwert 2018a; Selk and Lee 2017;
Zielinski 2019). Rather than simply being "conventional" and "demonstrative" protest events (Kriesi et al. 1995), fascist rallies serve as an opportunity to intimidate political opponents and attempt to demobilize them through violence.

The ideological imperative toward fascist violence

Violence is an essential and consistent component of the fascist tactical repertoire. While movement tactics change as a result of shifts in historical and cultural contexts as well as access to resources (Jenkins 1983; McCarthy and Zald 1977; Tilly 2006; Tilly and Tarrow 2006), fascist movements consistently deploy violence in attempts to achieve their ideological goals (Belew 2018; Dobratz and Waldner 2012). For this movement in particular, this is the result of the unique ideological position that violence plays in fascism. Violence is central to fascist ideology as both a means of achieving the world of inequality, hierarchy, and domination they envision, and as the end result of a world where that domination is produced and reproduced through explicit force. For fascists, violent action is a moral good in and of itself, and it defines the fascist as superior to his ideological opponents. The fascist is morally and spiritually a better person because he is willing to impose his will through force (Berlet 1992; Eco 1995; Paxton 2004). In this dynamic, violence is an ideological imperative for fascists because it is explicitly proscribed by the movement's belief system as the key form of action.[6]

The examples of fascist violence described in this chapter are the product of fascist ideology not only because it privileges violent action, but also because it centers inequality and domination. Barbara Perry (2001) refers to this process of violence in bias crime as "doing difference." She argues that bias crimes serve to construct the identities of both perpetrator and victim, ultimately asserting the dominant and subordinate social position of each. This dynamic is laid bare in fascist ideology that asserts innate biological differences based on categories of race and sex, and seeks to enforce those differences through force (Burley 2017). "Within the essentialist understanding of identities, there is very little space for ambiguity, or crossing the boundaries between categories of difference" (Perry 2001, 54). Fascist violence seeks to wipe away any possibility of ambiguity consistent with the dualistic frame discussed in the previous chapter (Berlet 2004a; Berlet and Vysotsky 2006). Violence, therefore, serves to assert the dominant position of the fascist and reassert hegemonic control.

This also drives the terrorist aspect of fascist violence as the movement seeks to reassert domination in reaction to the societal gains made by historically marginalized groups of people (Perry 2001). The sense of entitlement to domination is embodied in the preferred terrorist tactic of American fascists in the Trump era – the mass shooting. Eric Madfis (2014, 68) asserts that acts of mass homicide are driven by an intersectional entitlement regarding life outcomes based on whiteness, masculinity, heterosexuality, and middle class status combined with "disappointing life course events." While these acts of mass violence may not be new, the ideological cognizance of their perpetrators is a novel phenomenon. Mass shootings now serve as a weaponized manifestation of fascist ideology.

The reliance on violence as a social movement tactic by fascists reflects the most direct manifestation of "ideologically structured action" where belief informs social movement activity (Mayer N. Zald 2000). Fascist ideology centers violence as the preferred means of achieving movement goals and the violent individual as superior. Violence serves as a means of asserting domination for an ideology that venerates essentialized inequality. It, therefore, becomes a primary tactic in the repertoire of the movement.

The antifascist tactical repertoire

Antifa activism is more than punching fascists. During my period of ethnographic research, New City Antifa engaged in non-violent activism focusing much more on tactics that rely on public shaming than public confrontation. The campaigns devised by Old City Antifa were also similarly focused on "outing" fascist activists and organizers in their community. What makes these groups, and other antifascists, militant is their willingness to engage in unconventional and confrontational forms of activity against fascists. In my formal interviews with antifa activists, there was universal approval for confrontational tactics as well as less confrontational approaches such as educational campaigns and symbolic actions such as pamphleting or picketing campaigns. Darby explained the dynamic that defines antifa as militant:

> I think that there is no place for forms of moralism over pacifism or other forms of tactics. That it's really simply a question of what will effectively politically incapacitate and also militarily incapacitate these [fascist] organizations .... You have to recognize that these groupings typically ... interact with a political base and they have some sort of military support structure ... that's inherent in them. You have to confront the political structure, the political base ... and you have to confront the military apparatus that is sustained by that political base and that means confronting it with whatever tactics you have at your disposal.

Antifa activists often frame their tactical preferences in terms of practical activity toward the strategic goal of demobilizing fascists. Therefore, they are just as likely to use non-militant tactics as militant and confrontational ones in service of that goal.

Non-militant antifascist tactics

Tactics that are categorized as non-militant generally fall within the bounds of what is considered acceptable social movement activity by mainstream political and movement actors (Fitzgerald and Rodgers 2000; Jasper 1997; Kriesi et al. 1995). These types of activities are generally uncontroversial and adopted by a number of different social movements across a variety of ideological positions. As historian Mark Bray (2017) notes in his overview of militant antifascism, the vast majority of what antifa activists do is relatively unexciting, non-confrontational, and nonviolent. In part because of its mundanity, this type of activism and the tactics that it employs are rarely acknowledged or analyzed. The "mundane" tactics at the core of the antifascist repertoire consist of information and intelligence gathering, education campaigns, public shaming campaigns, and the construction of antifascist culture.

Information and intelligence gathering

Amelia, a member of Old City Antifa, called her fellow member Max with an idea. She found the public contact information for the local chapter of a national supremacist organization and thought that she could use this to get more information about the leadership and members in Old City. The two met to hatch a plan to make contact with the group and gather information, then brought it to a group meeting. The antifa group was excited to develop this knowledge and work to publicly expose the fascists in their community with the aim of subverting the supremacists' organizing activities. Thus began a complex operation to gather intelligence on a major fascist organization through infiltration. This approach of in-person information gathering was used by Old City Antifa until its dissolution.

New City Antifa were masters of the public records search. Many members of the group became regulars at county courthouses and extremely adept at searching through online public records for information on the criminal histories of fascists in their community. Their meetings would frequently consist of lengthy discussions about the information gathered and how it could be put to use to subvert the activities of supremacists. Members would pore through documents in order to gain information such as home addresses, telephone numbers, places of employment, and criminal records. The group developed elaborate processes for corroborating this information that relied on direct confirmation ranging from telephone calls to fascists' homes or places of employment to lengthy stakeouts. The information was then leveraged into public campaigns designed to shame fascist leaders and activists and increase the costs of their participation in supremacist movements.

These types of information and intelligence gathering practices are the core of antifascist activism, and are not solely the domain of antifa activists. National watch-dog organizations such as the Southern Poverty Law Center and Anti-Defamation League monitor the activities of supremacist groups and leaders. Antifa activists engage in similar monitoring and intelligence gathering on a local level. This is based on the immediacy of threat that fascists pose to the communities in which militant antifascists organize. Additionally, the information gathering conducted by antifa activists requires either penetrating into or bringing to light the underground activities of fascists. Much of the activity engaged in by supremacists occurs outside of the sight of the majority of people. The combination of public stigma and the shift to new social movement style countercultural activity places most fascist activism in underground spaces (Berlet and Vysotsky 2006; Daniels 2009; Simi and Futrell 2010; Vysotsky and Dentice 2008). Information gathering regarding these activities, therefore, takes on a more clandestine character as militant antifascists work to penetrate closed, subterranean networks. The information gathered through such activity is then made public in order to educate communities and enforce public shaming as a control on fascist activism.

Education

On a mid-summer day, members of Old City Antifa met at a local coffee shop to discuss their latest project. The group decided to produce a pamphlet outlining the ideology and activity of contemporary supremacists as a means of informing people about the scope and threat of fascism. New City antifa produced a series of educational materials ranging from a flyer explaining fascist symbols to a history of fascist activity in the city to information about local and national fascist organizations. Large-scale antifascist gatherings serve as educational events as much as organizing ones, with numerous conference sessions open to the public that inform attendees about the scope of fascist organizing and the nature and nuance of fascist ideology. With the growth of social media, antifascist education efforts have expanded to a complex network of formal and informal blogs, Facebook pages, and Twitter accounts.

Social movements, including opposing movements, typically engage in education campaigns in order to persuade a certain audience or construct a particular frame on an issue for them (Benford and Snow 2000; Meyer and Staggenborg 1996; Zald and Useem 1987). Antifascists engage in educational campaigns as a form of activism in and of itself. Informing a community, or the public more broadly, about the nature of fascist ideology and activity is its own end because it is considered a means of inoculation against fascist organizing and mobilization efforts. Militant antifascists use education as a means of inspiring people to engage in additional actions designed to demobilize fascists such as public shaming and protest.

Public shaming

The intelligence gathering projects undertaken by militant antifascists come to full fruition in public dissemination of the information gathered. Amelia's infiltration of a supremacist group resulted in the gathering of personal information about its leader, which was made public in a leafletting campaign on the college campus where the fascists held clandestine meetings. New City Antifa's first major action consisted of a demonstration and leafletting campaign in the neighborhood of the leader of a local neo-Nazi group, which was followed by a telephone campaign to his workplace. The antifa group was prolific, and successful, in its efforts to "out" fascists in their community. Such campaigns to publicly identify fascists expanded with the growth of online activity and social media. Long before the proliferation of blogs and social media outlets, One People's Project was publishing tabloid-style news stories about fascist activity and antifascist opposition as well as the details of fascist activists' personal information in their "Rogues Gallery." By 2010, a number of formal antifascist groups were operating blogs that engaged in "doxing" of fascists and this practice has expanded with antifa activists moving into social media platforms such as Facebook and Twitter.

The practice of doxing, as performed by militant antifascists, involves the public dissemination of personal information such as the name, photograph, personal phone number, address, and employer of fascists along with a descriptive narrative about the individual's activism in the supremacist movement. These types of campaigns often come with a call to pressure employers and landlords to cut their ties with fascist activists. This pressure is sometimes accompanied by protests at or near fascists' homes or workplaces that are designed to increase pressure and mobilize social stigma.

The tactic of outing or doxing serves multiple strategic goals for militant antifascists. As an extension of the educational efforts discussed above that provide a community with details about the extent of fascist activity in its midst, the information regarding fascists is part of a broader campaign to inform communities about the extent of fascist activity that they face in order to motivate oppositional activism. The educational component in this case is also designed to marshal public pressure on supremacists in order to increase the cost of participation consistent with countermovement dynamics (Zald and Useem 1987), or as the slogan of One People's Project states, "hate has consequences." Kam described the countermovement strategy of public shaming in the following way,

> finding out where the Nazis in town that are organizing logistics are living and working and trying to get them evicted from their houses and fired from their jobs because if they don't have a job or a house, it's a lot harder for them to organize.

Eowyn explained that public pressure has the potential to motivate fascists to disengage from activism, "letting their neighbors, bosses, and everyone else know they are involved with hate groups might be enough to make them back off." While the Trump era has brought fascist discourse and mobilization into the public eye, there remains a great deal of stigma associated with overt expressions of bigotry typical of supremacist movements. Fascist activists and hardcore movement members often take great pains to avoid the stigma associated with their ideological position and activity (Simi and Futrell 2009). Exposing fascists to the public forces them to confront the "activist stigma" of their identity and reckon with the consequences of their movement involvement. Landlords, employers, and the broader community are also put in a position to be abe to proactively repudiate fascist activism and ideology. Doxing, therefore, serves as a means of pressuring fascists to make a choice between their ideological position and engaging with normative familial, work, and social activities. By encouraging community mobilization in opposition to the fascism in its midst, such campaigns also contribute to building a broader culture of antifascism.

Antifascist culture

Although it may seem like a fringe movement, antifa is everywhere. If you look closely, you will see it on buttons and t-shirts, light poles and walls, even marked on people's bodies. This is the result of a conscious tactic of deploying culture in order to challenge the fascist movement. Like many contemporary antifa groups, both Old City Antifa and New City Antifa engaged in a variety of cultural activities as part of their antifascist activism. "Merchandizing! That's where the real money is antifascism is made!" Max, a member of Old City Antifa, would joke, paraphrasing a line from Mel Brooks' film *Spaceballs* in reference to the sheer volume of cultural products the group produced and distributed. The group intentionally printed hoodies and t-shirts with its name and distinctive logo on them that were distributed at punk shows, anarchist gatherings, and in the local radical bookstore. They also printed a series of vinyl stickers with the slogan "No Nazis in Our Neighborhood," and encouraged members and supporters to place them around the city to mark it as antifascist territory. Old City Antifa would also host social events such as monthly antifascist film nights. New City Antifa similarly produced a variety of items that demonstrated affiliation with militant antifascism and marked public and private space as antifascist. The group sold t-shirts and buttons with antifa imagery and slogans and produced a series of stickers and posters encouraging the public to share information about fascist activity in their area. They also organized benefit music events to raise money for antifascists who faced repression from the state or fascist violence. Other antifa groups engage in similar work along with direct subcultural participation through the production and distribution of music by sympathetic artists. These examples are just a sample of the cultural activity militant antifascists engage in as part of their activism. The breadth of this activity will be discussed in Chapter 4.

Cultural work as a tactic deployed by social movements is a distinct feature of contemporary activism. The NSM perspective in particular outlines the importance of culture as a form of activism. Contemporary social movements often turn to the development of culture as a way of not only transmitting movement ideas or recruiting new members, but also as an end in itself because it is designed to prefigure an ideal society (Jasper 1997; Johnston, Laraña, and Gusfield 1994; McAdam 1994). By focusing on culture as a crucial element of social movement work, contemporary movements often overlap with subcultures and countercultures with the most radical movements turning to alternative cultures as an expressive form of their activism (Kriesi et al. 1995). This is clearly the pattern for the fascist movement in its participation in subcultures as a distinct manifestation of its ideological goals (Blazak 2001; Berlet and Vysotsky 2006; Simi and Futrell 2010; Vysotsky and Dentice 2008). Antifascists, as direct opponents, operate both within similar subcultures and as their own unique subcultures, often constructing a distinct antifascist culture positioned as an alternative to fascist organizing and subcultural efforts. These activities expand into the broader culture through the public display of antifascist imagery and information. To some extent, antifascist culture is a form of activism in and of itself since it marks individuals and spaces as opposing fascism. In its simplest form, antifa activism can take the form of symbolic representation displayed by people and places opposed to manifestations of fascist activism. In this sense, the subcultural form of antifascist activism manifests itself as a "lifestyle movement" that focuses on individual level identity rather than organized movement participation (Haenfler, Johnson, and Jones 2012). Culture, therefore, facilitates both informal and formal antifascist activism.

Non-militant tactics as militant antifascism

If most antifa activity consists of non-militant tactics similar to those employed by watchdog groups, journalists, and even law enforcement, then what distinguishes these actions as militant? The answer to this question lies in the style with which these activities are performed and the ideology that drives them. When antifa activists engage in non-militant tactics, they do so in a manner that is often aggressive and confrontational. As anti-authoritarians, militant antifascists choose tactics that intentionally circumvent bureaucratic and legal avenues to address their concerns as a form of direct action (Shantz 2011; Sturgeon 1995; D. M. Williams 2019).

The militant antifascist style of activism takes on a confrontational tone even when applied to non-militant tactics. Educational campaigns designed to inform the general public often are accompanied by an explicit encouragement for people to take action against individuals who display fascist symbols or other forms of affiliation with fascist groups. Public shaming and doxing campaigns are conducted in a tabloid-like manner that belittles and mocks individual fascists for their ideology and activism. Antifa culture venerates confrontation, often relying on aggressive and violent imagery. Compared to the milquetoast style of more mainstream oriented and non-militant antifascists who act within the boundaries of conventional activism, militant antifascist activities, even those that aren't confrontational, appear relatively aggressive.

The aggressive and confrontational style of militant antifascists is also driven in part by ideological orientation. Antifa activists challenge the monopoly on legitimacy claimed by mainstream watchdog groups and law enforcement agencies consistent with their radical orientation (Fitzgerald and Rodgers 2000). As Chapter 2 indicated, militant antifascism is informed by anarchist and anti-authoritarian ideology, which drives its confrontational style even in non-militant activity. By engaging in activities ranging from intelligence gathering to construction of culture, militant antifascists challenge the control of these undertakings by centralized, bureaucratic organizations embodied in state and non-state actors. This position is evident in the major plank of all militant antifascist networks' points of unity, "we don't rely on cops or courts to do our work for us." This sentiment extends to mainstream antifascist watchdog and activist groups which are viewed by militant activists with distrust and disdain. In a formal interview, Damon articulated that distrust as follows:

> I just think all of the larger ones, Southern Poverty Law Center, etc., are just so tied in with the FBI that any tendency to work with them is going to discredit those of us who think that the state … continues to generate its own forms of white supremacy that are equally or more destructive than any of the neo-fascist groups.

Antifa activists choose instead to take on even the most non-militant activities as a path toward a society without centralized political and social organization consistent with anarchist ideology and radical social movement orientation (Fitzgerald and Rodgers 2000; Shantz 2011). This results in the criminalization of antifa activism even when it does not involve direct or violent confrontation with fascists because anarchist countercultural and prefigurative practices frequently come into conflict with the "legitimate" actions of the state and civil society (Ferrell 1997a; Ferrell 1998; Ferrell 2001; Fitzgerald and Rodgers 2000; Jasper 1997; Kriesi et al. 1995). In this sense, even the most banal antifascist activities take on a much more aggressive and confrontational tone when performed by militant antifascists because they are in the service of a larger radical ideological agenda.

Militant antifascist tactics

Despite their relative rarity, it is the militant tactics engaged in by antifa activists that bring them the most notoriety and distinguish them from other types of antifascists. What makes antifa activists militant is their willingness to include disruptive, destructive, and confrontational (including violent) activities in their tactical repertoire. Militant antifascists not only accept such tactics as legitimate or strategic, but also as necessary in their opposition to fascist mobilizations and organizing efforts. These tactics can best be understood as belonging to two complimentary categories: disruption and confrontation.

Disruption of fascist activities

On June 26, 2016, the neo-Nazi Traditionalist Worker's Party, Golden State Skinheads, and other assorted white supremacists planned a rally on the California Capitol steps in Sacramento. Antifascists, militant and non-militant alike, organized a mass counter-rally and disruption. Since the fascist rally was planned for that afternoon, the antifascists organized to occupy the location as a means of disrupting the supremacist event by occupying the Capitol steps early in the morning. As scheduled, a large crowd of antifascist protesters arrived on the Capitol grounds and took over the steps intending to use force, if necessary, to defend the space from fascist rally attendees. As fascists began to arrive, scuffles broke out between them and antifascists. The clashes resulted in the stabbing of seven antifascists by supremacists and numerous injuries to activists on both sides. Despite the violence and injuries to counter-protesters, the antifascists declared the protest a success because the Traditionalist Worker's Party and Golden State Skinheads were unable to hold their rally.

While this is an extreme example of militant antifascist disruption, it serves to demonstrate many of the dynamics involved in the deployment of this tactic. Antifa activists engage in disruption by directly preventing fascist events from occurring. The specific means by which this is achieved varies for each event, but often involve some form of direct action in order to impede the fascists from meeting and carrying out their gathering. In many instances, this type of disruption involves damage to the facility or confrontations with attendees. Regardless of the level of confrontation and conflict, this strategy relies on venue owners, managers, or the state intervening and canceling the event.

In formal interviews, militant antifascists consistently supported the use of property destruction and damage as a means of disrupting fascist events. Speaking about the procedure for stopping a fascist rally, Lydia stated that "you should find out where it is and completely do everything within your power to destroy it …. I would say whatever means necessary to keep them from coming to town." Antifa activists asserted that such tactics are effective because "it's physically impossible for them to hold it at that same venue and if they try to do it at some other place, you can go after those places as well" (Kam). Ultimately, the purpose of such disruptions is to discourage both the immediate and future mobilizations. For example, Eowyn asserted that destruction or damage to a venue "sends the message that people who allow white supremacists to rally will be held accountable, and discourages them from continuing support, with a venue, anyway, and makes it harder for them to rally."

Not all disruptive activity employed by militant antifascists requires the use of violence or destruction. In fact, such tactics are generally deployed only when other methods fail to shut down fascist events. In general, antifa activists rely on much less invasive tactics for disruption. The most common disruptive tactic combines intelligence gathering, education campaigns, and public shaming to pressure venues to cancel events before the scheduled date and time. Antifa groups routinely pressure venue owners and managers through mass call in, email, and social media campaigns that accompany the release of information about upcoming fascist events. New City Antifa routinely engaged in such activities by encouraging supporters to make phone calls to venues that hosted racist skinhead music events, talks by Holocaust deniers, and speeches by anti-Semites. In a formal interview Kam described the process antifa activists use:

> The most appropriate and effective response is to try and get that event cancelled. You can do that by finding out where the venue is and going after the owners of the venue … talking to whoever owns it. Usually people that own it don't know what the venue is actually used for …. The owners usually don't know. If they're informed, the majority of the time they'll cancel the event outright. If there is opposition, you can bring community support and show opposition to the venue, make it bad for business, and usually that'll work. If it's bad for business, then almost anyone, even if they're a white supremacist, will end up canceling.

For antifa activists the use of disruptive tactics is ultimately borne out in the impact they have on fascist mobilization and organizing efforts. Consistent with Zald and Useem's (1987) framework of countermovement tactics, occupying fascist rallying space or forcing the cancellation of fascist events serves to disrupt movement activity in favor of countermovement goals.

Confronting fascists

Old City Antifa was the product of confrontational, sometimes violent interactions between its members and supremacists. The founding members of the group participated in a number of clashes between fascist and antifascists in the eastern part of the United States as part of their anarchist organizing. They also engaged in informal antifascism at parties, punk shows, and on the streets of Old City by confronting individuals who displayed supremacist tattoos or imagery on their clothing. By forming the antifascist group, these activists solidified their pre-existing activity into a formal organization that prioritized antifascist activism as the core of its mission. Confronting fascists, whether in a formal rally setting or informal public settings, is a key element of militant antifascist activism that distinguishes antifa activists from non-militant antifascists. Like the process of disruption, militant antifascists do not immediately rely on violence as a tactic in confrontations with fascists. Confronting fascists often begins with verbal challenges and a kind of information gathering to determine how committed an individual is to fascist ideology and movement activity. Mark describes the process of discerning the ideological and movement commitment of an individual fascist as follows:

> I think the first thing would be in like a really assertive way [saying], "what's up with your shirt?" The only explanations I think I could get that would suggest further conversation would be … "oh, I'm just trying to be shocking or piss people off" like some kind of ridiculous things like that or maybe there are some people who don't really know, particularly with some kinds of racist music and stuff like that, particularly I think with some of the [national socialist black] metal shit or something like that. You know, that's kind of like a kitschy kind of sub-genre to be into right now and people don't even realize that some of these bands really have a serious even historically violent, racist message that they're sending so they might be just like wearing the shirt to be ironic that they listen to [black] metal. Maybe they really are [black] metal fans and don't realize that this is the message of the music. And then you would see what happens from there.

If it is established that an individual is in fact affiliated with a fascist group or ideology, the interactive dynamic shifts to one that becomes more aggressive in order to dissuade them from participation. Damon elaborated on this process by describing the policy his organization developed for interrogating these types of individuals:

> the rule that we tried to put forth was do not attack people while they're alone. And the reason for this was that we believed that individual Nazis, boneheads, whatever could be converted, and some of them were. But we felt that if you took a gang of anti-racists and attacked these folks that, attacked them physically and by that, I mean people with baseball bats and stuff jumping out of the car and beating the shit out of them, that it would drive them further into their neo-Nazi brotherhood. And so, what we tried to put forth was once people get the tattoos that signals a certain level of membership so it was ok to talk with them, it was ok to approach them in a group and say, "Why are you wearing these? Why did you get those and why are you in this

town? What do those mean to you?" It was ok to confront them and to tell them that they should not be exposing [fascist symbols] and if they continue to expose them, that they would get beat down. And it was also ok if they had been known to be part of gangs which were attacking people, that we would retaliate and we did retaliate against individuals after they'd been warned that if they attacked people, if they were known to be part of gangs which I meant by that groups of 3 or 4 or 5 boneheads who would attack people and do so in a very public manner, in clubs or other places.

The level of commitment that an individual has toward fascist activity clearly aligns with antifascists' confrontational response. Antifa activists engage in violent confrontation when the individual in question has asserted a deep and unabiding commitment to fascism. This dynamic explains why militant antifascists are less likely to engage in dialogue with attendees at fascist events and move straight to confrontational violence. Attendees at fascist events demonstrate a commitment to the movement because they must be linked to key organizers through networks of underground communication and their willingness to attend such events demonstrates a certain amount of desire to be involved in movement activity (Futrell and Simi 2004; Simi and Futrell 2009). On its blog, Southside Chicago Anti-Racist Action describes a number of these violent confrontations with users of the Daily Stormer white supremacist forum, individual neo-Nazis involved in violent attacks on antifascists, and members of the "Western chauvinist" Proud Boys. Antifa activists routinely clash with fascist attendees of speeches by movement leaders whether they are held in surreptitiously rented public libraries, restaurants, hotel ballrooms or on university campuses.

The use of violence by antifascist activists is intended to "increase the cost of participation" (Zald and Useem 1987, 260) in fascist movements. Militant antifascists contend that confrontation and the threat or use of violence forces fascists to make a calculation regarding their continued public membership in the movement. As Damon described above, such confrontations force people to make a commitment to the movement, which then results in certain types of outcomes – social stigma and potential violence. The purpose of antifascist violence is to demobilize fascists in both the short and long term. In the short term, violent confrontation serves to disrupt fascist events as indicated above. In the long term, confrontation contributes in part to demobilization (Bowen 2008; Linden and Klandermans 2006).

Although the tactics of disruption and confrontation are deployed relatively rarely by antifa activists, they often signify the core distinction between them and other non-militant antifascists. Antifa activists' willingness, and at times insistence, on incorporating such tactics in their repertoire places them apart from other types of antifascist activists. This distinction also gives them a notoriety because it draws media attention to confrontational protests and disruptive clashes. It also informs the culture and style of antifa activism as discussed above and in greater detail in Chapter 4. While violence isn't the defining characteristic of antifa activism, it is clearly the distinguishing one.

Tactical decision-making

Any discussion of militant antifascist tactics must be grounded in an understanding that there is no universal set of tactics that all antifa groups adhere to. Every militant antifascist group has direct autonomy when it comes to tactical choices and makes decisions regarding tactics in a direct democratic manner. In the case of mass mobilizations, militant blocs come together in the spirit of tactical unity and similar tactical sentiment. Yet, the process of decision-making with regard to tactics is one that reflects the radical orientation of antifa groups. Tactical decisions are often made in small affinity groups that prioritize direct democracy and strive for consensus.

When Amelia and Max developed a plan to gather intelligence as described above, they didn't simply set out on their own. As members of a formal antifa group, they brought it to the whole collective for discussion in a meeting. The relative benefits and dangers were discussed by all of the meeting attendees and a vote was taken regarding whether to go forward with the operation. Once it was unanimously approved, group members volunteered for various roles in the project. Those members formed a separate "affinity group" that met to discuss operations and provided updates to the complete membership of Old City Antifa during meetings. All of the projects that the group engaged in went through similar processes. A member would bring an idea to the group, the idea would be discussed, the discussion would lead to a call for consensus or vote, and the approved action would be taken by the group as a whole or volunteer members. The process described is typical of antifa groups. New City Antifa used a similar one in decision-making, and policy decisions for national antifascist networks relied on direct democratic processes at meetings or via electronic communication.

The key component to any tactical decisions is direct democracy. Like many other radical or new social movement participants, antifa activists are deeply committed to an egalitarian process that stresses direct democratic decision-making (Fitzgerald and Rodgers 2000; Jasper 1997; Polletta 2007). For militant antifascists, the process of determining tactics is as important as the tactics themselves because it reflects a distinct ideological and identity orientation. Because many members of formal antifa groups identify as anarchists or anti-authoritarians, the way in which their group comes to decisions is reflective of that orientation. For anarchists the form of any collective endeavor must prefigure the society that they desire to build, which results in non-hierarchical organizations (Day 2005; Graeber 2002; D. M. Williams 2018). Contemporary anarchists prioritize direct democratic processes and the development of consensus over the expediency of hierarchical management. Antifascists in particular are committed to these types of processes in order to model an alternative to the explicit and implicit authoritarianism of their fascist opposition. It, therefore, is incumbent upon antifa activists to engage in democratic processes and transparency even when their activity requires secrecy. Antifa activists are responsible to their fellow collective members and antifa groups often have direct democratic ties to wider radical communities that hold them accountable for their decisions. Through these practices, militant antifascists model a non-hierarchical, directly democratic society.

Antifa tactics and strategy

As an ideal typical countermovement, militant antifascism has a clear goal: stopping fascist movements. Antifa strategy focuses on direct intervention whenever possible in order to demobilize fascists. The tactics deployed by militant antifascists reflect this rather simple strategic formulation. The breadth of the antifa tactical repertoire is designed to achieve the movement's goals by using whatever methods are available to intervene against fascist mobilizing and organizing efforts. This orientation results in militant antifascists developing a relatively diverse tactical repertoire that encourages a variety of approaches and innovations in response to fascist maneuvers.

Although antifa activists are notorious for the use of violence against fascists, the majority of their repertoire consists of non-militant activities such as intelligence gathering, education campaigns, public shaming, and cultural construction. Antifa activists engage in these tactics because they are effective in mobilizing public opinion against fascist activists and movements. What distinguishes militant antifascists from their non-militant comrades is often the style with which they deploy these tactics. Antifa activists bring a confrontational and aggressive edge to non-militant tactics that differentiates them from other more mainstream antifascists. This style is a product of their anti-authoritarian ideology and subcultural background, which puts them in conflict with mainstream groups and law enforcement as well as fascists.

The use of violent tactics by antifascists is equally driven by pragmatic and strategic concerns. Militant antifascists are committed to demobilizing fascists by any means. Disruptive and confrontational tactics are employed when non-militant approaches appear to be ineffective at directly intervening against fascist activity. Militant antifascists, unlike their non-militant counterparts, are willing to physically disrupt or confront fascists in order to stop them. These direct confrontations may result in violence. From a strategic antifascist perspective, however, that violence is viewed as a necessary countermovement tactic because it increases the cost of participation for fascists and forces them to make a calculation regarding their continued involvement.

Antifa activists do not make tactical decisions lightly. Militant groups are organized around an affinity group model that stresses direct democracy and accountability. Tactical decisions are made collectively by group members in meetings where their relative merits and disadvantages are thoroughly discussed. Group members vote on potential actions striving for consensus in decision-making in order to maintain maximum tactical unity. The internal processes of antifa groups reflect more than a desire for collective reinforcement, but are driven by a commitment to decentralizing power and avoiding hierarchical control. In this sense, the very process of tactical choice is fundamentally antifascist.

Notes

1 The continued presence of fascist users and groups on Facebook, Twitter, and YouTube is the result of a number of technological, logistical, and ideological factors. Constructing algorithms that can distinguish context for hate symbols and hate speech is a challenge that these platforms are working to address, but current capabilities are limited and end up punishing opponents of fascism, researchers, and journalists for drawing attention to hate (Neiwert 2019). In order to achieve accurate content moderation, social media sites would need to employ and properly train individuals who could distinguish context and understand the ever-changing landscape of coded fascist imagery and language. Finally, the ideological dimension is twofold: the biases of coders and moderators as well as the ideological overlap between fascist and mainstream right-wing political positions. Many tech workers subscribe at least in part to a libertarian position in regard to hate speech that either ignores or excuses some aspects or draws false equivalence between far-right and far-left expression labeling both as examples of hate speech (Guynn 2019). Additionally, insiders indicate that enforcing policies against hate speech would result in the deactivation of accounts by mainstream conservatives, including President Trump (O'Brien 2019).

2 This term was popularized by *New York Times* columnist Bari Weiss in reference to a number of online personalities who were allegedly "locked out" by mainstream media for their controversial philosophies. These individuals, who generally self-identify as classical liberals, often express reactionary ideas regarding innate biological differences in race and gender, the incompatibility of Islam with Western cultural values and institutions, and a general derision of multiculturalism (Farrell 2018). In doing so, they frequently serve as an entry point for individuals to exposure to fascist content online (Lewis 2018; Roose 2019).

3 The 14 words – "We must secure the existence of our people and a future for white children" – were coined by David Lane, a member of the notorious neo-Nazi terrorist group the Order, who served as a major influence in the fascist movement even after his incarceration for activity with the group.

4 Pepe the frog was created by cartoonist Matt Furie in 2005 without any racist or anti-Semitic intent. The character was appropriated as an alt-right symbol and effectively became the face of online bigotry. After a valiant effort to reclaim the character from the alt-right that included lawsuits for copyright infringement, Furie killed the comic character effectively conceding its appropriation (Hunt 2017). The Moon Man meme is an appropriation of a 1980s McDonald's advertising character, Mac the Night, that was used as an avatar for YouTube rap "parodies" that contain gruesome racist imagery and racial epithets. It is also used in violent memes and far-right avatars (Caffier 2017).

5 LARP is an acronym for live action role play, a type of fantasy role-playing game where participants dress in costumes to represent their characters and engage in face-to-face combat with opponents using foam weapons. The term is used in both left- and right-wing activist circles to refer to individuals who privilege appearance and staged conflict over what is perceived to be the "real work" of the social movement.

6 I use the gendered pronoun here intentionally because the patriarchal character of fascism exalts violence as a masculine attribute and renders superiority upon men for their innate desire to be violent. Fascist masculinity is, therefore, defined by violence, and fascism is defined by its masculinity (Daniels 1997; Ferber 1999).

Works cited

Allaway, Jennifer. 2014. "#Gamergate Trolls Aren't Ethics Crusaders; They're a Hate Group." *Jezebel.* https://jezebel.com/gamergate-trolls-arent-ethics-crusaders-theyre-a-hate-1644984010.

Anti-Defamation League. 2019a. "Murder and Extremism in the United States in 2018." *Anti-Defamation League.* https://www.adl.org/murder-and-extremism-2018.

Anti-Defamation League. 2019b. "White Supremacists Increase College Campus Recruiting Efforts for Third Straight Year." *Anti-Defamation League*. https://www.adl.org/news/press-relea ses/white-supremacists-increase-college-campus-recruiting-efforts-for-third.

Anti-Defamation League. 2019c. "Despite YouTube Policy Update, Anti-Semitic, White Supremacist Channels Remain." *Anti-Defamation League*. https://www.adl.org/blog/desp ite-youtube-policy-update-anti-semitic-white-supremacist-channels-remain.

Belew, Kathleen. 2018. *Bring the War Home: The White Power Movement and Paramilitary America*. Cambridge, MA: Harvard University Press.

Benford, Robert D., and David A. Snow. 2000. "Framing Processes and Social Movements: An Overview and Assessment." *Annual Review of Sociology* 26 (1): 611–639.

Berbrier, Mitch. 1998. "White Supremacists and the (Pan)-Ethnic Imperative: On 'European-Americans' and 'White Student Unions.'" *Sociological Inquiry* 68 (4): 498–516.

Berbrier, Mitch. 1999. "Impression Management for the Thinking Racist: A Case Study of Intellectualization as Stigma Transformation in Contemporary White Supremacist Discourse." *The Sociological Quarterly* 40 (3): 411–433.

Berbrier, Mitch. 2000. "The Victim Ideology of White Supremacists and White Separatists in the United States." *Sociological Focus* 33 (2): 175–191.

Berlet, Chip. 1992. "Fascism!" *Political Research Associates*. https://www.politicalresearch.org/ 1992/09/28/fascism.

Berlet, Chip. 2004a. "Mapping the Political Right: Gender and Race Oppression in Right-Wing Movements." In *Home-Grown Hate: Gender and Organized Racism*, edited by Abby L. Ferber, 19–48. New York, NY: Routledge.

Berlet, Chip, and Mathew N. Lyons. 2000. *Right-Wing Populism in America: Too Close for Comfort*. New York, NY: Guilford Press.

Berlet, Chip, and Stanislav Vysotsky. 2006. "Overview of US White Supremacist Groups." *Journal of Political and Military Sociology* 34 (1): 11.

Blazak, Randy. 2001. "White Boys to Terrorist Men: Target Recruitment of Nazi Skinheads." *American Behavioral Scientist* 44 (6): 982–1000.

Blee, Kathleen M. 2003. *Inside Organized Racism: Women in the Hate Movement*. Berkeley, CA: University of California Press.

Borgeson, Kevin, and Robin Valeri. 2004. "Faces of Hate." *Journal of Applied Sociology* 21 (2): 99–111.

Bowen, Derek. 2008. *"Patterns of Skinhead Violence."* Ph.D. Dissertation, Durham, NH: University of New Hampshire.

Bray, Mark. 2017. *Antifa: The Antifascist Handbook*. Brooklyn, NY: Melville House Publishing.

Burghart, Devin. 1999. *Soundtracks to the White Revolution: White Supremacist Assaults on Youth Subcultures*. Chicago, IL: Center for New Community.

Burley, Shane. 2017. *Fascism Today – What It Is and How to End It*. Chico, CA: AK Press.

Burley, Shane. 2019. "Patriot Prayer Is Building a Violent Movement in Portland." *Salon*. https://www.salon.com/2019/07/04/patriot-prayer-is-building-a-violent-movem ent-in-portland_partner/.

Burris, Val, Emery Smith, and Ann Strahm. 2000. "White Supremacist Networks on the Internet." *Sociological Focus* 33 (2): 215–235.

Caffier, Justin. 2017. "Get to Know the Memes of the Alt-Right and Never Miss a Dog-Whistle Again." *Vice*. https://www.vice.com/en_us/article/ezagwm/get-to-know-the-m emes-of-the-alt-right-and-never-miss-a-dog-whistle-again.

Cai, Weiyi, Troy Griggs, Jason Kao, Juliette Love, and Joe Ward. 2019. "White Extremist Ideology Drives Many Deadly Shootings." *The New York Times*, August 4, sec. U.S. https:// www.nytimes.com/interactive/2019/08/04/us/white-extremist-active-shooter.html.

Corte, Ugo, and Bob Edwards. 2008. "White Power Music and the Mobilization of Racist Social Movements." *Music and Arts in Action* 1 (1): 4–20.

Cox, Joseph, and Jason Koebler. 2019. "Twitter Won't Treat White Supremacy Like ISIS Because It'd Have to Ban Some GOP Politicians Too." *Vice*. https://www.vice.com/en_us/article/a3xgq5/why-wont-twitter-treat-white-supremacy-like-isis-because-it-would-mean-banning-some-republican-politicians-too.

Daniels, Jessie. 1997. *White Lies: Race, Class, Gender, and Sexuality in White Supremacist Discourse*. New York, NY: Routledge.

Daniels, Jessie. 2009. *Cyber Racism: White Supremacy Online and the New Attack on Civil Rights*. Lanham, MD: Rowman & Littlefield.

Day, Richard J.F. 2005. *Gramsci Is Dead: Anarchist Currents in the Newest Social Movements*. Ann Arbor, MI: Pluto Press.

Dobratz, Betty A., and Stephanie L. Shanks-Meile. 1997. *White Power, White Pride!: The White Separatist Movement in the United States*. New York, NY: Prentice Hall.

Dobratz, Betty A., and Lisa Waldner. 2012. "Repertoires of Contention: White Separatist Views on the Use of Violence and Leaderless Resistance." *Mobilization: An International Quarterly* 17 (1): 49–66. doi:10.17813/maiq.17.1.3282448743272632.

Eco, Umberto. 1995. "Ur-Fascism." *The New York Review of Books*, June 22. https://www.nybooks.com/articles/1995/06/22/ur-fascism/.

Ezekiel, Raphael S. 1995. *The Racist Mind: Portraits of American Neo-Nazis and Klansmen*. New York, NY: Viking.

Farrell, Henry. 2018. "The 'Intellectual Dark Web,' Explained: What Jordan Peterson Has in Common with the Alt-Right." *Vox*. https://www.vox.com/the-big-idea/2018/5/10/17338290/intellectual-dark-web-rogan-peterson-harris-times-weiss.

Ferber, Abby L. 1999. *White Man Falling: Race, Gender, and White Supremacy*. Lanham, MD: Rowman & Littlefield.

Ferrell, Jeff. 1997a. "Youth, Crime, and Cultural Space." *Social Justice* 24 (4): 21–38.

Ferrell, Jeff. 1998. "Against the Law: Anarchist Criminology." *Social Anarchism* 24: 5–15.

Ferrell, Jeff. 2001. *Tearing Down the Streets: Adventures in Urban Anarchy*. New York, NY: Palgrave.

Fitzgerald, Kathleen J., and Diane M. Rodgers. 2000. "Radical Social Movement Organizations: A Theoretical Model." *Sociological Quarterly* 41 (4): 573–592.

Futrell, Robert, and Pete Simi. 2004. "Free Spaces, Collective Identity, and the Persistence of U.S. White Power Activism." *Social Problems* 51 (1): 16–42.

Gardell, Mattias. 2003. *Gods of the Blood: The Pagan Revival and White Separatism*. Durham, NC: Duke University Press.

Gerstenfeld, Phyllis B., Diana R. Grant, and Chau-Pu Chiang. 2003. "Hate Online: A Content Analysis of Extremist Internet Sites." *Analyses of Social Issues and Public Policy* 3 (1): 29–44. doi:10.1111/j.1530-2415.2003.00013.x.

Graeber, David. 2002. "The New Anarchists." *New Left Review* 13: 61–73.

Green, Donald P., Dara Z. Strolovitch, and Janelle S. Wong. 1998. "Defended Neighborhoods, Integration, and Racially Motivated Crime." *American Journal of Sociology* 104 (2): 372–403. doi:10.1086/210042.

Gupta, Arun. 2019. "Portland's Andy Ngo Is the Most Dangerous Grifter in America." *Jacobin*. https://jacobinmag.com/2019/08/andy-ngo-right-wing-antifa-protest-portland-bigotry.

Guynn, Jessica. 2019. "Facebook While Black: Users Call It Getting 'Zucked,' Say Talking About Racism Is Censored as Hate Speech." *USA Today*, April 24. https://www.usatoday.com/story/news/2019/04/24/facebook-while-black-zucked-users-say-they-get-blocked-racism-discussion/2859593002/.

Haenfler, Ross. 2014. *Subcultures the Basics*. New York, NY: Routledge.

Haenfler, Ross, Brett Johnson, and Ellis Jones. 2012. "Lifestyle Movements: Exploring the Intersection of Lifestyle and Social Movements." *Social Movement Studies* 11 (1): 1–20.

Hamm, Mark S. 1993. *American Skinheads: The Criminology and Control of Hate Crime.* Westport, CT: Praeger.

Hatewatch. 2017. "White Nationalist Flyering on American College Campuses." *Southern Poverty Law Center.* https://www.splcenter.org/hatewatch/2017/10/17/white-nationalist-flyering-american-college-campuses.

Hayden, Michael Edison. 2019. "Far-Right Extremists Are Calling for Terrorism on the Messaging App Telegram." *Southern Poverty Law Center.* https://www.splcenter.org/hatewatch/2019/06/27/far-right-extremists-are-calling-terrorism-messaging-app-telegram.

Hegghammer, Thomas. 2017. "Introduction: What Is Jihadi Culture and Why Should We Study It?" In *Jihadi Culture: The Art and Social Practices of Militant Islamists*, edited by Thomas Hegghammer, 1–21. New York, NY: Cambridge University Press.

Hern, Alex. 2019. "Facebook Ban on White Nationalism Too Narrow, Say Auditors." *The Guardian*, July 1, sec. Technology. https://www.theguardian.com/technology/2019/jul/01/facebook-ban-on-white-nationalism-too-narrow-say-auditors.

Hunt, Elle. 2017. "Pepe the Frog Creator Kills Off Internet Meme Co-Opted by White Supremacists." *The Guardian*, May 8, sec. World News. https://www.theguardian.com/world/2017/may/08/pepe-the-frog-creator-kills-off-internet-meme-co-opted-by-white-supremacists.

Iganski, Paul. 2001. "Hate Crimes Hurt More." *American Behavioral Scientist* 45 (4): 626–638. doi:10.1177/0002764201045004006.

Jasper, James M. 1997. *The Art of Moral Protest: Culture, Biography, and Creativity in Social Movements.* Chicago, IL: University of Chicago Press.

Jenkins, J. Craig. 1983. "Resource Mobilization Theory and the Study of Social Movements." *Annual Review of Sociology* 9: 527–553.

Johnston, Hank, Enrique Laraña, and Joseph R. Gusfield. 1994. "Identities, Grievances, and New Social Movements." In *New Social Movements: From Ideology to Identity*, edited by Enrique Laraña, Hank Johnston, and Joseph R. Gusfield, 3–35. Philadelphia, PA: Temple University Press.

Kriesi, Hanspeter, Ruud Koopmans, Jan Willem Duyvendak, and Marco G. Guigni. 1995. *New Social Movements in Western Europe: A Comparative Analysis.* Minneapolis, MN: University of Minnesota Press.

Langton, Lynn, and Madeline Masucci. 2017. *Hate Crime Victimization, 2004–2015.* Washington, DC: Bureau of Justice Statistics. https://www.bjs.gov/index.cfm?ty=pbdetail&iid=5967.

Lee, Elissa, and Laura Leets. 2002. "Persuasive Storytelling by Hate Groups Online Examining Its Effects on Adolescents." *American Behavioral Scientist* 45 (6): 927–957.

Levin, Brian. 2002. "Cyberhate: A Legal and Historical Analysis of Extremists' Use of Computer Networks in America." *American Behavioral Scientist* 45 (6): 958–988. doi:10.1177/0002764202045006004.

Levin, Jack, and Jack McDevitt. 2002. *Hate Crimes Revisited: America's War against Those Who Are Different.* Boulder, CO: Westview.

Levin, Jack, and Jim Nolan. 2017. *The Violence of Hate: Understanding Harmful Forms of Bias and Bigotry.* Lanham, MD: Rowman & Littlefield.

Lewis, Rebecca. 2018. *Alternative Influence: Broadcasting the Reactionary Right on YouTube.* New York, NY: Data and Society Research Institute.

Linden, Annette, and Bert Klandermans. 2006. "Stigmatization and Repression of Extreme-Right Activism in the Netherlands." *Mobilization: An International Journal* 11 (2): 213–228.

Lyons, Matthew N. 2017. *Ctrl-Alt-Delete: The Origins and Ideology of the Alternative Right*. Somerville, MA: Political Research Associates. https://www.politicalresearch.org/2017/01/20/ctrl-alt-delete-report-on-the-alternative-right/.

Lytvynenko, Jane, Craig Silverman, and Alex Boutilier. 2019. "White Nationalist Groups Banned by Facebook Are Still on the Platform." *BuzzFeed News*. https://www.buzzfeednews.com/article/janelytvynenko/facebook-white-nationalist-ban-evaded.

Madfis, Eric. 2014. "Triple Entitlement and Homicidal Anger: An Exploration of the Intersectional Identities of American Mass Murderers." *Men and Masculinities* 17 (1): 67–86. doi:10.1177/1097184X14523432.

McAdam, Doug. 1994. "Culture and Social Movements." In *New Social Movements: From Ideology to Identity*, edited by Enrique Laraña, Hank Johnston, and Joseph R. Gusfeld, 36–57. Philadelphia, PA: Temple University Press.

McCarthy, John D., and Mayer N. Zald. 1977. "Resource Mobilization and Social Movements: A Partial Theory." *American Journal of Sociology* 82 (6): 1212–1241.

McDevitt, Jack, Jennifer M. Balboni, Susan Bennett, Joan C. Weiss, Stan Orchowsky, and Lisa Walbot. 2003. "Improving the Quality and Accuracy of Bias Crime Statistics Nationally: An Assessment of the First Ten Years of Bias Crime Data Collection." In *Hate and Bias Crime: A Reader*, edited by Barbara Perry, 77–89. New York, NY: Routledge.

Meyer, David S., and Suzanne Staggenborg. 1996. "Movements, Countermovements, and the Structure of Political Opportunity." *American Journal of Sociology* 101 (6): 1628–1660.

Miller-Idriss, Cynthia. 2019. "Selling Extremism: Nationalist Streetwear and the Rise of the Far Right." *CNN Style*. https://www.cnn.com/style/article/right-wing-fashion-streetwear/index.html.

Nagle, Angela. 2017. *Kill All Normies: The Online Culture Wars from Tumblr and 4chan to the Alt-Right and Trump*. Washington, DC: Zero Books.

Neiwert, David. 2018a. "Freedom to Bash Heads." *The Baffler*. https://thebaffler.com/latest/freedom-to-bash-heads-niewert.

Neiwert, David. 2018b. "Is That an Ok Sign? A White Power Symbol? Or Just a Right-Wing Troll?" *Southern Poverty Law Center – Hatewatch*, September 18. https://www.splcenter.org/hatewatch/2018/09/18/ok-sign-white-power-symbol-or-just-right-wing-troll.

O'Brien, Luke. 2019. "Twitter Still Has a White Nationalist Problem." *Huffington Post*. https://www.huffpost.com/entry/twitter-white-nationalist-problem_n_5cec4d28e4b00e036573311d.

Paxton, Robert O. 2004. *The Anatomy of Fascism*. New York, NY: Alfred A. Knopf.

Peleg, Samuel. 2000. "Peace Now or Later?: Movement–Countermovement Dynamics and the Israeli Political Cleavage." *Studies in Conflict and Terrorism* 23 (4): 235–254.

Perry, Barbara. 2000. "'Button-Down Terror': The Metamorphosis of the Hate Movement." *Sociological Focus* 33 (2): 113–131.

Perry, Barbara. 2001. *In the Name of Hate: Understanding Hate Crimes*. New York, NY: Routledge.

Perry, Barbara, and Shahid Alvi. 2012. "'We Are All Vulnerable': The *in Terrorem* Effects of Hate Crimes." *International Review of Victimology* 18 (1): 57–71. doi:10.1177/0269758011422475..

Polletta, Francesca. 2007. *Freedom Is an Endless Meeting: Democracy in American Social Movements*. Chicago, IL: University of Chicago Press.

Roose, Kevin. 2019. "The Making of a YouTube Radical." *The New York Times*, June 8, sec. Technology. https://www.nytimes.com/interactive/2019/06/08/technology/youtube-radical.html.

Schiano, Chris. 2019. "Neo-Nazis Use Discord Chats to Promote New Zealand Copycat Shootings." *Unicorn Riot*. https://unicornriot.ninja/2019/neo-nazis-use-discord-chats-to-promote-new-zealand-copycat-shootings/.

Selk, Avi, and Michelle Ye Hee Lee. 2017. "The Berkeley Rally Aftermath: Mass Arrests, a Stabbing and Weaponized Pepsi." *Washington Post*, April 16, sec. Grade Point. https://www.washingtonpost.com/news/grade-point/wp/2017/04/16/the-berkeley-rally-afterm ath-mass-arrests-a-stabbing-and-weaponized-pepsi/.

Shantz, Jeff. 2011. *Active Anarchy: Political Practice in Contemporary Movements*. Lanham, MD: Lexington Books.

Sherr, Ian, and Daniel Van Boom. 2019. "8chan Is Struggling to Stay Online in Wake of El Paso Massacre." *CNET*. https://www.cnet.com/news/8chan-is-struggling-to-stay-onli ne-in-wake-of-el-paso-massacre/.

Simi, Pete, and Robert Futrell. 2009. "Negotiating White Power Activist Stigma." *Social Problems* 56 (1): 89–110.

Simi, Pete, and Robert Futrell. 2010. *American Swastika: Inside the White Power Movement's Hidden Spaces of Hate*. Lanham, MD: Rowman & Littlefield.

Southern Poverty Law Center. 2019. "Richard Bertrand Spencer." *Southern Poverty Law Center*. Accessed August 27. https://www.splcenter.org/fighting-hate/extremist-files/indi vidual/richard-bertrand-spencer-0.

Sturgeon, Noel. 1995. "Theorizing Movements: Direct Action and Direct Theory." In *Cultural Politics and Social Movements*, edited by Marc Darnovsky, Barbara L. Epstein, and Richard Flacks, 35–51. Philadelphia, PA: Temple University Press.

Tenold, Vegas. 2018. *Everything You Love Will Burn: Inside the Rebirth of White Nationalism in America*. New York, NY: Nation Books.

Tilly, Charles. 2006. *Regimes and Repertoires*. Chicago, IL: University of Chicago Press.

Tilly, Charles, and Sidney G. Tarrow. 2006. *Contentious Politics*. Boulder, CO: Paradigm Publishers.

Unicorn Riot. 2017. "Charlottesville Violence Planned Over Discord Servers." *Unicorn Riot*. https://unicornriot.ninja/2017/charlottesville-violence-planned-discord-servers-uni corn-riot-reports/.

Valeri, Robin, and Kevin Borgeson. 2005. "Identifying the Face of Hate." *Journal of Applied Sociology* 22 (1): 91–104.

Vysotsky, Stanislav, and Dianne Dentice. 2008. "The Continuing Evolution of the White Supremacist Movement: A New Social Movement." In *Social Movements: Contemporary Perspectives*, edited by Dianne Dentice and James L. Williams, 86–97. Newcastle upon Tyne, UK: Cambridge Scholars Publishing.

Vysotsky, Stanislav, and Eric Madfis. 2014. "Uniting the Right: Anti-Immigration, Orga- nizing, and the Legitimation of Extreme Racist Organizations." *Journal of Hate Studies* 12 (1): 129. doi:10.33972/jhs.106.

Vysotsky, Stanislav, and Adrienne L. McCarthy. 2017. "Normalizing Cyberracism: A Neu- tralization Theory Analysis." *Journal of Crime and Justice* 40 (4): 446–461. doi:10.1080/ 0735648X.2015.1133314.

Ward, Justin. 2019. "Day of the Trope: White Nationalist Memes Thrive on Reddit's r/ The_Donald." *Southern Poverty Law Center*. https://www.splcenter.org/hatewatch/2018/ 04/19/day-trope-white-nationalist-memes-thrive-reddits-rthedonald.

Wendling, Mark. 2018. *Alt-Right: From 4chan to the White House*. London: Pluto Press.

Williams, Dana M. 2018. "Contemporary Anarchist and Anarchistic Movements." *Sociology Compass* 12 (6): 1–17.

Williams, Dana M. 2019. "Tactics: Conceptions of Social Change, Revolution, and Anar- chist Organisation." In *The Palgrave Handbook of Anarchism*, edited by Carl Levy and Matthew S. Adams, 107–123. New York, NY: Palgrave.

Williams, J. Patrick. 2011. *Subcultural Theory: Traditions & Concepts*. Chichester: Polity Press.

Zald, Mayer N. 2000. "Ideologically Structured Action: An Enlarged Agenda for Social Movement Research." *Mobilization* 5 (1): 1–16.

Zald, Meyer N., and Bert Useem. 1987. "Movement and Countermovement Interaction: Mobilization, Tactics and State Involvement." In *Social Movements in an Organizational Society: Collected Essays*, edited by Meyer N. Zald and John D. McCarthy. New Brunswick, NJ: Transaction Books.

Zielinski, Alex. 2019. "Undercover in Patriot Prayer: Insights From a Vancouver Democrat Who's Been Working Against the Far-Right Group from the Inside." *Portland Mercury*. https://www.portlandmercury.com/blogtown/2019/08/26/27039560/undercover-in-pa triot-prayer-insights-from-a-vancouver-democrat-whos-been-working-against-the-far-rig ht-group-from-the-inside.

4

"SOMETIMES ANTI-SOCIAL, ALWAYS ANTIFASCIST"

Antifa culture

Antifascist symbolism is intentionally iconic. Contemporary American antifa activists intentionally appropriate the symbolism of the German social democratic activists who originally opposed Nazis in the 1930s – the three arrows (Drei Pfeile) of the Iron Front and the overlapping flags of the original Antifascist Action – to symbolize militant antifascism. These symbols serve as the tip of an iceberg of antifascist culture and subculture that covertly and overtly mark the world as opposing fascism. Militant antifascism is as much a cultural movement as it is a political one.

Since the 1960s, social movements have increasingly engaged in cultural activity and construction as a core element of their activism (Jasper 1997; McAdam 1994; Roy 2010). These new social movements were often directly linked to newly formed subcultures that reflect similar resistant orientations (Kriesi et al. 1995; McKay 2004; Moore and Roberts 2009; St. John 2004; Weiß 2015). In true countermovement fashion, fascist encroachment into subcultures is met with significant antifascist resistance in the form of distinct music, artwork, and style. Such efforts signify for other participants that the most authentic expression of the subculture is antifascist.

Social movement participation also results in the construction of unique movement culture (Hart 1996; Jasper 1997; Kriesi et al. 1995; McAdam 1994; Reed 2005; Roy 2010). While contemporary American militant antifascism is rooted in subcultural activism and maintains strong ties to resistant subcultures, it is an independent movement with its own unique cultural practices. Antifa activists contribute to a broad visual culture of images that represent the movement and convey movement themes. Antifascist art celebrates militant opposition to fascism by appropriating popular cultural imagery to encourage active, even violent, resistance. This work serves to denigrate opponents as well as encourage mobilization against fascists. Movement culture also involves a number of social events and relationships. Social events allow antifa activists to celebrate the movement, fundraise, and build solidarity with one another and the broader community. Culture, therefore, is fundamental to movement success.

Antifascist culture is geared toward the public sphere as much as subterranean subcultures and activist scenes. Militant antifascist visual imagery is often distributed to the general public in the form of flyers, posters, and stickers placed in conspicuous public locations. Graffiti artists affiliated with the movement produce pieces that mark territory, honor prisoners and martyrs, or cover fascist graffiti. Finally, antifa social events are often open to the public intentionally in order to demonstrate mass appeal.

Culture and social movements

Culture is an especially varied concept in the social sciences ranging from the material objects to the non-material norms and values of a society. The concept is similarly applied to the study of social movements (Hart 1996; Jasper 2017; Johnston 2009; McAdam 1994; R. H. Williams 2007). One of the foremost avenues for the study of culture has been the extensive work on the concept of framing, which analyzes the processes of meaning-making and messaging by social movements (Benford and Snow 2000; Gamson 2002). Hank Johnston (2009) classifies the breadth of research into the intersections of social movements and culture into three categories: performances, artifacts, and ideations. Performances consist of the activity of social movements as actions and interactions of social movement participants and the movements more broadly. Artifacts are the material products of social movement activity such as music or texts. Finally, ideation represents the beliefs of social movement members, often reflected in movement ideology. Rhys Williams (2007) widens the context of culture to encompass the "cultural environment" in which social movements operate that set the "boundedness," or limitations of appropriate social movement cultural activity, and "resonance," or the degree of acceptance of the cultural elements of social movement activity.

Social movement culture frequently occurs in distinct spaces. Frequently conceived as "free" spaces, social movement cultures are viewed as locations where participants can experiment with new social forms and facilitate movement mobilization (Polletta 1999). Darcy Leach and Sebastian Haunss (2009) implicitly articulate an intersection between the cultural study of social movements and subculture studies in their conception of social movement scenes.[1] The scene consists of "*a network of people* who share a common identity and a common set of subcultural or countercultural beliefs, values, norms, and convictions as well as *a network of physical spaces* where members of that group are known to congregate" (Leach and Haunss 2009, 259, emphasis in original). The degree of linkage between cultural practice and movement activity distinguishes types of scenes. Social movement scenes represent a tight connection between subculture and movement activity and identity. Countercultural scenes are politicized insofar as they seek to transform the dominant culture, and subcultural scenes may be politicized or simply expressions of lifestyle. Social movement scenes are defined by three distinct characteristics: a unique culture, flexible boundaries, and networks of people as well as spaces. The functions of a scene for social movements include the facilitation of mobilization, the development of identity and lifestyle practices, and the maintenance of movement longevity. The scene is manifested in cultural artifacts, individual practices, events, and distinct spaces ranging from homes to community institutions to neighborhoods. The delineation of scene spaces is marked by distinct symbolic and stylistic elements (Creasap 2012; Leach and Haunss 2009). The scene, therefore, serves as a means of incorporating a variety of beliefs and cultural practices into a cohesive movement.

The culture of militant antifascism discussed in this chapter presents some affinity with the scene concept, but does not align entirely. Antifascism is discussed as an ideological component of the social movement scene as articulated by Leach and Haunss (2009), but it is only one of a number of orientations that are part of a broader left-oriented community. In this framework, antifa activism is, therefore, just a piece of the puzzle of a wider social movement scene. Militant antifascism also defies clear categorization in the framework described above. The antifascism of punks, skinheads, and metal fans would likely be described as part of a subcultural scene, yet the more politicized (and explicitly antifascist) anarcho-punks and red and anarchist skinheads[2] are part of a countercultural scene, and still there is a wider culture of antifascism that transcends these subcultural forms creating a genuine movement scene. Antifa culture is both scene and subculture, and may best be understood by applying concepts of subcultural resistance and authenticity as much as social movement culture.

Subcultures, resistance and authenticity

The concept of resistance is central to many interpretations of subculture. Albert Cohen's (1955) groundbreaking work *Delinquent Boys* identified the subculture of adolescent deviance as a form of resistance to strain through the creation of an alternative culture with its own status and activity requirements. Other American scholars of subculture conceived of these types of cultural formations as active forms of resistance to normative society that posit alternative forms of social organization (K. A. Roberts 1978; Yinger 1960). Yet, much of the work that constructs subculture as a form of active resistance to economic, political, and social structures is embedded in the new social movements research and theory discussed in earlier chapters (J. P. Williams 2011). The dominant frameworks in subculture theory largely conceive of resistance as either purely symbolic (Hall and Jefferson 1976; Hebdige 1979) or secondary to the expressive and hedonistic aspects of subcultural practice and presentation (Muggleton 2000; Muggleton and Weinzierl 2003). Recent work by J. Patrick Williams (2011) and Ross Haenfler (2014) systematically critiques these "grand theories" of subculture embodied in the CCCS (developed at the Centre for Contemporary Cultural Studies at the University of Birmingham) and post-subcultures perspectives on resistance; and, more importantly, develops frameworks for understanding the ways in which subcultures engage in acts of opposition.

) synthesizes scholarship on subcultures and social movements in a multidimensional model for subcultural resistance that exists passive ↔ active, micro ↔ macro, and overt ↔ covert. In this tural activity exists at various points along these axes in the unique forms that it takes. The first axis of passive ↔ active "draws attention to the intentions that underlie [subcultural] acts of resistance, rather than the consequences of those acts" (J. P. Williams 2011, 94). By focusing on consumption, most subculture theory places resistance on the passive end of the continuum, yet interviews with subculture participants indicate that their stylistic presentation and actions may be designed as acts of resistance even if they are ineffectual or largely symbolic. Additionally, subculturalists may not be engaging in active forms of resistance, but authority figures may interpret those acts as forms of active defiance. The micro ↔ macro axis indicates the direction in which resistance is applied. Micro-level resistance involves interpersonal activity that defies the norms established by immediate peers and authority figures (parents, teachers, bosses, etc.). Meso-level resistance, which exists between micro and macro, occurs at the small group scope of interaction where collective activities by subculturalists, ranging from a group of friends hanging out together to a small musical event in a basement or bar to a large festival that brings together hundreds or thousands of people, serve to construct and reinforce oppositional values among participants. "Mesa-oriented analyses of resistance may call attention to collective identity, how resistance may represent conflicts and contestations among young people's overlapping social networks, or to the policing of subcultural boundaries from outsiders" (J. P. Williams 2011, 101). Finally, macro-level resistance targets large-scale institutions, often through active forms of defiance oriented toward economic, political, or social change. Williams' (2011) final axis of overt ↔ covert indicates the audience for and interpretation of subcultural acts of resistance. Overt resistance is, as the term implies, actions that are specifically designed to be oppositional and recognized as such by both the participants and observers. Conversely, covert acts of resistance are still oppositional, but designed to be undetectable by authorities or outsiders from the subculture. Overt resistance involves subcultural norms of political participation in social movements or the construction of prefigurative practices that model ideological goals in immediate activity. Covert acts of resistance either reflect deep insider meaning that only other subculturalists can understand or occur outside of the view of normative society. Williams (2011) further notes that the resistance may not be so easily placed at either end of the continuum and may occur in both as certain subcultural acts can have both internal subcultural meaning and external impacts on observers and the larger society.

Building on the framework of resistance described above, Ross Haenfler (2014) presents not only distinct examples of subcultural actions that constitute active, mesa and micro-level, as well as overt forms of resistance, but also the ways in which subcultures perform a series of crucial social movement functions. Subcultures often engage in a number of concerted activities that blend style and identity with pro-social engagement in the form of charitable or non-profit work

from raising money for charitable causes to donating their time t(
nities in need. At the micro-level of resistance, many subcultu
impetus for individuals to engage in lifestyle movements, "
collectivities in which participants advocate lifestyle change as a pri
social change, politicizing daily life while pursuing morally coherent 'authentic'
identities" (Haenfler, Johnson, and Jones 2012, 14). Subculturalists also engage in
resistance by constructing prefigurative practices where movement participants
attempt to construct their ideal world that reflects an ideological and/or moral
vision within the infrastructure of the subculture. Finally, subcultures provide a
series of functions for social movements. Related to prefigurative practices, many
subcultures provide "free spaces relatively removed from (and safe from the
surveillance of) dominant groups in which activists can build collective identity and
even develop tactics" (Haenfler 2014, 54). Similarly, subcultures serve as "sub-
merged networks" which combine prefigurative practices and free spaces in a series
of structures and interactions where new models for a future society can be created.
Lastly, subcultures may operate as "abeyance structures" where ideologies and
movement practices can be maintained during periods when activity and general
support declines ensuring that the movement continues despite setbacks. This presents a practical understanding of the intersections between social movement
activity and subculture.

The question of authenticity has been central to subcultural theory at least since
the work of the CCCS in the 1970s (Hall and Jefferson 1976; Hebdige 1979). This
work framed the symbolic resistance of subcultural practice as easily commodified
and stripped of its authenticity by mass marketing in a capitalist system. Subcultures
often aren't inherently ideological, but represent a kind of magical transformation
of mundane life in a capitalist society into a resistant pose against the hegemonic
expectations of young people. In this framework, the only authentic representation
of a subculture exists in its original incarnation, and all subsequent iterations lose
their resistant quality as a result of capitalist reproduction. While scholars of the
CCCS questioned the authenticity and resistant quality of subcultures beyond their
inception, they conceived of them as relatively static forms with distinct styles and
interactive dynamics. In response to the static conception of subculture of the
CCCS, a postmodern perspective on subculture, the post-subculture paradigm,
developed by asserting that identity and authenticity are fluid concepts (Bennett
1999; Muggleton 2000; Muggleton and Weinzierl 2003). Rather than presenting
subcultures as distinct forms with their own style or ideology, this perspective
instead conceives of a diverse field of "neo-tribes" or local and/or temporary
"scenes." In the post-subculture framework, authenticity is constructed as an ideal
type by subcultural participants rather than as an achievable outcome of participation (Muggleton 2000). Individuals involved in subculture often accumulate "subcultural capital" in relation to others through the acquisition of knowledge,
artifacts, and stylistic representations (Thornton 2013). This perspective, therefore,
views authenticity as a consistently shifting set of standards that vary from scene to
scene and era to era.

Yet, analyses of certain subcultures, particularly punk and skinhead where conflicts between fascists and antifascists have occurred, presents a model of subcultural authenticity that challenges both the CCCS and post-subculture frameworks. Katherine Fox's (1987) groundbreaking work on punk subculture revealed not only a status hierarchy, but also a set of standards and expectations for authentic expression of subcultural values. Unlike the dance-oriented subcultures that serve as the basis for the post-subculture perspective, punk and skinhead put great value on authentic performance of identity. This is the product of the relationship of these subcultures with mass media and marketing. Each subculture has experienced diffusion through the spread of its style and identity beyond its original adherents and defusion through the moderation of subcultural values as it gains mass appeal. In response to these processes, many subcultures assert an authentic, often underground, expression that serves to resist processes of commodification (Daschuk 2011; Force 2011; Spracklen and Spracklen 2014; J. P. Williams 2006). Punk, especially, developed in a dialectical relationship to mainstream commodification and representation by constructing an underground network of bands, music distribution systems, and promoters outside of corporate and normative structures (Clark 2003; Daschuk 2011; Force 2011). The process of maintaining authenticity serves as a means of defining and retaining subcultural boundaries (Force 2011; J. P. Williams 2006; J. P. Williams and Copes 2011). Antifascism is often a core component of authentic subcultural identity for punks and skinheads who view fascist ideology and elements as interlopers in what are defined as politicized, prefigurative, or simply working-class spaces (Goodyer 2003; Marshall 1994; M. J. Roberts and Moore 2009; Travis and Hardy 2012; Wood 1999). The contest over subcultural authenticity drives a great deal of antifascist militancy ranging from cultural signifiers and conflicts over space to the boundaries of subcultural participation and safety.

Subculture as antifa

Antifascists have a long-standing symbiotic relationship with subcultures, particularly punk and skinhead.[2] Contemporary antifascism arose in large part as a response to white supremacist organizing efforts within these subcultures. In the UK, Rock Against Racism organized major and minor musical events and published a fanzine specifically geared toward the blending of youth culture and antifascist attitudes (Bray 2017; Goodyer 2003; Moore and Roberts 2009; Renton 2001; M. J. Roberts and Moore 2009). The more militant Anti-Fascist Action found support among punks and skinheads who were often on the front line in conflicts with fascists. This relationship between antifascist groups and subculture was even stronger in the United States where Skinheads Against Racial Prejudice (SHARP) and Anti-Racist Action were formed specifically as subcultural responses to the rise of racist skinheads (Bray 2017; Sarabia and Shriver 2004; Wood 1999). This legacy of subcultural participation in antifascist activity continues to this day.

Subcultures are especially appealing for both fascist and antifascist activists because they are frequently developed as sites of resistance, even if it is largely symbolic, against normative society and existing structures of power. Scholars have identified subcultures as alternatively inherently resistant or simply sites for individual expressions of resistance (Haenfler 2014; J P. Williams 2011). Punk in particular presented a novel approach to subcultural resistance with its combination of bricolage and outward-facing expressions of shock and outrage (Hebdige 1979). This subculture developed an even more distinctive resistant position as it gained public attention by producing a vibrant underground that was increasingly politicized (Clark 2003; Daschuk 2011; Force 2011). Fundamental to the process of maintaining underground authenticity was a focus on maintaining control over the production of culture (music, magazines, art, etc.) within the subculture through a "do-it-yourself" (DIY) process of creation and distribution (Jeppesen 2018). This dynamic proved to be extremely appealing for fascists because of the freedom that it offers subcultural participants to produce and distribute materials.

Punk subculture also provided fascist recruiters with a ready-made group of alienated youth to appeal to in their recruitment processes. The anger of punk music and lyrics combined with the aggression of punk shows gave fascists a space to enact violence without potential repercussions (Blazak 2001; Simi and Futrell 2010). The DIY process of creating and distributing punk culture enabled fascists to spread their message without relying on mainstream music businesses that would be averse to association with fascism. Through records and fanzines distributed on existing and newly created underground networks, subcultural fascists around the globe distributed their ideology and built their membership (Corte and Edwards 2008; Futrell, Simi, and Gottschalk 2006). Fascist musical and artistic endeavors have the added benefit of diverting criticism under the guise of free expression. By developing a fascist subculture, the movement creates a space for individual adherence and decentralized organization (Berlet and Vysotsky 2006; Haenfler, Johnson, and Jones 2012; Simi and Futrell 2010). The shift toward subculture both sustained fascist movements in abeyance and allowed them to thrive and spread (Berlet and Vysotsky 2006; Simi and Futrell 2010).

The fascist participation and infiltration in punk subculture spurred large scale resistance. For example, Rock Against Racism in the UK shifted its focus away from expressions of fascist sympathy by mainstream musicians toward building a popular opposition to fascist participation in punk and skinhead subculture (Bray 2017; Goodyer 2003; Moore and Roberts 2009; Renton 2001; M. J. Roberts and Moore 2009). However, most of the opposition to fascist participation in subculture occurred through the informal, underground efforts of punks and skinheads who provided a distinct antifascist tendency within the subculture that more closely aligned with its core left-wing ideology. From its earliest incarnations punk subculture contained an aggressive left-wing and anarchist ideological orientation (Ferrell 2001; O'Hara 1999) that positions fascist activity within it as fundamentally inauthentic. The subcultural response to fascist activity within the punk scene took the form of everyday resistance that will be discussed in detail in Chapter 6 and cultural expression in the form of music and style.

Punk antifascism manifests itself most viscerally in the myriad of songs dedicated to antifascist commitment. Some, like the Dead Kennedy's "Nazi Punks Fuck Off," have become so iconic that they transcend the underground and have mainstream recognition; while others such as Aus Rotten's "Fuck Nazi Sympathy" are iconic within the subculture. These anthems are designed to not only demonstrate a band's commitment to antifascism, but also serve as rallying cries to mobilize antifascists. Certain sub-genres of punk, such as left-wing Oi! or anarcho-punk, specialize in taking strong antifascist stances with bands at times being associated or actively involved with antifascist activism. Yet, the songs are more than rallying cries; they frequently operate as signals or opportunities to oppose a fascist presence at a show or in a local punk scene. Bands with distinctly antifascist songs will play them if they learn that fascists are in the audience or as victory hymns after fascists have been ejected from a punk show. The music, therefore, serves as a sonic antifascist weapon of its own. It challenges fascist encroachment into the subculture, rallies antifascist activism, and celebrates antifascist success.

Punk style is laden with intentional and unintentional ideological signifiers (S. Cohen 1980; Hebdige 1979). Punk clothing in particular is used to convey ideological messages through the display of slogans and symbols; antifascism being chief among them. A standard of punk aesthetic consists of the display of band names and artwork on clothing whether it is a t-shirt, a patch on existing clothing, or design painted onto clothing. Because bands often convey distinct ideological associations, the mere presence of their name or logo on one's person carries symbolic meaning. Antifascist bands whose names do not directly convey their ideological orientation like Oi Polloi and the Oppressed represent much deeper meanings among punks and skinheads who can read the covert symbolism as overt expressions of antifascist resistance (J. P. Williams 2011). It's also common for punk bands to use antifascist symbolism in their artwork to directly convey their position. The cover of Aus Rotten's aforementioned record featured an image of a patch on a punk's jacket showing a common militant antifascist symbol of a fist punching a swastika. This cover, with its message opposing fascist appeasement has been reproduced itself on patches, t-shirts, and buttons worn by punks. It is also relatively common for punks and skinheads to demonstrate their antifascism by displaying antifascist imagery as its own ideological statement. The Iron Front symbol, Antifascist Action flags, all manner of swastikas and other fascist icons being crossed out or destroyed, and a variety of other antifascist symbols can be found adorning the clothing of subcultural antifascists. The ultimate purpose of these displays is both internal to the subculture and external to outside observers (J. P. Williams 2011) in its representation of opposition to fascism.

The more covert symbols serve as internal subcultural markers designed to be read by fellow subculturalists in order to distinguish antifascism and assert authenticity. Overt symbols and slogans are clear signifiers for the general public that the individual is an antifascist and should not be confused with aesthetically similar, though ideologically different, fascists. This is of particular concern for skinheads who after several decades of media moral panic must often publicly display their anti-racism and antifascism as an assertion not only of their sub-cultural authenticity, but also of their relationship to society at large (Sarabia and Shriver 2004; Wood 1999).

Such covert expressions of style extend to entire subcultural "presentations of self" (Goffman 1959). The fascist variations of skinhead style in the United States, particularly in the era before global supply chains and internet marketing, were frequently remarkably poor simulations of an authentic appearance. This style often represented a copy of "traditional" skinhead aesthetic combined with even more militarized elements beyond the recognizable bomber jacket such as military combat boots, as opposed to Doc Martens work boots, and camouflage military trousers. In juxtaposition, the aesthetic of the traditional skinhead represents not only an authentic expression of the subculture, but also a distinctly symbolic anti-fascism. Traditional skinheads, who identify their subcultural origins in Jamaican ska music and rude boy subculture, often display such affiliations in overt and covert symbolism. Stylistic references to first wave ska, such as the Trojan record label, and the "two-tone" movement of ska's second wave are designed not just to signal subcultural authenticity, but at minimum a nominal commitment to anti-racism, if not outright antifascism. The very act of authentic stylistic presentation may, therefore, be enough to distinguish a fascist from an antifascist.

Just as clothing serves as a marker of ideological subcultural orientation, so too does the body. Tattoos are a common ritual and signifier of fascist orientation (Blazak 2001; Futrell and Simi 2004; Simi and Futrell 2010), and reading of the tattooed body is a common practice among antifascists in order to gauge the ideological position of an individual. Subcultural markers can be obscure; with a number of punk, Oi!, and metal musical acts being consumed by both fascist and antifascist audiences. Secondary markers are necessary in such situations to dis-tinguish the ideological orientation of an individual. Antifascists also use such markers to distinguish themselves from subculturalists who may present with a similar style, but not a similar ideological position. Just as with clothing, tattoos of band logos and antifascist imagery are commonplace. Many members of New City Antifa had tattoos of antifascist symbols. At my first national gathering of militant antifascists during the formal research period, I observed how these tat-toos served as a means of bonding among antifa activists. An anarchist skinhead struck up a conversation with Elias, a member of New City Antifa, over their similar Iron Front tattoos and their placement on their arms. This relatively common ritual among antifascists involves discussion of choice of symbols and placement on the body similar to conversations between other tattooed indivi-duals (Sanders and Vail 2008). What made this conversation, and others that I observed, uniquely antifascist is the tattoos in question. In all such conversations, antifascists are able to read each other's bodies in order to understand everything from time spent in the movement (age of tattoos) to regional affiliation (formal antifa group symbolism) to subcultural distinctions (punk vs skinhead vs general antifascist symbols). These markings make the body both a site and symbol of antifascist resistance (Ferrell 1997a; Langman 2008).

Engaging in subculture is a key component of antifascist cultural work. Sub-cultures are key sites of fascist activity, and antifascist resistance within those spaces takes on distinct cultural forms. Antifascist themes permeate lyrics and artwork produced by bands that choose to take a stand against fascism within their subculture. These bands often intentionally become symbols of antifascism and a means of distinguishing the ideological orientation of subculturalists. Subcultural style further reflects these ideological distinctions as symbolic repre-sentation in clothing and tattoos further reveals the antifascist cultural orientation of individuals within the subculture. Depending on how they are deployed, the subcultural practices described above demonstrate the dynamics of resistance outlined by Williams (2011) through active and passive deployment of covert and overt symbolism in micro-, meso-, and macro-level interactions. Subcultures also serve as points of entry for individuals into the antifascist movement and spaces of prefigurative antifascist practice (Haenfler 2014). By aligning authentic sub-cultural identity with antifascism, such cultural practices construct subcultures as spaces of ideological contention.

Antifa as subculture

While contemporary antifa culture has its origins in subcultural trends of the 1970s and 1980s, it has developed an autonomous culture of its own synthesizing styles from numerous subcultures, popular culture, and radical political culture. Like many other contemporary social movements, militant antifascism involves the construction and maintenance of a distinct culture that is both internally and externally oriented (Jasper 1997; Kriesi et al. 1995; McAdam 1994). Antifa groups and individual activists produce a great deal of unique graphic design that plays on subcultural and popular cultural themes in order to disparage fascists and motivate action. Militant antifascists also host a number of social events designed to raise funds, promote group ideology and membership, and encourage group cohesion.

Antifa visual style

In the highly mediated world of the early 21st century, antifa activism is as branded as any major corporation. The distinctive symbols of militant antifascism – three arrows and overlapping flags – are frequently featured in antifascist artwork, leaflets, stickers, clothing, and social media profile photos. Antifa groups modify these symbols in unique ways to fit their target audience, their local context, or their ideological orientation. The symbol designed for Northeast Antifascists in the early 2000s, which combined the flags and arrows with a laurel wreath and gear, served to represent both a working-class orientation and subcultural leanings. This parti-cular design has outlived its original context, having been reproduced on numerous antifascist items and in innumerable contexts. Portland's Rose City Antifa take a more localized approach to their logo by featuring roses with the usual antifascist imagery; whereas Philly Antifa combine a set of eyes with the three arrows to indicate that they are ever watchful of fascist activity and threats. The consistent visual style of antifa symbols creates a common point of reference that activists, fascists, and the general public can recognize and understand.

Antifa imagery is more than just a series of clever logos. The majority of militant antifascist imagery takes the form of poster, flyer, and meme images that serve to convey information and motivate people to action. In the tradition of "culture jamming" practiced by many radical and anarchist activists (Ferrell 2001; Morrison and Isaac 2012; Sandlin and Callahan 2009), antifascists regularly transform popular cultural images into symbols of resistance. A favorite among militant antifascists is the Adidas logo because it combines references to hip hop and street style with covert antifa symbolism. The three stripes corporate logo becomes a subtle reference to the three arrows of militant antifascism. The three-syllable corporate name also lends itself to détournement; replaced by antifa on t-shirts, stickers, patches, and buttons. Images from film and television are also popular subjects for antifascist representations. Films with clear antifascist themes such as *Inglourious Basterds* and *Raiders of the Lost Ark* are especially popular because of their overt content; their themes of literally fighting Nazis have been reproduced in a number of memes shared online and on posters encouraging antifascist mobilizations. Buffy the Vampire Slayer represents another, more covert, symbol because of her feminist iconography as an empowered woman who must use force against pure evil. Images from anime are similarly subject to détournement both for their visual style and resistance to increasing fascist appropriation. Recently, there has been a revival of Second World War era comic book images of heroes like Captain America and Wonder Woman fighting Nazis which have found great popularity among antifascists. There is also the ironic appropriation of "cutesy" imagery such as Care Bears and cartoon unicorns as a reversal of fascist taunting, a challenge to accusations of machismo, and queer signaling. The use of popular culture images provides a common cultural point of reference for antifascists and a broader audience that operates outside of the often-covert meanings of movement subculture.

Militant antifascists also create images that are wholly original. Contemporary antifa artwork includes classical images such as a variety of figures and items smashing fascist symbols or fighting fascists, as well as works that capitalize on historical inspiration and graphic design trends. In the 1990s, Anti-Racist Action produced and reproduced a series of hand drawn images of individuals destroying fascist symbols. Iconic images such as an anti-racist skinhead destroying a swastika with a baseball bat and a young person kicking a fascist to the ground are replicated to this day. The ubiquitous slogan "good night, white pride" encircled around an image of antifascist violence is reproduced in variations so numerous that it is impossible to catalogue them all. Antifascist cartoons follow a common theme of either denigrating prominent fascists like Richard Spencer or Matthew Heimbach or simply enacting violence upon them. Original antifa art also takes inspiration from historical antifascism of the interwar period and Second World War Propaganda. Contemporary artists produce work that references Soviet futurism as well as propaganda posters from the Spanish Civil War and the American, British, and

Soviet war effort. Such artwork, whether on posters for protests or standalone art encourages militant resistance by harkening to historical use of force in opposition to fascism. Finally, contemporary antifa artists capitalize on graphic design trends that incorporate bold color and font combinations to represent militant slogans. These works represent both the familiar and cutting edge in terms of their style as well as references that are movement specific and universal.

Proof of death and proof of life

One of the more shocking aspects of militant antifascist culture for observers outside of the movement is the consumption and trade of violent images. Pictures of fascists being beaten or bloodied in addition to memes that extol the virtue of antifascist violence or mock injured fascists are a common element of antifa culture. In some ways, this is an extension of the broader anarchist practice of exchanging images of "riot porn," a self-deprecating term coined for the vicarious consumption of protest violence. Yet, antifascist consumption takes on a different tone in a movement that has direct contact with its opposition. These images serve as an inspiration and motivation for militant action, but they may best be understood through the lens of "proof of death" and "proof of life" (Linnemann 2017) in the conflict between fascists and antifascists.

These violent antifascist images could be understood as similar to the police "trophy shot" and its placement as a proof of death similar to the images that hunters collect with their prey as a form of narcissistic display of violence and control. Police regularly collect and display trophy shots as a means of exerting their position of power over criminalized populations and society as a whole (Linnemann 2017). The images serve as a display of their power to wield their monopoly on the use of force. In Chapter 6, I argue that antifascist activists serve as a force of radical policing by engaging in many of the practices claimed by law enforcement. Like policing practice, antifascism takes on the characteristics of hunting, with its pursuit of fascists and its intelligence operations and patrols of communities and spaces where fascists are known to congregate. The title of a 2008 documentary of Parisian antifascist activities in the 1980s that was popular in the movement, *Antifa: Chasseurs de Skins*, translates as Skinhead Hunters. It is, therefore, appropriate to consider the litany of violent imagery transmitted by antifa as a kind of set of trophy shots.

On their own, devoid of context, the images appear as grim depictions of human suffering. Young men with blood streaming from head wounds, individuals set upon by groups of armed protesters, an endless parade of cartoon violence; to the outside observer these seem like a ghastly collection of misery. Anyone who would consume such things with delight appears to be a sadist reveling in the pain of others, unwilling to acknowledge the humanity of those hurt in such conflicts. For many critics, it is a mirror image of the kind of violence seen in alt-right memes celebrating Pinochet's torture and fascist street violence. If antifa is a form of policing, then is there any difference between these and police trophy shots that assert domination?

The antifa trophy shot and violent meme are less a mirror image than the "upside down" of their counterparts, a world similar to the one we recognize, but different. While the antifa trophy shot glorifies violence, we must ask to what end? In the spirit of "criminological verstehen" (Ferrell 1997b) and the cultural criminological process of "visual ethnography" (Ferrell, Hayward, and Young 2008), we must understand the context to understand the function of the image.

Images of bloody, broken, defeated fascists are, in fact, a proof of death. Like their counterparts for hunters or law enforcement, they demonstrate an accomplishment (Linnemann 2017). Yet, the subject is relatively different in the image of the antifa trophy shot. In this case, the person portrayed in the image has made a conscious decision to affiliate with an ideology and a movement that at its core has an imperative to violence (Berlet 1992; Eco 1995; Paxton 2004). Fascist ideology exalts violence against its enemies in the form of at best forcible repatriation of historically marginalized racial, ethnic, and religious groups and at worst their genocidal elimination; and it reserves no sympathy for those it deems gender or sexual deviants. Fascists glorify violence as not just strategically useful or practical, but as an end in itself; celebrating the violent individual as spiritually and personally better than the non-violent or even hesitant. And so, the image of fascists recoiling in fear and pain carries with it a bitter irony; a proof that they are failures in their spiritual quest. For antifascists, such images demonstrate that fascists, despite their tough talk and frightening demeanor, can and will be defeated; and that force works to destroy the fascist self-image as a violent "Übermensch."

Proof of death is also strategically important for antifascists. The images must be understood in the context of a social movement conflict. If antifa activism serves as a countermovement to fascist mobilizations and activities, its actions must be viewed as part of that struggle. As proof of death, such images serve to fulfill Zald and Useem's (1987) first and second tactical approaches of countermovements: damage or destruction of the other group and preemption or dissuasion of group mobilization. The images of injured and overpowered fascists serve as visual proof that the movement has sustained significant damage and destruction. Such images are used to celebrate antifascist victories and indicate that fascists have been successfully routed in their attempts at public mobilization or organizing. In some cases, such public relations failures led fascists to admit defeat as in the case of "Unite the Right" organizer Christopher Cantwell, who cried on camera in the wake of the deadly fiasco, and Richard Spencer, who admitted that public speaking events became "no fun" because of antifa militancy. As the final months of 2017 demonstrate, images of fascist getting trounced served to preempt and dissuade participation. Would be attendants to fascist events must take into consideration the possibility of violence and potential public humiliation. This increased cost of participation for anyone involved with the fascist movement is made public with a series of images and memes. Knowing that one might face antifascist confrontation serves at least in part to encourage desistance from far-right movement participation (Linden and Klandermans 2006).

Images of antifascist violence are also a peculiar form of trophy shot because they lack the narcissism seen in the work of the hunter or the law enforcement agent (Linnemann 2017). The antifa trophy shot is rarely documented by antifascists and often comes from journalists and other observers of the conflict. In many cases, the aggressor is often missing from the antifascist proof of death having fled the scene of violence or having been separated from the subject of violence by police attempts to restore order. The stark bloody fascist is drastically different from the image of the hunter or police officer smiling with their quarry. When the antifascist is featured, whether in documented photos and videos or artwork and memes, the person is unidentifiable with all black attire and a face masked as part of a "black bloc" strategy to avoid prosecution. As testament, the individual who punched Richard Spencer walks free to this day. Committed militant antifascists will never publicly lay claim to a particular assault even if it is lauded by the movement. An essential component of antifa action is anonymity. Such images are not about the ego of individual activists, they are about the collective power of a movement.

It is in that collective power that we see the greatest difference between antifa trophy shots and their counterparts. As much as they are proof of death, they are also a "proof of life" (Linnemann 2017); a mediated image of the resilience and power of resistance. As stated earlier, fascism presents itself as the superior wielder of violence and force against opposition from racial, gender, and sexual inferiors where even cisgender heterosexual male leftists are constructed as "cucks" and "betas." But, the images of the victorious antifa activist, whether in the act or in the aftermath of the act of antifascist violence, serve to prove the power of opposition. They assert the strength and vigor, the very life, of antifascist resistance by confronting fascist violence head on. The images are consumed by antifascists as much for their inspiration and proof of victory as they are for *Schadenfreude* and proof of fascist defeat. Images of antifascist violence serve to empower would be resisters and committed activists alike; invigorating them for the struggles to come as much as celebrating the triumphs of the past. They also serve as proof of life for the myriad of historically marginalized people targeted by supremacist violence. The bloody fascist or the violent meme serve as a reminder that they are survivors and fighters against the onslaught of fascist violence; that they can fight back, or that there are those who will stand with them to defend them. As such, antifa memes serve to signal defense as much as offense. As proof of the life of antifascists, their cultural production and reproduction is a core component of the movement.

Beyond the image and the gaze: antifa cultural events

As part of an outreach and general cultural strategy, Old City Antifa organized a monthly film event. The group hosted screenings of a variety of movies ranging from the aforementioned *Raiders of the Lost Arc* to the classic documentary on the white supremacist movement, *Blood in the Face*, to the dramatic allegory of the assassination of Alan Berg, *Talk Radio*. The films were screened at a radical book store and open to the public. Some of the films were designed to generate discussion on antifascist issues, others simply to entertain the audience as they reveled in the defeat of fictional fascists. Film events are a common component of antifa culture with formal groups routinely hosting screenings of movies with antifascist themes. The antifa watch list of popular movies that celebrate fascist defeat through violent resistance and documentaries about fascist movements is now supplemented by a series of documentaries focused specifically on militant antifascism. European documentaries like the above-mentioned *Antifa: Chasseurs de Skins* (France), *Sad But True: Ivan. In Memory of Our Friend* (Russia), and *The Antifascists* (Sweden) are staples of militant antifascist film events. Such movies are celebrated because they portray militant antifascism in a positive and sympathetic light, and serve to convey a frame that is counter to mainstream discourse on the movement.

Antifa activists are more than just film buffs, and movement cultural events reflect a variety of social opportunities to demonstrate that there is more to militant antifascism than rowdy protests and punching supremacists. In an overlap with the subcultural manifestations of antifascism, formal antifa groups frequently host musical events in a variety of genres from the predictable punk and ska to hip hop and metal. In addition to music, there are art shows as well as speaker and book events to fill out an antifascist's social calendar. Antifa cultural events provide an opportunity to raise funds for movement activism or medical or legal costs incurred by antifascists domestically or abroad, generate awareness regarding fascist and antifascist activity, and build camaraderie among activists and supporters. In true countermovement fashion, the antifascist social events serve a series of functions similar to those of events for the fascist movement (Futrell and Simi 2004; Simi and Futrell 2010).

Militant antifascist culture also involves a great deal of informal activity. Events and spaces become antifascist simply because activists are present en masse either formally as group members or informally as attendees. New City Antifa members often congregated at a number of local bars on designated evenings or on the spontaneous whim of a handful of people. While these bars may not have been formally antifascist spaces, they developed a reputation among activists and subculturalists as effectively antifa spaces. Members regularly attended DJ nights at other bars and were active supporters of the city's soccer team. Antifascist activity in social settings allows the activists to build relationships with individuals and groups that generate support for militant antifascists. The presence of a critical mass of antifa activists also transforms a space or event into one that is functionally antifascist since the activists remained on alert for a fascist presence even in the most benign of settings.

The distinct culture of militant antifascism shares many of the characteristics of a social movement scene (Creasap 2012; Leach and Haunss 2009). There are distinct movement artifacts, elements of visual style, aspects of prefigurative behaviors, and even spatial dimensions. Yet, the concept of scene, whether developed by post-subculture or social movement theorists, explicitly relies on a fluidity of identity and belief. Social movement scenes in particular reflect a series of concerns under the umbrella of an oppositional orientation (Creasap 2012; Leach and Haunss 2009). Antifascist culture, however, is rooted in a clear and stable concern and ideological orientation – an opposition to fascism rooted in left-wing anti-authoritarianism. In their ideological stability and iconographic consistency, antifa cultural practices constitute an activist subculture (Haenfler, Johnson, and Jones 2012).

The public eye:antifa culture in the public sphere

Not all antifa cultural activity is internally focused. Like most social movements, antifascists engage with the general public who may hold a variety of positions on the movement. Countercultural new social movements, like antifa, generally engage with actors outside of their sphere of influence in a hostile or confrontational manner (Kriesi et al. 1995). Yet, the cultural work of militant antifascists in the public sphere tends much more toward persuasive framing (Benford and Snow 2000) rather than hostile challenges to dominant discourses typical of radical and anarchist movements (Ferrell 2001; Fitzgerald and Rodgers 2000). Antifascist fliers, posters, and stickers engage the public to educate them about fascist activity, elicit assistance in information gathering, or attend protest events. These cultural products and antifa graffiti mark space as antifascist or reclaim it from fascists engaging in similar actions in the public sphere (Creasap 2016; Ferrell 2001; Gerbaudo 2013; Waldner and Dobratz 2013). Regardless of its form, antifascist culture outside of the bounds of subcultural or activist space marks the public sphere as hostile to fascist activism and ideology.

Militant antifascists regularly engage in campaigns to poster or flyer a community. Sky News reporter, Hannah Thomas-Peter (2018) followed members of Rose City Antifa as they engaged in one such activity. The antifascists stapled two distinct items to lamp posts in a Portland neighborhood – a flier informing the community about a fascist resident and a poster that stated "FIGHT RACISM" with an image of raised fists and a crossed-out swastika. These types of activities are typical of formal antifa groups that seek to engage the general public. Antifascist activists regularly place flyers, posters, and stickers in public view distributing their message to communities. In the Portland case, the intent was to educate a community about an active fascist in their midst. Other antifa groups commonly post stickers that ask community members to provide information on fascist activity. These stickers frequently feature antifascist artwork in addition to the solicitations for information; a tactic observed in the activity of both New City and Old City Antifa. In periods preceding a fascist mobilization, militant antifascists will advertise counter-protests with a diversity of artistic media. The antifascist counter-protest of an alt-right mobilization by activist Joey Gibson's Patriot Prayer and the Proud Boys in Portland on August 4, 2018 generated dozens of posters and flyers in the various graphic design styles discussed above. This practice of marking public space exists in a liminal state between legal advertising and defacing of property (Ferrell 2001; Ferrell, Hayward, and Young 2008; Waldner and Dobratz 2013).

Antifascist graffiti, however, exists almost entirely as a criminal cultural activity (Ferrell 1996; Ferrell, Hayward, and Young 2008). Like any other form of graffiti, the type created by militant antifascists spans the gamut of styles and forms. In its simplest form, it can be three arrows or a crossed-out swastika drawn in permanent marker as well as antifa written as a tag. Larger works featuring the term antifa or antifascist in the throw up or blockbuster style of urban street art may be put up when time is not of the essence. Antifa stencil art can range from simple images to complex layer work typical of street artists. Antifascist graffiti artists have also been known to do murals in homage to resistance or as memorials to prisoners or victims of fascist violence.

The street art campaigns, whether posters or graffiti, ultimately serve to designate space as antifascist (Creasap 2016; Gerbaudo 2013; Waldner and Dobratz 2013). An antifascist tag or sticker in a dive bar signifies the space as welcoming to activists and hostile to fascists. Antifa posters or stickers on lamp posts or walls in a community show that at minimum there is an active militant antifascist group operating in the area. Antifa graffiti can assert a similar claim to public space. An antifascist cultural presence in a community effectively asserts a public commitment to multiculturalism and progressive values.

Public displays of antifascist cultural work are not simply assertions of activism and marking of space; they are also the product of a clear contest over space. Fascist activism routinely involves public campaigns similar to those of antifascists described above. It is not uncommon for fascist groups to put up flyers or stickers either in recruitment efforts or as a means of intimidating a community. Fascist graffiti similarly marks a space as having a supremacist presence. The antifascist response to these types of campaigns is to remove or cover the offending fascist material.[3] Antifascist flyers, posters, stickers, and even graffiti are commonly used to challenge fascist control of public space (Waldner and Dobratz 2013). In some cases, antifa activists produce material that indicates that fascist material was present as a means of raising public consciousness of supremacist activity.[4] In most cases, it is the cultural remnant staking out the space as antifascist.

Antifa culture, social movements, and space

Culture is an essential aspect of contemporary social movements. Militant antifascism, like many other radical movements, involves participation in culture as well as the construction of its own unique movement culture. As a counterculturally oriented social movement, antifa activism maintains strong historical and functional ties to punk and skinhead subculture. Yet, the culture of militant antifascism branches out beyond these subcultures to build ties with sympathetic elements across a variety of subcultural forms. Additionally, militant antifascists create a culture that is original to the movement through the appropriation and détournement of popular culture. Antifascist culture extends beyond these visual forms that are consumed by activists as a means of bolstering their commitment to militancy, and manifests itself in a variety of social events and gatherings. Rather than being completely insular, antifa culture extends to the public sphere in order to mobilize the public to oppose fascism and mark space as hostile to fascist activity.

Militant antifascist overlap with subculture is more than simply the result of histor-ical precedent (Bray 2017; Goodyer 2003; Moore and Roberts 2009; M. J. Roberts and Moore 2009). Contemporary subcultures arose in the post-Second World War era as sites of resistance to capitalism and mainstream social uniformity (Haenfler 2014; Hall and Jefferson 1976; Muggleton 2000; J. P. Williams 2011). While much of the resistant quality of subcultures has been symbolic, certain subcultural forms have been active, even core participants, in social movement organization and mobilization (Ferrell 2001; Kriesi et al. 1995; Magaña 2016; McKay 2004; St. John 2004; D. M. Williams 2018). Contemporary fascist movements have specifically engaged in recruitment and movement building through subcultural participation (Berlet and Vysotsky 2006; Blazak 2001; Simi and Futrell 2010), which resulted in vigorous anti-fascist opposition. Punk and skinhead subcultures responded to these ideological incursions by developing a strong antifascist culture that is manifested in music and style with song lyrics, band names, stage performances, artwork, fashion, and even tattoos dedicated to bold, militant antifascism. In this respect, these subcultures, among others, serve as distinct antifascist countercultures.

While contemporary militant antifascist culture owes a great deal to its sub-cultural roots and foundation, it has taken on a life of its own. Like so many social movements, militant antifascism constructs its own original culture that is unique to the movement (Danaher 2010; Fitzgerald and Rodgers 2000; Jasper 1997; Leach and Haunss 2009; Morrison and Isaac 2012; Reed 2005). Antifa culture is driven by a distinct visual culture of symbols designed to clearly mark groups, content, and space as antifascist. Militant antifascist culture greatly relies on détournement of popular cultural imagery, in the spirit of "culture jamming" (Ferrell 2001; Sandlin and Callahan 2009) to encourage radical opposition to fascism. Antifascist artwork routinely reconfigures popular cultural figures and themes into bold messages of militant confrontation, but also features a number of original images relying on the graphic design trends of the moment. A great deal of militant antifascist culture involves the consumption of graphic violence as a form of celebrating the "proof of death" of fascist opponents and the "proof of life" of the antifa movement (Lin-nemann 2017). However, antifascist culture is not simply limited to visual repre-sentations. Antifa culture contains a series of private and public interactive elements. Militant antifascists routinely organize cultural and social events that allow the movement to interact with supporters and the broader society. Through these practices, militant antifascism constitutes a unique activist subculture.

Social movement culture operates in a truly unique manner in the service of countermovements. As we have seen, cultural moves and innovations operate in relation to moves by opposing movements (Meyer and Staggenborg 1996). Antifa activism, from subcultural participation to public postering campaigns, routinely matches moves by fascist activists in the spirit of the first principle of US antifa networks: "We go where they go." Whether subcultural or movement specific in form, antifa culture signifies a distinct opposition to fascist mobilization. Public campaigns serve to "preempt or dissuade the other group from mobilizing" (Zald and Useem 1987, 260) by creating a climate, whether cultural or physical, that is overtly hostile to fascism. The culture of militant antifascism also serves to mobilize opposition to fascist activity. For sympathetic individuals and activists, it serves to reinforce existing inclinations. For uncommitted members of the general public, antifascist culture serves as a means of framing the movement and its actions as legitimate in its opposition to fascism.

Lastly, antifascist culture serves to ideologically mark public and social space. The next chapter will discuss fascist and antifascist conflicts over space in detail, however, culture is a major indicator of the group that dominates a particular space. Within subcultural spaces, the predominance of antifascist culture serves to dissuade fascists from organizing or taking action because it marginalizes them in relation to dominant tendencies in the subculture consistent with countermovement goals (Zald and Useem 1987). In public spaces, antifascist culture often comes as a response to fascist presence. Antifa activists frequently find themselves removing and covering fascist symbolism in the public sphere in a move that asserts that the space, and wider community, are not welcoming to fascist ideology and organizing. By building a public culture of antifascism, activists effectively serve to marginalize fascist movements and ensure continuing opposition.

Notes

1   In subculture studies, the concept of scene is associated with the post-subcultures perspective, which views musical and stylistic expressions as fragmented, fluid, and individualistic (Bennett 1999, 2011; Muggleton 2000; Muggleton and Weinzierl 2003). The concept of scene is juxtaposed against the more stable notion of subculture. Scenes incorporate a diversity of people and perspectives around common experiences. A scene, therefore, is a cross-class experience that is shared by individuals based on music or style that is consistently evolving and may be transient in nature (Bennett 2011; Bennett and Peterson 2004; Hodkinson and Deicke 2009; Straw 1991). The concept of scene incorporates both the practices of the individuals involved and the spatial component of the location in which those practices occur (Bennett and Peterson 2004; Straw 1991).

2   The ideological positions of certain subcultures are highly contested. Punk and skinhead represent such contestations in part because of the role of fascists within them. These subcultures are frequently fractionalized along ideological lines with distinct scenes developing in relation to the participant's ideological orientation. Within punk, anarchist, or anarcho-, punks represent the most radical, left-orientated faction by advocating for gender, racial, and sexual orientation equality, environmental concerns, animal rights, and non-capitalist economic systems (Cross 2010; O'Hara 1999; Worley 2017). This position is fundamentally oppositional to the fascist presence in punk subculture, and the ideological pole that it represents. A similar dynamic is evident among skinheads whose subculture has been associated with fascism in the public imagination. For many skinheads, the fascist orientation constitutes a hijacking of a subculture whose origins lie in a multiracial blend of Jamaican rude boy and British mod subcultures (Marshall 1994; Travis and Hardy 2012). These "traditional" skinheads base their identity in part on a (passive) nonracism or (active) anti-racism. In juxtaposition, fascist skinheads are considered an inauthentic expression of the subculture because of the virulent racism at the core of their belief system. Among the actively anti-racist factions of skinheads are far-left participants who actively identify as socialist, communist, or anarchist. While there may be ideological distinctions among them, these red and anarchist skinheads construct a subcultural identity as the most directly oppositional to fascist participation in the subculture.

3 The practice of covering up fascist graffiti or propaganda with antifascist imagery provides an opportunity for informal forms of everyday antifa activism. It is not uncommon for individuals who may not otherwise write graffiti to take it upon themselves to overwrite or remove fascist imagery or propaganda.
4 Antifascists have been so successful in their response to fascist flyers, graffiti, posters, and stickers in certain American cities that they were removing and replacing the material before the community even had a sense of the fascist presence. Antifascist propaganda, therefore, began to appear seemingly out of context for these communities. In response, antifa activists produce material that states in some variation that "fascist propaganda was here" in order to underscore the necessity for antifascist response and activism.

Works cited

Benford, Robert D., and David A. Snow. 2000. "Framing Processes and Social Movements: An Overview and Assessment." *Annual Review of Sociology* 26 (1): 611–639.

Bennett, Andy. 1999. "Subcultures or Neo-Tribes? Rethinking the Relationship between Youth, Style and Musical Taste." *Sociology* 33 (3): 599–617. doi:10.1177/S0038038599000371.

Bennett, Andy. 2011. "The Post-Subcultural Turn: Some Reflections 10 Years On." *Journal of Youth Studies* 14 (5): 493–506. doi:10.1080/13676261.2011.559216.

Bennett, Andy, and Richard A. Peterson. 2004. *Music Scenes: Local, Translocal and Virtual.* Nashville, TN: Vanderbilt University Press.

Berlet, Chip. 1992. "Fascism!" *Political Research Associates.* https://www.politicalresearch.org/1992/09/28/fascism.

Berlet, Chip, and Stanislav Vysotsky. 2006. "Overview of US White Supremacist Groups." *Journal of Political and Military Sociology* 34 (1): 11.

Blazak, Randy. 2001. "White Boys to Terrorist Men: Target Recruitment of Nazi Skinheads." *American Behavioral Scientist* 44 (6): 982–1000.

Bray, Mark. 2017. *Antifa: The Antifascist Handbook.* Brooklyn, NY: Melville House Publishing.

Clark, Dylan. 2003. "The Death and Life of Punk, the Last Subculture." In *The Post Subcultures Reader*, edited by David Muggleton and Rupert Weinzierl, 233–238. New York, NY: Berg.

Cohen, Albert K. 1955. *Delinquent Boys: The Culture of the Gang.* Glencoe, IL: The Free Press.

Cohen, Stanley. 1980. *Folk Devils and Moral Panics: The Creation of the Mods and Rockers.* New York, NY: St. Martin's Press.

Corte, Ugo, and Bob Edwards. 2008. "White Power Music and the Mobilization of Racist Social Movements." *Music and Arts in Action* 1 (1): 4–20.

Creasap, Kimberly. 2012. "Social Movement Scenes: Place-Based Politics and Everyday Resistance." *Sociology Compass* 6 (2): 182–191. doi:10.1111/j.1751-9020.2011.00441.x.

Creasap, Kimberly. 2016. "Finding the Movement: The Geographies of Social Movement Scenes." *The International Journal of Sociology and Social Policy* 36 (11/12): 792–807.

Danaher, William F. 2010. "Music and Social Movements." *Sociology Compass* 4 (9): 811–823. doi:10.1111/j.1751-9020.2010.00310.x.

Daschuk, Mitch Douglas. 2011. "The Significance of Artistic Criticism in the Production of Punk Subcultural Authenticity: The Case Study of Against Me!" *Journal of Youth Studies* 14 (5): 605–626. doi:10.1080/13676261.2011.559215.

Eco, Umberto. 1995. "Ur-Fascism." *The New York Review of Books*, June 22. https://www.nybooks.com/articles/1995/06/22/ur-fascism/.

Ferrell, Jeff. 1996. *Crimes of Style: Urban Graffiti and the Politics of Criminality*. Boston, MA: Northeastern University Press.

Ferrell, Jeff. 1997a. "Youth, Crime, and Cultural Space." *Social Justice* 24 (4): 21–38.

Ferrell, Jeff. 1997b. "Criminological *Verstehen*: Inside the Immediacy of Crime." *Justice Quarterly* 14 (1): 3–23. doi:10.1080/07418829700093201.

Ferrell, Jeff. 2001. *Tearing Down the Streets: Adventures in Urban Anarchy*. New York, NY: Palgrave.

Ferrell, Jeff, Keith J. Hayward, and Jock Young. 2008. *Cultural Criminology: An Invitation*. Thousand Oaks, CA: Sage Publications.

Fitzgerald, Kathleen J., and Diane M. Rodgers. 2000. "Radical Social Movement Organizations: A Theoretical Model." *Sociological Quarterly* 41 (4): 573–592.

Force, William Ryan. 2011. "Consumption Styles and the Fluid Complexity of Punk Authenticity." *Symbolic Interaction* 32 (4): 289–309. doi:10.1525/si.2009.32.4.289.

Fox, Kathryn J. 1987. "Real Punks and Pretenders: The Social Organization of a Counterculture." *Journal of Contemporary Ethnography* 16 (3): 344–370. doi:10.1177/0891241687163006.

Futrell, Robert, and Pete Simi. 2004. "Free Spaces, Collective Identity, and the Persistence of U.S. White Power Activism." *Social Problems* 51 (1): 16–42.

Futrell, Robert, Pete Simi, and Simon Gottschalk. 2006. "Understanding Music in Movements: The White Power Music Scene." *Sociological Quarterly* 47 (2): 275–304.

Gamson, William A. 2002. *Talking Politics*. New York, NY: Cambridge University Press.

Gerbaudo, Paolo. 2013. "Spikey Posters." *Space and Culture*, October. doi:10.1177/1206331213501127.

Goffman, Erving. 1959. *The Presentation of Self in Everyday Life*. New York, NY: Anchor Books.

Goodyer, Ian. 2003. "Rock against Racism: Multiculturalism and Political Mobilization, 1976–81." *Immigrants & Minorities* 22 (1): 44–62.

Haenfler, Ross. 2014. *Subcultures: The Basics*. New York, NY: Routledge.

Haenfler, Ross, Brett Johnson, and Ellis Jones. 2012. "Lifestyle Movements: Exploring the Intersection of Lifestyle and Social Movements." *Social Movement Studies* 11 (1): 1–20.

Hall, Stuart, and Tony Jefferson. 1976. *Resistance through Rituals: Youth Subcultures in Post-War Britain*. Abingdon: Routledge.

Hart, Stephen. 1996. "The Cultural Dimension of Social Movements: A Theoretical Reassessment and Literature Review." *Sociology of Religion* 57 (1): 87.

Hebdige, Dick. 1979. *Subculture: The Meaning of Style*. New York, NY: Routledge.

Hodkinson, Paul, and Wolfgang Deicke. 2009. *Youth Cultures: Scenes, Subcultures and Tribes*. New York, NY: Routledge.

Jasper, James M. 1997. *The Art of Moral Protest: Culture, Biography, and Creativity in Social Movements*. Chicago, IL: University of Chicago Press.

Jasper, James M. 2017. "Cultural Approaches in the Study of Social Movements." In *Handbook of Social Movements Across Disciplines*, edited by Bert Klandermans and Conny Roggeband, 59–109. New York, NY: Springer International Publishing.

Jeppesen, Sandra. 2018. "DIY." In *Anarchism: A Conceptual Approach*, edited by Benjamin Franks, Nathan Jun, and Leonard Williams, 203–218. New York, NY: Routledge.

Johnston, Hank. 2009. "Protest Cultures: Performances, Artifacts, and Ideations." In *Culture, Social Movements, and Protest*, edited by Hank Johnston, 3–29. Burlington, VT: Ashgate.

Kriesi, Hanspeter, Ruud Koopmans, Jan Willem Duyvendak, and Marco G. Guigni. 1995. *New Social Movements in Western Europe: A Comparative Analysis*. Minneapolis, MN: University of Minnesota Press.

Langman, Lauren. 2008. "Punk, Porn and Resistance: Carnivalization and the Body in Popular Culture." *Current Sociology* 56 (4): 657–677. doi:10.1177/0011392108090947.

Leach, Darcy K., and Sebastian Haunss. 2009. "Scenes and Social Movements." In *Culture, Social Movements, and Protest*, edited by Hank Johnston, 255–276. Burlington, VT: Ashgate.

Linden, Annette, and Bert Klandermans. 2006. "Stigmatization and Repression of Extreme-Right Activism in the Netherlands." *Mobilization: An International Journal* 11 (2): 213–228.

Linnemann, Travis. 2017. "Proof of Death: Police Power and the Visual Economies of Seizure, Accumulation and Trophy." *Theoretical Criminology* 21 (1): 57–77. doi:10.1177/1362480615622533.

Magaña, Maurice Rafael. 2016. "From the Barrio to the Barricades: Grafiteros, Punks, and the Remapping of Urban Space." *Social Justice* 42 (3/4): 170–183.

Marshall, George. 1994. *Spirit of '69: A Skinhead Bible*. Dunoon, UK: S.T. Publishing.

McAdam, Doug. 1994. "Culture and Social Movements." In *New Social Movements: From Ideology to Identity*, edited by Enrique Laraña, Hank Johnston, and Joseph R. Gusfeld, 36–57. Philadelphia, PA: Temple University Press.

McKay, George. 2004. "Subcultural Innovations in the Campaign for Nuclear Disarmament." *Peace Review* 16 (4): 429–438. doi:10.1080/1040265042000318653.

Meyer, David S., and Suzanne Staggenborg. 1996. "Movements, Countermovements, and the Structure of Political Opportunity." *American Journal of Sociology* 101 (6): 1628–1660.

Moore, Ryan, and Michael Roberts. 2009. "Do-It-Yourself Mobilization: Punk and Social Movements." *Mobilization: An International Journal* 14 (3): 273–291.

Morrison, Daniel R., and Larry W. Isaac. 2012. "Insurgent Images: Genre Selection and Visual Frame Amplification in IWW Cartoon Art." *Social Movement Studies* 11 (1): 61–78. doi:10.1080/14742837.2012.640530.

Muggleton, David. 2000. *Inside Subculture the Postmodern Meaning of Style*. New York, NY: Berg.

Muggleton, David, and Rupert Weinzierl. 2003. *The Post-Subcultures Reader*. New York, NY: Berg.

O'Hara, Craig. 1999. *The Philosophy of Punk: More than Noise*. Edinburgh: AK Press.

Paxton, Robert O. 2004. *The Anatomy of Fascism*. New York, NY: Alfred A. Knopf.

Polletta, Francesca. 1999. "'Free Spaces' in Collective Action." *Theory & Society* 28 (1): 1.

Reed, T.V. 2005. *The Art of Protest: Culture and Activism from the Civil Rights Movement to the Streets of Seattle*. Minneapolis: University of Minnesota Press.

Renton, Dave. 2001. *This Rough Game: Fascism and Anti-Fascism*. Stroud: Sutton.

Roberts, Keith A. 1978. "Toward a Generic Concept of Counter-Culture." *Sociological Focus* 11 (2): 111–126.

Roberts, Michael James, and Ryan Moore. 2009. "Peace Punks and Punks Against Racism: Resource Mobilization and Frame Construction in the Punk Movement." *Music and Arts in Action* 2 (1): 21–36.

Roy, William. 2010. "How Social Movements Do Culture." *International Journal of Politics, Culture & Society* 23 (2/3): 85–98. doi:10.1007/s10767-010-9091-7.

Sanders, Clinton, and D. Angus Vail. 2008. *Customizing the Body: The Art and Culture of Tattooing*. Philadelphia, PA: Temple University Press.

Sandlin, Jennifer A., and Jamie L. Callahan. 2009. "Deviance, Dissonance, and Détournement: Culture Jammers' Use of Emotion in Consumer Resistance." *Journal of Consumer Culture* 9 (1): 79–115. doi:10.1177/1469540508099703.

Sarabia, Daniel, and Thomas E. Shriver. 2004. "Maintaining Collective Identity in a Hostile Environment: Confronting Negative Public Perception and Factional Divisions Within the Skinhead Subculture." *Sociological Spectrum* 24 (3): 267–294. doi:10.1080/02732170390258614.

Simi, Pete, and Robert Futrell. 2010. *American Swastika: Inside the White Power Movement's Hidden Spaces of Hate*. Lanham, MD: Rowman & Littlefield.

Spracklen, Karl, and Beverley Spracklen. 2014. "The Strange and Spooky Battle over Bats and Black Dresses: The Commodification of Whitby Goth Weekend and the Loss of a Subculture." *Tourist Studies* 14 (1): 86–102. doi:10.1177/1468797613511688.

St. John, Graham. 2004. "Counter-Tribes, Global Protest and Carnivals of Reclamation." *Peace Review* 16 (4): 421–428. doi:10.1080/1040265042000318644.

Straw, Will. 1991. "Systems of Articulation, Logics of Change: Communities and Scenes in Popular Music." *Cultural Studies* 5 (3): 368–388. doi:10.1080/09502389100490311.

Thomas-Peter, Hannah. 2018. "Fascist Fighters or Criminals? On the Streets with Portland's Antifa Group." *Sky News*. https://news.sky.com/story/fascist-fighters-or-criminals-on-the-streets-with-portlands-antifa-group-11217880.

Thornton, Sarah. 2013. *Club Cultures: Music, Media and Subcultural Capital*. Cambridge: Polity Press.

Travis, Tiffini A., and Perry Hardy. 2012. *Skinheads: A Guide to an American Subculture*. Santa Barbara, CA: Greenwood.

Waldner, Lisa K., and Betty A. Dobratz. 2013. "Graffiti as a Form of Contentious Political Participation." *Sociology Compass* 7 (5): 377–389. doi:10.1111/soc4.12036.

Weiß, Peter Ulrich. 2015. "Civil Society from the Underground: The Alternative Antifa Network in the GDR." *Journal of Urban History* 41 (4): 647–664. doi:10.1177/0096144215579354.

Williams, Dana M. 2018. "Contemporary Anarchist and Anarchistic Movements." *Sociology Compass* 12 (6): 1–17.

Williams, J. Patrick. 2006. "Authentic Identities: Straightedge Subculture, Music, and the Internet." *Journal of Contemporary Ethnography* 35 (2): 173–200. doi:10.1177/0891241605285100.

Williams, J. Patrick. 2011. *Subcultural Theory: Traditions & Concepts*. Chichester: Polity Press.

Williams, J. Patrick, and Heith Copes. 2011. "'How Edge Are You?' Constructing Authentic Identities and Subcultural Boundaries in a Straightedge Internet Forum." *Symbolic Interaction* 28 (1): 67–89. doi:10.1525/si.2005.28.1.67.

Williams, Rhys H. 2007. "The Cultural Contexts of Collective Action: Constraints, Opportunities, and the Symbolic Life of Social Movements." In *The Blackwell Companion to Social Movements*, 91–115. Malden, MA: Wiley-Blackwell. doi:10.1002/9780470999103.ch5.

Wood, Robert T. 1999. "The Indigenous, Nonracist Origins of the American Skinhead Subculture." *Youth & Society* 31 (2): 131–151. doi:10.1177/0044118X99031002001.

Yinger, J. Milton. 1960. "Contraculture and Subculture." *American Sociological Review* 25 (5): 625–635.

Zald, Meyer N., and Bert Useem. 1987. "Movement and Countermovement Interaction: Mobilization, Tactics and State Involvement." In *Social Movements in an Organizational Society: Collected Essays*, edited by Meyer N. Zald and John D. McCarthy. New Brunswick, NJ: Transaction Books.

5

FASCIST THREAT AND ANTIFASCIST ACTION

The experience of being face-to-face in a social setting with a person who is ideologically committed to harming or killing you is surreal. The first time this happened to me was largely by accident. I was 16 years old and entered a local record store, ironically owned by a Jewish person, that sold racist Oi! records among its punk selection. A group of three racist skinheads were there to sell wholesale overtly racist and anti-Semitic records. There would be other such experiences throughout the years at punk and metal shows, on the street and on public transportation, on airline flights, and eventually, at antifascist protests. Being mere feet away from a fascist who has declared it their mission to rid the world of you and others like you generates a series of intense emotions: fear, anger, frustration, hatred, and innumerable others. For those who have had the misfortune to have such an experience, it leaves an indelible mark. This chapter is about those emotions and the response of militant antifascists to the threats they face from their fascist opposition. The militant tactics associated with antifa activism, particularly the use of force and violence, are in many respects driven by the threat that fascists pose directly to antifascist activists and to the broader communities in which they live.

Whereas many social movements approach the use of violence as a strategic method to achieve an economic, political, or social goal, violence is a goal in and of itself for fascists. The most benign policy proscriptions put forth by contemporary fascists would result in structural dislocation or forcible repatriation of historically marginalized groups, and the extreme ones call for genocide. Violence isn't simply the outcome of fascist ideology, it is at its core. Fascists uphold violence as an end in itself, often venerating the violent individual as a spiritually superior being (Berlet 1992; Eco 1995; Paxton 2004). Violence against political opponents is especially celebrated as an integral part of their "mission," and "the violence of hate" serves as a means of "doing difference" by imposing inequality and domination through force (Levin and McDevitt 2002; Levin and Nolan 2017; Perry

2001). Contemporary fascists celebrate violence on social media with memes that mock victims and honor perpetrators (Caffier 2017; Futrelle 2017). Fascists, however, are not just bold talk and keyboard warriors. While it is impossible to estimate how many bias crimes are committed in a given year by hardcore "hatemongers" (Levin and Nolan 2017), supremacists routinely engage in bias crimes that are unreported (McDevitt et al. 2003) as well as violence against antifascists in everyday and protest settings. Antifa activists not only face, but comprehend, a unique threat that drives their activism and tactical choices.

Social movements are frequently motivated by existential threat or the participants' sense of ontological insecurity (Jasper 1997). In most cases, the threat is born of structural conditions or policy decisions rather than specific segments of a population. Antifascism is unique among both social movements and countermovements in that the primary threat that is perceived comes directly from the activity of the fascist movement. As this chapter will outline, the threats that militant antifascists encounter are often immediate and direct, which necessitates very specific tactical responses. The threats described by activists and witnessed as part of my research take on three distinct forms: physical, political, and spatial. Physical threat is a fear of direct physical harm or danger at the hands of fascist activists that stems from the individual being a member of a category of people targeted for fascist violence. Political threat takes the form of attacks on the political activity of activists because of their support for an ideology that is directly conflicting with fascism. Finally, spatial threat appears when fascist activity encroaches into subcultures and social spaces that are sites of contestation with antifascists. While each form of threat is unique, the forms are not mutually exclusive and may intersect with one another for individual antifascists. Intersecting threats may increase the perceived danger that fascists pose, warranting a militant response.

A sociology of threat

The concept of threat is increasingly becoming a subject of study for sociologists, particularly those interested in social movement activism. Much of the work on threat as it relates to social movements has been developed by political process theorists who are interested in the structural conditions that lead to social movement success or failure such as the role of government, alliances with elites and other social movements, or changes in the economy. In this framework, threat was initially viewed as a polar opposite to the concept of opportunity, but it has increasingly been understood as operating independently of and in conjunction with increasing opportunity (Almeida 2003, 2008, 2019; Einwohner and Maher 2011; Goldstone and Tilly 2001; Maher 2010; Tilly 1978). This concept has been elaborated especially in relation to repressive environments where governments present a unique danger to people's lives and livelihoods (Almeida 2003, 2008; Einwohner and Maher 2011; Maher 2010; Soyer 2014). Paul Almeida (2019) indicates that threats may also stem from economic-related problems, environmental and public health decline, as well as the erosion of basic rights.

The political process model of threat, however, has limited utility in under-standing the actions of militant antifascists. As non-state actors in opposition to other non-state actors, the primary threats faced by antifa activists come from the violent actions of fascists rather than the state. This dynamic results in an existential rather than political threat. Sociologists have studied a number of movements that are driven by such mortal threats including AIDS activism (Gould 2001, 2009; Jennings and Andersen 1996; Tester 2004), anti-nuclear power activism (Jasper 1997), and environmental activism (Johnson and Frickel 2011; Shriver, Adams, and Longo 2015). These types of threats generate strong emotional responses in activists who work to mediate these feelings through movement participation (Gould 2009; Goodwin and Pfaff 2001; Jasper 1997). Militant antifascist activism is driven by a unique set of existential threats posed by fascist mobilization and activity.

Of some interest to the study of fascist/antifascist dynamics is the role of threat in mobilizing far-right movements. These movements often marshal racist and xeno-phobic perceptions of people of color and immigrants as key organizing and mobilizing factors (Burley 2017; Van Dyke and Soule 2002; M. Ward 2013, 2017). African Americans and Latinx people are portrayed in far-right propaganda as taking jobs that white Americans are entitled to and subverting wages by over-whelming job markets. Structural changes such as deindustrialization and wage stagnation are thus blamed on people of color rather the structural maneuvers of capitalism (Levin and Nolan 2017; Levin and Rabrenovic 2004). Additionally, demographic shifts are identified by the far-right as a threat to the political influ-ence of white Americans (Burley 2017; Van Dyke and Soule 2002). These per-ceptions of threat are filtered through a conspiracist frame that interprets demographic, economic, and political shifts as the product of anti-Semitic beliefs in secret Jewish control of government and the economy (Berlet and Vysotsky 2006; Burley 2017; E. K. Ward 2017). For contemporary fascists, an additional dynamic of threat lies in gender and sexuality. The far-right has long viewed the moderate reforms of gender inequality and social acceptance of homosexuality and trans-gender identity as threats to traditional, often defined as natural or intrinsic, gender and sexuality (Blee 2003; Daniels 1997; Ferber 1999). The alt-right in particular has reacted to these perceived threats by mobilizing especially virulent forms of misogyny, homophobia, and transphobia (Burley 2017; Lyons 2017; Neiwert 2017; Wendling 2018). As we shall see in this chapter, these fascist perceptions of threat result in direct targeting of individuals, political organizing maneuvers, and social and cultural spaces that then generate a sense of threat among antifascist activists.

Recent social movement scholarship on Jewish resistance to Nazi extermination, although not a direct corollary, serves as a key analytical framework for the role of threat in militant antifascist mobilizations. Aside from the similarity of source of threat (fascist violence), the sociological principles of threat experienced by Jewish resistors may be echoed in contemporary, militant antifascist mobilizations. The rare cases of active, militant Jewish defiance occurred when populations were confronted with the reality of ghetto and concentration camp liquidation (Ein-wohner and Maher 2011; Maher 2010; Soyer 2014). Thomas Maher (2010) indicates that a threat must be perceived as "total" if it is to spur resistance. A total threat is one that is understood to be both lethal and immediate. Prisoner rebellions at Sobibor, Treblinka, and Auschwitz concentration camps, as well as the Warsaw and Lachwa ghetto uprisings were driven by a sense that annihilation was inevitable and survival unlikely (Einwohner and Maher 2011; Maher 2010; Soyer 2014). In the case of the Lachwa ghetto revolt, microsocial ties such as family and close friend networks were activated by "an alignment of specific structural circumstances, such as strong leadership, shared cultural schemata, spatial proximity, a functioning under-ground movement, and the lack of any other opportunities for survival [that] allowed for an unequivocal perception of immediate and lethal threat" (Soyer 2014, 61). This dynamic resulted in resistance being viewed as the most likely means of ensuring the survival of the microsocial unit. Finally, in order to mobilize militant resistance, threats must be perceived as severe (likely to result in death), imminent (immediate vs. eventual), applicable (affecting the people perceiving the threat), malleable (impacted by people's activity), and credible (verifiable) (Einwohner and Maher 2011; Soyer 2014). The threats experienced by militant antifascists described below, despite being relatively less lethal, demonstrate many similar dynamics.

Threat intensity

For many people, fascist activism and violence is an abstraction. It is something that they read about or see in news reports; something that they may hear about from others; a cautionary tale about a group of criminal deviants that they never have to interact with. Those fascists gather in bars that they will never frequent; attend music events they'll never go to; protest in the streets of faraway cities. For the militant antifascist activists that I interviewed and spent time with, the threat posed by fascists was much closer to home and very real. The antifa experience is defined in part by an intimate understanding of not only the fascist ideological commit-ment to violence, but fascist activists' willingness to use it. This level of threat in part drives antifascist militancy as a form of self-defense.

To be an antifascist is to essentially live life under threat. The vast majority of antifa activists whom I interviewed reported feeling threatened by fascists. The most common form of threat made by fascists was verbal or written. Verbal threats from fascists typically occurred in either social or protest settings. As discussed in Chapter 4 and in detail below, antifascists and fascists often find themselves in similar social locations by virtue of subcultural affiliations and other lifestyle choi-ces. Other antifa activists experience threats as a result of their being members of historically marginalized groups that are targets of fascist violence. Still others receive threats because of their notoriety as activists. Written threats are far more common because of the ease with which they can be issued, especially in an age of social media and electronic communication. New City Antifa's email, designed to receive information on fascist activity and to communicate with the public, routi-nely received threats from fascists using both anonymous and verifiable addresses. Individual activists also receive threatening emails and written messages. Eowyn described a time when fascists modified an antifa flyer and used it to threaten her and her partner because of their antifascist activity:

> What we discovered was that the Nazis had torn down as many [antifascist flyers] as possible and altered our images. The kid stomping on the swastika [in the original flyer] was now stomping on a hammer and sickle, a circled A, and the three antifa arrows. It now said "communist scum not welcome here …." What was scary is that they put a bunch outside our apartment on a pole where we hadn't put any posters before. We felt like maybe they had followed us home from [a nearby bar known as an antifascist meeting place] and that it was a message telling us that they knew where we lived.

While this was a somewhat unusual form of written threat, it is not uncommon for fascists to dox antifa activists with flyers similar to antifascist information and shaming campaigns. Fascist doxing is a routine threat faced by antifascists in the era of social media with activist information commonly passed around fascist message boards, social media accounts, and even semi-public forums such as 4chan and 8chan. Whereas antifascist flyer and online doxing campaigns are designed to educate communities and leverage social stigma against fascist activists, fascist doxing is effectively a violent threat. Online doxing posts by fascists garner replies that at best allude to violence in the form of violent images and memes and at worst directly threaten it. While people may disagree with militant antifascist tactics, an antifa identity simply doesn't carry the kind of stigma that comes with being an avowed bigot. Flyering campaigns, therefore, serve to put antifa activists on notice that fascists know where they live and work, and that they must beware of potentially violent retribution.

The threatening nature of fascist doxing campaigns is made evident when fascist activists actually come to the homes of antifascists and other critics. This has become a prominent tactic of the Proud Boys who organized a late night "visit" to the home of Gwen Snyder, a Philadelphia activist who has been doxing fascists and indicating their connections to local conservative politics, and several "visits" to the home of comedy video editor Vic Berger, who has made videos mocking the group, among others (Sommer 2019). Unlike the daytime "house demo" protests occasionally organized by antifascists that are designed to educate and leverage social stigma, the threatening character of such "house visits" is made clear by their timing – generally after dark or in the middle of the night – and the message sent – the Proud Boys who came to Snyder's home allegedly informed her neighbor "You tell that fat bitch she better stop" (Sommer 2019). As a final threatening gesture, the Proud Boys also left stickers on light poles near the house marking the territory as having a fascist presence. The fascist home visit tactic operates as an intermediary threat between the written and verbal threats of doxing campaigns and the actual use of violent force. By going to the home of an antifascist activist, the fascists are demonstrating that they have the ability to leverage violence against them under the right circumstances.

It may be easy to dismiss the verbal and written threats levied by fascists as hollow acts of cowardly blowhards; however, antifascists often face direct violent attacks. In an interview, Darby, an anti-racist skinhead and long-time antifascist activist, described how threats from fascists often lead to violence, "I've been beaten by them, too, so they've followed through on those [verbal and written] threats." The most notorious of these violent acts was the murder of Daniel Shersty and Lin "Spit" Newborn, two members of Anti-Racist Action from Las Vegas, who were murdered by racist skinheads in 1998 (Terry 1998). In 2010, Luke Querner, a prominent anti-racist skinhead in Portland, OR, was shot leaving his birthday party at a local bar (Bernstein 2010). The attack was, fortunately, not fatal, but left him paralyzed. Within weeks of the attack on Querner, the home of antifascist activists in Vancouver, Canada was firebombed (Salerno 2010). Probably the most infamous contemporary attack on antifascist activists was the intentional ramming of counter-protesters against the "Unite the Right" rally in Charlottes-ville, VA by James Alex Fields, an affiliate of the neo-Nazi group Vanguard America (now known as Patriot Front), which killed Heather Heyer and injured 19 others (Burley 2017). While these are some of the most extreme examples, antifa activists routinely face violence from fascists. Attacks on antifascists are so commonplace that they are considered part of the experience of being an activist.

Even if violence at the hands of fascists is a routine part of antifascist activity, it results in serious emotional impacts. Kam described his emotional reaction to receiving direct threats of violence as follows:

> It feels shitty cause … if you're threatened, some of the times you can't do [anything] because usually they'll only threaten you if they feel like they can, if they outnumber you or if they're physically larger than you … and if they're physically larger than you, you're feeling threatened by them, you start getting a bunch of adrenaline and you start being scared because you could get hurt, you could get hurt bad because they could stomp you, possibly even kill you, so it's scary.

That level of fear is amplified when antifascists actually experience violence. Helena, a militant antifascist with a reputation for being confrontational, explained that she struggled with post-traumatic stress disorder (PTSD) after an especially vicious street attack by fascists. Although the level of violence experienced by antifa activists elevates their feelings of anxiety regarding their overall safety, it does not discourage them from continuing with their activism. As Lydia stated after recounting an incident of fascist violence, "[they] just make me feel like we need to get organized." Her trauma notwithstanding, Helena described her motivation for continuing to engage in militant antifascist activism:

> I think that all sorts of people live in terror all the time all over the world and here in the United States – I think about black people being lynched or something, I think I can take this on …. I think that's what really makes you

an ally is when you say like, "no, I'm joining this team." I guess getting your ass kicked by a bunch of white supremacists is when you're on that team. It's like we talk a lot about no race and trying to get rid of your whiteness and blah, blah, blah, I guess that's to me that's what really did it. It's like, it is really renouncing it in that way... it's just too core to who I am to wanna be fighting injustice.

Whether in formal interviews or informal conversations, antifa activists consistently indicated that the intensity of the threat they felt was a key motivating factor for their activism. This motivation may stem from a need to protect their "ontological security," an ideological impetus, or a political maneuver. The threats described above meet the criteria for severity, timeliness, applicability, and credibility (Einwohner and Maher 2011; Maher 2010; Soyer 2014). Regardless of individual motivation, militant antifascists consistently indicated that it was crucial to stop fascist organizing and mobilizing efforts through a diverse set of tactics, including the use of force. This conviction arises from a desire to defend themselves and others targeted for fascist violence.

Physical threat

The concept of physical threat stems from the existential danger that fascists pose to individuals. Fascist ideology is predicated on the violent control and elimination of a number of historically marginalized groups of people based on race and ethnicity, religious affiliation, sexual orientation, and disability status to name a few. Militant antifascists experience a strong perception of this threat because they are identified as targeted "minorities" or "race traitors" by fascist activists.

In Chapter 2, I discussed the demographics of militant antifascist groups in this study as well as the alliances between formal antifa groups and other militant activists. For queer, transgender, or gender non-conforming activists, fascist movements often represent a viable and imminent threat because they are predicated on violent control and/or elimination of individuals labeled as "sexually deviant." Contemporary movements are particularly fixated on control of sexuality and heterosexual domination (Daniels 1997; Ferber 1999). Individuals who are willing to be "out" regarding their queer sexual orientation or transgender or gender nonconforming identity, or those who are just perceived as non-heterosexual or nonconforming, become rightful targets of fascist violence (Levin and McDevitt 2002; Perry 2001). For queer antifa activists, like formal interview respondents Adria and Lydia, being "queer bashed" by racist skinheads on several occasions over the course of their lives presents a sense of urgency to their activism that is driven by direct experiences of violence based on their identity.

A similar sense of physical threat is faced by people of color and members of religious minority groups. The significant proportion of people of color active in New City Antifa, as well as other antifa groups, reflects the visceral racism of fascist groups in the United States. Contemporary fascist groups tap into a historical legacy of white supremacy and racialized violence (Dobratz and Shanks-Meile 1997; Novick 1995). The antifascist dynamics of racial violence were made evident in some of the clashes that occurred in Charlottesville, VA. Some of the most vicious attacks targeted African Americans such as the attempted shooting of Corey Long and beating of DeAndre Harris (Hauser and Jacobs 2018). People of color come to militant antifascist activism precisely because popular fascist mobilizations represent an escalation in the dynamics of white supremacist violence.

This sense of historic threat also informs militant antifascists from Jewish back-grounds. Contemporary fascist movements are predicated on anti-Semitism as the driving force for their worldview (Berlet and Vysotsky 2006; Burley 2017; E. K. Ward 2017). For populist fascist movements, entire narratives are reduced to secretive Jewish conspiracies. Within the movement, white supremacist frames such as fear of black crime and concerns about undocumented migration leading to unemployment are explained as the products of a Jewish conspiracy of control (Ezekiel 1995). The Jewish members of Old City Antifa all acknowledged the same basic reality that I came face to face with in that record store and every encounter with fascists since – the fact of our Jewishness makes us targets for fascist violence regardless of our political ideology or level of observance. Under such circum-stances, antifascism becomes a practice of self-defense.

Fascist violence, however, extends as much to antifascists who are white, het-erosexual, cisgender, and from Christian backgrounds as it does to members of historically marginalized groups. Often branded as "traitors," these antifascists pose an especially serious threat because they consciously resist supremacist narratives and frames. For example, Eowyn's sense of physical threat was rooted in her part-ner's Jewish identity and her strong connections to antifa activists. In response to being asked whether she felt threatened by fascist activists, she stated the following:

> Yes. Maybe not so much for myself by myself, but my partner is Jewish and we are both active in anti-racist politics and ultra-left or anarchist organizing, and we live with each other and near other activists. I do not think this is the same threat that a person of color feels every day of their life and I am not trying to make that comparison for myself, but yes, I do feel that [fascists] would do me or my partner or my friends or my neighbors serious harm.

As an antifascist activist, Eowyn is aware that her relationship with a Jewish person is clear violation of fascist dictates for white women (Daniels 1997; Ferber 1999), which makes her the target for potential retributive violence, and points out that her activist work places her at risk of retaliation. The threat that militants face should not be underestimated as Damon indicated when he described a direct threat levied against him:

> When the police report on the small group of <city> boneheads[1] who were pulled over by the cops was turned over to us … they listed what they found in the car. So, here's 4 young boneheads and they had 6 guns: 1 revolver, 3

semi-automatics, 1 shotgun, 1 rifle …, 3 baseball bats; a crow bar, every one of them had at least one knife, maybe a couple of them had 2 knives, and they were looking for us. They weren't looking for unnamed individuals. They named who they were looking for because a lot of the boneheads weren't very smart …. But yeah, they've said they're going to kill me in particular and people that I hang out with a number of times and they've made those attempts in great seriousness so I think I have to at least respect their intentions.

The attack that triggered Helena's PTSD discussed earlier in this chapter was similarly motivated by fascist elimination of "traitors." She and a friend experienced a potentially deadly attack because of the friend's decision to leave fascist activism and move to militant antifascism, "my friend was a former Nazi in England who had turned Red Skin[2] so they were, you know, they wanted to murder him, basically. So, they knew who we were at the time." As a traitor to the cause, Helena's friend was especially vilified and his associates were similarly despised.

As "sexual deviants," "subhumans," or "traitors," antifa activists face a distinctly direct threat of physical harm at the hands of fascists. Militant antifascists are targeted in a very public manner and experience the danger of potential fascist violence daily. The intensity of this type of threat creates a situation where the potential for violence becomes an everyday reality for antifa activists. Because they are activists who advocate a radical response to fascist violence, militant antifascists generally cannot, or ideologically will not, turn to the police for assistance because they will simply be classified as a rival gang (Porter 2017; Pyrooz and Densley 2018). From the perspective of militant antifascists, relying on police protection is an ineffective strategy because they arrive after an act of violence has occurred at best, and are sympathetic to fascist ideology at worst. Confrontational approaches to addressing fascist threats also arise out of an ideological commitment to "direct action" that stems from antifa activists' anarchist or anti-authoritarian beliefs (Apoifis 2017; Shantz 2011; D. M. Williams 2018, 2019). Antifa activists, therefore, consider the use of violent and confrontational tactics to be a key component of any program of "self-defense" that ensures both personal and community safety (Clark 2018). From a social movements perspective, the use of confrontational tactics assures that fascist threats are neutralized by effectively engaging in the countermovement strategy of damage or disruption of movement activity (Zald and Useem 1987). When fascist movements cannot mobilize, they effectively cannot engage in violence or threats of violence against individuals and communities that they would typically target, thus ensuring their safety.

Political threat

The physical threats faced by militant antifascists are effectively the product of a political conflict. The ideological positions of fascist and antifascists places them in direct opposition to one another in a manner that makes them an ideal model of countermovements (Meyer and Staggenborg 1996; Zald and Useem 1987). The two groups adhere to diametrically opposing political ideologies that place them in constant contention over a variety of economic, political, and social issues. The threat that fascists pose, therefore, becomes more than simply one of physical safety, it is also a danger to entire social movements as they struggle to achieve a trans-formative or revolutionary outcome (Bray 2017; Burley 2017). Antifa activists acknowledge that fascists pose a unique threat because they are often in competi-tion to win over a similar political base and mobilize populations toward broader social change. The fascist threat is based on their reactionary critique of the existing system and eagerness to utilize violence to dominate public discourse.

For many mainstream observers, the political threat of fascism lies in its potential to subvert the liberal values of freedom and legal equality; however, militant antifascists perceive a more existential threat. Historically, fascist movements have arisen as a direct political opposition to the organizing efforts of anarchist, communist, and socialist movements; often building from similar bases of support within working-class communities and engaging in similar issue sets (Bray 2017; Burley 2017; Copsey 2000; Hamerquist 2002; Ross 2017). Militant antifascist movements organize out of a sense of political self-preservation because fascists actively work to subvert movements on the left (Bray 2017; Burley 2017; Testa 2015). As discussed in Chapters 2 and 3, fas-cism is predicated on violent suppression of ideological opponents and their organizing efforts. To the extent that fascism represents a physical threat as described above, it does so in large part because of the political work that antifascists engage in.

While some observers indicate the superficial similarity in political bases and ideological concerns between leftist and far-right movements under the guise of "horseshoe theory," it is more appropriately understood as a "creep" of fascist ideology into leftist discourse and organizing (Burley 2017; Ross 2017). In a formal interview, Darby explains this dynamic by stating,

> [fascist] ideals are typically some form of cultural trapping that ... are a window dressing for routing people away from really addressing more funda-mental, structural grievances that are typically oriented around economy, community, culture, and over who has a right to determine power relation-ships and dynamics within those spheres of existence.

As fascist movements develop ideologically to address contemporary concerns, they move into territory that has been the preserve of the left. For militant antifascists, the threat of fascism is one that extends to their political work on broader social issues.

Fascist political organizing efforts often aim for a similar base of support as leftists. Helena explains this "battle of ideas" during a formal interview as follows:

> in the town where I grew up there was definitely a pretty big Nazi population in the city across the river. It was very like 'the other side of the tracks,' you know, and it was basically because of the loss of blue collar jobs like a bunch of industry had moved out so there's all these white men who were angry

because they couldn't get the same kinds of jobs that their dad did and the property value there declined … and it was like really ripe for recruiters and there would be these creepy, middle-aged men that would come in and start hanging out with the teenagers [in the punk scene] …. There was a real fascist presence there and so they were intermingled …. And for me, always I felt like there was this real ideological war, like it was all these working-class people were being recruited into fascism and those were the same people that could be potential revolutionaries and just got totally derailed into this asinine world view. So, I felt like it was this ideological war, like they were taking all of our potential anarchist [recruits] and turning [them] into boneheads.

Antifa activists came to this movement in part as a result of political organizing on broader economic and social issues. They found that antifascism was an extension of that political work because of the threat that fascists pose to their organizing efforts. The "target recruitment" of young people experiencing forms of economic and social strain (Blazak 2001; Van Dyke and Soule 2002) places fascists in political conflict with leftist organizers. Successful fascist recruitment creates additional foot soldiers in a political war with the left. Because the fascist movement has an ideological imperative toward violence, organizing success on its part becomes a direct physical threat as discussed above. Militancy, therefore, becomes a defensive strategy against the political organizing efforts of the far-right.

Militancy also undermines the ideological message of fascist movements as a superior form of political organization because they are able to leverage violence against their opponents. Antifa activists demonstrate that people will not be cowed into silence by the mere presence of fascist organizers and will resist. When supremacists construct their movement as one that has superior strength, defeat by antifascists subverts an aspect of their ideology and key recruitment tactic (Blazak 2001). By mounting a militant defense of their political organizing work, antifa activists undermine the effectiveness of the political threat of fascism.

Spatial threat

Physical space represents a key dimension of social movement mobilization (Leitner, Sheppard, and Sziarto 2008; Martin and Miller 2003; Polletta 1999; Tilly 2000, 2003). Charles Tilly (2000) indicates that contention occurs in some form of physical space, spatial distributions greatly affect the potential for mobilization, and these spaces have significant meaning to social movement actors. Social movements often establish "safe" spaces where they can operate outside of the control of state and other bureaucratic institutions (Tilly 2000). "Free" spaces are "small-scale settings within a community or movement that are removed from the direct control of dominant groups, are voluntarily participated in, and generate the cultural challenge that precedes or accompanies political mobilization" (Polletta 1999, 1). The spatial dimensions of fascist threat operate at both a micro and macro level. At the micro level, antifascists often find themselves in close physical proximity to

fascists in part as a result of subcultural participation. The m
manifests itself in the use of subcultures as "safe" or "free'
mainstream values. Fascists and antifascists engage in a cor
control of such spaces and ideological hegemony within the..
is extended further into public space as fascists attempt to engage .
public spaces and claim them as fascist territory.

The scenario described at the beginning of this chapter illustrates the physical
proximity that many antifascists have with fascists. For many subculturalists, contact
with fascists may occur simply as part of the process of normal, everyday activities.
The physical threats described above often occur because fascists and antifascists
find themselves in the same spaces, which generates tension and conflict. This is
largely the product of the similar lifestyles of individuals involved in both movements. As Ross Haenfler's (2014; Haenfler, Johnson, and Jones 2012) research
indicates, social movement activity can take the form of distinct lifestyle choices,
including subcultural expression. As discussed in Chapters 2 and 3, fascists and
antifascists both participate in distinct subcultures. The kinds of "alternative" lifestyles that come with non-normative tastes generate distinct types of social activity
that occur in spaces outside of the experience of "ordinary" individuals. This form
of subcultural participation brings both movements together in similar social spaces.
This type of proximity increases the possibility of conflict between these opposing
movements.

The conflicts that Helena has described throughout this chapter are the product
of interactions in shared social space. The attack on her and her friend that resulted
in PTSD occurred in a park that was a typical hangout for people involved in
subcultures. Fascists recognized the antifascists in this space and attacked them
because of their activism. Her local punk scene, like many others, experienced
increased levels of violence because of supremacist activity. Research by Randy
Blazak (2001) indicates that fascists routinely deploy violence in subcultural spaces
in order to assert their ideological and physical control of those spaces. The focus
on violence as an ideological imperative in fascist movements, combined with
violent subcultural norms (Bowen 2008; Hamm 1993), easily and rapidly transforms subcultures into spaces that are dangerous for everyone except the fascist
brutes who control them. Militant antifascist activity, whether formal or informal,
serves as a countervailing force to this violence.

The presence of fascists transforms subcultures into ideologically contested spaces
as they attempt to present their beliefs as authentic expressions of subcultural
rebellion (Madfis and Vysotsky 2020). Subcultures often serve as sites of resistance
for their participants (Haenfler 2014; J. P. Williams 2011), which designates the
spaces that they occupy as potentially "safe" spaces for antifascists or the "prefigurative" spaces of supremacists (Simi and Futrell 2010; Tilly 2000). As discussed
in Chapter 4, there is an ideological contest over subculture as a meta-space. The
ideological orientation of a subculture provides a number of benefits for social
movements such as serving as an abeyance structure for movements in decline,
offering a potential recruitment pool, and even generating revenue for movement

,vity. Fascist and antifascists have, therefore, competed over subcultural meaning nd authenticity since the 1970s (Bray 2017; Burley 2017; Copsey 2000; Renton 2001; Testa 2015). Anti-Racist Action built its base of militant opposition through a consistent presence at punk, metal, and other "alternative" subcultural events. New City Antifa regularly set up a merchandise table at subcultural events to maintain an antifascist presence, and routinely organized benefit shows for anti-fascist causes. Such efforts are designed to specifically mark subcultures as antifascist spaces. This sentiment regarding subcultures as spaces that either welcome or resist fascist organizing attempts was expressed clearly by a speaker at an antifa benefit, "My attitude is Nazi see, Nazi go! We gotta make it clear they're not welcome here. Not their scene, not their city, not their society!"

Militant antifascism as a response to threat

This chapter outlined the key threats faced by antifa activists from fascists, which are identified as physical, political, and spatial. The physical threat that fascists pose is based on their ideological imperative to engage in violence in order to establish and maintain inequality, as well as to intimidate their political opponents. Political threat is identified as efforts on the part of fascists to undermine the activist work of leftists by appealing to a similar recruitment base and engaging with similar issues. Finally, spatial threat may be understood as stemming from the physical proximity of fascist and antifascist activists that results from similar lifestyle and subcultural participation. This threat may also be applied to subcultures as a whole because they serve as unique spaces of resistance, organizing, and prefigurative practice. Antifascist militancy in part stems from these threats that activists face because it is a strategic response to the conditions and emotions that they generate.

From a sociological perspective, the militant antifascist response reflects the dynamics of threat identified in historical research on antifascist resistance, specifically by Jewish people facing extermination (Einwohner and Maher 2011; Maher 2010; Soyer 2014). The concept of total threat (Maher 2010) is clearly demonstrated by both the intensity of the threat posed by fascists and in the concept of physical threat. Though not lethal as defined by Maher (2010; Einwohner and Maher 2011), the level and frequency of violence experienced by antifa activists is severe enough to be of grave concern. The physical and spatial threats described in this chapter also speak to the immediacy of threat experienced by militant anti-fascists (Einwohner and Maher 2011; Maher 2010). For antifa activists, fascists do not represent an abstract ideological opponent, but a tangible menace that may directly impact them. Physical and political threats as described above clearly indicate applicability, that the threat affects the individuals who perceive it (Einwohner and Maher 2011). Fascists are explicit in their intent and action against people who identify as queer, transgender, gender non-conforming, people of color, religious minorities, and any other identity they view as inferior. Similarly, just as they have historically, contemporary fascists mobilize violence against their political opponents. Both the history of fascist violence and the immediate experiences of antifascists indicate that the threats they face are indeed credible (Einwohner and Maher 2011). The militant response, therefore, is designed to neutralize the total threat that fascists pose; a position that indicates the malleability of the threat (Einwohner and Maher 2011).

Social movement analysis recognizes the importance of emotions as factors in mobilization (Goodwin, Jasper, and Polletta 2001, 2007; Jasper 1997). Central to militant mobilization, such as that of antifa activists, is the concept of fear. Existential threats where individuals fear for their lives or safety often drive activists toward more militant tactics (Gould 2001; Gould 2009; Jasper 1997; Jennings and Andersen 1996; Tester 2004). Activists who face the most intense forms of threat often rely of the most militant tactics to address it (Jennings and Andersen 1996). The physical threats discussed in this chapter represent such an existential threat because activists are often not only directly targeted, but targeted specifically based on their identity. Jeff Goodwin and Steven Pfaf (2001) indicate that social movement activity serves as a means of managing the fear that individuals may experience as targets of existential threat. In a formal interview, Damon spoke to this phenomenon when he described a clash with a Klansman at a protest, "When the head of the (state) KKK had his hands around my throat trying to strangle me at that point, yes, I felt threatened. After I knocked him down and attempted to break his nose, no, I did not feel threatened." Militancy in opposition to fascist mobilization serves to empower antifa activists, but also provides an immediate protection for activists, which will be discussed in detail in the following chapter.

Notes

1 Bonehead is a common derisive term for a racist skinhead. It originated in traditional and anti-racist skinhead subculture to distinguish between authentic members from inauthentic racists. Because skinhead subculture has its roots in Jamaican immigration to England in the late 1960s, it is often viewed by its members as authentically non-racist or actively anti-racist (Marshall 1994; Sarabia and Shriver 2004; Travis and Hardy 2012; Wood 1999). Racist skinheads are, therefore, viewed as an aberration from authentic expression of the subculture.
2 Red Skin, short for Red Skinhead, is a term used to identify skinheads who are active in leftist politics, specifically socialism, communism, and anarchism. The moniker is intended to differentiate leftist anti-racist skinheads from other anti-racist skinheads who may hold less radical political beliefs or identify as "non-political" on issues other than racism. It is not intended as a term of derision for Indigenous people. The moniker has somewhat fallen out of favor because of its racist implications with many left-wing skinheads identifying as Skinheads Against Racial Prejudice (SHARP) or Red and Anarchist Skinheads (RASH).

Works cited

Almeida, Paul D. 2003. "Opportunity Organizations and Threat-Induced Contention: Protest Waves in Authoritarian Settings." *American Journal of Sociology* 109 (2): 345–400. doi:10.1086/378395.

Almeida, Paul D. 2008. *Waves of Protest: Popular Struggle in El Salvador: 1925–2005*. Minneapolis, MN: University of Minnesota Press.

Almeida, Paul D. 2019. "The Role of Threat in Collective Action." In *The Wiley Blackwell Companion to Social Movements*, edited by David A. Snow, Sarah A. Soule, Hanspeter Kriesi, and Holly J. McCammon, 2nd Edition, 43–62. Hoboken, NJ: John Wiley & Sons.

Apoifis, Nicholas. 2017. *Anarchy in Athens: An Ethnography of Militancy, Emotions and Violence*. Manchester, UK: Manchester University Press.

Berlet, Chip. 1992. "Fascism!" *Political Research Associates*. https://www.politicalresearch.org/1992/09/28/fascism.

Berlet, Chip, and Stanislav Vysotsky. 2006. "Overview of US White Supremacist Groups." *Journal of Political and Military Sociology* 34 (1): 11.

Bernstein, Maxine. 2010. "Anti-Racist Group Argues Shooting of Portland Man Was a Neo-Nazi Attack." *OregonLive.com*, April 2. www.oregonlive.com/portland/index.ssf/2010/04/anti-racist_group_argues_shoot.html.

Blazak, Randy. 2001. "White Boys to Terrorist Men: Target Recruitment of Nazi Skinheads." *American Behavioral Scientist* 44 (6): 982–1000.

Blee, Kathleen M. 2003. *Inside Organized Racism: Women in the Hate Movement*. Berkeley, CA: University of California Press.

Bowen, Derek. 2008. "*Patterns of Skinhead Violence*." Ph.D. Dissertation, Durham, NH: University of New Hampshire.

Bray, Mark. 2017. *Antifa: The Antifascist Handbook*. Brooklyn, NY: Melville House Publishing.

Burley, Shane. 2017. *Fascism Today – What It Is and How to End It*. Chico, CA: AK Press.

Caffier, Justin. 2017. "Get to Know the Memes of the Alt-Right and Never Miss a Dog-Whistle Again." *Vice*. https://www.vice.com/en_us/article/ezagwm/get-to-know-the-memes-of-the-alt-right-and-never-miss-a-dog-whistle-again.

Clark, J. 2018. "Three-Way Fight: Revolutionary Anti-Fascism and Armed Self-Defense." In *Setting Sights: Histories and Reflections on Community Armed Self-Defense*, edited by Scott Crow, 49–67. Oakland, CA: PM Press.

Copsey, Nigel. 2000. *Anti-Fascism in Britain*. New York, NY: St. Martin's Press.

Daniels, Jessie. 1997. *White Lies: Race, Class, Gender, and Sexuality in White Supremacist Discourse*. New York, NY: Routledge.

Dobratz, Betty A., and Stephanie L. Shanks-Meile. 1997. *White Power, White Pride!: The White Separatist Movement in the United States*. New York, NY: Prentice Hall.

Eco, Umberto. 1995. "Ur-Fascism." *The New York Review of Books*, June 22. https://www.nybooks.com/articles/1995/06/22/ur-fascism/.

Einwohner, Rachel L., and Thomas V. Maher. 2011. "Threat Assessment and Collective-Action Emergence: Death-Camp and Ghetto Resistance During the Holocaust." *Mobilization: An International Quarterly* 16 (2): 127–146. doi:10.17813/maiq.16.2.j263166u14286024.

Ezekiel, Raphael S. 1995. *The Racist Mind: Portraits of American Neo-Nazis and Klansmen*. New York, NY: Viking.

Ferber, Abby L. 1999. *White Man Falling: Race, Gender, and White Supremacy*. Lanham, MD: Rowman & Littlefield.

Futrelle, David. 2017. "Nazi Memelords Mock the Murder of Heather Heyer by One of Their Own." *We Hunted the Mammoth*. www.wehuntedthemammoth.com/2017/08/13/nazi-memelords-mock-the-murder-of-heather-heyer-by-one-of-their-own/.

Goldstone, Jack A., and Charles Tilly. 2001. "Threat (And Opportunity): Popular Action and State Response in the Dynamics of Contentious Action." In *Silence and Voice in the Study of Contentious Politics*, edited by Ronald R. Aminzade, Jack A. Goldstone, Doug McAdam, Elizabeth J. Perry, William H.Sewell, Jr., Sidney G. Tarrow, and Charles Tilly, 179–194. New York, NY: Cambridge University Press.

Goodwin, Jeff, James M. Jasper, and Francesca Polletta. 2001. "Introduction: Why Emotions Matter." In *Passionate Politics: Emotions and Social Movements*, edited by Jeff Goodwin, James M. Jasper, and Francesca Polletta, 1–24. Chicago, IL: University of Chicago Press.

Goodwin, Jeff, James M. Jasper, and Francesca Polletta. 2007. "Emotional Dimensions of Social Movements." In *The Blackwell Companion to Social Movements*, 413–432. Malden, MA: Wiley-Blackwell. doi:10.1002/9780470999103.ch18.

Goodwin, Jeff, and Steven Pfaff. 2001. "Emotion Work in High-Risk Social Movements: Managing Fear in the U.S. and East German Civil Rights Movements." In *Passionate Politics: Emotions and Social Movements*, edited by Jeff Goodwin, James M. Jasper, and Francesca Polletta, 282–302. Chicago, IL: University of Chicago Press.

Gould, Deborah B. 2001. "Rock the Boat, Don't Rock the Boat, Baby: Ambivalence and the Emergence of Militant AIDS Activism." In *Passionate Politics: Emotions and Social Movements*, edited by Jeff Goodwin, James M. Jasper, and Francesca Polletta, 135–157. Chicago, IL: University of Chicago Press.

Gould, Deborah B. 2009. *Moving Politics: Emotion and Act Up's Fight Against AIDS*. Chicago, IL: University of Chicago Press.

Haenfler, Ross. 2014. *Subcultures: The Basics*. New York, NY: Routledge.

Haenfler, Ross, Brett Johnson, and Ellis Jones. 2012. "Lifestyle Movements: Exploring the Intersection of Lifestyle and Social Movements." *Social Movement Studies* 11 (1): 1–20.

Hamerquist, Don. 2002. "Fascism and Anti-Fascism." In *Confronting Fascism: Discussion Documents for a Militant Movement*, edited by Anti Racist Action Chicago. Montréal: Kersplebedeb.

Hamm, Mark S. 1993. *American Skinheads: The Criminology and Control of Hate Crime*. Westport, CT: Praeger.

Hauser, Christine, and Julia Jacobs. 2018. "Three Men Sentenced to Prison for Violence at Charlottesville Rally." *The New York Times*, August 25, sec. U.S. https://www.nytimes.com/2018/08/23/us/kkk-charlottesville-richard-preston.html.

Jasper, James M. 1997. *The Art of Moral Protest: Culture, Biography, and Creativity in Social Movements*. Chicago, IL: University of Chicago Press.

Jennings, M. Kent, and Ellen Ann Andersen. 1996. "Support for Confrontational Tactics among AIDS Activists: A Study of Intra-Movement Divisions." *American Journal of Political Science* 40 (2): 311–334. doi:10.2307/2111626.

Johnson, Erik W., and Scott Frickel. 2011. "Ecological Threat and the Founding of U.S. National Environmental Movement Organizations, 1962–1998." *Social Problems* 58 (3): 305–329. doi:10.1525/sp.2011.58.3.305.

Leitner, Helga, Eric Sheppard, and Kristin M. Sziarto. 2008. "The Spatialities of Contentious Politics." *Transactions of the Institute of British Geographers* 33 (2): 157–172.

Levin, Jack, and Jack McDevitt. 2002. *Hate Crimes Revisited: America's War Against Those Who Are Different*. Boulder, CO: Westview.

Levin, Jack, and Jim Nolan. 2017. *The Violence of Hate: Understanding Harmful Forms of Bias and Bigotry*. Lanham, MD: Rowman & Littlefield.

Levin, Jack, and Gordana Rabrenovic. 2004. *Why We Hate*. Amherst, NY: Prometheus Books.

Lyons, Matthew N. 2017. *Ctrl-Alt-Delete: The Origins and Ideology of the Alternative Right*. Somerville, MA: Political Research Associates. https://www.politicalresearch.org/2017/01/20/ctrl-alt-delete-report-on-the-alternative-right/.

Madfis, Eric, and Stanislav Vysotsky. 2020. "Exploring Subcultural Trajectories: Racist Skinhead Desistance and Countercultural Value Persistence." *Sociological Focus*.

Maher, Thomas V. 2010. "Threat, Resistance, and Collective Action: The Cases of Sobibor, Treblinka, and Auschwitz." *American Sociological Review* 75 (2): 252–272. doi:2048/10.1177/0003122410365305.

Marshall, George. 1994. *Spirit of '69: A Skinhead Bible*. Dunoon, UK: S.T. Publishing.

Martin, Deborah, and Byron Miller. 2003. "Space and Contentious Politics." *Mobilization: An International Quarterly* 8 (2): 143–156. doi:10.17813/maiq.8.2.m886w54361j81261.

McDevitt, Jack, Jennifer M. Balboni, Susan Bennett, Joan C. Weiss, Stan Orchowsky, and Lisa Walbot. 2003. "Improving the Quality and Accuracy of Bias Crime Statistics Nationally: An Assessment of the First Ten Years of Bias Crime Data Collection." In *Hate and Bias Crime: A Reader*, edited by Barbara Perry, 77–89. New York, NY: Routledge.

Meyer, David S., and Suzanne Staggenborg. 1996. "Movements, Countermovements, and the Structure of Political Opportunity." *American Journal of Sociology* 101 (6): 1628–1660.

Neiwert, David. 2017. *Alt-America: The Rise of the Radical Right in the Age of Trump*. New York, NY: Verso.

Novick, Michael. 1995. *White Lies, White Power: The Fight Against White Supremacy and Reactionary Violence*. Monroe, ME: Common Courage Press.

Paxton, Robert O. 2004. *The Anatomy of Fascism*. New York, NY: Alfred A. Knopf.

Perry, Barbara. 2001. *In the Name of Hate: Understanding Hate Crimes*. New York, NY: Routledge.

Polletta, Francesca. 1999. "'Free Spaces' in Collective Action." *Theory & Society* 28 (1): 1.

Porter, Tom. 2017. "Berkeley's Mayor Wants Antifa to Be Classified as a Gang." *Newsweek*. https://www.newsweek.com/berkeley-mayor-calls-antifa-be-classified-crime-gang-after-clashes-sunday-656286.

Pyrooz, David C., and James A. Densley. 2018. "On Public Protest, Violence, and Street Gangs." *Society* 55 (3): 229–236. doi:10.1007/s12115-018-0242-1.

Renton, Dave. 2001. *This Rough Game: Fascism and Anti-Fascism*. Stroud: Sutton.

Ross, Alexander Reid. 2017. *Against the Fascist Creep*. Chico, CA: AK Press.

Salerno, Rob. 2010. "UPDATE: Anti-Racism Activist's House Firebombed." *Xtra*. https://www.dailyxtra.com/update-anti-racism-activists-house-firebombed-10670.

Sarabia, Daniel, and Thomas E. Shriver. 2004. "Maintaining Collective Identity in a Hostile Environment: Confronting Negative Public Perception and Factional Divisions Within the Skinhead Subculture." *Sociological Spectrum* 24 (3): 267–294. doi:10.1080/02732170390258614.

Shantz, Jeff. 2011. *Active Anarchy: Political Practice in Contemporary Movements*. Lanham, MD: Lexington Books.

Shriver, Thomas E., Alison E. Adams, and Stefano B. Longo. 2015. "Environmental Threats and Political Opportunities: Citizen Activism in the North Bohemian Coal Basin." *Social Forces* 94 (2): 699–722.

Simi, Pete, and Robert Futrell. 2010. *American Swastika: Inside the White Power Movement's Hidden Spaces of Hate*. Lanham, MD: Rowman & Littlefield.

Sommer, Will. 2019. "Far Right Proud Boys Attempt to Menace Critic with Late-Night Threat." *The Daily Beast*, July 29, sec. Politics. https://www.thedailybeast.com/far-right-proud-boys-attempt-to-menace-critic-with-late-night-threat.

Soyer, Michaela. 2014. "'We Knew Our Time Had Come': The Dynamics of Threat and Microsocial Ties in Three Polish Ghettos Under Nazi Oppression." *Mobilization: An International Quarterly* 19 (1): 47–66. doi:10.17813/maiq.19.1.6618khh78976h112.

Terry, Don. 1998. "Skinhead Split on Racism Is Seen in Killing of 2 Friends." *The New York Times*, August 29, sec. U.S. https://www.nytimes.com/1998/08/29/us/skinhead-split-on-racism-is-seen-in-killing-of-2-friends.html.

Testa, M. 2015. *Militant Anti-Fascism: A Hundred Years of Resistance*. Oakland, CA: AK Press.

Tester, Griff M. 2004. "Resources, Identity, and the Role of Threat: The Case of AIDS Mobilization, 1981–1986." *Research in Political Sociology* 13: 47–75.

Tilly, Charles. 1978. *From Mobilization to Revolution*. New York, NY: McGraw-Hill.

Tilly, Charles. 2000. "Spaces of Contention." *Mobilization: An International Quarterly* 5 (2): 135–159. doi:10.17813/maiq.5.2.j6321h02n200h764.

Tilly, Charles. 2003. "Contention Over Space and Place." *Mobilization: An International Quarterly* 8 (2): 221–225. doi:10.17813/maiq.8.2.f1429714767152km.

Travis, Tiffini A., and Perry Hardy. 2012. *Skinheads: A Guide to an American Subculture.* Santa Barbara, CA: Greenwood.

Van Dyke, Nella, and Sarah A. Soule. 2002. "Structural Social Change and the Mobilizing Effect of Threat: Explaining Levels of Patriot and Militia Organizing in the United States." *Social Problems* 49 (4): 497–520. doi:10.1525/sp.2002.49.4.497.

Ward, Eric K. 2017. "Skin in the Game: How Antisemitism Animates White Nationalism." *Public Eye*, June 29. https://www.politicalresearch.org/2017/06/29/skin-in-the-game-how-antisemitism-animates-white-nationalism/.

Ward, Matthew. 2013. "Mobilising 'Minutemen': Predicting Public Support for Anti-Immigration Activism in the United States." *Sociological Research Online* 18 (4): 1–18. doi:10.5153/sro.3141.

Ward, Matthew. 2017. "Opportunity, Resources, and Threat: Explaining Local Nativist Organizing in the United States." *Sociological Perspectives* 60 (3): 459–478. doi:10.1177/0731121416655994.

Wendling, Mark. 2018. *Alt-Right: From 4chan to the White House.* London: Pluto Press.

Williams, Dana M. 2018. "Contemporary Anarchist and Anarchistic Movements." *Sociology Compass* 12 (6): 1–17.

Williams, Dana M. 2019. "Tactics: Conceptions of Social Change, Revolution, and Anarchist Organisation." In *The Palgrave Handbook of Anarchism*, edited by Carl Levy and Matthew S. Adams, 107–123. New York, NY: Palgrave.

Williams, J. Patrick. 2011. *Subcultural Theory: Traditions & Concepts.* Chichester: Polity Press.

Wood, Robert T. 1999. "The Indigenous, Nonracist Origins of the American Skinhead Subculture." *Youth & Society* 31 (2): 131–151. doi:10.1177/0044118X99031002001.

Zald, Meyer N., and Bert Useem. 1987. "Movement and Countermovement Interaction: Mobilization, Tactics and State Involvement." In *Social Movements in an Organizational Society: Collected Essays*, edited by Meyer N. Zald and John D. McCarthy. New Brunswick, NJ: Transaction Books.

6

THE ANARCHY POLICE (REVISITED)

A critical criminology of antifa

Antifa is self-defense. This is the position of militant antifascists in regard to the countermovement moves that they make in response to fascist threats. The threats outlined in the previous chapter are so significant in their intensity and immediacy that they warrant some form of defensive response (Maher 2010). The immediacy of supremacist threats faced by antifascists provides little opportunity for recourse to structural means of defense such as calling the police. Additionally, because much of the interaction between fascists and militant antifascists occurs outside of the purview of legal authorities, they are unlikely to intervene; and in the cases where they do, it is often to the detriment of antifascists. To complicate this dynamic further, the anti-authoritarian ideological orientation of most antifa activists discourages reliance on police and the state to intervene against fascists and encourages direct action; as the Anti-Racist Action and Torch Antifa Network point of unity says, "We don't rely on the cops or courts to do our work for us." In this context, militant antifascism becomes more than simply a social movement or subcultural phenomenon; it is a form of radical community protection and social control.

As radical activists, militant antifascists are critical of the structural role of police in society. Police are identified as enforcers of systems of domination through their use of force and selective enforcement of the law (Vitale 2017; Williams 2015). This perception is reinforced during interactions with police that are marked by activists' historically marginalized identities, subcultural affiliation, or protest repression. Antifa activists often experience criminalization and repression of their protest activity and accuse police of colluding with and being sympathetic to fascists. Under such circumstances, militant antifascists frame their actions as defensive because they perceive that they cannot rely on law enforcement for protection from fascist threat.

Ironically, the defensive activities engaged in by antifa activists replicate some of the duties of law enforcement. The protective work of antifa activists takes two distinct forms: preventative action and direct confrontation actions on the part of militant antifascists involve a series of activit ward off supremacist threats by serving as security personnel f people threatened by fascists. When antifa activists engage in direct ᴄᴏᴎᴛᴏᴎᴛᴀᴛᴉᴏᴎ of fascists, they are taking steps to remove an immediate fascist threat through verbal opposition or the physical use of force. These activities represent some of the illiberal aspects of militant antifascism (Bray 2017); however, the manner in which they are deployed and the function that they provide within subcultures and for the broader left are consistent with general anarchist principles of spontaneity, direct democracy, direct action, and prefigurative practice. As such, the proactive activity of militant antifascists presents an anti-authoritarian model for engaging in community protection that contributes to the theoretical development of anarchist criminology.

By taking on the investigative and protective activities of law enforcement in a radical, direct democratic manner, antifascist activists challenge the claim to a monopoly on the use of force by the state (Weber [1910] 1998). In doing so, the actions of antifa activists challenge the legitimacy of the state, which ultimately results in efforts to criminalize antifascism. By criminalizing antifa activism, the state not only reasserts its commitment to law and order, but also reaffirms its legitimacy to the exclusive use of force.

A critical criminology of antifa

An analysis of militant antifascism from an orthodox criminological perspective is relatively simple. Antifa activists are violent actors in society, a threat to norms of civility of protest in American society, and clearly engage in criminal activity. Recent criminological assessments of militant antifascism are relatively one-dimensional in their focus on the most spectacular displays of protest violence, and they argue that it may be understood as either a terrorist group or street gang (Pyrooz and Densley 2018; Short and Hughes 2018). The most cogent critique of this position has to date been historical rather than social scientific; focusing on the broad contours of antifascism as an ideological position (Copsey 2018) rather than the essence of militant antifascist organizational structure and activity. In addition to the sociological perspectives on social movements and subculture presented in this book, a critical, and specifically anarchist, criminological perspective presents a more nuanced understanding of the defensive character of antifascist confrontation.

Anarchist criminology

Although anarchists have been strong on critique of the criminal justice system, there has been relatively little theoretical or practical development of alternatives consistent with the ideology's call for prefigurative practice. The key exception to this is work on restorative justice (Pepinsky 1978; Pepinsky and Quinney 1991; Sullivan and Tifft 2010; L. Tifft and Sullivan 1980). This needs-based approach to resolving the conflict that arises out of the harm created by crime stresses addressing all parties involved in a criminal act – people who are harmed, people who have harmed, and the entire community. This approach rejects a system of justice based on punishment in favor of building strong community relationships central to the non-hierarchical vision anarchists hold of social organization.

Anarchist criminologists, however, rarely consider approaches to address issues of public order and safety as they occur, in part because this may require the use of force or assertion of power that is antithetical to anarchist values. The rare cases of research and theoretical work in this area are consistently rooted in a pacifist approach to maintaining social order (Niman 2011; Ferrell 2011). Anarchist practices of maintaining social order involve de-escalation of tension and conflict in a manner that is spontaneous, non-hierarchical, and collective. Individuals who become aggressive and disruptive are isolated by members of the community and encouraged to regain their composure (Niman 2011). Similarly, an anarchist practice of controlling the boundaries of an event can protect participants and outsiders from engaging in conflict and acts of aggression (Niman 2011; Ferrell 2011). The key anarchist principle in these approaches is that there is no formal structure that engages in social control. Participants are neither selected nor elected, but voluntarily join efforts at de-escalation; so theoretically, anyone is free to engage in such acts. These actions are temporally limited, and people who participate have no special power or status within the community. This approach generates three key conditions for proactive anarchist social control: it should be relatively spontaneous based on the disruptive event, it should be directly democratic and open to all in its structure, and it should provide no power to the individuals engaging in it beyond the immediate event. Finally, as a radical alternative to existing social and political structures, anarchist practice is designed to "prefigure" a model of a future society, often designed to build "dual power" that challenges existing institutions (Ferrell 2001; Graeber 2002; Shantz 2011).

Militant antifascism in the United States is primarily driven by an anarchist or anti-authoritarian ideology that seeks a broader economic, political, and social transformation. The defensive practices of antifa activists embody the principles of anarchism that many of them adhere to. This chapter also argues that by embodying these practices, militant antifascists present a model for maintaining community safety beyond the confines of existing state models of law enforcement and criminal justice. By challenging the state's role in community protection through the use of force, militant antifascists are subjected to criminalization and repression.

The prevention of threat

Much of the activity of militant antifascists is designed to preempt fascist activity, including the violence and threats presented in the previous chapter. A great deal of these types of actions involve relatively non-militant tactics such as intelligence gathering, education, and public shaming campaigns. The physical manifestation of preemptive, or preventative, activity involves the deployment of activists in order to protect individuals and spaces from potential or immediate threats posed by fascists.

The most visceral threat that fascists present is one of physical violence. It is at the core of their ideology and often manifests itself in the values of the sub-cultures that they are involved in or create (Berlet 1992; Blazak 2001; Bowen 2008; Burley 2017; Hamm 1993; Neiwert 2009). Mobilization and a show of force by antifa activists serves a dual purpose: protecting people who are threatened and potentially preventing supremacist violence. Militant antifascists often take on the responsibility of providing protection to individuals and households facing a fascist threat regardless of their ideological position or stance on the use of force or confrontation.

When fascists make direct threats against specific individuals, antifa activists will answer the call to assist in defending them. In some cases, people who are threatened will approach an antifa group; but in others, militant antifascists will reach out to the subjects of threats. When racist skinheads attacked a punk rock house party, Old City Antifa reached out to offer assistance. The residents asked for people to come to the house to provide protection in the event that fascists returned. The antifa activists found themselves among a motley crew of defenders, including relatively apolitical punks and a diverse crew of skinheads that included openly gay and African American participants. The residents of the house repeatedly thanked the antifa activists for answering their call for assistance, and indicated that this provided a kind of protection that the police could not.

The members of New City Antifa participated in a more elaborate protection plan for an activist who was the target of a threatening supremacist leafletting campaign. After militant antifascists successfully shut down a racist skinhead gathering, doxed a supremacist leader, and held a mass, non-violent unity rally, local fascists were looking for revenge. Unable to accurately identify members of the antifa group, they targeted a left-wing videographer who posted a video of the antifascist rally online. Supremacists posted flyers in the individual's neighborhood identifying him as "anti-white" and listing his home address. As discussed in the previous chapter, fascist doxing campaigns are not designed to leverage shame, but to indicate that supremacists know where a person lives and that they may be subject to violence. New City had a history of fascist violence, including attacks on antifascists, so this person contacted the antifa group seeking assistance. Members of New City Antifa and allies from an anarchist group developed a plan to provide overnight protection for the targeted household because this was determined to be the time of maximum risk of fascist attack. Militant antifascist activists mobilized a series of proactive measures to defend the home with activists stationed inside the house and on the front porch, vehicle-based surveillance of the blocks near the house, and patrols through the neighborhood. While this was probably the most elaborate defensive activity that I experienced, militant antifascists routinely employ at least one of the tactics described when protecting a person or household from fascist attack.

Preventative actions are also employed in the defense of spaces and events targeted by fascists. Militant antifascists frequently serve as formal and informal security forces with a visible presence that is designed to signal to potential fascist assailants that a gathering is not vulnerable to attack. One of the approaches to this kind of defense is mass mobilization of antifascists willing to confront supremacists who may turn up to subcultural or protest events. Informal militant antifascism regularly occurs in such contexts, especially in punk and skinhead scenes where rumors of fascist attendance at shows may be addressed by attendees preparing to confront them. Formal antifa groups also engage in mass spontaneous and planned defensive gatherings.

A notable example of impromptu defense by formal antifa groups occurred when members of Old City Antifa attended a regional gathering of antifascists in the Mid-Atlantic. Fascists had been actively organizing in the city where the gathering was taking place, and attending punk shows with the express intent of attacking participants in order to intimidate leftist elements in the scene. These supremacists indicated that they were going to attend a punk show that was coincidentally scheduled for the evening of the antifa gathering, but was not affiliated with the event, in part because at least one of the bands playing took an explicitly antifascist stance and had leftist skinheads as members. Show organizers reached out to local antifa activists for assistance with defense of the event, so many of the militant antifascists who attended the meeting mobilized to defend the show. Activists spent the evening inside the venue and in the adjacent parking lot preparing for possible confrontation with supremacists. A similar dynamic existed in New City where a regular ska music DJ night that was a reliable gathering for anti-racist skinheads and militant antifascist activists often presented an easy target for fascist threats and violence. Although the venue had paid security, this was supplemented by an unofficial security detail that consisted of anti-racist skinheads and antifa activists who maintained a regular presence outside to signal that any attempts to attack the event would be opposed.

These types of preventative mass gatherings are often supplemented by proactive patrols by militant antifascists of the area surrounding the event to explicitly identify fascist threats. Such activity expands the scope of antifascist protection beyond the immediate venue and operates as a means of potentially limiting confrontation and violence at the event itself. This tactic may be deployed in a number of scenarios ranging from individual protection, as described above, to subcultural and protest events. For example, the rally filmed by the videographer discussed above was a mass, non-militant protest against supremacist activity and organizing in New City. Security for the rally was coordinated by militant antifascists who organized patrols of the site and surrounding area in the event that supremacists chose to antagonize or threaten the event. This particular rally was organized in protest against a national gathering of white supremacists, which was expected to draw hundreds of attendees. The critical mass of supremacists in the city created the possibility that they may threaten the antifascist rally either in small numbers or en masse. Militant antifascists patrolled the perimeter of the park in which the protest rally was held with the intention of intervening if fascists arrived. If a fascist threat is identified, patrolling activists will confront it and contact others either for reinforcements or to prepare for mass defense.

This tactic, whether deployed to defend subcultural or protest events, shifts the location of conflict between fascists and antifascists. By confronting fascists in the street, antifa activists protect venues and individuals who are under threat. Additionally, patrols are a signal to fascists that their plans for intimidation or attack will be confronted by an expressly antifascist force. In doing so, patrols serve to enhance mass defensive gatherings.

Confrontation and conflict as defense

The mass gatherings and patrols described above are largely designed to inhibit confrontation and violence through displays of mass antifascist opposition. Just as with the discussion of tactics in Chapter 3, what makes these relatively non-militant actions militant is the possibility of confrontation. Antifa activists approach the situations described so far with the knowledge and preparedness that they may escalate into conflict. Militant antifascists do not shy away from confrontation or the use of force in opposition to fascist threat, which ultimately distinguishes them from other antifascist activists. For antifa activists, these confrontations are ultimately framed as defensive actions. Militant antifascists deploy force as a means of mediating or eliminating the types of fascist threats discussed in the previous chapter.

The most common type of defensive confrontation is spontaneous and represents an informal form of militant antifascism. These confrontations frequently take place in the subcultural spaces and contexts discussed in Chapters 4 and 5. Although they are spontaneous and informal, these clashes often represent a key aspect of militant antifascism as both a starting point for activism (see Helena's narrative in the previous chapter) and as a means of self-defense. A typical scenario involves fascists entering or being identified at a subcultural event, usually musical in nature, or space such as a bar, record or clothing store, or designated hangout. A group of antifascist-oriented individuals, sometimes affiliated with a formal group, will organize a response to the fascist presence that can range in size from a small group of people to the attendees of an entire venue addressing the potential threat. The initial confrontation will take the form of the fascist interlopers being commanded, sometimes quite forcefully, to leave. Because fascists often attend such events specifically to demonstrate some form of aggression and intimidation (Blazak 2001; Bowen 2008; Hamm 1993; see also Chapter 5), they are unlikely to leave; even less so if asked politely. This oppositional stance on the part of fascists escalates the conflict to necessitate the use of force to remove them, resulting in fights between supremacists and their antifascist opposition or the forcible ejection of the fascists. In a best-case scenario, the fascists leave and the event continues; in a worst-case scenario, police arrive and the event is shut down. In either case, the action is largely viewed by participants as a defense of the space and ideological integrity of the subculture.

Members of formal antifa groups are regularly at the vanguard of these informal confrontations. Militant antifascists generally have an acute awareness of the often obscure or covert signifiers of fascist affiliation (Miller-Idriss 2019) and the identities of fascist organizers, which gives them an advantage in identifying fascists in subcultural or public spaces. Old City Antifa was founded in part because its original members were consistently moved to confront low-key fascist presence in social settings. Individuals who displayed fascist tattoos and symbols on clothing were consistently questioned and challenged; in some cases, resulting in violent conflict. New City Antifa members engaged in similar approaches to addressing potential fascists within the city's punk, skinhead, and metal subcultures, as well as its soccer supporter scene. Individuals attending local soccer matches and other soccer supporter events who were perceived to be fascist would be vigorously questioned and at times expelled under threat of force in order to assert this particular subculture and space as antifascist, as well as maintain the safety of participants.

Most of these types of conflicts are routine elements of subcultural participation and take the form of "everyday antifascism" (Bray 2017; Burley 2017). Because such clashes take place within the context of everyday activities for the antifa activists involved, they rarely are discussed outside of affinity group or activist interactions. South Side Chicago Anti-Racist Action, however, publicly detailed one such confrontation that resulted in the hospitalization of a fascist punk with known ties to the Proud Boys, as well as the Portland-based Volksfront International, who had claimed to be responsible for shooting and paralyzing an antifascist activist. Antifa activists identified the fascist in a Chicago bar, and the ensuing confrontation led to a violent conflict.

> [The supremacist] was confronted by Chicago antifascists who believe that neo-nazis (sic) are not to be debated with, but rather pushed out of any community or scene. If someone's beliefs are based of (sic) the oppression of others, that belief poses a bigger threat to our society than the discomfort or pain experienced by those who hold them.
>
> *(South Side Anti-Racist Action 2017)*

Of course, the most well-known confrontations between fascists and militant antifascists are the public skirmishes that occur as a result of supremacist events. Public perception of antifa activism is largely guided by these conflicts and the sensational images circulated in mass and social media, as well as by antifascists and their supporters. The defensive orientation of antifascist confrontation is evident in the framing of counter-protests. The language of defense is consistently deployed when mobilizing against fascists; evident in posts to blogs and social media calling for protesters to "Defend Portland," "Defend the Bay [Area]," even "Defend Appalachia" from fascist threat. For militant antifascists, these clashes are both a strategic countermovement maneuver designed to demobilize their opponents (Zald and Useem 1987) and a response to the threat of fascist activity (see Chapter 5). Clashes with supremacist protesters are designed to break up the fascist event and lead to the dispersal of its participants.

Some of the most high-profile skirmishes between fascists and antifa activists demonstrate this effect. From the "Battle of York" in 2002 where militant anti-fascists, including members of Old City Antifa, were joined by community members to disrupt a rally by the National Alliance and Creativity Movement (Bray 2017) to the ostensible "March 4 Trump" in Berkeley in 2017, which was inundated with fascist and far-right attendees (NoCARA 2017), clashes between opposing protesters have served to effectively end far-right mobilizations. In York, PA militant antifascists circumvented a police cordon, with the assistance of local residents, to disrupt the fascist rally. By using this tactic, and with the support of the community, the fascists were dispersed and the rally's attendees were forced to flee the scene with antifa activists and residents in pursuit (Bray 2017). Militant antifascists in Berkeley preempted the planned far-right rally by occupying its location and clashing with far-right activists, which effectively led to the right-wing event's cancellation (NoCARA 2017). Clashes between antifa activists and fascist rally attendees serve to disrupt the intended purpose of far-right rallies and their long-term organizing functions, which effectively constitutes a form of repression in a countermovement dynamic. By utilizing force to disrupt fascist rallies and events, militant antifascists are effectively engaging in an activity that mirrors the repressive actions of the state in the interest of maintaining civil order and adherence to legal principles (Bourne 2011; della Porta 2008; Earl 2007; Gillham 2011; Noakes, Klocke, and Gillham 2005; Starr, Fernandez, and Scholl 2011). As anti-authoritarians, antifa activists engage in repression to demobilize an opposing movement in the long term and ensure the immediate safety of threatened populations and spaces in the short term.

Confrontations also serve a defensive function by focusing fascist violence on militant antifascists and away from vulnerable demonstrators or populations. The starkest example of this occurred at the now infamous "Unite the Right" rally in Charlottesville, VA where non-militant protesters, many of whom were people of color, were protected from an attack by fascist protesters by militant antifascists (Goodman 2017). In an interview just days after the rally, renowned scholar and activist, Cornel West summarized the defensive dynamic:

> those 20 of us who were standing, many of them clergy, we would have been crushed like cockroaches if it were not for the anarchists and the anti-fascists who approached, over 300, 350 anti-fascists. We just had 20. And we're singing "This Little Light of Mine," you know what I mean? So … the anti-fascists, and then, crucial, the anarchists, because they saved our lives, actually. We would have been completely crushed, and I'll never forget that.
>
> *(Goodman 2017)*

A similar dynamic occurred in Portland. OR on May Day in 2019 when fascists aligned with Patriot Prayer attacked revelers at Cider Riot, a bar that regularly hosted antifascist events. Clashes between the fascist attackers and militant antifascist defenders allowed time for more vulnerable people to enter the bar for safety. The fascists were kept at bay by militant resistance and ultimately driven off (Anon 2019). In this case, both the physical and spatial threat of fascist violence was addressed by confrontational resistance.

When militant antifascists engage in confrontational and violent tactics, they are understood as defensive moves. By virtue of their ideology, fascists represent a unique threat to specific individuals and social spaces. This ideological position, coupled with a predominant culture of oppositional defiance results in a dynamic where fascists ignore and even scoff at attempts at de-escalation and non-confrontational forms of resistance. The tactics discussed in this chapter represent an attempt by antifa activists to ensure the safety of individuals, spaces, subcultures, events, and communities from fascist threat. Militant antifascists engage in a number of preemptive practices that are designed to provide security. What makes these largely non-violent activities militant is the preparedness of participants to engage in confrontation or violence should the need arise. The tactical deployment of confrontation serves to protect spaces and individuals from fascist violence. In this regard, antifa activists serve as a defense for subcultures and activist communities. This dynamic allows us to analyze militant antifascism as a prefigurative form of radical self-defense.

Anarchist self-defense

This chapter began with a simple assertion: antifa is self-defense. From preemptive activities such as providing protection to directly engaging with fascist violence, militant antifascists provide a form of protection from threats posed by supremacists. Of course, there is already a structural means that people can resort to for protection from threats, the police. Ostensibly, the role of law enforcement is in part to ensure the safety of the public (Moore and Kelling 1983; Moskos 2008). For antifa activists this is as much an impractical proposal as it is an affront to their ideological sensibilities. In response, militant antifascists indicate that their actions are both a pragmatic response to the immediacy and intensity of fascist threat as well as one that is consistent with their radical, anti-authoritarian vision of "community self-defense" (Clark 2018). In this sense, militant antifascist activity serves as a means of social control and security based on anarchist principles of spontaneity, direct democracy, and direct action.

As a practical matter, relying on the police to intervene when faced with a fascist threat is simply unrealistic. Police response to emergency calls varies greatly, and more often than not, they arrive on the scene after an incident has occurred, even when it is considered "in progress," for a number of structural and personal reasons (Moskos 2008). In the scenarios described above and in the previous chapter, by the time police have arrived to a call for service, it is unlikely that they will be able to intervene to prevent fascist violence because it will have already occurred, and likely been dealt with. Such was the case with the attack on Cider Riot described above where police reportedly did not arrive for over an hour after the incident occurred despite being stationed only blocks away from the scene (Anon 2019). This dynamic is further complicated by the reality that fascist threats and violence often occur within subcultural spaces, which operate outside of the observation and control of official regulation (Ferrell 1997a; Ferrell 2001). Essentially, calling the police to mediate an unwelcome fascist presence or in response to violence has the potential to negatively impact the subculture by at best resulting in the cancellation of the event and at worst the closure of an essential venue. Police intervention at protest events generally results in social movement repression, especially for the most "radical" or "countercultural" factions at such events (della Porta 2008; Earl 2007; King 2013; Kriesi et al. 1995). Militant antifascist counter-protesters routinely face arrest and aggressive dispersal by police in protest situations against fascists where no confrontation or violence has occurred (Flynn 2018; Wilson 2018). To further underscore the futility of antifa activists relying on law enforcement to intervene on their behalf in conflicts with supremacists, they point to evidence of cooperation, collaboration, and even potential collusion between fascists and police (Knox 2019; Levin 2018; Shepherd 2019; Unicorn Riot 2018). This presents a conundrum for activists who face an immediate and serious threat of violence: how do they ensure their safety when they cannot credibly rely on existing structures and processes in a manner that is consistent with their values? Antifa activists in effect become the protective force for their subculture and activist community.

By acting to protect vulnerable people and spaces and employing force, militant antifascists simultaneously usurp the role of law enforcement as protectors of safety and social order as well as challenge the legitimacy of the state's claim to a monopoly on that role and the use of force. These actions on the part of antifa activists, however, do not constitute an authoritarian imposition of their will (Beinart 2017); but rather a series of prefigurative practices that are consistent with non-hierarchical principles of "self-help" (Barclay 1990; Black 1983, 2004). The confrontations described in this book constitute a form of "moralistic violence" designed to maintain order through the use of force, which is ultimately structurally similar to law (Black 2004). The means by which militant antifascists organize and deploy these acts of force reinforces their anarchist quality.

Anarchist theory has long valued spontaneity in opposition to the rigidity of the restrictions placed on individuals by social institutions such as the family, religion, the state, and work (Ferrell 2001). Spontaneous actions in the interest of collective and social order as well as the safety of individuals in non-hierarchical spaces and activities are therefore theorized as anarchist forms of social control (Ferrell 2011; Niman 2011). The informal, and in some cases even formal, antifascist activities described above reflect this quality of spontaneity. Certainly, the militant antifascist defense of spaces where fascists are present, even when performed by members of formal antifa groups, are relatively spontaneous. After all, who can predict what event or social space fascists might choose to attend? Even when such predictions are possible, as was the case when Old City Antifa members and other antifa activists stood on guard for fascists threatening a punk show described earlier, militant antifascists may be called upon at the last minute to intervene. Confrontations with fascists in subcultural spaces are rarely preplanned or highly organized because they often appear without the prior knowledge of event organizers or participants, generally intent on intimidation or violence (Blazak 2001; Bowen 2008). In these situations, confrontation is organized suddenly and informally to repel the fascist threat. Rather than following a set of bureaucratic procedures or relying on law enforcement to intervene, decisions are made in the moment about the most appropriate and effective means of maintaining order and people's safety. By acting spontaneously, the antifascist action is performed in a manner that prevents any individual or group from holding unwarranted power in this situation because participation in the confrontation is open to anyone. Although the use of force may be an exertion of power, it is one that is temporary and situational. The individuals engaging in militant antifascist confrontation and use of force are given no special status or social power, and their activity is certainly not institutionalized in any form, which gives them no overarching authority (Bakunin 1970; Barclay 1990; Ferrell 2011; Niman 2011). In general, power is decentralized because it is temporary and not invested in a durable institution. As a form of anarchist practice, militant antifascist confrontation is spontaneous and decentralized thereby ensuring that authority and power are not entrenched.

Even though the actions described in this chapter are spontaneous and decentralized, they are not chaotic or disorganized. Consistent with anarchist principles, the decision-making processes of antifa groups and activists are directly democratic. Anarchists advocate directly democratic deliberative processes based on the principle of "self-management" in which workers and communities take control of the processes of production and life in general (Guérin 1970). Consistent with other examples of anarchist social control and defense (Ferrell 2011; Niman 2011), antifa actions, particularly spontaneous mass ones, are open to anyone who is willing to participate in them, while simultaneously not compelling anyone to engage in them. The mass confrontations of fascists in subcultural spaces described above are functionally inclusive of everyone in the space who wishes to confront the immediate fascist threat. Actions that require a greater level of organization, such as protection of an individual or securing a space under fascist threat, are also the product of direct democratic decision-making on the part of the groups and individuals involved. Formal antifascist groups and organizations are less open in terms of membership because of security concerns stemming from threats posed by fascists and law enforcement; however, their deliberative processes are equally non-hierarchical and directly democratic. In the case of the protection New City Antifa provided for the videographer threatened by supremacists, the members of the group and their allies met collectively to decide whether to provide assistance, what strategies should be employed, how to implement them, and who would take on specific roles. These decisions were made through formal votes of the membership which were unanimous. Individual roles in the action were assumed voluntarily by antifa activists based on a number of factors including, but not limited to, individuals' ability, skills, and willingness to participate. Because antifa affinity groups have no formal leadership, all decisions are made collectively by the group. This process is consistent whether in small, local groups or regional and national organizations. In the spirit of non-hierarchal direct democracy, militant antifascist deliberative bodies, regardless of scale, strive for consensus or a super-majority to ratify decisions. Individuals who dissent from collective decisions are free to decline participation. By embodying the core anarchist principle of direct democratic decision-making, antifa activists are effectively prefiguring an alternative model of organization and applying it to "community self-defense" against fascist threat. Finally, such deliberative processes reflect broader radical and prefigurative social movement practices (Fitzgerald and Rodgers 2000; Franks 2018; Polletta 2007).

The principle of direct action is fundamentally embodied in the militant antifascist defense from supremacist threat. While the concept of direct action is utilized by a variety of contemporary social movements, especially those that are classified as countercultural or radical (Fitzgerald and Rodgers 2000; Jasper 1997; Kriesi et al. 1995; Polletta 2007), it is a key pillar of anarchist activism. Because anarchists categorically reject enacting change through existing structures and mechanisms, they prioritize forms of activism that directly and radically transform social institutions and practices (Franks 2018; Ordóñez 2018). These forms of direct action are specifically designed to reject the authority of the state and other structures of power. Rather than relying on government intervention or the slow process of electoral reform, anarchists advocate for the construction of social structures that are designed to supplant them in the present as a foundation for future social change (Ehrlich 1996; Ferrell 2001; Ordóñez 2018; Shantz 2011; Williams and Lee 2012; Williams 2018). From this perspective, militant antifascist confrontation is a form of direct action. In its simplest form, militant confrontation is a pragmatic response to a distinct need. As discussed in this and the previous chapter, the immediacy of fascist threat creates a protective void that must be filled. Antifa activists take on the protective role of law enforcement in a manner that reflects their radical ideology and non-hierarchical values. By providing protective services for people, events, and spaces, militant antifascists directly intervene against supremacists without "outsourcing" the use of force to the state (Rimel 2017). In doing so, militants take on the responsibility for their own safety and that of the communities of which they are a part. Additionally, as a form of direct action, antifa activism serves as a means of personal empowerment (Clark 2018). Militant antifascism demonstrates that subcultures, communities, and movements can self-organize for their own security without reliance on the state.

Anarchist theory broadly, and anarchist criminological theory specifically, has prioritized critique of the state and the ways in which it constructs and controls crime (Ferrell 1998; Pepinsky 1978; L. L. Tifft 1979); however, there has been very little theoretical development to answer this critique. Groundbreaking anarchist criminologists have been at the forefront of developing processes of restorative justice as a remedy to the punitive aspects of the criminal justice system (Pepinsky and Quinney 1991; Sullivan and Tifft 2010), but these do not address the issue of how to proactively tackle immediate concerns of public order and safety. Those who have theorized practical responses do so in a context that is already ideologically predisposed to non-hierarchical resolution of disputes and from a pacifist perspective (Ferrell 2011; Niman 2011). Militant antifascists confront an ideologically oppositional threat to public safety with the possibility or direct application of force. They do so in a manner that is decidedly non-hierarchical and decentralized, which reflects an anti-authoritarian orientation. The confrontations described in this chapter, and generally in this book, are spontaneous and directly democratic forms of direct action that are consistent with anarchist principles. As such, they represent a theoretical contribution to anarchist criminology by proposing a framework for self-defense outside of existing structures. From this perspective, militancy not only challenges the state's claim to a legitimate monopoly on the use of force, but also prefigures a framework for community safety and self-defense that is an alternative to existing police structures.

The criminalization of antifa

While antifa activists assert that their actions are a form of self-defense that may be analyzed as justifiable "moralistic violence" (Black 2004), the state response to militant antifascism has been marked by repression. Antifa activism is stigmatized by being framed as inherently criminal; and, therefore, a legitimate target for harsh forms of state repression. As this chapter has indicated, militant antifascists assert the use of force in repressive and defensive activity against fascists, which usurps the state's claim to a monopoly on violence. They do so in a manner that is driven by and reflects anarchist principles which represent a radical framework for proactive community defense. This radical challenge to the legitimacy of the state represents the true threat that militant antifascism poses.

The social movement militancy of antifa activists has been alternately portrayed as gang or terrorist activity by government officials and agencies (Porter 2017; Meyer 2017). Such claims focus entirely on the limited acts of violence committed by militant antifascists and ignore the countermovement dynamics that are the subject of this book.[1] By focusing on violence, assertions by political leaders and state agencies are consistent with a broader pattern of social movement framing. Mainstream media contributes to this framing process by constructing a "protest paradigm" where "the press emphasizes the negative, violent, and irrational elements of protest and protesters while legitimating figures of authority by quoting them and therefore tacitly supporting their accounting of events" (Corrigall-Brown and Wilkes 2012, 224). Framing protest movements as violent or disruptive, as well as protesters as "freaks" are key strategies for discrediting participants and challenging the legitimacy of their claims (Boykoff 2006). For militant antifascists who assert that their actions are defensive, such processes serve to undermine the claim of self-help. The portrayal of antifa activism as criminal gang or terrorist activity serves as a *criminalization frame* that associates a social movement with non-protest oriented antisocial criminal activity as a means of discrediting, delegitimizing, and deprecating protest activity; ultimately justifying repression.

Repression is a common aspect of the dynamic between social movements and the state, especially for radical or countercultural movements (della Porta 1995; Earl 2003; King 2013; Kriesi et al. 1995). Police have largely responded aggressively to militant antifascist mobilizations even when they have been relatively non-confrontational and non-violent. Some of the most aggressive repression of militant antifascists has occurred in Portland, OR where police have repeatedly used force to disperse militant antifascist protesters in situations where no violence or conflict has occurred. On June 4, 2017, fascists gathered ostensibly under the guise of a "Free Speech Trump Rally." This event occurred just over one week after Jeremy Christian, an attendee at previous fascist rallies in the city, fatally stabbed two people and seriously injured a third on a light rail train when they confronted his harassment of two young women of color, one of whom was wearing a hijab (Wamsley 2017). Despite pressure from antifascist and other community activists, rally organizers chose to proceed with their event, which motivated extensive opposition. Three counter-protests were organized to surround the fascist rally; two decidedly non-militant and one that would create space for militant antifascists. The day was a major victory for antifascists of all stripes due to its mass mobilization and largely non-violent opposition of supremacists. At the conclusion of the fascist rally, Portland police summarily declared the counter-protest an unlawful assembly, attempted to disperse antifascist counter-protesters using "chemical and impact munitions," and engaged in mass detention and arrests based on ideology (ACLU 2017; Rose City Antifa 2017; Templeton 2018). This case established a pattern of police response to antifascist protest in the city culminating in an aggressive dispersal of counter-protesters on August 4, 2018 during which an antifascist protester was struck in the head by a projectile fired by police (Wilson 2018). While this has been some of the most extreme and consistent repression of antifascist mobilization, it is also indicative of a broader pattern of police response. The repression deployed against militant antifascists is not only disproportionate based on the level of violence that they employ, but it is also unique in that it involves state intervention into a conflict between opposing movements effectively for the protection of fascists.

The criminalization frame justifies repression of social movements by leveraging the violence and disruption frames (Boykoff 2006) to portray movement participants as lawbreakers. Police use of force against individuals who are perceived to be criminal is often considered legitimate, particularly by individuals who have an authoritarian or right-wing ideological orientation (Arthur and Case 1994; Barkan and Cohn 1998; Perkins and Bourgeois 2006; Gerber and Jackson 2017). Yet, the scale of repression wielded against militant antifascists is disproportionate to the extent of violence they engage in; more so when placed in the context of countermovement response to fascist threats and use of violence. Police response to militant antifascists without a concomitant approach to fascists becomes a functional support for one side in the dynamic between opposing movements. From Huntington Beach, CA to New York, fascists have attacked antifascist counter-protesters with impunity (Brazil 2017; Moynihan and Winston 2018). Police intervention and criminal prosecution in both of these cases only occurred after public outrage forced law enforcement to act. In Portland, OR police stood by as a fascist march attacked antifascist protestors resulting in four people being hospitalized. When law enforcement finally declared a riot, they turned their force toward the antifascist victims of violence rather than the fascist perpetrators (Benderev 2018). From a critical criminological perspective, the actions of police in response to antifa activism are unsurprising. The application of the law is viewed as unequal because it reflects the existing dynamics of power (Chambliss 1975; Ferrell 1998; Pepinsky 1978; Quinney 1974; L. L. Tifft 1979). In their radicalism, militant antifascists explicitly challenge those dynamics and institutions of power. By engaging in violent conflict with fascists, antifa activists assert a claim to the use of legitimate force. This claim challenges the power and authority of police, and ultimately the state, which designates antifa activists as a threat rather than fascists who frequently express a populist frame in support of police and the abstract power of the state (Berlet 2004a; Paxton 2004).

It is precisely this populist framing that provides a pretext for the official criminalization of antifa activism in the form of legislative moves and official declarations by right-wing politicians such as Senator Ted Cruz and President Trump (Aleem 2019; Sunshine 2019a). Militant antifascists make a convenient scapegoat for mainstream politicians seeking to mobilize conservative constituencies and fascist movements looking to make a populist appeal. The defensive use of force by antifascists discussed in this and the preceding chapter is framed as offensive by far-right actors who employ a "victimization" frame that presents them as underdogs (Berbrier 2000). Because fascists utilize a populist frame that depicts them as patriotic American activists (Berlet and Lyons 2000; Paxton 2004), attacks against them can be portrayed as unnecessarily aggressive, authoritarian, and dangerous (Beinart 2017). This maneuver allows fascists to build structural ties with mainstream politicians and legitimize their movement by aligning with conservative concerns (Vysotsky and Madfis 2014). Such an alignment then serves as a means of not only criminalizing antifascism, but also a broad swath of activism on the mainstream left (Sunshine 2019a). As antifa activists assert their right to engage in militant self-defense, they are further criminalized precisely because they position themselves in radical opposition to normative values of civility and the legitimacy of the state monopoly on the use of force.

The power of government is effectively defined by its ability to maintain a monopoly on the legitimate use of force within the territory under its control. "The state is considered the sole source of the 'right' to use violence" (Weber [1910] 1998, 78). In an ironic tautology, challenges to the state's assertion of the use of force are criminalized and subjected to the power of the state, which legitimizes the initial assertion of monopoly of that right. By serving as a defensive structure within subcultures and leftist spaces, militant antifascists assert a legitimacy to the use of force that exists outside of the boundaries of existing legal structures. As discussed in this chapter, militant antifascists perform the defensive and repressive functions of the state, which ultimately serve as a potential model for such activities in a non-hierarchical social order. Since the subjects of antifascist violence are fascist activists and organizers, the societal danger that the movement poses is functionally limited. Because of this dynamic, militant antifascism is not so much a challenge to the norms of civility in discourse and social movement activism, but to the very essence of the state. It is this defiance of the legitimacy of the state that makes antifa activism truly anarchic.

The anarchy police re-revisited

In light of the threats posed by fascists discussed in Chapter 5, militant antifascist practice is framed as a defensive position to protect activists and others from fascist violence. The confrontational activity of militant antifascists serves two key functions: preemption and repression of fascist activity. Antifa activists actively offer support to those in need when they learn of fascist threats or potential attacks. These defensive moves can take the form of spontaneous, informal antifascist mobilizations or the formal work of providing security services. Confrontational tactics are designed to demobilize fascist activity and ultimately to repress the movement in its nascent stages. In providing protection and suppressing fascist activity, militant antifascists take on activities that are reserved exclusively for the state and its law enforcement arm. The actions of antifa activists, therefore, represent a type of radical alternative model of "community self-defense" rooted in anarchist and anti-authoritarian principles (Clark 2018; Niman 2011). It is precisely this radical practice of defensive force that represents the threat of antifa activism in American society because it challenges the state's monopoly on the use of force, which drives campaigns to criminalize antifascism.

The confrontational tactics of militant antifascists may be understood as a form of "moralistic violence" (Black 2004) designed to maintain social order, but outside of the legitimate organs of the state. As such, it serves as a means of demonstrating a prefigurative practice of community defense that represents key aspects of radical, anarchist, and anti-authoritarian ideals. The militant antifascist practices described in this chapter, and this book as a whole, are frequently spontaneous, decentralized, and directly democratic. Spontaneity is evident in the practices of "everyday antifascism" (Bray 2017; Burley 2017) or in the informal antifascism demonstrated in subcultural responses to fascist incursion. Even formal antifa activity contains elements of spontaneity in that activists are open to mobilization with little notice, or may act as the vanguard in acts of informal resistance. Antifa activism is decentralized because it is ultimately open to anyone. Informal forms of confrontation are open to everyone who chooses to engage in them. There is no formal leadership in such actions and any authority or power is temporary and doesn't extend beyond that particular moment. Formal antifa groups are intentionally non-hierarchical and operate on direct democratic principles at the local, regional, and even national levels. Direct democracy is also practiced in informal antifascism as decisions about how best to address fascist threats are made on the spot by people in a space or subculture. By maintaining spontaneity, decentralization, and direct democratic practice, militant antifascists present an alternative framework for exerting force as a means of community protection.

It is precisely this radical challenge to the state's monopoly to the use of force that drives the hostility toward and attempted criminalization of militant antifascism. Attempts to label antifa activism as a form of gang or terrorist activity are designed to delegitimize not only the actions of militant antifascists, but also the prefigurative practices of self-defense that they engage in. These representations of antifa activism are consistent with the "protest paradigm" of media framing that serves to delegitimize social movements by presenting them as violent, disruptive freaks (Boykoff 2006; Corrigall-Brown and Wilkes 2012). The focus on antifa violence additionally serves to construct a criminalization frame where a social movement is associated with non-protest forms of antisocial criminal activity. These framing strategies serve to justify the repression of antifascist activity and the state's assertion of the use of force. Ironically, by engaging in criminalization of antifascism, politicians and scholars reinforce the victimization frame deployed by fascist movements to garner sympathy and legitimize their activity and ideology. If antifa activism is a radical form of self-defense, then it is in a "three-way fight" against the fascist movement and the state (Burley 2017; Clark 2018).

Note

1 The focus on antifascist violence is particularly disingenuous in light of the scope and scale of fascist violence. While antifascist activists clearly engage in acts of protest and confrontational violence against fascists, it rarely exceeds acts of simple assault. In comparison, fascists have a track record of engaging in acts of fatal violence against both antifascists and people whom they target for elimination that is described throughout this book. The justification for the criminalization of militant antifascism under the guise of addressing "antifa violence" draws a false equivalence between the eliminationist violence of fascist movements and the defensive violence of antifascists that ultimately serves to empower and embolden the far-right and the state (Sunshine 2019a, 2019b; Vysotsky 2017).

Works cited

ACLU. 2017. "Analyzing the Police Response to the June 4th Protests in Portland." *ACLU of Oregon*. https://www.aclu-or.org/en/news/analyzing-police-response-june-4th-protests-portland.

Aleem, Zeeshan. 2019. "Ahead of a Far-Right Rally in Portland, Trump Tweets a Warning to Antifa." *Vox*. https://www.vox.com/policy-and-politics/2019/8/17/20810221/portland-rally-donald-trump-alt-right-proud-boys-antifa-terror-organization.

Anon. 2019. "The Cider Riot Rules: One Person's May Day Account." *Idavox*. http://idavox.com/index.php/2019/05/09/the-cider-riot-rules-one-persons-may-day-account/.

Arthur, John A., and Charles E. Case. 1994. "Race, Class and Support for Police Use of Force." *Crime, Law and Social Change* 21 (2): 167–182. doi:10.1007/BF01307910.

Bakunin, Mikhail A. 1970. *God and the State*. New York, NY: Dover Publications.

Barclay, Harold B. 1990. *People Without Government: An Anthropology of Anarchy*. Seattle, WA: Left Bank Books.

Barkan, Steven E., and Steven F. Cohn. 1998. "Racial Prejudice and Support by Whites for Police Use of Force: A Research Note." *Justice Quarterly* 15 (4): 743–753. doi:10.1080/07418829800093971.

Beinart, Peter. 2017. "The Rise of the Violent Left." *The Atlantic*, September. https://www.theatlantic.com/magazine/archive/2017/09/the-rise-of-the-violent-left/534192/.

Benderev, Chris. 2018. "Police Declare a Riot After Far-Right and Antifa Groups Clash in Portland, Ore." *NPR*. https://www.npr.org/2018/07/01/625095869/police-declare-a-riot-after-far-right-and-antifa-groups-clash-in-portland.

Berbrier, Mitch. 2000. "The Victim Ideology of White Supremacists and White Separatists in the United States." *Sociological Focus* 33 (2): 175–191.

Berlet, Chip. 1992. "Fascism!" *Political Research Associates*. https://www.politicalresearch.org/1992/09/28/fascism.

Berlet, Chip. 2004a. "Mapping the Political Right: Gender and Race Oppression in Right-Wing Movements." In *Home-Grown Hate: Gender and Organized Racism*, edited by Abby L. Ferber, 19–48. New York, NY: Routledge.

Berlet, Chip, and Mathew N. Lyons. 2000. *Right-Wing Populism in America: Too Close for Comfort*. New York, NY: Guilford Press.

Black, Donald. 1983. "Crime as Social Control." *American Sociological Review* 48 (1): 34–45. doi:10.2307/2095143.

Black, Donald. 2004. "Violent Structures." In *Violence: From Theory to Research*, edited by Margaret A. Zahn, Henry H. Brownstein, and Shelly L. Jackson, 145–158. Newark, NJ: LexisNexis Anderson Publishers.

Blazak, Randy. 2001. "White Boys to Terrorist Men: Target Recruitment of Nazi Skinheads." *American Behavioral Scientist* 44 (6): 982–1000.

Bourne, Kylie. 2011. "Commanding and Controlling Protest Crowds." *Critical Horizons* 12 (2): 189–210. doi:10.1558/crit.v12i2.189.

Bowen, Derek. 2008. *"Patterns of Skinhead Violence."* Ph.D. Dissertation, Durham, NH: University of New Hampshire.

Boykoff, Jules. 2006. "Framing Dissent: Mass-Media Coverage of the Global Justice Movement." *New Political Science* 28 (2): 201–228. doi:10.1080/07393140600679967.

Bray, Mark. 2017. *Antifa: The Antifascist Handbook*. Brooklyn, NY: Melville House Publishing.

Brazil, Ben. 2017. "Violence Breaks Out at Pro-Trump Rally in Huntington Beach." *Los Angeles Times*, March 25. https://www.latimes.com/socal/daily-pilot/news/tn-dpt-me-0326-maga-march-20170325-story.html.

Burley, Shane. 2017. *Fascism Today – What It Is and How to End It*. Chico, CA: AK Press.

Chambliss, William J. 1975. "Toward a Political Economy of Crime." *Theory and Society* 2 (1): 149–170. doi:10.1007/BF00212732.

Clark, J. 2018. "Three-Way Fight: Revolutionary Anti-Fascism and Armed Self-Defense." In *Setting Sights: Histories and Reflections on Community Armed Self-Defense*, edited by Scott Crow, 49–67. Oakland, CA: PM Press.

Copsey, Nigel. 2018. "Militant Antifascism: An Alternative (Historical) Reading." *Society* 55 (3): 243–247. doi:10.1007/s12115-018-0245-y.

Corrigall-Brown, Catherine, and Rima Wilkes. 2012. "Picturing Protest: The Visual Framing of Collective Action by First Nations in Canada." *American Behavioral Scientist* 56 (2): 223–243. doi:10.1177/0002764211419357.

della Porta, Donatella. 1995. *Social Movements, Political Violence, and the State: A Comparative Analysis of Italy and Germany*. Cambridge: Cambridge University Press.

della Porta, Donatella. 2008. "Research on Social Movements and Political Violence." *Qualitative Sociology* 31 (3): 221–230.

Earl, Jennifer. 2003. "Tanks, Tear Gas, and Taxes: Toward a Theory of Movement Repression." *Sociological Theory* 21 (1): 44–68. doi:10.1111/1467-9558.00175.

Earl, Jennifer. 2007. "The Cultural Consequences of Social Movements." In *The Blackwell Companion to Social Movements*, 508–530. Malden, MA: Wiley-Blackwell. doi:10.1002/9780470999103.ch22.

Ehrlich, Howard J. 1996. *Reinventing Anarchy, Again*. San Francisco, CA: AK Press.

Ferrell, Jeff. 1997a. "Youth, Crime, and Cultural Space." *Social Justice* 24 (4): 21–38.

Ferrell, Jeff. 1998. "Against the Law: Anarchist Criminology." *Social Anarchism* 24: 5–15.

Ferrell, Jeff. 2001. *Tearing Down the Streets: Adventures in Urban Anarchy*. New York, NY: Palgrave.

Ferrell, Jeff. 2011. "Corking as Community Policing." *Contemporary Justice Review* 14 (1): 95–98. doi:10.1080/10282580.2011.541079.

Fitzgerald, Kathleen J., and Diane M. Rodgers. 2000. "Radical Social Movement Organizations: A Theoretical Model." *Sociological Quarterly* 41 (4): 573–592.

Flynn, Meagan. 2018. "Georgia Police Invoke Law Made for KKK to Arrest Anti-Racism Protesters." *Washington Post*, April 23, sec. Morning Mix. https://www.washingtonpost.com/news/morning-mix/wp/2018/04/23/georgia-police-invoke-anti-mask-law-made-for-kkk-to-arrest-racism-protesters/.

Franks, Benjamin. 2018. "Prefiguration." In *Anarchism: A Conceptual Approach*, edited by Benjamin Franks, Nathan Jun, and Leonard Williams, 28–43. New York, NY: Routledge.

Gerber, Monica M., and Jonathan Jackson. 2017. "Justifying Violence: Legitimacy, Ideology and Public Support for Police Use of Force." *Psychology, Crime & Law* 23 (1): 79–95. doi:10.1080/1068316X.2016.1220556.

Gillham, Patrick F. 2011. "Securitizing America: Strategic Incapacitation and the Policing of Protest Since the 11 September 2001 Terrorist Attacks." *Sociology Compass* 5 (7): 636–652. doi:10.1111/j.1751-9020.2011.00394.x.

Goodman, Amy. 2017. "Cornel West & Rev. Traci Blackmon: Clergy in Charlottesville Were Trapped by Torch-Wielding Nazis." *Democracy Now!*https://www.democracynow.org/2017/8/14/cornel_west_rev_toni_blackmon_clergy.

Guérin, Daniel. 1970. *Anarchism: From Theory to Practice*. New York, NY: Monthly Review Press.

Hamm, Mark S. 1993. *American Skinheads: The Criminology and Control of Hate Crime*. Westport, CT: Praeger.

Jasper, James M. 1997. *The Art of Moral Protest: Culture, Biography, and Creativity in Social Movements*. Chicago, IL: University of Chicago Press.

King, Mike. 2013. "Disruption Is Not Permitted: The Policing and Social Control of Occupy Oakland." *Critical Criminology* 21 (4): 463–475. doi:10.1007/s10612-013-9198-z.

Knox, Liam. 2019. "Recently Released Records Show Portland Police Bureau Targeted Counter-Protesters, Ignored Armed Alt-Right Demonstrators at 'Patriot Prayer' Rally." *MuckRock*. https://www.muckrock.com/news/archives/2019/apr/24/pbb-patriot-prayer-logs/.

Kriesi, Hanspeter, Ruud Koopmans, Jan Willem Duyvendak, and Marco G. Guigni. 1995. *New Social Movements in Western Europe: A Comparative Analysis*. Minneapolis, MN: University of Minnesota Press.

Levin, Sam. 2018. "California Police Worked with Neo-Nazis to Pursue 'Anti-Racist' Activists, Documents Show." *The Guardian*, February 9, sec. World News. https://www.theguardian.com/world/2018/feb/09/california-police-white-supremacists-counter-protest.

Maher, Thomas V. 2010. "Threat, Resistance, and Collective Action: The Cases of Sobibor, Treblinka, and Auschwitz." *American Sociological Review* 75 (2): 252–272. doi:2048/10.1177/0003122410365305.

Meyer, Josh. 2017. "FBI, Homeland Security Warn of More 'Antifa' Attacks." *Politico*. https://www.politico.com/story/2017/09/01/antifa-charlottesville-violence-fbi-242235.

Miller-Idriss, Cynthia. 2019. "Selling Extremism: Nationalist Streetwear and the Rise of the Far Right." *CNN Style*. https://www.cnn.com/style/article/right-wing-fashion-streetwear/index.html.

Moore, Mark H., and George L. Kelling. 1983. "'To Serve and Protect': Learning from Police History." *Public Interest* 70: 49–65.

Moskos, Peter. 2008. *Cop in the Hood: My Year Policing Baltimore's Eastern District*. Princeton, NJ: Princeton University Press.

Moynihan, Colin, and Ali Winston. 2018. "Far-Right Proud Boys Reeling After Arrests and Scrutiny." *The New York Times*, December 23, sec. New York. https://www.nytimes.com/2018/12/23/nyregion/gavin-mcinnes-proud-boys-nypd.html.

Neiwert, David. 2009. *The Eliminationists: How Hate Talk Radicalized the American Right*. Sausalito, CA: PoliPoint Press.

Niman, Michael I. 2011. "The Shanti Sena 'Peace Center' and the Non-Policing of an Anarchist Temporary Autonomous Zone: Rainbow Family Peacekeeping Strategies." *Contemporary Justice Review* 14 (1): 65–76. doi:10.1080/10282580.2011.541077.

Noakes, John A., Brian V. Klocke, and Patrick F. Gillham. 2005. "Whose Streets? Police and Protester Struggles over Space in Washington, DC, 29–30 September 2001." *Policing and Society* 15 (3): 235–254. doi:10.1080/10439460500168576.

NoCARA. 2017. "Piss, Kilts, and Sticks: How Violent Trump Supporters Are Merging with the Alt-Right." *Northern California Anti-Racist Action (NoCARA)*. https://nocara.blackblogs.org/2017/03/16/piss-kilts-and-sticks-how-violent-trump-supporters-are-merging-with-the-alt-right/.

Ordóñez, Vicente. 2018. "Direct Action." In *Anarchism: A Conceptual Approach*, edited by Benjamin Franks, Nathan Jun, and Leonard Williams, 74–85. New York, NY: Routledge.

Paxton, Robert O. 2004. *The Anatomy of Fascism*. New York, NY: Alfred A. Knopf.

Pepinsky, Harold E. 1978. "Communist Anarchism as an Alternative to the Rule of Criminal Law." *Contemporary Crises* 2 (3): 315–334. doi:10.1007/BF02741899.

Pepinsky, Harold E., and Richard Quinney. 1991. *Criminology as Peacemaking*. Bloomington, IN: Indiana University Press.

Perkins, James E., and Martin J. Bourgeois. 2006. "Perceptions of Police Use of Deadly Force." *Journal of Applied Social Psychology* 36 (1): 161–177. doi:10.1111/j.0021-9029.2006.00056.x.

Polletta, Francesca. 2007. *Freedom Is an Endless Meeting: Democracy in American Social Movements*. Chicago, IL: University of Chicago Press.

Porter, Tom. 2017. "Berkeley's Mayor Wants Antifa to Be Classified as a Gang." *Newsweek*. https://www.newsweek.com/berkeley-mayor-calls-antifa-be-classified-crime-gang-after-clashes-sunday-656286.

Quinney, Richard. 1974. *Critique of Legal Order; Crime Control in Capitalist Society*. Boston, MA: Little and Brown.

Rimel, Logan. 2017. "My 'Nonviolent' Stance Was Met with Heavily Armed Men." *Radical Discipleship*. https://radicaldiscipleship.net/2017/08/23/my-nonviolent-stance-was-met-with-heavily-armed-men/.

Rose City Antifa. 2017. "*From Far-Right to Nazi – Report Back from the June 4 Stand Against Fascism*." https://rosecityantifa.org/articles/report-back-june-4-2017/.

Shantz, Jeff. 2011. *Active Anarchy: Political Practice in Contemporary Movements.* Lanham, MD: Lexington Books.

Shepherd, Katie. 2019. "Texts Between Portland Police and Patriot Prayer Ringleader Joey Gibson Show Warm Exchange." *Willamette Week.* https://www.wweek.com/news/courts/2019/02/14/texts-between-portland-police-and-patriot-prayer-ringleader-joey-gibson-show-warm-exchange/.

Short, James F., and Lorine A. Hughes. 2018. "Antifa, Street Gangs, and the Importance of Group Processes." *Society* 55 (3): 253–255. doi:10.1007/s12115-018-0247-9.

South Side Anti-Racist Action. 2017. "Known White Supremacist Tom Christensen Sent to Hospital by Antifa." *South Side Anti-Racist Action.* http://southsideantifa.blogspot.com/2017/05/known-white-supremacist-tom-christensen.html.

Starr, Amory, Luis A. Fernandez, and Christian Scholl. 2011. *Shutting down the Streets: Political Violence and Social Control in the Global Era.* New York, NY: New York University Press.

Sullivan, Dennis, and Larry Tifft. 2010. *Restorative Justice: Healing the Foundations of Our Everyday Lives.* Boulder, CO: Lynne Rienner Publishers.

Sunshine, Spencer. 2019a. "Ted Cruz's 'Antifa Are Terrorists' Resolution Seeks to Stifle the Left." *Truthout.* https://truthout.org/articles/ted-cruzs-antifa-are-terrorists-resolution-seeks-to-stifle-the-left/.

Sunshine, Spencer. 2019b. "Antifa Panic." *Battleground.Eu.* https://www.thebattleground.eu/articles/2019/08/05/antifa-panic/.

Templeton, Amelia. 2018. *"Review Faults Portland Police for June 2017 Mass Detention of Protesters."* https://www.opb.org/news/article/portland-police-protesters-detention-patriot-prayer-rally/.

Tifft, Larry L. 1979. "The Coming Redefinitions of Crime: An Anarchist Perspective." *Social Problems* 26 (4): 392–402. doi:10.2307/800503.

Tifft, Larry, and Dennis Sullivan. 1980. *The Struggle to Be Human: Crime, Criminology, and Anarchism.* Sanday: Cienfuegos Press.

Unicorn Riot. 2018. "Georgia Police Used Fake News from Militia to Plan for Nazi Rally, Emails Show." *Unicorn Riot.* https://unicornriot.ninja/2018/georgia-police-used-fake-news-from-militia-to-plan-for-nazi-rally-emails-show/.

Vitale, Alex S. 2017. *The End of Policing.* New York, NY: Verso.

Vysotsky, Stanislav. 2017. "Drawing Equivalencies Between Fascists and Anti-Fascists Is Not Just Wrong—It's Dangerous – in These Times." https://inthesetimes.com/article/20427/false-equivalency-white-supremacist-nazis-fascists-antifa-Charlottesville.

Vysotsky, Stanislav, and Eric Madfis. 2014. "Uniting the Right: Anti-Immigration, Organizing, and the Legitimation of Extreme Racist Organizations." *Journal of Hate Studies* 12 (1): 129. doi:10.33972/jhs.106.

Wamsley, Laurel. 2017. "White Supremacist Charged with Killing 2 in Portland, Ore., Knife Attack." *NPR.Org.* https://www.npr.org/sections/thetwo-way/2017/05/27/530351468/2-dead-1-injured-after-stabbing-in-portland-ore.

Weber, Max. [1910] 1998. "Politics as a Vocation." In *From Max Weber: Essays in Sociology,* translated by H.H. Gerth and C. Wright Mills, 77–128. New York, NY: Routledge.

Williams, Dana M. 2018. "Contemporary Anarchist and Anarchistic Movements." *Sociology Compass* 12 (6): 1–17.

Williams, Dana M., and Matthew T. Lee. 2012. "Aiming to Overthrow the State (Without Using the State): Political Opportunities for Anarchist Movements." *Comparative Sociology* 11 (4): 558–593.

Williams, Kristian. 2015. *Our Enemies in Blue: Police and Power in America.* Oakland, CA: AK Press.

Wilson, Jason. 2018. "Portland Far-Right Rally: Police Charge Counterprotesters with Batons Drawn." *The Guardian*, August 5, sec. US News. https://www.theguardian.com/us-news/2018/aug/04/patriot-prayer-to-carry-guns-at-portland-rally-as-fears-of-violence-rise.

Zald, Meyer N., and Bert Useem. 1987. "Movement and Countermovement Interaction: Mobilization, Tactics and State Involvement." In *Social Movements in an Organizational Society: Collected Essays*, edited by Meyer N. Zald and John D. McCarthy. New Brunswick, NJ: Transaction Books.

7

ANTIFA UNMASKED

A sociological and criminological understanding

Antifa activism as portrayed in mass media and the popular imagination is a caricature; personified as a black-clad malcontent hell bent on creating chaos and disorder in flagrant disregard for the norms of civility or law and order. By applying a sociological and criminological analysis to the tactics, culture, and practices of militant antifascists, we can look beyond this simplification for an understanding of the complexity of this form of activism. The complexity of antifa activism may be explained by synthesizing perspectives from social movement studies, subculture studies, and critical criminology. As a social movement, antifascism operates with a distinct structure of informal and formal as well as non-militant and militant forms of activism. It is this militant form that constitutes what we understand as activism under the antifa label. At its core, the movement analyzed in this book represents a distinct radical opposition to the fascist movement. Militant antifascists engage in this opposition with a broad tactical repertoire that is marked by a confrontational style and actions. Yet, antifa activism is more than just punching fascists. Militant antifascism operates within subcultures and as its own movement subculture constructing practices, artifacts, and ideas that rebuke fascism in all its manifestations. At the intersection of social movements, subcultures, and the sociology of emotions, antifascist militancy is driven in part by distinct threats that fascists pose to people, social movements, and spaces. The antifascist practices that respond to these threats serve as a form of self-defense that represents a critical criminological model of prefigurative practices to ensure safety and social control. Antifa activists are, therefore, criminalized precisely because they engage in use of force and thus challenge the state's monopoly on violence.

Militant antifascism represents an ideal type of countermovement rather than the opposing movements model articulated by social movement scholars. The prevailing model for opposing movement dynamics is rooted in social movements' contest against one another in relation to state or corporate policy makers (Dixon

2008; Gale 1986; Lo 1982; Meyer and Staggenborg 1996; Mottl 1980; Peleg 2000; Zald and Useem 1987). Both fascist and antifascist movements stand in opposition to existing state and corporate structures. Historical and contemporary fascist movements present themselves as insurrectionary fighters against governments that they frame as illegitimate (Belew 2018; Berlet 1992; Burley 2017; Dobratz and Waldner 2012; Paxton 2004). Militant antifascists, however, do not stand in support of the state in opposition to fascists. In the words of the Anti-Racist Action and Torch Antifa networks, "We don't rely on the cops or courts to do our work for us." Antifa activists oppose fascism from the far left with roots in anarchist and anti-authoritarian ideology. This places militant antifascists in a "three-way fight" against fascists and the state (Burley 2017, 112). As a countermovement, this orients the focus of antifascists exclusively on the activity and maneuvers of the fascist movement, while opposing state intervention in that dynamic.

The tactics of antifascist activists are focused on the key countermovement strategy of demobilizing the fascist movement by delegitimizing it and increasing the costs of participation for members (Zald and Useem 1987). The antifascist tactical repertoire consists of a number of activities that are designed to preempt fascist mobilization through non-violent and non-confrontational activity: information gathering, educational efforts, and cultural work. Antifascists also leverage the social stigma associated with fascist activism through public pressure campaigns and public shaming in the form of doxing. What distinguishes militant from non-militant forms of these types of activism is often the style with which they are deployed. Militant antifascist campaigns are marked by a confrontational style that is lacking in their non-militant versions. Ultimately, it is the willingness to use force in confrontations with fascists that delineates antifa activism. The tactical repertoire for militant antifascists is therefore much broader than non-militant activists because of their radical orientation (Fitzgerald and Rodgers 2000). Because of their anti-authoritarian position, antifa activists are not constrained by the necessity to maintain financial and allied backing from mainstream activists or political institutions. The antifa tactical repertoire is ultimately a series of strategic, radical countermovement responses to fascist activity and mobilizations.

Culture plays a central role in the struggle between fascists and antifascists as both a tactical manifestation and metaphorical and literal space of struggle. The cultural work of antifa activists serves as a form of resistance and assertion of authentic identity expression within oppositional subcultures. Antifascist activism is a core component of punk, skinhead, metal, and other subcultures because of fascist participation and activism within them. Since the late 1970s, fascists have participated in these types of subcultures as both a means of recruitment and construction of prefigurative movement spaces (Blazak 2001; Hamm 1993; Simi and Futrell 2010). The antifascist response to this encroachment was swift and militant, resulting in an ideological contest over the orientation of the subculture (Bray 2017; Copsey 2000; Goodyer 2003; Moore and Roberts 2009; Renton 2001; Roberts and Moore 2009; Madfis and Vysotsky 2020). Antifascism in subcultures manifests itself in the distinct performances, artifacts, and ideations

(Johnston 2009) evident in the practices of participants. Antifascist representations are manifested in expressions of subcultural style, the content of music, and even in the performances of subcultural gatherings in a manner that serves as both a covert and an overt form of resistance (Williams 2011) to fascist activity and ideology. When such forms of antifascist activity are successful, they subvert fascist activity to such an extent that it is driven out of the subculture.

Antifascist culture, however, is not exclusively an underground phenomenon, and manifests itself in public expressions of opposition to fascism. Antifa activists routinely engage in activity that marks public space as hostile to fascist activity through graffiti, leafletting, postering, and stickering campaigns. These may be mobilized in response to similar fascist propaganda campaigns, proactive attempts at public shaming, or simply preemptive cultural activity. These practices place antifascist iconography in the public sphere and clearly demarcate public space as sympathetic to the movement (Creasap 2016; Gerbaudo 2013; Waldner and Dobratz 2013). Antifa activists also generate a series of memes that celebrate militant resistance to fascism and use of force that are shared widely on social media. The celebration of violence in antifa memes serves as a "proof of death" of the fascist movement in their imagery of defeat and a "proof of life" through declarations of antifascist victory (Linnemann 2017). Becoming involved in antifa activism introduces a person to a series of covert symbolic representations of resistance from specific forms of street style to numeric and linguistic codes. This collection of public representations of militant antifascism serves to construct a distinct activist subculture that is marked by a stable ideological orientation and base set of practices.

The countermovement and cultural dynamics between antifascist and fascist movements construct an elevated level of threat for antifa activists. Consistent with the sociological research on the dynamics between emotion and social movement mobilization (Emirbayer and Goldberg 2005; Goodwin, Jasper, and Polletta 2007, 2001; Jasper 1998), the militant response of antifa activists is driven in part by the threats they perceive from the fascist movement. These threats are understood as existential for activists and the broader network of movements and subcultures that they participate in which can be classified as physical, political, and spatial. Physical threat consists of the fear of direct harm or danger from fascists as a result of an individual being categorized as a target for fascist violence. Antifa activists represent a diversity of gender, racial, religious, and sexual orientation identities that fascists target for elimination. Even for white, cisgender, heterosexual antifascists, the identification as oppositional activists marks them as "traitors" to fascist ideology and legitimate targets for violence. These threats are borne out as antifa activists routinely experience attacks from fascists such as arson, assault, and even murder. Political threat consists of assaults on the political activity of activists that represents an ideological challenge to fascism. Fascists and antifascists frequently seek to organize a similar demographic and subcultural base, which places them in direct ideological conflict. For fascists, this challenge is resolved through the use of violence against their opponents, which escalates the sense of threat. Finally, spatial threat is the result of the direct proximity between antifascist and fascist activists in subcultural and social spaces. The cultural activity of fascists involves a fundamental transformation of subcultures to reflect fascist ideology as a prefigurative space (Futrell and Simi 2004; Simi and Futrell 2010), which threatens the ideological integrity of subcultures that are constructed as resisting dominant hierarchies of gender, race, and sexuality. Fascists, therefore, pose a threat to the participants of the subculture, the local scene, and the trans-local identity of the subculture as a whole. The militant position of antifa activists represents a strategic response to the severe, imminent, applicable, malleable, and credible threat posed by fascist activism and ideology (Einwohner and Maher 2011; Maher 2010; Soyer 2014). Antifascist militancy serves as a means of directly addressing the threats posed by fascists.

The militant antifascist response to the threats effectively operates as a form of self-defense or "self-help" (Black 2004; Clark 2018). Since a great deal of fascist activity occurs outside of the purview of normative institutions of social control, antifa activists must rely on themselves to protect individuals and spaces from threats of violence. The defensive activities of militant antifascists may be categorized as preventative or repressive. Antifa activists act to prevent fascist violence by providing direct protective services to people and spaces threatened by supremacists. Confrontations between militant antifascists and supremacists are ultimately designed to repress the activity of fascist activists and force demobilization. These antifascist defensive actions mimic many of the protective and repressive activities engaged in by law enforcement. The defensive actions of antifa activists represent a form of self-help in a situation where individuals cannot or will not rely on law enforcement for protection (Barclay 1990; Black 1983, 2004).

As a form of self-defense, antifascist militancy represents a unique contribution to anarchist criminology by modeling a prefigurative set of practices for maintaining social order and safety (Barclay 1990; Ferrell 2011; Niman 2011). Militant anti-fascist actions adhere to core anarchist principles of spontaneity, decentralization, and direct democracy. The confrontational tactics that are the hallmark of antifa activism are frequently on the spot reactions to the presence of fascists in sub-cultural and other social spaces. Even more formal counter-protest actions are defined in the moment rather than as pre-planned or premeditated actions. As such, they allow for a fluidity of actions and wide breadth of the antifascist tactical repertoire. Antifa activity is fundamentally decentralized in that it is open to anyone who identifies as an antifascist. Whether it is forms of informal, "everyday antifascism" (Bray 2017; Burley 2017) or the work of formal affinity groups operating under the antifa banner, there is no central organization coordinating the work of militant antifascists. Formal antifa groups are organized in a loose network structure with local collectives being given a great deal of autonomy in choosing the focus of their activism and the tactics that they deploy. Finally, antifa activism is fundamentally directly democratic. Everything from the spontaneous decision to eject fascists from an event to the sustained activity of formal antifa groups is conducted in a manner where the direct input of participants guides the form of the action. Formal antifa groups and networks rely in particular on the direct plebiscite of their members to make binding decisions with the consensus or a super-majority serving as the threshold. In this respect, militant antifascism reflects a radical assertion of the use of force in community defense.

Antifascist militancy ultimately challenges the monopoly on the legitimate use of force reserved for the state and enacted by law enforcement. As a result, antifa activism represents a direct challenge to the very essence of the state – the state's unique ability to deploy legitimate force in defense of a population. The danger of militant antifascism is that it undermines the state's claims to protect vulnerable populations, and maintain order and safety. The possibility that there are alternative means for people to protect themselves from fascist violence is the threat that antifa activists pose to society. The attempts to criminalize antifascist activism are rooted in precisely this fear. Militant antifascism is presented by politicians and pundits through a criminalization frame that associates activism with antisocial crime and violence as a means of delegitimizing dissent. Attempts to designate antifa activists as gangs or terrorists are meant to repress their activity and assert the power of the state rather than curb incidents of violence. By defying the state's assertion of the monopoly on the use of force, militant antifascists engage in truly radical activity.

Sitting at the crossroads of social movement, subculture, and radical criminological practice militant antifascism follows the patterns of mobilization and demobilization of each of these phenomena. As a countermovement to fascist activism, antifascism will exist as long as the movement it opposes exists. Antifa activism operates in the spaces and subcultures that fascism seeks to control and mobilizes the people who are most directly threatened by it. Antifa activists will act in defense of themselves, their movements, and their spaces from fascist assault. They will do so out of necessity and ideological commitment, and will use a wide-ranging set of tactics in a radical assertion of the need for self-defense. In this dynamic, antifa activists also demobilize when fascist movements are in decline. So, the surest means of reducing militant antifascist activism, and related violence, is quite simple – stop fascism.

Works cited

Barclay, Harold B. 1990. *People Without Government: An Anthropology of Anarchy.* Seattle, WA: Left Bank Books.

Belew, Kathleen. 2018. *Bring the War Home: The White Power Movement and Paramilitary America.* Cambridge, MA: Harvard University Press.

Berlet, Chip. 1992. "Fascism!" *Political Research Associates.* https://www.politicalresearch.org/1992/09/28/fascism.

Black, Donald. 1983. "Crime as Social Control." *American Sociological Review* 48 (1): 34–45. doi:10.2307/2095143.

Black, Donald. 2004. "Violent Structures." In *Violence: From Theory to Research*, edited by Margaret A. Zahn, Henry H. Brownstein, and Shelly L. Jackson, 145–158. Newark, NJ: LexisNexis Anderson Publishers.

Blazak, Randy. 2001. "White Boys to Terrorist Men: Target Recruitment of Nazi Skinheads." *American Behavioral Scientist* 44 (6): 982–1000.

Bray, Mark. 2017. *Antifa: The Antifascist Handbook*. Brooklyn, NY: Melville House Publishing.

Burley, Shane. 2017. *Fascism Today – What It Is and How to End It*. Chico, CA: AK Press.

Clark, J. 2018. "Three-Way Fight: Revolutionary Anti-Fascism and Armed Self-Defense." In *Setting Sights: Histories and Reflections on Community Armed Self-Defense*, edited by Scott Crow, 49–67. Oakland, CA: PM Press.

Copsey, Nigel. 2000. *Anti-Fascism in Britain*. New York, NY: St. Martin's Press.

Creasap, Kimberly. 2016. "Finding the Movement: The Geographies of Social Movement Scenes." *The International Journal of Sociology and Social Policy* 36 (11/12): 792–807.

Dixon, Marc. 2008. "Movements, Countermovements and Policy Adoption: The Case of Right-to-Work Activism." *Social Forces* 87 (1): 473–500. doi:10.1353/sof.0.0076.

Dobratz, Betty A., and Lisa Waldner. 2012. "Repertoires of Contention: White Separatist Views on the Use of Violence and Leaderless Resistance." *Mobilization: An International Quarterly* 17 (1): 49–66. doi:10.17813/maiq.17.1.3282448743272632.

Einwohner, Rachel L., and Thomas V. Maher. 2011. "Threat Assessment and Collective-Action Emergence: Death-Camp and Ghetto Resistance During the Holocaust." *Mobilization: An International Quarterly* 16 (2): 127–146. doi:10.17813/maiq.16.2.j263166u14286024.

Emirbayer, Mustafa, and Chad Goldberg. 2005. "Pragmatism, Bourdieu, and Collective Emotions in Contentious Politics." *Theory & Society* 34 (5/6): 469–518. doi:10.1007/s11186-005-1619-x.

Ferrell, Jeff. 2011. "Corking as Community Policing." *Contemporary Justice Review* 14 (1): 95–98. doi:10.1080/10282580.2011.541079.

Fitzgerald, Kathleen J., and Diane M. Rodgers. 2000. "Radical Social Movement Organizations: A Theoretical Model." *Sociological Quarterly* 41 (4): 573–592.

Futrell, Robert, and Pete Simi. 2004. "Free Spaces, Collective Identity, and the Persistence of U.S. White Power Activism." *Social Problems* 51 (1): 16–42.

Gale, Richard P. 1986. "Social Movements and the State: The Environmental Movement, Countermovement, and Government Agencies." *Sociological Perspectives* 29 (2): 202–240. doi:10.2307/1388959.

Gerbaudo, Paolo. 2013. "Spikey Posters." *Space and Culture*, October. doi:10.1177/1206331213501127.

Goodwin, Jeff, James M. Jasper, and Francesca Polletta. 2001. "Introduction: Why Emotions Matter." In *Passionate Politics: Emotions and Social Movements*, edited by Jeff Goodwin, James M. Jasper, and Francesca Polletta, 1–24. Chicago, IL: University of Chicago Press.

Goodwin, Jeff, James M. Jasper, and Francesca Polletta. 2007. "Emotional Dimensions of Social Movements." In *The Blackwell Companion to Social Movements*, 413–432. Malden, MA: Wiley-Blackwell. doi:10.1002/9780470999103.ch18.

Goodyer, Ian. 2003. "Rock against Racism: Multiculturalism and Political Mobilization, 1976–81." *Immigrants & Minorities* 22 (1): 44–62.

Hamm, Mark S. 1993. *American Skinheads: The Criminology and Control of Hate Crime*. Westport, CT: Praeger.

Jasper, James M. 1998. "The Emotions of Protest: Affective and Reactive Emotions In and Around Social Movements." *Sociological Forum* 13 (3): 397.

Johnston, Hank. 2009. "Protest Cultures: Performances, Artifacts, and Ideations." In *Culture, Social Movements, and Protest*, edited by Hank Johnston, 3–29. Burlington, VT: Ashgate.

Linnemann, Travis. 2017. "Proof of Death: Police Power and the Visual Economies of Seizure, Accumulation and Trophy." *Theoretical Criminology* 21 (1): 57–77. doi:10.1177/1362480615622533.

Lo, Clarence Y.H. 1982. "Countermovements and Conservative Movements in the Contemporary US." *Annual Review of Sociology*, 107–134.

Madfis, Eric, and Stanislav Vysotsky. 2020. "Exploring Subcultural Trajectories: Racist Skinhead Desistance and Countercultural Value Persistence." *Sociological Focus*.

Maher, Thomas V. 2010. "Threat, Resistance, and Collective Action: The Cases of Sobibor, Treblinka, and Auschwitz." *American Sociological Review* 75 (2): 252–272. doi:2048/10.1177/0003122410365305.

Meyer, David S., and Suzanne Staggenborg. 1996. "Movements, Countermovements, and the Structure of Political Opportunity." *American Journal of Sociology* 101 (6): 1628–1660.

Moore, Ryan, and Michael Roberts. 2009. "Do-It-Yourself Mobilization: Punk and Social Movements." *Mobilization: An International Journal* 14 (3): 273–291.

Mottl, Tahi L. 1980. "The Analysis of Countermovements." *Social Problems* 27 (5): 620–635. doi:10.2307/800200.

Niman, Michael I. 2011. "The Shanti Sena 'Peace Center' and the Non-Policing of an Anarchist Temporary Autonomous Zone: Rainbow Family Peacekeeping Strategies." *Contemporary Justice Review* 14 (1): 65–76. doi:10.1080/10282580.2011.541077.

Paxton, Robert O. 2004. *The Anatomy of Fascism*. New York, NY: Alfred A. Knopf.

Peleg, Samuel. 2000. "Peace Now or Later?: Movement–Countermovement Dynamics and the Israeli Political Cleavage." *Studies in Conflict and Terrorism* 23 (4): 235–254.

Renton, Dave. 2001. *This Rough Game: Fascism and Anti-Fascism*. Stroud: Sutton.

Roberts, Michael James, and Ryan Moore. 2009. "Peace Punks and Punks Against Racism: Resource Mobilization and Frame Construction in the Punk Movement." *Music and Arts in Action* 2 (1): 21–36.

Simi, Pete, and Robert Futrell. 2010. *American Swastika: Inside the White Power Movement's Hidden Spaces of Hate*. Lanham, MD: Rowman & Littlefield.

Soyer, Michaela. 2014. "'We Knew Our Time Had Come': The Dynamics of Threat and Microsocial Ties in Three Polish Ghettos Under Nazi Oppression." *Mobilization: An International Quarterly* 19 (1): 47–66. doi:10.17813/maiq.19.1.66l8khh78976h112.

Waldner, Lisa K., and Betty A. Dobratz. 2013. "Graffiti as a Form of Contentious Political Participation." *Sociology Compass* 7 (5): 377–389. doi:10.1111/soc4.12036.

Williams, J. Patrick. 2011. *Subcultural Theory: Traditions & Concepts*. Chichester: Polity Press.

Zald, Meyer N., and Bert Useem. 1987. "Movement and Countermovement Interaction: Mobilization, Tactics and State Involvement." In *Social Movements in an Organizational Society: Collected Essays*, edited by Meyer N. Zald and John D. McCarthy. New Brunswick, NJ: Transaction Books.

APPENDIX – AGAINST METHODOLOGY

Ethnography, autoethnography, and the intimately familiar

I did not intend to study militant antifascist activists. My scholarly trajectory was focused on their opponents in the fascist movement. I began my academic career by studying the far-right and maintain an active interest in its dynamics. The idea for this project came shortly after the protest known in antifa circles as "the Battle of York" (Bray 2017). The militant antifascist conflict that routed the National Alliance and Creativity movement and disrupted their rally was criticized by many of the scholars of far-right movements who served as my mentors, which I expected. They based their critique on a social psychological assessment of the function of such rallies for fascists, which indicates that rallies provide them with attention and negative reinforcement; and therefore, should be ignored or protested in a festive manner away from the site. It was ultimately a critique of militant antifascism from the noted anarchist sociologist, Howard Ehrlich (2002), that inspired this project. Unlike other scholars, Ehrlich's critique begins with an acknowledgment of the militant antifascist position from his own radical standpoint and implicit connections to such activists, but still repeated the position that centers the fascist perspective. At the time, as a budding radical sociologist and scholar of supremacist movements, I felt that there were some things missing from this discussion – the perspective of militant antifascists and the social movement component of their activity – and so, the seeds of this research were planted.

The seeds of this study into militant antifascism germinated when the time came to conduct my dissertation research. When my original idea of a longitudinal study of the changes in fascist ideology and movement structure fell through due to a insufficient access to an archive of supremacist materials, I returned to the idea of antifascism. As discussed briefly in the introduction of this book, I had the distinct benefit of access to militant antifascist activists as a result of my own history of activism and subcultural participation. This unique position made a qualitative study of antifa activists a feasible project that could be completed within a reasonable period of time. Thus began the research that is the foundation of this book.

ed a "spiral model" where "the researcher engages in the analytic circles rather than using a linear approach" (Creswell ial project consisted of formal interviews with non-militant and activists. Shortly after the completion of those interviews, I rmal ethnographic study with antifa activists. As I began to pub- f my research, autoethnographic reflections of my own history of informa rmal antifa activism became relevant data points; and, ultimately, as militant antifascists mobilized in response to an emboldened fascist movement in the Trump era, a visual ethnography of antifascist social media and mass media representations served to validate and update my existing data.

The interview process was based on a non-probability sample of antifascist activists. As the first and second chapters of this book indicate, it is virtually impossible to estimate the size of the antifascist movement because of the variability of informal and formal activism as well as non-militant and militant organizing efforts. Beyond non-profit organizations that monitor "hate group" activity, there are few formal, non-militant antifascist groups in the United States. At the time that the interview research was conducted in 2007, the American antifascist movement, and its formal, militant wing in particular, was at its nadir. As a result, I utilized a non-probability snowball sampling methodology to secure interviews with militant activists. I contacted member groups of the Anti-Racist Action network to solicit interviews and relied on my personal networks from my own activist experiences to build a pool of potential interviewees. Ultimately, 15 interviews were conducted with militant antifascists who were based in every region of the United States.

The interviews were conducted in order to understand the dynamics that drive antifascist militancy with an eye toward ideology and threat. In the process of conducting interviews, other dynamics of antifascism became clear that are featured throughout this book such as the distinct culture of militant antifascism (Chapter 4) and its manifestation as a prefigurative form of community and self-defense (Chapter 6). In order to triangulate my initial findings and build on the interview data, I chose to engage in ethnographic research with militant antifascists by observing their activity in "the field." From late 2007 until late 2010, I observed the activity of New City antifa as they organized against fascists in their community. This process involved attending group meetings, formal and informal antifascist events such as parties, benefit and other shows, DJ nights, and even protest events. The reflexive process of ethnographic study prompted me to consider my experiences with formal antifascist activism as a member of Old City antifa between 2002 and 2005 in light of the dynamics identified in the field and through the process of writing. This process of autoethnography involves "retrospectively and selectively [writing] about epiphanies that stem from, or are made possible by, being part of a culture and/or by possessing a particular cultural identity" (Ellis, Adams, and Bochner 2010). These past experiences served to reaffirm the processes and dynamics that are discussed throughout this book.

The final component to the research strategy for this book was a visual ethnography of contemporary militant antifascist blogs, social media, and mass media content. The process of visual ethnography applies the reflexive and subjective experiences of field research to the analysis of visual media (Ardèvol 2012; Pink 2001, 2012a; Postill and Pink 2012). A particular value of internet content as a source of ethnographic data is its ability to extend the experiences of the ethnographer in the field into the online realm where depictions reflect activities that occur off-line (Pink 2012b). In the case of militant antifascism, the contents of blogs published by formal antifa groups, social media content, and mass media coverage reflect off-line movement activities and dynamics. As a researcher of militant antifascism, I maintained a consistent engagement with these online activities and representations after formally leaving the field of ethnographic study. The reflexive process of engaging with this content presented another point of triangulation of data from interviews, ethnography, and auto-ethnography, and updates the data to incorporate information that is contemporaneous to the writing of this book.

Insider research

There is an expectation among the positivist and scientific approaches to social science research that investigators be outsiders from the groups and social phenomena that they study and that those studies follow a structured, ideally quantitative approach in order to maintain objectivity (Merton 1972; Mills 1959; Young 2011). The rise of postmodern, feminist, and critical theoretical perspectives and methodologies has challenged this assumption and indicated the crucial role of the subjective experience of the researcher in the process. Building on these assertions, social scientists increasingly rely on their own experiences with the groups and phenomena that they study as a resource in the research process (Bennett 2003; Ferrell 1996, 2001; Ferrell, Hayward, and Young 2008; Hodkinson 2005; Roseneil 1993; Taylor 2011). The logic of the "insider principle" was described by Robert Merton (1972, 15) as follows:

> Only through continued socialization in the life of a group can one become fully aware of its symbolisms and socially shared realities; only so can one understand the fine-grained meanings of behavior, feelings, and values; only so can one decipher the unwritten grammar of conduct and the nuances of cultural idiom.

One of the key benefits of insider research is the unique ability of individuals with experience in subcultures, social movements, or acts of crime and deviance to access fields and participants that are inaccessible to the outside researcher (Bennett 2003; Ferrell 1996, 2001; Hodkinson 2005; Roseneil 1993). Insider researchers can leverage their "subcultural capital" (Thornton 2013) as a means of gaining access to spaces where outsiders would be unwelcome or treated with suspicion and hostility (Hodkinson 2005). A researcher who has experience with the group that they are studying is "liable, to some degree, already to share with respondents an internalised language and a range of experiences," which facilitates their ability to navigate the field with "cultural competence" (Hodkinson 2005, 137–138; see also Roseneil 1993). Insider researchers may also be able to identify participants and fields of study that are simply not available to outsiders because of the guarded nature of the subjects of their study. In the cases of studies of groups outside of the normative structures of society, the insider knows who constitutes a reliable and authentic source and who doesn't (Bennett 2003; Hodkinson 2005; Roseneil 1993).

The interview process is also greatly facilitated by insider status. The insider researcher is able to build a rapport and trust with their interviewee because they are viewed as equals with at least some base of common experience that serves to level some of the dynamics of power in the research process (Hodkinson 2005; Roseneil 1993). The researcher comes into the field with the status and structural advantages of legitimate social institutions that may intimidate or alienate potential interviewees. The insider brings with them a series of experiences that, while they may not eliminate the dynamics of power, serve to bridge the social distance between researcher and participant (Hodkinson 2005; Roseneil 1993). Paul Hodkinson (2005, 139) notes that "An ability to share subcultural gossip, anecdotes and observations with respondents further enhanced initial rapport, as well as offering an invaluable and effective additional stimulus for conversation during the interviews themselves." This level of rapport enables interviewees to share information that would otherwise be unavailable to outsiders who are kept at a distance.

Finally, the insider researcher possesses a unique perspective based on their own experiences that allows them to design an appropriate method of study, critically assess interview responses and probe for additional information, as well as engage in interpretation that reflects the perspective of the group or phenomenon under study. The past experience of the researcher as participant in a subculture, social movement, or even criminal or deviant activity provides the insider researcher with knowledge about which methods and frames of analysis may be the most effective in gaining understanding of their research subject (Bennett 2003; Hodkinson 2005; Roseneil 1993). The choice of field and participants for insider researchers reflects past knowledge and avoids the potential pitfalls of false starts and pilot studies, as well as the possibility of applying inappropriate frameworks for analysis (Hodkinson 2005). Because they have "experienced activities, motivations, feelings and affiliations that are liable, at least, to be comparable with those of many respondents, [insider researchers] have a significant extra pool of material with which to compare and contrast what they see and hear during the research process" (Hodkinson 2005, 143). The insider researcher is able to gauge the validity and authenticity of respondents' statements based on their own experience with the subject of study (Bennett 2003; Hodkinson 2005). As someone with intimate experience of the group or phenomenon being studied, the inside researcher is able to uniquely apply a scholarly framework to their own experiences as well as those being proffered by interviewees or other research subjects (Hodkinson 2005; Roseneil 1993).

As discussed throughout this book, this study of militant antifascism constitutes insider research because it is informed by my own experiences as an activist. From the inspiration to the process of writing interview questions to the access to formal antifascist groups for ethnographic observation to the analysis of antifa media, every aspect of this study is linked to my own experiences with informal and formal militant antifascism. Access to militant antifascists was the core benefit of my insider position as a researcher. Militant antifascists understandably are reticent to speak to researchers and other interviewers for fear that they may be agents of the state, fascist infiltrators, or opportunists who will misrepresent their positions (Bray 2017). A related concern was that even a sympathetic researcher might provide "insider" information to law enforcement in their presentation of data. I found a similar reticence among some of my potential interviewees, but was able to reassure them by leveraging my own subcultural or movement capital. My own history of informal activism in the punk scene and formal activism as part of radical social movements provided me with a reputation of being someone who could be trusted. I could also rely on activist networks and other militant antifascist activists to "vouch" for my credibility as I approached participants. In interviews and ethnographic field research, trust and rapport were evident in the ease with which I was able to interact with militant activists. The insider knowledge that I brought to these interactions facilitated interviews that were conversational as activists "talked shop" with me about the processes and dynamics of antifa activism. Similarly, in the various interactions with activists in the field, I was viewed as a fellow antifascist first and a researcher second. This allowed me to be privy to high-risk activities such as the defensive work described in Chapter 6. Finally, as someone with experience of militant antifascist activism, I was able to interpret my own experience, both in the past and in the field, through a scholarly lens that is sensitive to the nuances of movement activity and the perspectives of movement members. By being an insider researcher, I was able to conduct a holistic study of militant antifascism that would have been impossible for an outsider.

Edgework and risk

Studying militant antifascists is a risky business. As such, the research I conducted that is assembled in this book constitutes a form of "edgework" or "voluntary risk taking" (Lyng 1990, 855). For social science researchers, the process of edgework involves engaging in activities related to the research process that involve some element of personal risk (Ferrell and Hamm 1998a). This is particularly true for qualitative researchers of crime and deviance who seek to develop "criminological verstehen," or an understanding of the experience and meaning of criminalized activity rather than simply describe its causal variables (Ferrell 1997b; Ferrell and Hamm 1998a; Ferrell, Hayward, and Young 2008). These processes of edgework research produce a series of risks for the researcher as well as potential research subjects that must be negotiated carefully in order to ensure the safety of all parties (Hamm and Ferrell 1998). The research conducted for this book demonstrates these distinct risks and points to the methodological intersections of research into radical social movements and the critical criminological method.

In the conclusion of their edited volume on edgework in criminology, Mark Hamm and Jeff Ferrell (1998) outline five key dangers evident in the process of edgework research: legal, stigma, ethical, emotional, and physical. Legal danger consists of the risks of legal sanction that are related to engagement in the process of research. For criminologists and even radical social movement researchers, involvement with individuals and groups that violate the law presents a potential risk of criminal prosecution. Mitigating such risks requires a complex interplay of "personal survival skills" (Hamm and Ferrell 1998, 257) and cultural capital to avoid severe legal repercussions. The danger of stigma involves becoming the "the brunt of prejudice and discrimination based on stereotypical views of one's identity or group affiliation" (Hamm and Ferrell 1998, 258). In the cases described, researchers find themselves being negatively associated with the subjects of their studies and being forced to navigate processes of negative perceptions and their outcomes in the field. Additionally, researchers are similarly stigmatized by fellow scholars who view their work with skepticism at best and disdain at worst.

> [Field] researchers who share cultural space with crack 'house girls' and street gang members, who intentionally place themselves in situations of shady legality and unconventional morality, push at the very boundaries of professionally acceptable scholarly inquiry. They risk having their research denigrated on the grounds of bias, subjectivity, over-involvement, and 'overrapport.'
>
> *(Ferrell and Hamm 1998b, 4)*

Ethical danger takes the form of the conflict between a researcher's obligations as defined by codes of conduct, institutional review boards, or legal compulsions and responsibilities to the subjects of their study. These can vary from airing acts of injustice committed by public officials and criminal justice professionals whom the researcher relies on for information to acts of subterfuge designed to protect research subjects from criminal prosecution or other sanctions for their activity. The skilled researcher must attend to these concerns while also avoiding personal danger. The risk of emotional danger is manifested in the feelings that arise from the process of research which can range from exhilaration and empathy to anger and revulsion. Part of the reflexive process of research is the acknowledgment and mediation of these emotional responses. Finally, physical danger consists of the potential for injury or death as a result of engaging in research. For criminologists, such risks often reflect the very nature of the subjects of their study. Fieldwork on acts of crime and deviance places one in the situational context of violence, which must be mediated in order to avoid personal harm or additional harm for one's research subjects. By intentionally taking on the dangers described above, edge-work researchers are not only able to develop unique insights, but also push the boundaries of social scientific research.

In the process of studying antifa activists, I have come to experience each of the dangers described. As discussed in Chapter 6, militant antifascism is a criminalized form of activism. Studying antifa opens a researcher to legal sanction and scrutiny. My research subjects were informed of this danger and my legal obligation to comply with any criminal investigation as part of the consent statement for interviews. I have been fortunate not to face that legal dilemma. Because of the controversy over militant antifascism, there is a great risk of stigma associated with this research. I have already faced accusations of sympathy, bias, and worse based on public scholarship and the promotion of this book. These have been largely partisan in nature, but are likely to include the type of scholarly derision identified by Ferrell and Hamm above. The primary ethical danger of this research constitutes airing information that may harm individuals engaged in antifa activism either through criminal prosecution or fascist retribution. This is minimized through a series of strategies throughout this work. Interview subjects have been given pseudonyms and are not associated with any identifying information. Most readers will notice that this book lacks the "thick description" (Geertz 1973) of most ethnographies. This is an intentional strategy designed to obscure the individuals and events while maintaining accuracy in their description in order to avoid identifying the individuals involved. This is a crucial ethical decision designed to protect antifascists from any potential harm. The emotional and physical dangers of research into antifa activism mirror those faced by the activists themselves as discussed in Chapter 5. As an insider researcher, I have had the experience of fear of fascist violence and its potential and the exhilaration and relief of its mitigation through activism. Having "outed" myself as an insider researcher, I write this book with the distinct knowledge that I will be subject to doxing and targeted harassment campaigns as a result of the production of this work. Although the mitigation of those dangers is beyond the scope of this volume, it provides a unique opportunity for future autoethnographic and other forms of research.

As a work of edgework research, this book provides a unique contribution to informing this methodological approach. It is unique in that it acknowledges the dangers associated with the study of radical social movement activism. Social movement scholars have built fine careers on the study of historical movements and quantitative datasets of news accounts. Even in the case of those who have conducted qualitative and field research, it has generally been with non-violent movements, even militant ones. To the extent that scholars study radical social movements, they may wish to look to the field of critical criminology for methodological inspiration and to take on some risk in order to achieve the benefits of understanding.

Militant research and bias

Scholarship in the service of social change, social justice, or simply social movements is not new. Whether in the form of militant anthropology, militant ethnography, or participatory action research, academic work has often served the needs
of social movements (Chevalier and Buckles 2012; Juris 2007; Scheper-Hughes
1995). Such research is designed to advance the activities and agenda of the groups
that the researcher is affiliated with. An additional line of research involves scholarship designed to further the theoretical development of social movements
through scholarly analysis (Juris 2007; Loadenthal 2017). A final approach to
movement research applies the theoretical frameworks of social science from a
sympathetic or "partisan" position (Apoifis 2017; Green 1993; Roseneil 1993).
Inevitably, any research in the service of social movements is likely to be framed as
biased, yet the links between researchers and the subjects of their research are likely
to yield unique and highly valid results (Green 1993; Roseneil 1993).

Accusations of researcher bias are fraught with controversy. Even in the most
quantitative, positivist approaches to research, the construction of survey questions
or choice of variables for analysis is indicative of potential researcher biases. Yet,
these biases are rarely acknowledged, or even explored (Mills 1959; Young 2011).
Howard Becker (1967, 240) explained the power dynamic behind issues of bias,
"the accusation arises, in one important class of cases, when the research gives
credence, in any serious way, to the perspective of the subordinate group in some
hierarchical relationship." The relative property of bias is based on a "hierarchy of
credibility" in which individuals and institutions with legitimacy and social power
are given greater credence than those who lack such status (Becker 1967, 241).
This hierarchical dynamic manifests in apolitical and political forms based on the
relative acquiescence of the subordinate groups. In the apolitical model, there is
little contest over the perception of the subordinate group, and they do not present
an organized challenge to dominant forces in the society. In these cases, the accusation of bias against researchers occurs when they represent social dynamics from
the point of view of the subordinate group, which challenges the hierarchy of
credibility. In the political model, accusations of bias arise from "interested parties"
who are likely to take issue with the results of the research, even if they do not
arise from scholars themselves (Becker 1967, 244). Another dynamic of bias exists
when researchers are viewed as being "too close" or ideologically aligned to the
subjects of their research (Green 1993; Roseneil 1993). The validity of their data is
called into question because it is assumed that it is collected through an ideological
filter. In all such cases, accusations of bias are rarely wielded against researchers who
represent or reinforce dominant or hegemonic positions.

For anyone who has read this book, my position on militant antifascism is pretty
clear. As discussed above, this research was based on and conducted as insider
experience with antifascism. As a "partisan" or "militant" research project (Green
1993; Juris 2007), this work is designed to give voice to antifa activists through the
interview excerpts. Its analysis of culture, threat, and practices of self-defense are

meant not only to apply sociological and criminology theory to the movement, but to provide a point of departure for theoretical discussion within the movement. This work, therefore, represents an antifascist scholarship, but accusations of bias in the validity of the content of the research reflect the apolitical and political approaches described by Becker summarized above.

The apolitical form of the accusation is the product of the relative lack of credibility of both the people represented in this research and the researcher himself. Antifa activists have few supporters with formal credentials and legitimacy nor do they any official spokespeople or organizational structure to advance their perspective. Much of this is the product of the structural and movement dynamics described in this book. The potential for fascist violence means that few people go public as antifa activists. The decentralized structure of formal antifascism means that there can be no official antifa spokesperson for no one can speak for a loose network as a whole. The voices of antifascists, therefore, carry little credibility outside of the movement and its informal, often subcultural and radical network of supporters. Any attempt to give credence to their position contradicts the credible position on militant antifascism that views the use of force in countermovement activity as illegitimate. The political accusation of bias is levied from those who would utilize the criminalization frame discussed in Chapter 6. These critics who have a vested interest in the suppression of any movements on the left or a commitment to the existing model of law and order will find little in this work to reinforce their point of view; and therefore, would judge it as biased in favor of the antifascist movement that they condemn.

To these critics and potential accusations of bias, I respond with the words of Sasha Roseneil (1993, 192, emphasis in original) whose research was also informed by reflexive social movement participation, "I claim a high level of validity for my findings *because of*, not in spite of, my own involvement." This research represents an accurate depiction of the militant antifascist movement because it is written by someone with a history of participation and connection to it. As an insider researcher, I was able to access a movement that is closed to outsiders and establish, as well as maintain, a rapport and trust with its participants. The data presented in this book reflects that unique insider position and represents the voices of movement participants. In doing fieldwork with antifa activists, this study presents a clear example of edgework ethnography because of the risks associated not just with studying a militant social movement from the inside but the affiliation with it in the public eye. By taking a militant research approach, this work represents the position of movement participants with a high level of validity not likely to be achieved through the "objectivity" of scholarly distance.

The methodological approach of this research, which combines an insider and edgework approach with a militant perspective, represents not only a unique approach to the study of social movements, but also a combination of traditional sociological methods with a radical cultural and critical criminological sensibility. In doing so, this research presents a model for future studies of radical social movements as well as criminalized social practices from a critical perspective.

Works cited

Apoifis, Nicholas. 2017. *Anarchy in Athens: An Ethnography of Militancy, Emotions and Violence*. Manchester: Manchester University Press.

Ardèvol, Elisenda. 2012. "Virtual/Visual Ethnography: Methodological Crossroads at the Intersection of Visual and Internet Research." In *Advances in Visual Methodology*, edited by Sarah Pink, 74–93. Los Angeles, CA: Sage.

Becker, Howard S. 1967. "Whose Side Are We On?" *Social Problems* 14 (3): 239–247. doi:10.2307/799147.

Bennett, Andy. 2003. "The Use of Insider Knowledge in Ethnographic Research on Contemporary Youth Music Scenes." In *Researching Youth*, edited by Andy Bennett, Mark Cieslik, and Steven Miles, 186–200. New York, NY: Palgrave Macmillan.

Bray, Mark. 2017. *Antifa: The Antifascist Handbook*. Brooklyn, NY: Melville House Publishing.

Chevalier, Jacques M., and Daniel Buckles. 2012. *Participatory Action Research: Theory and Methods for Engaged Inquiry*. New York, NY: Routledge.

Creswell, John W. 1998. *Qualitative Inquiry and Research Design: Choosing Among Five Traditions*. Thousand Oaks, CA: Sage Publications.

Ehrlich, Howard J. 2002. "When Hate Groups Come to Town." *Onward*, March 1. https://onwardnewspaper.wordpress.com/volume-2-issue-4-spring-2002/when-hate-groups-come-to-town/.

Ellis, Carolyn, Tony E. Adams, and Arthur P. Bochner. 2010. "Autoethnography: An Overview." *Forum Qualitative Sozialforschung / Forum: Qualitative Social Research* 12 (1). doi:10.17169/fqs-12.1.1589.

Ferrell, Jeff. 1996. *Crimes of Style: Urban Graffiti and the Politics of Criminality*. Boston, MA: Northeastern University Press.

Ferrell, Jeff. 1997b. "Criminological *Verstehen*: Inside the Immediacy of Crime." *Justice Quarterly* 14 (1): 3–23. doi:10.1080/07418829700093201.

Ferrell, Jeff. 2001. *Tearing Down the Streets: Adventures in Urban Anarchy*. New York, NY: Palgrave.

Ferrell, Jeff, and Mark S. Hamm, eds. 1998a. *Ethnography at the Edge: Crime, Deviance, and Field Research*. Boston, MA: Northeastern University Press.

Ferrell, Jeff, and Mark S. Hamm. 1998b. "True Confessions: Crime, Deviance, and Field Research." In *Ethnography at the Edge: Crime, Deviance, and Field Research*, edited by Jeff Ferrell and Mark S. Hamm, 2–19. Boston, MA: Northeastern University Press.

Ferrell, Jeff, Keith J. Hayward, and Jock Young. 2008. *Cultural Criminology: An Invitation*. Thousand Oaks, CA: Sage Publications.

Geertz, Clifford. 1973. *The Interpretation of Cultures: Selected Essays*. New York, NY: Basic Books.

Green, Penny. 1993. "Taking Sides: Partisan Research on the 1984–1985 Miners' Strike." In *Interpreting the Field: Accounts of Ethnography*, edited by Dick Hobbs and Tim May, 99–117. Oxford: Oxford University Press.

Hamm, Mark S., and Jeff Ferrell. 1998. "Confessions of Danger and Humanity." In *Ethnography at the Edge: Crime, Deviance, and Field Research*, edited by Jeff Ferrell and Mark S. Hamm, 254–272. Boston, MA: Northeastern University Press.

Hodkinson, Paul. 2005. "'Insider Research' in the Study of Youth Cultures." *Journal of Youth Studies* 8 (2): 131–149. doi:10.1080/13676260500149238.

Juris, Jeffrey S. 2007. "Practicing Militant Ethnography with the Movement for Global Resistance in Barcelona." In *Constituent Imagination: Militant Investigations. Collective Theorization*, edited by Stevphen Shukaitis, David Graeber, and Erika Biddle, 164–176. Oakland, CA: AK Press.

Loadenthal, Michael. 2017. *The Politics of Attack: Communiqués and Insurrectionary Viole.* Manchester: Manchester University Press.

Lyng, Stephen. 1990. "Edgework: A Social Psychological Analysis of Voluntary Risk Taking." *American Journal of Sociology* 95 (4): 851–886. doi:10.1086/229379.

Merton, Robert K. 1972. "Insiders and Outsiders: A Chapter in the Sociology of Knowledge." *American Journal of Sociology* 78 (1): 9–47.

Mills, C. Wright. 1959. *The Sociological Imagination.* London: Oxford University Press.

Pink, Sarah. 2001. *Doing Visual Ethnography: Images, Media and Representation in Research.* Thousand Oaks, CA: Sage.

Pink, Sarah. 2012a. "Advances in Visual Methodology: An Introduction." In *Advances in Visual Methodology*, edited by Sarah Pink, 3–16. Los Angeles, CA: Sage.

Pink, Sarah. 2012b. "Visual Ethnography and the Internet: Visuality, Virtuality and the Spatial Turn." In *Advances in Visual Methodology*, edited by Sarah Pink, 113–130. Los Angeles, CA: Sage.

Postill, John, and Sarah Pink. 2012. "Social Media Ethnography: The Digital Researcher in a Messy Web." *Media International Australia* 145 (1): 123–134. doi:10.1177/1329878X1214500114.

Roseneil, Sasha. 1993. "Greenham Revisited: Researching My Self and My Sisters." In *Interpreting the Field: Accounts of Ethnography*, edited by Dick Hobbs and Tim May, 177–208. Oxford: Oxford University Press.

Scheper-Hughes, Nancy. 1995. "The Primacy of the Ethical." *Current Anthropology* 36 (3): 409–440. doi:10.1086/204378.

Taylor, Jodie. 2011. "The Intimate Insider: Negotiating the Ethics of Friendship When Doing Insider Research." *Qualitative Research* 11 (1): 3–22. doi:10.1177/1468794110384447.

Thornton, Sarah. 2013. *Club Cultures: Music, Media and Subcultural Capital.* Cambridge: Polity Press.

Young, Jock. 2011. *The Criminological Imagination.* Malden, MA: Polity.

APHY

ACLU. 2017. "Analyzing the Police Response to the June 4th Protests in Portland." *ACLU of Oregon.* https://www.aclu-or.org/en/news/analyzing-police-response-june-4th-protests-portland.

Aleem, Zeeshan. 2019. "Ahead of a Far-Right Rally in Portland, Trump Tweets a Warning to Antifa." *Vox.* https://www.vox.com/policy-and-politics/2019/8/17/20810221/portland-rally-donald-trump-alt-right-proud-boys-antifa-terror-organization.

Allaway, Jennifer. 2014. "#Gamergate Trolls Aren't Ethics Crusaders; They're a Hate Group." *Jezebel.* https://jezebel.com/gamergate-trolls-arent-ethics-crusaders-theyre-a-hate-1644984010.

Almeida, Paul D. 2003. "Opportunity Organizations and Threat-Induced Contention: Protest Waves in Authoritarian Settings." *American Journal of Sociology* 109 (2): 345–400. doi:10.1086/378395.

Almeida, Paul D. 2008. *Waves of Protest: Popular Struggle in El Salvador: 1925–2005.* Minneapolis, MN: University of Minnesota Press.

Almeida, Paul D. 2019. "The Role of Threat in Collective Action." In *The Wiley Blackwell Companion to Social Movements*, edited by David A. Snow, Sarah A. Soule, Hanspeter Kriesi, and Holly J. McCammon, 2nd Edition, 43–62. Hoboken, NJ: John Wiley & Sons.

Anon. 2019. "The Cider Riot Rules: One Person's May Day Account." *Idavox.* http://idavox.com/index.php/2019/05/09/the-cider-riot-rules-one-persons-may-day-account/.

Anti-Defamation League. 2017. "Behind the American Guard: Hardcore White Supremacists." *Anti-Defamation League.* https://www.adl.org/blog/behind-the-american-guard-hardcore-white-supremacists.

Anti-Defamation League. 2019a. "Murder and Extremism in the United States in 2018." *Anti-Defamation League.* https://www.adl.org/murder-and-extremism-2018.

Anti-Defamation League. 2019b. "White Supremacists Increase College Campus Recruiting Efforts for Third Straight Year." *Anti-Defamation League.* https://www.adl.org/news/press-releases/white-supremacists-increase-college-campus-recruiting-efforts-for-third.

Anti-Defamation League. 2019c. "Despite YouTube Policy Up‹ Supremacist Channels Remain." *Anti-Defamation League.* https:/ ite-youtube-policy-update-anti-semitic-white-supremacist-chann‹

Apoifis, Nicholas. 2017. *Anarchy in Athens: An Ethnography of Militanc* Manchester: Manchester University Press.

Ardèvol, Elisenda. 2012. "Virtual/Visual Ethnography: Methodolog. Intersection of Visual and Internet Research." In *Advances in Visual 1.* Sarah Pink, 74–93. Los Angeles, CA: Sage.

Arel, Dan. 2017. "New Atheism's Move from Islamophobia to White Nationalism." *The New Arab.* https://www.alaraby.co.uk/english/comment/2017/7/12/new-atheisms-move-from-islamophobia-to-white-nationalism.

Arena, Michael P., and Bruce A. Arrigo. 2000. "White Supremacist Behavior: Toward an Integrated Social Psychological Model." *Deviant Behavior* 21 (3): 213–244. doi:10.1080/016396200266243.

Arthur, John A., and Charles E. Case. 1994. "Race, Class and Support for Police Use of Force." *Crime, Law and Social Change* 21 (2): 167–182. doi:10.1007/BF01307910.

Bakunin, Mikhail A. 1970. *God and the State.* New York, NY: Dover Publications.

Barclay, Harold B. 1990. *People Without Government: An Anthropology of Anarchy.* Seattle, WA: Left Bank Books.

Barkan, Steven E. 1979. "Strategic, Tactical and Organizational Dilemmas of the Protest Movement Against Nuclear Power." *Social Problems* 27 (1): 19–37. doi:10.2307/800014.

Barkan, Steven E., and Steven F. Cohn. 1998. "Racial Prejudice and Support by Whites for Police Use of Force: A Research Note." *Justice Quarterly* 15 (4): 743–753. doi:10.1080/07418829800093971.

Barkun, Michael. 1997. *Religion and the Racist Right: The Origins of the Christian Identity Movement.* Chapel Hill, NC: University of North Carolina Press.

Barkun, Michael. 2013. *A Culture of Conspiracy Apocalyptic Visions in Contemporary America.* Berkeley, CA: University of California Press.

Becker, Howard S. 1967. "Whose Side Are We On?" *Social Problems* 14 (3): 239–247. doi:10.2307/799147.

Beamish, Thomas D., and Amy J. Luebbers. 2009. "Alliance Building across Social Movements: Bridging Difference in a Peace and Justice Coalition." *Social Problems* 56 (4): 647–676. doi:10.1525/sp.2009.56.4.647.

Beinart, Peter. 2017. "The Rise of the Violent Left." *The Atlantic*, September. https://www.theatlantic.com/magazine/archive/2017/09/the-rise-of-the-violent-left/534192/.

Belew, Kathleen. 2018. *Bring the War Home: The White Power Movement and Paramilitary America.* Cambridge, MA: Harvard University Press.

Benderev, Chris. 2018. "Police Declare a Riot After Far-Right and Antifa Groups Clash in Portland, Ore." *NPR.* https://www.npr.org/2018/07/01/625095869/police-declare-a-riot-after-far-right-and-antifa-groups-clash-in-portland.

Benford, Robert D., and David A. Snow. 2000. "Framing Processes and Social Movements: An Overview and Assessment." *Annual Review of Sociology* 26 (1): 611–639.

Bennett, Andy. 1999. "Subcultures or Neo-Tribes? Rethinking the Relationship between Youth, Style and Musical Taste." *Sociology* 33 (3): 599–617. doi:10.1177/S0038038599000371.

Bennett, Andy. 2003. "The Use of Insider Knowledge in Ethnographic Research on Contemporary Youth Music Scenes." In *Researching Youth*, edited by Andy Bennett, Mark Cieslik, and Steven Miles, 186–200. New York, NY: Palgrave Macmillan.

Bennett, Andy. 2011. "The Post-Subcultural Turn: Some Reflections 10 Years On." *Journal of Youth Studies* 14 (5): 493–506. doi:10.1080/13676261.2011.559216.

ett, Andy, and Richard A. Peterson. 2004. *Music Scenes: Local, Translocal and Virtual.* Nashville, TN: Vanderbilt University Press.

Berbrier, Mitch. 1998. "White Supremacists and the (Pan)-Ethnic Imperative: On 'European-Americans' and 'White Student Unions.'" *Sociological Inquiry* 68 (4): 498–516.

Berbrier, Mitch. 1999. "Impression Management for the Thinking Racist: A Case Study of Intellectualization as Stigma Transformation in Contemporary White Supremacist Discourse." *The Sociological Quarterly* 40 (3): 411–433.

Berbrier, Mitch. 2000. "The Victim Ideology of White Supremacists and White Separatists in the United States." *Sociological Focus* 33 (2): 175–191.

Berlet, Chip. 1992. "Fascism!" *Political Research Associates.* https://www.politicalresearch.org/1992/09/28/fascism.

Berlet, Chip. 2004a. "Mapping the Political Right: Gender and Race Oppression in Right-Wing Movements." In *Home-Grown Hate: Gender and Organized Racism*, edited by Abby L. Ferber, 19–48. New York: Routledge.

Berlet, Chip. 2004b. "Christian Identity: The Apocalyptic Style, Political Religion, Palingenesis and Neo-Fascism." *Totalitarian Movements & Political Religions* 5 (3): 469–506. doi:10.1080/1469076042000312221.

Berlet, Chip, and Mathew N. Lyons. 2000. *Right-Wing Populism in America: Too Close for Comfort.* New York, NY: Guilford Press.

Berlet, Chip, and Stanislav Vysotsky. 2006. "Overview of US White Supremacist Groups." *Journal of Political and Military Sociology* 34 (1): 11.

Biehl, Janet, and Peter Staudenmaier. 1995. *Ecofascism: Lessons from the German Experience.* Edinburgh: AK Press.

Berninger, Dieter George. 1988. "Milwaukee's German-American Community and the Nazi Challenge of the 1930's." *Wisconsin Magazine of History* 71 (2): 118–142.

Bernstein, Arnie. 2014. *Swastika Nation: Fritz Kuhn and the Rise and Fall of the German-American Bund.* New York, NY: Picador.

Bernstein, Maxine. 2010. "Anti-Racist Group Argues Shooting of Portland Man Was a Neo-Nazi Attack." *OregonLive.com*, April 2. www.oregonlive.com/portland/index.ssf/2010/04/anti-racist_group_argues_shoot.html.

Black, Donald. 1983. "Crime as Social Control." *American Sociological Review* 48 (1): 34–45. doi:10.2307/2095143.

Black, Donald. 2004. "Violent Structures." In *Violence: From Theory to Research*, edited by Margaret A. Zahn, Henry H. Brownstein, and Shelly L. Jackson, 145–158. Newark, NJ: LexisNexis Anderson Publishers.

Blazak, Randy. 2001. "White Boys to Terrorist Men: Target Recruitment of Nazi Skinheads." *American Behavioral Scientist* 44 (6): 982–1000.

Blee, Kathleen M. 2003. *Inside Organized Racism: Women in the Hate Movement.* Berkeley, CA: University of California Press.

Bonilla-Silva, Eduardo. 2018. *Racism without Racists: Color-Blind Racism and the Persistence of Racial Inequality in America.* Lanham, MD: Rowman & Littlefield.

Borgeson, Kevin, and Robin Valeri. 2004. "Faces of Hate." *Journal of Applied Sociology* 21 (2): 99–111.

Bourne, Kylie. 2011. "Commanding and Controlling Protest Crowds." *Critical Horizons* 12 (2): 189–210. doi:10.1558/crit.v12i2.189.

Bowen, Derek. 2008. *"Patterns of Skinhead Violence."* Ph.D. Dissertation, Durham, NH: University of New Hampshire.

Boykoff, Jules. 2006. "Framing Dissent: Mass-Media Coverage of the Global Justice Movement." *New Political Science* 28 (2): 201–228. doi:10.1080/07393140600679967.

Bray, Mark. 2017. *Antifa: The Antifascist Handbook*. Brooklyn, NY: Melville House Publishing.

Brazil, Ben. 2017. "Violence Breaks out at Pro-Trump Rally in Huntington Beach." *Los Angeles Times*, March 25. https://www.latimes.com/socal/daily-pilot/news/tn-dpt-me-0326-maga-march-20170325-story.html.

Breines, Wini. 1989. *Community and Organization in the New Left, 1962–1968: The Great Refusal*. New Brunswick, NJ: Rutgers University Press.

Burghart, Devin. 1999. *Soundtracks to the White Revolution: White Supremacist Assaults on Youth Subcultures*. Chicago, IL: Center for New Community.

Burley, Shane. 2017. *Fascism Today – What It Is and How to End It*. Chico, CA: AK Press.

Burley, Shane. 2018. "*How White Nationalists Hide in Academia*." www.truth-out.org/news/item/43117-how-white-nationalists-hide-in-academia.

Burley, Shane. 2019. "Patriot Prayer Is Building a Violent Movement in Portland." *Salon*. https://www.salon.com/2019/07/04/patriot-prayer-is-building-a-violent-movem ent-in-portland_partner/.

Burris, Val, Emery Smith, and Ann Strahm. 2000. "White Supremacist Networks on the Internet." *Sociological Focus* 33 (2): 215–235.

Caffier, Justin. 2017. "Get to Know the Memes of the Alt-Right and Never Miss a Dog-Whistle Again." *Vice*. https://www.vice.com/en_us/article/ezagwm/get-to-know-the-m emes-of-the-alt-right-and-never-miss-a-dog-whistle-again.

Cai, Weiyi, Troy Griggs, Jason Kao, Juliette Love, and Joe Ward. 2019. "White Extremist Ideology Drives Many Deadly Shootings." *The New York Times*, August 4, sec. U.S. http s://www.nytimes.com/interactive/2019/08/04/us/white-extremist-active-shooter.html.

Carroll, William K., and Robert S. Ratner. 1996. "Master Frames and Counter-Hegemony: Political Sensibilities in Contemporary Social Movements." *Canadian Review of Sociology & Anthropology* 33 (4): 407.

Castle, Tammy. 2012. "Morrigan Rising: Exploring Female-Targeted Propaganda on Hate Group Websites." *European Journal of Cultural Studies* 15 (6): 679–694. doi:10.1177/1367549412450636.

Castle, Tammy, and Meagan Chevalier. 2011. "The Women of Stormfront: An Examina-tion of White Nationalist Discussion Threads on the Internet." *The Internet Journal of Criminology*, 1–14.

Chambliss, William J. 1975. "Toward a Political Economy of Crime." *Theory and Society* 2 (1): 149–170. doi:10.1007/BF00212732.

Chevalier, Jacques M., and Daniel Buckles. 2012. *Participatory Action Research: Theory and Methods for Engaged Inquiry*. New York, NY: Routledge.

Clark, Dylan. 2003. "The Death and Life of Punk, the Last Subculture." In *The Post Sub-cultures Reader*, edited by David Muggleton and Rupert Weinzierl, 233–238. New York, NY: Berg.

Clark, J. 2018. "Three-Way Fight: Revolutionary Anti-Fascism and Armed Self-Defense." In *Setting Sights: Histories and Reflections on Community Armed Self-Defense*, edited by Scott Crow, 49–67. Oakland, CA: PM Press.

Cobb, Charles E. 2014. *This Nonviolent Stuff'll Get You Killed: How Guns Made the Civil Rights Movement Possible*. New York, NY: Basic Books.

Cohen, Albert K. 1955. *Delinquent Boys: The Culture of the Gang*. Glencoe, IL: The Free Press.

Cohen, Jean L. 1985. "Strategy or Identity: New Theoretical Paradigms and Contemporary Social Movements." *Social Research* 52 (4): 663–716.

Cohen, Stanley. 1980. *Folk Devils and Moral Panics: The Creation of the Mods and Rockers*. New York, NY: St. Martin's Press.

Copsey, Nigel. 2000. *Anti-Fascism in Britain*. New York, NY: St. Martin's Press.

Copsey, Nigel. 2018. "Militant Antifascism: An Alternative (Historical) Reading." *Society* 55 (3): 243–247. doi:10.1007/s12115-018-0245-y.

Corte, Ugo, and Bob Edwards. 2008. "White Power Music and the Mobilization of Racist Social Movements." *Music and Arts in Action* 1 (1): 4–20.

Cox, Joseph, and Jason Koebler. 2019. "Twitter Won't Treat White Supremacy Like ISIS Because It'd Have to Ban Some GOP Politicians Too." *Vice*. https://www.vice.com/en_us/article/a3xgq5/why-wont-twitter-treat-white-supremacy-like-isis-because-it-would-mean-banning-some-republican-politicians-too.

Creasap, Kimberly. 2012. "Social Movement Scenes: Place-Based Politics and Everyday Resistance." *Sociology Compass* 6 (2): 182–191. doi:10.1111/j.1751-9020.2011.00441.x.

Creasap, Kimberly. 2016. "Finding the Movement: The Geographies of Social Movement Scenes." *The International Journal of Sociology and Social Policy* 36 (11/12): 792–807.

Creswell, John W. 1998. *Qualitative Inquiry and Research Design: Choosing Among Five Traditions*. Thousand Oaks, CA: Sage Publications.

Cross, Rich. 2010. "'There Is No Authority but Yourself': The Individual and the Collective in British Anarcho-Punk." *Music and Politics* 4 (2). doi:10.3998/mp.9460447.0004.203.

Danaher, William F. 2010. "Music and Social Movements." *Sociology Compass* 4 (9): 811–823. doi:10.1111/j.1751-9020.2010.00310.x.

Daniels, Jessie. 1997. *White Lies: Race, Class, Gender, and Sexuality in White Supremacist Discourse*. New York, NY: Routledge.

Daniels, Jessie. 2009. *Cyber Racism: White Supremacy Online and the New Attack on Civil Rights*. Lanham, MD: Rowman & Littlefield.

Daschuk, Mitch Douglas. 2011. "The Significance of Artistic Criticism in the Production of Punk Subcultural Authenticity: The Case Study of Against Me!" *Journal of Youth Studies* 14 (5): 605–626. doi:10.1080/13676261.2011.559215.

Day, Richard J.F. 2005. *Gramsci Is Dead: Anarchist Currents in the Newest Social Movements*. Ann Arbor, MI: Pluto Press.

della Porta, Donatella. 1995. *Social Movements, Political Violence, and the State: A Comparative Analysis of Italy and Germany*. Cambridge: Cambridge University Press.

della Porta, Donatella. 2008. "Research on Social Movements and Political Violence." *Qualitative Sociology* 31 (3): 221–230.

Dixon, Marc. 2008. "Movements, Countermovements and Policy Adoption: The Case of Right-to-Work Activism." *Social Forces* 87 (1): 473–500. doi:10.1353/sof.0.0076.

Dobratz, Betty A. 2002. "The Role of Religion in the Collective Identity of the White Racialist Movement." *Journal for the Scientific Study of Religion* 40 (2): 287–302. doi:10.1111/0021-8294.00056.

Dobratz, Betty A., and Stephanie L. Shanks-Meile. 1997. *White Power, White Pride!: The White Separatist Movement in the United States*. New York, NY: Prentice Hall.

Dobratz, Betty A., and Lisa Waldner. 2012. "Repertoires of Contention: White Separatist Views on the Use of Violence and Leaderless Resistance." *Mobilization: An International Quarterly* 17 (1): 49–66. doi:10.17813/maiq.17.1.3282448743272632.

Earl, Jennifer. 2003. "Tanks, Tear Gas, and Taxes: Toward a Theory of Movement Repression." *Sociological Theory* 21 (1): 44–68. doi:10.1111/1467-9558.00175.

Earl, Jennifer. 2007. "The Cultural Consequences of Social Movements." In *The Blackwell Companion to Social Movements*, 508–530. Malden, MA: Wiley-Blackwell. doi:10.1002/9780470999103.ch22.

Eco, Umberto. 1995. "Ur-Fascism." *The New York Review of Books*, June 22. https://www.nybooks.com/articles/1995/06/22/ur-fascism/.

Ehrlich, Howard J. 1996. *Reinventing Anarchy, Again*. San Francisco, CA: AK Press.

Ehrlich, Howard J. 2002. "When Hate Groups Come to Town." *Onward*, March 1. https://onwardnewspaper.wordpress.com/volume-2-issue-4-spring-2002/when-hate-groups-come-to-town/.

Einwohner, Rachel L., and Thomas V. Maher. 2011. "Threat Assessment and Collective-Action Emergence: Death-Camp and Ghetto Resistance During the Holocaust." *Mobilization: An International Quarterly* 16 (2): 127–146. doi:10.17813/maiq.16.2.j263166u14286024.

Ellis, Carolyn, Tony E. Adams, and Arthur P. Bochner. 2010. "Autoethnography: An Overview." *Forum Qualitative Sozialforschung / Forum: Qualitative Social Research* 12 (1). doi:10.17169/fqs-12.1.1589.

Ellwood, Robert. 2000. "Nazism as a Millennialist Movement." In *Millennialism, Persecution, and Violence: Historical Cases*, edited by Catherine Lowman Wessinger, 241–260. Syracuse, NY: Syracuse University Press.

Emirbayer, Mustafa, and Chad Goldberg. 2005. "Pragmatism, Bourdieu, and Collective Emotions in Contentious Politics." *Theory & Society* 34 (5/6): 469–518. doi:10.1007/s11186-005-1619-x.

Ezekiel, Raphael S. 1995. *The Racist Mind: Portraits of American Neo-Nazis and Klansmen*. New York, NY: Viking.

Fantasia, Rick, and Kim Voss. 2004. *Hard Work: Remaking the American Labour Movement*. Berkeley, CA: University of California Press.

Farrell, Henry. 2018. "The 'Intellectual Dark Web,' Explained: What Jordan Peterson Has in Common with the Alt-Right." *Vox*. https://www.vox.com/the-big-idea/2018/5/10/17338290/intellectual-dark-web-rogan-peterson-harris-times-weiss.

Ferber, Abby L. 1999. *White Man Falling: Race, Gender, and White Supremacy*. Lanham, MD: Rowman & Littlefield.

Ferree, Myra Marx, and Beth B. Hess. 2000. *Controversy and Coalition: The New Feminist Movement Across Three Decades of Change*. New York, NY: Routledge.

Ferrell, Jeff. 1996. *Crimes of Style: Urban Graffiti and the Politics of Criminality*. Boston, MA: Northeastern University Press.

Ferrell, Jeff. 1997a. "Youth, Crime, and Cultural Space." *Social Justice* 24 (4): 21–38.

Ferrell, Jeff. 1997b. "Criminological *Verstehen*: Inside the Immediacy of Crime." *Justice Quarterly* 14 (1): 3–23. doi:10.1080/07418829700093201.

Ferrell, Jeff. 1998. "Against the Law: Anarchist Criminology." *Social Anarchism* 24: 5–15.

Ferrell, Jeff. 2001. *Tearing Down the Streets: Adventures in Urban Anarchy*. New York, NY: Palgrave.

Ferrell, Jeff. 2011. "Corking as Community Policing." *Contemporary Justice Review* 14 (1): 95–98. doi:10.1080/10282580.2011.541079.

Ferrell, Jeff, and Mark S. Hamm, eds. 1998a. *Ethnography at the Edge: Crime, Deviance, and Field Research*. Boston: Northeastern University Press.

Ferrell, Jeff, and Mark S. Hamm. 1998b. "True Confessions: Crime, Deviance, and Field Research." In *Ethnography at the Edge: Crime, Deviance, and Field Research*, edited by Jeff Ferrell and Mark S. Hamm, 2–19. Boston, MA: Northeastern University Press.

Ferrell, Jeff, Keith J. Hayward, and Jock Young. 2008. *Cultural Criminology: An Invitation*. Thousand Oaks, CA: Sage Publications.

Fitzgerald, Kathleen J., and Diane M. Rodgers. 2000. "Radical Social Movement Organizations: A Theoretical Model." *Sociological Quarterly* 41 (4): 573–592.

Flynn, Meagan. 2018. "Georgia Police Invoke Law Made for KKK to Arrest Anti-Racism Protesters." *Washington Post*, April 23, sec. Morning Mix. https://www.washingtonpost.com/news/morning-mix/wp/2018/04/23/georgia-police-invoke-anti-mask-law-made-for-kkk-to-arrest-racism-protesters/.

Force, William Ryan. 2011. "Consumption Styles and the Fluid Complexity of Punk Authenticity." *Symbolic Interaction* 32 (4): 289–309. doi:10.1525/si.2009.32.4.289.

Fox, Kathryn J. 1987. "Real Punks and Pretenders: The Social Organization of a Counterculture." *Journal of Contemporary Ethnography* 16 (3): 344–370. doi:10.1177/0891241687163006.

Franks, Benjamin. 2018. "Prefiguration." In *Anarchism: A Conceptual Approach*, edited by Benjamin Franks, Nathan Jun, and Leonard Williams, 28–43. New York, NY: Routledge.

Futrell, Robert, and Pete Simi. 2004. "Free Spaces, Collective Identity, and the Persistence of U.S. White Power Activism." *Social Problems* 51 (1): 16–42.

Futrell, Robert, Pete Simi, and Simon Gottschalk. 2006. "Understanding Music in Movements: The White Power Music Scene." *Sociological Quarterly* 47 (2): 275–304.

Futrelle, David. 2017. "Nazi Memelords Mock the Murder of Heather Heyer by One of Their Own." *We Hunted The Mammoth*. www.wehuntedthemammoth.com/2017/08/13/nazi-memelords-mock-the-murder-of-heather-heyer-by-one-of-their-own/.

Gale, Richard P. 1986. "Social Movements and the State: The Environmental Movement, Countermovement, and Government Agencies." *Sociological Perspectives* 29 (2): 202–240. doi:10.2307/1388959.

Gamson, William A. 2002. *Talking Politics*. New York, NY: Cambridge University Press.

Gardell, Mattias. 2003. *Gods of the Blood: The Pagan Revival and White Separatism*. Durham, NC: Duke University Press.

Garvey, John, Beth Henson, Noel Ignatiev, Adam Sabra, Russell Banks, Derrick Bell, John Bracey, et al. 1999. "Renew the Legacy of John Brown." *Race Traitor* 10: 1–2.

Gattinara, Pietro Castelli, and Andrea L.P. Pirro. 2018. "The Far Right as Social Movement." *European Societies* 21 (4): 447–462. doi:10.1080/14616696.2018.1494301.

Geertz, Clifford. 1973. *The Interpretation of Cultures: Selected Essays*. New York, NY: Basic Books.

Gerbaudo, Paolo. 2013. "Spikey Posters." *Space and Culture*, October. doi:10.1177/1206331213501127.

Gerber, Monica M., and Jonathan Jackson. 2017. "Justifying Violence: Legitimacy, Ideology and Public Support for Police Use of Force." *Psychology, Crime & Law* 23 (1): 79–95. doi:10.1080/1068316X.2016.1220556.

Gerstenfeld, Phyllis B., Diana R. Grant, and Chau-Pu Chiang. 2003. "Hate Online: A Content Analysis of Extremist Internet Sites." *Analyses of Social Issues and Public Policy* 3 (1): 29–44. doi:10.1111/j.1530-2415.2003.00013.x.

Gillham, Patrick F. 2011. "Securitizing America: Strategic Incapacitation and the Policing of Protest Since the 11 September 2001 Terrorist Attacks." *Sociology Compass* 5 (7): 636–652. doi:10.1111/j.1751-9020.2011.00394.x.

Goffman, Erving. 1959. *The Presentation of Self in Everyday Life*. New York, NY: Anchor Books.

Goldman, Emma. 1969. *Anarchism and Other Essays Emma Goldman*. New York, NY: Dover Publications.

Goldstone, Jack A., and Charles Tilly. 2001. "Threat (and Opportunity): Popular Action and State Response in the Dynamics of Contentious Action." In *Silence and Voice in the Study of Contentious Politics*, edited by Ronald R. Aminzade, Jack A. Goldstone, Doug McAdam, Elizabeth J. Perry, William H.Sewell, Jr., Sidney G. Tarrow, and Charles Tilly, 179–194. New York, NY: Cambridge University Press.

Goodman, Amy. 2017. "Cornel West & Rev. Traci Blackmon: Clergy in Charlottesville Were Trapped by Torch-Wielding Nazis." *Democracy Now!*https://www.democracynow.org/2017/8/14/cornel_west_rev_toni_blackmon_clergy.

Goodwin, Jeff, and James M. Jasper. 2004. "Trouble in Paradigms.' Movements, edited by Jeff Goodwin and James M. Jasper, 75–9 Rowman & Littlefield.

Goodwin, Jeff, James M. Jasper, and Francesca Polletta. 2001. "Introdu Matter." In Passionate Politics: Emotions and Social Movements, edit James M. Jasper, and Francesca Polletta, 1–24. Chicago, IL: University of Chicago Press.

Goodwin, Jeff, James M. Jasper, and Francesca Polletta. 2007. "Emotional Dimensions of Social Movements." In The Blackwell Companion to Social Movements, 413–432. Malden, MA: Wiley-Blackwell. doi:10.1002/9780470999103.ch18.

Goodwin, Jeff, and Steven Pfaff. 2001. "Emotion Work in High-Risk Social Movements: Managing Fear in the U.S. and East German Civil Rights Movements." In Passionate Politics: Emotions and Social Movements, edited by Jeff Goodwin, James M. Jasper, and Francesca Polletta, 282–302. Chicago, IL: University of Chicago Press.

Goodyer, Ian. 2003. "Rock against Racism: Multiculturalism and Political Mobilization, 1976–81." Immigrants & Minorities 22 (1): 44–62.

Gould, Deborah B. 2001. "Rock the Boat, Don't Rock the Boat, Baby: Ambivalence and the Emergence of Militant AIDS Activism." In Passionate Politics: Emotions and Social Movements, edited by Jeff Goodwin, James M. Jasper, and Francesca Polletta, 135–157. Chicago, IL: University of Chicago Press.

Gould, Deborah B. 2009. Moving Politics: Emotion and Act Up's Fight Against AIDS. Chicago, IL: University of Chicago Press.

Graeber, David. 2002. "The New Anarchists." New Left Review 13: 61–73.

Green, Donald P., Dara Z. Strolovitch, and Janelle S. Wong. 1998. "Defended Neighbor-hoods, Integration, and Racially Motivated Crime." American Journal of Sociology 104 (2): 372–403. doi:10.1086/210042.

Green, Penny. 1993. "Taking Sides: Partisan Research on the 1984–1985 Miners' Strike." In Interpreting the Field: Accounts of Ethnography, edited by Dick Hobbs and Tim May, 99–117. Oxford: Oxford University Press.

Griffin, Roger. 1993. The Nature of Fascism. New York, NY: Routledge.

Griffin, Roger. 2003. "From Slime Mould to Rhizome: An Introduction to the Group-uscular Right." Patterns of Prejudice 37 (1): 27. doi:10.1080/0031322022000054321.

Guérin, Daniel. 1970. Anarchism: From Theory to Practice. New York, NY: Monthly Review Press.

Gupta, Arun. 2019. "Portland's Andy Ngo Is the Most Dangerous Grifter in America." Jacobin. https://jacobinmag.com/2019/08/andy-ngo-right-wing-antifa-protest-portland-bigotry.

Guynn, Jessica. 2019. "Facebook While Black: Users Call It Getting 'Zucked,' Say Talking About Racism Is Censored as Hate Speech." USA Today, April 24. https://www.usatoday.com/story/news/2019/04/24/facebook-while-black-zucked-users-say-they-get-blocked-racism-discussion/2859593002/.

Haenfler, Ross. 2014. Subcultures the Basics. New York, NY: Routledge.

Haenfler, Ross, Brett Johnson, and Ellis Jones. 2012. "Lifestyle Movements: Exploring the Intersection of Lifestyle and Social Movements." Social Movement Studies 11 (1): 1–20.

Hall, Stuart, and Tony Jefferson. 1976. Resistance through Rituals: Youth Subcultures in Post-War Britain. Abingdon: Routledge.

Hamerquist, Don. 2002. "Fascism and Anti-Fascism." In Confronting Fascism: Discussion Documents for a Militant Movement, edited by Anti Racist Action. Chicago and Montreal: Kersplebedeb.

Hamm, Mark S. 1993. American Skinheads: The Criminology and Control of Hate Crime. Westport, CT: Praeger.

Hamm, Mark S., and Jeff Ferrell. 1998. "Confessions of Danger and Humanity." In *Ethnography at the Edge: Crime, Deviance, and Field Research*, edited by Jeff Ferrell and Mark S. Hamm, 254–272. Boston, MA: Northeastern University Press.

Hart, Stephen. 1996. "The Cultural Dimension of Social Movements: A Theoretical Reassessment and Literature Review." *Sociology of Religion* 57 (1): 87.

Hatewatch. 2017. "White Nationalist Flyering on American College Campuses." *Southern Poverty Law Center*. https://www.splcenter.org/hatewatch/2017/10/17/white-nationalist-flyering-american-college-campuses.

Hauser, Christine, and Julia Jacobs. 2018. "Three Men Sentenced to Prison for Violence at Charlottesville Rally." *The New York Times*, August 25, sec. U.S. https://www.nytimes.com/2018/08/23/us/kkk-charlottesville-richard-preston.html.

Hayden, Michael Edison. 2019. "Far-Right Extremists Are Calling for Terrorism on the Messaging App Telegram." *Southern Poverty Law Center*. https://www.splcenter.org/hatewatch/2019/06/27/far-right-extremists-are-calling-terrorism-messaging-app-telegram.

Hebdige, Dick. 1979. *Subculture: The Meaning of Style*. New York, NY: Routledge.

Hegghammer, Thomas. 2017. "Introduction: What Is Jihadi Culture and Why Should We Study It?" In *Jihadi Culture: The Art and Social Practices of Militant Islamists*, edited by Thomas Hegghammer, 1–21. New York, NY: Cambridge University Press.

Hern, Alex. 2019. "Facebook Ban on White Nationalism Too Narrow, Say Auditors." *The Guardian*, July 1, sec. Technology. https://www.theguardian.com/technology/2019/jul/01/facebook-ban-on-white-nationalism-too-narrow-say-auditors.

Hesse, Monica, and Dan Zak. 2016. "Does This Haircut Make Me Look Like a Nazi?" *Washington Post*, November 30, sec. Arts and Entertainment. https://www.washingtonpost.com/news/arts-and-entertainment/wp/2016/11/30/does-this-haircut-make-me-look-like-a-nazi/.

Hill, Lance. 2004. *The Deacons for Defense: Armed Resistance and the Civil Rights Movement*. Chapel Hill, NC: University of North Carolina Press.

Hodkinson, Paul. 2005. "'Insider Research' in the Study of Youth Cultures." *Journal of Youth Studies* 8 (2): 131–149. doi:10.1080/13676260500149238.

Hodkinson, Paul, and Wolfgang Deicke. 2009. *Youth Cultures: Scenes, Subcultures and Tribes*. New York, NY: Routledge.

Hunt, Elle. 2017. "Pepe the Frog Creator Kills Off Internet Meme Co-Opted by White Supremacists." *The Guardian*, May 8, sec. World News. https://www.theguardian.com/world/2017/may/08/pepe-the-frog-creator-kills-off-internet-meme-co-opted-by-white-supremacists.

Iganski, Paul. 2001. "Hate Crimes Hurt More." *American Behavioral Scientist* 45 (4): 626–638. doi:10.1177/0002764201045004006.

Jasper, James M. 1997. *The Art of Moral Protest: Culture, Biography, and Creativity in Social Movements*. Chicago, IL: University of Chicago Press.

Jasper, James M. 1998. "The Emotions of Protest: Affective and Reactive Emotions in and around Social Movements." *Sociological Forum* 13 (3): 397.

Jasper, James M. 2010. "Social Movement Theory Today: Toward a Theory of Action?" *Sociology Compass* 4 (11): 965–976. doi:10.1111/j.1751-9020.2010.00329.x.

Jenkins, J. Craig. 1983. "Resource Mobilization Theory and the Study of Social Movements." *Annual Review of Sociology* 9: 527–553.

Jennings, M. Kent, and Ellen Ann Andersen. 1996. "Support for Confrontational Tactics among AIDS Activists: A Study of Intra-Movement Divisions." *American Journal of Political Science* 40 (2): 311–334. doi:10.2307/2111626.

Jeppesen, Sandra. 2018. "DIY." In *Anarchism: A Conceptual Approach*, edited by Benjamin Franks, Nathan Jun, and Leonard Williams, 203–218. New York, NY: Routledge.

Johnson, Erik W., and Scott Frickel. 2011. "Ecological Threat a. National Environmental Movement Organizations, 1962–1998 305–329. doi:10.1525/sp.2011.58.3.305.

Johnston, Hank. 2009. "Protest Cultures: Performances, Artifacts, an Social Movements, and Protest, edited by Hank Johnston, 3–29. Bur.

Johnston, Hank, Enrique Laraña, and Joseph R. Gusfield. 1994. "Idei New Social Movements." In New Social Movements: From Ideology Enrique Laraña, Hank Johnston, and Joseph R. Gusfield, 3–35. Phil. ...ia, PA: Temple University Press.

Juris, Jeffrey S. 2007. "Practicing Militant Ethnography with the Movement for Global Resistance in Barcelona." In Constituent Imagination: Militant Investigations. Collective Theorization, edited by Stevphen Shukaitis, David Graeber, and Erika Biddle, 164–176. Oakland, CA: AK Press.

Kilberg, Joshua. 2012. "A Basic Model Explaining Terrorist Group Organizational Structure." Studies in Conflict & Terrorism 35 (11): 810–830. doi:10.1080/1057610X.2012.720240.

King, Mike. 2013. "Disruption Is Not Permitted: The Policing and Social Control of Occupy Oakland." Critical Criminology 21 (4): 463–475. doi:10.1007/s10612-013-9198-z.

Knox, Liam. 2019. "Recently Released Records Show Portland Police Bureau Targeted Counter-Protesters, Ignored Armed Alt-Right Demonstrators at 'Patriot Prayer' Rally." MuckRock. https://www.muckrock.com/news/archives/2019/apr/24/pbb-patriot-prayer-logs/.

Kornhauser, William. 1959. The Politics of Mass Society. New Brunswick, NJ: Transaction.

Kriesi, Hanspeter, Ruud Koopmans, Jan Willem Duyvendak, and Marco G. Guigni. 1995. New Social Movements in Western Europe: A Comparative Analysis. Minneapolis, MN: University of Minnesota Press.

Kropotkin, Peter. 1904. Anarchism: Its Philosophy and Ideal. London: Freedom Press.

Langer, Elinor. 2003. A Hundred Little Hitlers: The Death of a Black Man, the Trial of a White Racist, and the Rise of the American Neo-Nazi Movement in America. New York, NY: Metropolitan Books.

Langman, Lauren. 2008. "Punk, Porn and Resistance: Carnivalization and the Body in Popular Culture." Current Sociology 56 (4): 657–677. doi:10.1177/0011392108090947.

Langton, Lynn, and Madeline Masucci. 2017. Hate Crime Victimization, 2004–2015. Washington, DC: Bureau of Justice Statistics. https://www.bjs.gov/index.cfm?ty=pbdetail&iid=5967.

Leach, Darcy K. 2013. "Culture and the Structure of Tyrannylessness." Sociological Quarterly 54 (2): 181–191. doi:10.1111/tsq.12014.

Leach, Darcy K., and Sebastian Haunss. 2009. "Scenes and Social Movements." In Culture, Social Movements, and Protest, edited by Hank Johnston, 255–276. Burlington, VT: Ashgate.

Lee, Elissa, and Laura Leets. 2002. "Persuasive Storytelling by Hate Groups Online Examining Its Effects on Adolescents." American Behavioral Scientist 45 (6): 927–957.

Lefkowith, Michele. 1999. "A Brief History of Skinheads." In Soundtracks to the White Revolution: White Supremacist Assaults on Youth Subcultures, edited by Devin Burghart, 41–42. Chicago, IL: Center for New Community.

Leitner, Helga, Eric Sheppard, and Kristin M. Sziarto. 2008. "The Spatialities of Contentious Politics." Transactions of the Institute of British Geographers 33 (2): 157–172.

Levin, Brian. 2002. "Cyberhate: A Legal and Historical Analysis of Extremists' Use of Computer Networks in America." American Behavioral Scientist 45 (6): 958–988. doi:10.1177/0002764202045006004.

Levin, Jack, and Jack McDevitt. 2002. Hate Crimes Revisited: America's War Against Those Who Are Different. Boulder, CO: Westview.

, Jack, and Jim Nolan. 2017. *The Violence of Hate: Understanding Harmful Forms of Bias and Bigotry.* Lanham, MD: Rowman & Littlefield.

Levin, Jack, and Gordana Rabrenovic. 2004. *Why We Hate.* Amherst, NY: Prometheus Books.

Levin, Sam. 2018. "California Police Worked with Neo-Nazis to Pursue 'anti-Racist' Activists, Documents Show." *The Guardian*, February 9, sec. World News. https://www.theguardian.com/world/2018/feb/09/california-police-white-supremacists-counter-protest.

Lewis, Rebecca. 2018. *Alternative Influence: Broadcasting the Reactionary Right on YouTube.* New York, NY: Data and Society Research Institute.

Linden, Annette, and Bert Klandermans. 2006. "Stigmatization and Repression of Extreme-Right Activism in the Netherlands." *Mobilization: An International Journal* 11 (2): 213–228.

Linnemann, Travis. 2017. "Proof of Death: Police Power and the Visual Economies of Seizure, Accumulation and Trophy." *Theoretical Criminology* 21 (1): 57–77. doi:10.1177/1362480615622533.

Lo, Clarence YH. 1982. "Countermovements and Conservative Movements in the Contemporary US." *Annual Review of Sociology*, 107–134.

Loadenthal, Michael. 2017. *The Politics of Attack: Communiqués and Insurrectionary Violence.* Manchester: Manchester University Press.

Lough, Adam Bhala. 2018. *Alt-Right: Age of Rage.* DVD. El Segundo, CA: Gravitas Ventures.

Lyng, Stephen. 1990. "Edgework: A Social Psychological Analysis of Voluntary Risk Taking." *American Journal of Sociology* 95 (4): 851–886. doi:10.1086/229379.

Lyons, Matthew N. 2017. *Ctrl-Alt-Delete: The Origins and Ideology of the Alternative Right.* Somerville, MA: Political Research Associates. https://www.politicalresearch.org/2017/01/20/ctrl-alt-delete-report-on-the-alternative-right/.

Lytvynenko, Jane, Craig Silverman, and Alex Boutilier. 2019. "White Nationalist Groups Banned by Facebook Are Still on the Platform." *BuzzFeed News.* https://www.buzzfeednews.com/article/janelytvynenko/facebook-white-nationalist-ban-evaded.

Madfis, Eric. 2014. "Triple Entitlement and Homicidal Anger: An Exploration of the Intersectional Identities of American Mass Murderers." *Men and Masculinities* 17 (1): 67–86. doi:10.1177/1097184X14523432.

Madfis, Eric, and Stanislav Vysotsky. 2020. "Exploring Subcultural Trajectories: Racist Skinhead Desistance and Countercultural Value Persistence." *Sociological Focus.*

Magaña, Maurice Rafael. 2016. "From the Barrio to the Barricades: Grafiteros, Punks, and the Remapping of Urban Space." *Social Justice* 42 (3/4): 170–183.

Maher, Thomas V. 2010. "Threat, Resistance, and Collective Action: The Cases of Sobibor, Treblinka, and Auschwitz." *American Sociological Review* 75 (2): 252–272. doi:2048/10.1177/0003122410365305.

Manne, Kate. 2018. *Down Girl: The Logic of Misogyny.* Oxford: Oxford University Press.

Marshall, George. 1994. *Spirit of '69: A Skinhead Bible.* Dunoon, UK: S.T. Publishing.

Martin, Deborah, and Byron Miller. 2003. "Space and Contentious Politics." *Mobilization: An International Quarterly* 8 (2): 143–156. doi:10.17813/maiq.8.2.m886w54361j81261.

McAdam, Doug. 1994. "Culture and Social Movements." In *New Social Movements: From Ideology to Identity*, edited by Enrique Laraña, Hank Johnston, and Joseph R. Gusfeld, 36–57. Philadelphia, PA: Temple University Press.

McAdam, Doug. 1999. *Political Process and the Development of Black Insurgency, 1930–1970.* Chicago, IL: University of Chicago Press.

McCarthy, John D., and Mayer N. Zald. 1977. "Resource Mobilization and Social Movements: A Partial Theory." *American Journal of Sociology* 82 (6): 1212–1241.

McDevitt, Jack, Jennifer M. Balboni, Susan Bennett, Joan C. Weiss, Stan Orchowsky, and Lisa Walbot. 2003. "Improving the Quality and Accuracy of Bias Crime Statistics Nationally: An Assessment of the First Ten Years of Bias Crime Data Collection." In *Hate and Bias Crime: A Reader*, edited by Barbara Perry, 77–89. New York, NY: Routledge.

McKay, George. 2004. "Subcultural Innovations in the Campaign for Nuclear Disarmament." *Peace Review* 16 (4): 429–438. doi:10.1080/1040265042000318653.

Melucci, Alaberto. 1985. "The Symbolic Challenge of Contemporary Movements." *Social Research* 52 (4): 789–816.

Merton, Robert K. 1972. "Insiders and Outsiders: A Chapter in the Sociology of Knowledge." *American Journal of Sociology* 78 (1): 9–47.

Meyer, David S., and Suzanne Staggenborg. 1996. "Movements, Countermovements, and the Structure of Political Opportunity." *American Journal of Sociology* 101 (6): 1628–1660.

Meyer, Josh. 2017. "FBI, Homeland Security Warn of More 'Antifa' Attacks." *Politico*. https://www.politico.com/story/2017/09/01/antifa-charlottesville-violence-fbi-242235.

Michael, George. 2012. *Lone Wolf Terror and the Rise of Leaderless Resistance*. Nashville, TN: Vanderbilt University Press.

Miller-Idriss, Cynthia. 2018. *The Extreme Gone Mainstream: Commercialization and Far Right Youth Culture in Germany*. Princeton, NJ: Princeton University Press.

Miller-Idriss, Cynthia. 2019. "Selling Extremism: Nationalist Streetwear and the Rise of the Far Right." *CNN Style*. https://www.cnn.com/style/article/right-wing-fashion-streetwear/index.html.

Mills, C. Wright. 1959. *The Sociological Imagination*. London: Oxford University Press.

Mooney, Patrick H., and Scott A. Hunt. 1996. "A Repertoire of Interpretations: Master Frames and Ideological Continuity in U.S. Agrarian Mobilization." *The Sociological Quarterly* 37 (1): 177–197.

Moore, Mark H., and George L. Kelling. 1983. "'To Serve and Protect': Learning from Police History." *Public Interest* 70: 49–65.

Moore, Ryan, and Michael Roberts. 2009. "Do-It-Yourself Mobilization: Punk and Social Movements." *Mobilization: An International Journal* 14 (3): 273–291.

Morrison, Daniel R., and Larry W. Isaac. 2012. "Insurgent Images: Genre Selection and Visual Frame Amplification in IWW Cartoon Art." *Social Movement Studies* 11 (1): 61–78. doi:10.1080/14742837.2012.640530.

Moskos, Peter. 2008. *Cop in the Hood: My Year Policing Baltimore's Eastern District*. Princeton, NJ: Princeton University Press.

Mottl, Tahi L. 1980. "The Analysis of Countermovements." *Social Problems* 27 (5): 620–635. doi:10.2307/800200.

Moynihan, Colin, and Ali Winston. 2018. "Far-Right Proud Boys Reeling After Arrests and Scrutiny." *The New York Times*, December 23, sec. New York. https://www.nytimes.com/2018/12/23/nyregion/gavin-mcinnes-proud-boys-nypd.html.

Muggleton, David. 2000. *Inside Subculture the Postmodern Meaning of Style*. New York, NY: Berg.

Muggleton, David, and Rupert Weinzierl. 2003. *The Post-Subcultures Reader*. New York, NY: Berg.

Nagle, Angela. 2017. *Kill All Normies: The Online Culture Wars from Tumblr and 4chan to the Alt-Right and Trump*. Washington, DC: Zero Books.

Neiwert, David. 2009. *The Eliminationists: How Hate Talk Radicalized the American Right*. Sausalito, CA: PoliPoint Press.

Neiwert, David. 2017. *Alt-America: The Rise of the Radical Right in the Age of Trump*. New York, NY: Verso.

Neiwert, David. 2018a. "Freedom to Bash Heads." *The Baffler.* https://thebaffler.com/latest/freedom-to-bash-heads-niewert.

Neiwert, David. 2018b. "Is that an OK Sign? A White Power Symbol? Or Just a Right-Wing Troll?" *Southern Poverty Law Center – Hatewatch*, September 18. https://www.splcenter.org/hatewatch/2018/09/18/ok-sign-white-power-symbol-or-just-right-wing-troll.

Neiwert, David. 2019. "Twitter Suspended My Account for Posting the Cover of My Book About the Radical Right." *Daily Kos.* https://www.dailykos.com/story/2019/6/11/1864093/-Twitter-suspended-my-account-for-posting-the-cover-of-my-book-about-the-radical-right.

Niman, Michael I. 2011. "The Shanti Sena 'Peace Center' and the Non-Policing of an Anarchist Temporary Autonomous Zone: Rainbow Family Peacekeeping Strategies." *Contemporary Justice Review* 14 (1): 65–76. doi:10.1080/10282580.2011.541077.

Noakes, John A., Brian V. Klocke, and Patrick F. Gillham. 2005. "Whose Streets? Police and Protester Struggles over Space in Washington, DC, 29–30 September 2001." *Policing and Society* 15 (3): 235–254. doi:10.1080/10439460500168576.

NoCARA. 2017. "Piss, Kilts, and Sticks: How Violent Trump Supporters Are Merging with the Alt-Right." *Northern California Anti-Racist Action (NoCARA).* https://nocara.blackblogs.org/2017/03/16/piss-kilts-and-sticks-how-violent-trump-supporters-are-merging-with-the-alt-right/.

Novick, Michael. 1995. *White Lies White Power: The Fight Against White Supremacy and Reactionary Violence.* Monroe, ME: Common Courage Press.

O'Brien, Luke. 2019. "Twitter Still Has a White Nationalist Problem." *Huffington Post.* https://www.huffpost.com/entry/twitter-white-nationalist-problem_n_5cec4d28e4b00e036573311d.

O'Hara, Craig. 1999. *The Philosophy of Punk: More than Noise.* Edinburgh: AK Press.

Obach, Brian K. 2004. *Labor and the Environmental Movement: The Quest for Common Ground.* Cambridge, MA: MIT Press.

Offe, Claus. 1985. "New Social Movements: Challenging the Boundaries of Institutional Politics." *Social Research* 52 (4): 817–868.

Oliver, Pamela E., and Hank Johnston. 2000. "What a Good Idea! Ideologies and Frames in Social Movement Research." *Mobilization* 5 (1): 37–54.

Olson, Benjamin Hedge. 2012. "Voice of Our Blood: National Socialist Discourses in Black Metal." *Popular Music History* 6 (1): 135–149. doi:10.1558/pomh.v6i1/2.135.

Omi, Michael, and Howard Winant. 2014. *Racial Formation in the United States.* New York, NY: Routledge.

Ordóñez, Vicente. 2018. "Direct Action." In *Anarchism: A Conceptual Approach*, edited by Benjamin Franks, Nathan Jun, and Leonard Williams, 74–85. New York, NY: Routledge.

Paxton, Robert O. 2004. *The Anatomy of Fascism.* New York, NY: Alfred A. Knopf.

Peleg, Samuel. 2000. "Peace Now or Later?: Movement–Countermovement Dynamics and the Israeli Political Cleavage." *Studies in Conflict and Terrorism* 23 (4): 235–254.

Pepinsky, Harold E. 1978. "Communist Anarchism as an Alternative to the Rule of Criminal Law." *Contemporary Crises* 2 (3): 315–334. doi:10.1007/BF02741899.

Pepinsky, Harold E., and Richard Quinney. 1991. *Criminology as Peacemaking.* Bloomington, IN: Indiana University Press.

Perkins, James E., and Martin J. Bourgeois. 2006. "Perceptions of Police Use of Deadly Force." *Journal of Applied Social Psychology* 36 (1): 161–177. doi:10.1111/j.0021-9029.2006.00056.x.

Perry, Barbara. 2000. "'Button-Down Terror': The Metamorphosis of the Hate Movement." *Sociological Focus* 33 (2): 113–131.

Perry, Barbara. 2001. *In the Name of Hate: Understanding Hate Crimes*. New York, NY: Routledge.

Perry, Barbara, and Shahid Alvi. 2012. "'We Are All Vulnerable': The in Terrorem Effects of Hate Crimes." *International Review of Victimology* 18 (1): 57–71. doi:10.1177/0269758011422475.

Phoenix, Tae. 2019. "Ban Antifa? I've Met Golden Retrievers Who Scared Me More." *Newsweek*. https://www.newsweek.com/ban-antifa-cruz-cassidy-golden-retrievers-1451271.

Pieslak, Jonathan R. 2015. *Radicalism and Music: An Introduction to the Music Cultures of Al-Qa'ida, Racist Skinheads, Christian-Affiliated Radicals, and Eco-Animal Rights Militants*. Middletown, CT: Wesleyan University Press.

Pink, Sarah. 2001. *Doing Visual Ethnography: Images, Media and Representation in Research*. Thousand Oaks, CA: Sage.

Pink, Sarah. 2012a. "Advances in Visual Methodology: An Introduction." In *Advances in Visual Methodology*, edited by Sarah Pink, 3–16. Los Angeles, CA: Sage.

Pink, Sarah. 2012b. "Visual Ethnography and the Internet: Visuality, Virtuality and the Spatial Turn." In *Advances in Visual Methodology*, edited by Sarah Pink, 113–130. Los Angeles, CA: Sage.

Polhemus, Ted. 1997. "In the Supermarket of Style." In *The Clubcultures Reader*, edited by Steve Redhead, Derek Wynne, and Justin O'Connor, 130–133. Malden, MA: Blackwell.

Polletta, Francesca. 1999. "'Free Spaces' in Collective Action." *Theory & Society* 28 (1): 1.

Polletta, Francesca. 2007. *Freedom Is an Endless Meeting: Democracy in American Social Movements*. Chicago, IL: University of Chicago Press.

Porter, Tom. 2017. "Berkeley's Mayor Wants Antifa to Be Classified as a Gang." *Newsweek*. https://www.newsweek.com/berkeley-mayor-calls-antifa-be-classified-crime-gang-after-clashes-sunday-656286.

Postill, John, and Sarah Pink. 2012. "Social Media Ethnography: The Digital Researcher in a Messy Web." *Media International Australia* 145 (1): 123–134. doi:10.1177/1329878X1214500114.

Pyrooz, David C., and James A. Densley. 2018. "On Public Protest, Violence, and Street Gangs." *Society* 55 (3): 229–236. doi:10.1007/s12115-018-0242-1.

Quinney, Richard. 1974. *Critique of Legal Order; Crime Control in Capitalist Society*. Boston, MA: Little and Brown.

Reed, T.V. 2005. *The Art of Protest: Culture and Activism from the Civil Rights Movement to the Streets of Seattle*. Minneapolis: University of Minnesota Press.

Rimel, Logan. 2017. "My 'Nonviolent' Stance Was Met With Heavily Armed Men." *Radical Discipleship*. https://radicaldiscipleship.net/2017/08/23/my-nonviolent-stance-was-met-with-heavily-armed-men/.

Renton, Dave. 1998. *The Attempted Revival of British Fascism: Fascism and Anti-Fascism 1945–51*. Sheffield: University of Sheffield.

Renton, Dave. 2001. *This Rough Game: Fascism and Anti-Fascism*. Stroud: Sutton.

Ridgeway, James. 1995. *Blood in the Face: The Ku Klux Klan, Aryan Nations, Nazi Skinheads and the Rise of a New White Culture*. New York, NY: Thunder's Mouth Press.

Rivers, Damian J. 2018. "Where Is the Love? White Nationalist Discourse on Hip-Hop." In *The Sociolinguistics of Hip-Hop as Critical Conscience: Dissatisfaction and Dissent*, edited by Andrew S. Ross and Damian J. Rivers, 101–129. Cham, Switzerland: Springer International Publishing. doi:10.1007/978-3-319-59244-2_5.

Roberts, Keith A. 1978. "Toward a Generic Concept of Counter-Culture." *Sociological Focus* 11 (2): 111–126.

Roberts, Michael James, and Ryan Moore. 2009. "Peace Punks and Punks Against Racism: Resource Mobilization and Frame Construction in the Punk Movement." *Music and Arts in Action* 2 (1): 21–36.

Rochon, Thomas R., and David S. Meyer. 1997. *Coalitions & Political Movements: The Lessons of the Nuclear Freeze*. Boulder, CO: Lynne Rienner.

Rogers, Thomas. 2014. "Nipsters: The German Neo-Nazis Trying to Put a Hipper Face on Hate." *Rolling Stone*. https://www.rollingstone.com/culture/news/heil-hipster-the-young-neo-nazis-trying-to-put-a-stylish-face-on-hate-20140623.

Roose, Kevin. 2019. "The Making of a YouTube Radical." *The New York Times*, June 8, sec. Technology. https://www.nytimes.com/interactive/2019/06/08/technology/youtube-radical.html.

Rose City Antifa. 2017. "From Far-Right to Nazi – Report Back from the June 4 Stand Against Fascism." https://rosecityantifa.org/articles/report-back-june-4-2017/.

Rose City Antifa. 2018a. "Portland Stands United Against Fascism." Accessed July 18. https://rosecityantifa.org/articles/call-out-to-oppose-warriors-for-freedom-llc/.

Rose City Antifa. 2018b. "Statement on Strategy and Tactics for June 4th Rally." Accessed July 18. https://rosecityantifa.org/articles/statment-on-strategy-and-tactics-for-june-4th-rally/.

Rose City Antifa. 2019. "Statement on the Far-Right's Attempt to Criminalize Protest of Concentration Camp Deaths and Hate Groups." http://rosecityantifa.org/articles/statement-against-criminalizing-protest/.

Roseneil, Sasha. 1993. "Greenham Revisited: Researching My Self and My Sisters." In *Interpreting the Field: Accounts of Ethnography*, edited by Dick Hobbs and Tim May, 177–208. Oxford: Oxford University Press.

Ross, Alexander Reid. 2017. *Against the Fascist Creep*. Chico, CA: AK Press.

Roy, William. 2010. "How Social Movements Do Culture." *International Journal of Politics, Culture & Society* 23 (2/3): 85–98. doi:10.1007/s10767-010-9091-7.

Rushton, J. Philippe. 1997. *Race, Evolution and Behavior: A Life History Perspective*. New Brunswick, NJ: Transaction Publishers.

Salerno, Rob. 2010. "UPDATE: Anti-Racism Activist's House Firebombed." *Xtra*. https://www.dailyxtra.com/update-anti-racism-activists-house-firebombed-10670.

Sanders, Clinton, and D. Angus Vail. 2008. *Customizing the Body the Art and Culture of Tattooing*. Philadelphia, PA: Temple University Press.

Sandlin, Jennifer A., and Jamie L. Callahan. 2009. "Deviance, Dissonance, and Détournement: Culture Jammers' Use of Emotion in Consumer Resistance." *Journal of Consumer Culture* 9 (1): 79–115. doi:10.1177/1469540508099703.

Sarabia, Daniel, and Thomas E. Shriver. 2004. "Maintaining Collective Identity in a Hostile Environment: Confronting Negative Public Perception and Factional Divisions Within the Skinhead Subculture." *Sociological Spectrum* 24 (3): 267–294. doi:10.1080/02732170390258614.

Scheper-Hughes, Nancy. 1995. "The Primacy of the Ethical." *Current Anthropology* 36 (3): 409–440. doi:10.1086/204378.

Schiano, Chris. 2019. "Neo-Nazis Use Discord Chats to Promote New Zealand Copycat Shootings." *Unicorn Riot*. https://unicornriot.ninja/2019/neo-nazis-use-discord-chats-to-promote-new-zealand-copycat-shootings/.

Selk, Avi, and Michelle Ye Hee Lee. 2017. "The Berkeley Rally Aftermath: Mass Arrests, a Stabbing and Weaponized Pepsi." *Washington Post*, April 16, sec. Grade Point. https://www.washingtonpost.com/news/grade-point/wp/2017/04/16/the-berkeley-rally-aftermath-mass-arrests-a-stabbing-and-weaponized-pepsi/.

Shantz, Jeff. 2011. *Active Anarchy: Political Practice in Contemporary Movements*. Lanham, MD: Lexington Books.

Shekhovtsov, Anton. 2009. "Apoliteic Music: Neo-Folk, Martial Industrial and 'Metapolitical Fascism'." *Patterns of Prejudice* 43 (5): 431–457.

Shepherd, Katie. 2019. "Texts Between Portland Police and Patriot Pray(Gibson Show Warm Exchange." *Willamette Week.* https://www.w courts/2019/02/14/texts-between-portland-police-and-patriot-prayer-n gibson-show-warm-exchange/.

Sherr, Ian, and Daniel Van Boom. 2019. "8chan Is Struggling to Stay Onli Paso Massacre." CNET. https://www.cnet.com/news/8chan-is-struggling-to-stay-onli ne-in-wake-of-el-paso-massacre/.

Short, James F., and Lorine A. Hughes. 2018. "Antifa, Street Gangs, and the Importance of Group Processes." *Society* 55 (3): 253–255. doi:10.1007/s12115-018-0247-9.

Shriver, Thomas E., Alison E. Adams, and Stefano B. Longo. 2015. "Environmental Threats and Political Opportunities: Citizen Activism in the North Bohemian Coal Basin." *Social Forces* 94 (2): 699–722.

Simi, Pete, and Robert Futrell. 2009. "Negotiating White Power Activist Stigma." *Social Problems* 56 (1): 89–110.

Simi, Pete, and Robert Futrell. 2010. *American Swastika: Inside the White Power Movement's Hidden Spaces of Hate.* Lanham, MD: Rowman & Littlefield Publishers.

Simi, Pete, Lowell Smith, and Ann M.S. Reeser. 2008. "From Punk Kids to Public Enemy Number One." *Deviant Behavior* 29 (8): 753–774. doi:10.1080/01639620701873905.

SmithIV, Jack. 2018. "This Is Fashwave, the Suicidal Retro-Futurist Art of the Alt-Right." *Mic.* https://mic.com/articles/187379/this-is-fashwave-the-suicidal-retro-futurist-art-of-the-alt-right#.VIpHlKt84.

Snow, David A., and Robert D. Benford. 1992. "Master Frames and Cycles of Protest." In *Frontiers in Social Movement Theory,* edited by Aldon D. Morris and Carol McClurg Mueller. New Haven, CT: Yale University Press.

Sommer, Will. 2019. "Far Right Proud Boys Attempt to Menace Critic With Late-Night Threat." *The Daily Beast,* July 29, sec. Politics. https://www.thedailybeast.com/far-right-p roud-boys-attempt-to-menace-critic-with-late-night-threat.

Southern Poverty Law Center. 2019. "Richard Bertrand Spencer." *Southern Poverty Law Center.* Accessed August 27. https://www.splcenter.org/fighting-hate/extremist-files/indi vidual/richard-bertrand-spencer-0.

South Side Anti-Racist Action. 2017. "Known White Supremacist Tom Christensen Sent to Hospital by Antifa." *South Side Anti-Racist Action.* http://southsideantifa.blogspot.com/2017/05/known-white-supremacist-tom-christensen.html.

Soyer, Michaela. 2014. "'We Knew Our Time Had Come': The Dynamics of Threat and Microsocial Ties in Three Polish Ghettos Under Nazi Oppression." *Mobilization: An International Quarterly* 19 (1): 47–66. doi:10.17813/maiq.19.1.6618khh78976h112.

Spracklen, Karl, and Beverley Spracklen. 2014. "The Strange and Spooky Battle over Bats and Black Dresses: The Commodification of Whitby Goth Weekend and the Loss of a Subculture." *Tourist Studies* 14 (1): 86–102. doi:10.1177/1468797613511688.

Springer, Simon. 2014. "Human Geography without Hierarchy." *Progress in Human Geography* 38 (3): 402–419. doi:10.1177/0309132513508208.

St. John, Graham. 2004. "Counter-Tribes, Global Protest and Carnivals of Reclamation." *Peace Review* 16 (4): 421–428. doi:10.1080/1040265042000318644.

Staggenborg, Suzanne. 2015. "Event Coalitions in the Pittsburgh G20 Protests." *Sociological Quarterly* 56 (2): 386–411. doi:10.1111/tsq.12090.

Starr, Amory, Amory Starr, Luis A. Fernandez, and Christian Scholl. 2011. *Shutting Down the Streets: Political Violence and Social Control in the Global Era.* New York, NY: New York University Press.

Stock, Catherine MacNicol. 1997. *Rural Radicals from Bacon's Rebellion to the Oklahoma City Bombing.* New York, NY: Penguin Books.

Straw, Will. 1991. "Systems of Articulation, Logics of Change: Communities and Scenes in Popular Music." *Cultural Studies* 5 (3): 368–388. doi:10.1080/09502389100490311.

Sturgeon, Noel. 1995. "Theorizing Movements: Direct Action and Direct Theory." In *Cultural Politics and Social Movements*, edited by Marc Darnovsky, Barbara L. Epstein, and Richard Flacks, 35–51. Philadelphia, PA: Temple University Press.

Sullivan, Dennis, and Larry Tifft. 2010. *Restorative Justice: Healing the Foundations of Our Everyday Lives.* Boulder, CO: Lynne Rienner Publishers.

Sunshine, Spencer. 2008. "Rebranding Fascism: National-Anarchists." *The Public Eye*, January 28. https://www.politicalresearch.org/2008/01/28/rebranding-fascism-national-anarchists.

Sunshine, Spencer. 2014. "The Right Hand of Occupy Wall Street." *The Public Eye*, February 24. https://www.politicalresearch.org/2014/02/23/the-right-hand-of-occupy-wall-street-from-libertarians-to-nazis-the-fact-and-fiction-of-right-wing-involvement.

Sunshine, Spencer. 2019a. "Ted Cruz's 'Antifa Are Terrorists' Resolution Seeks to Stifle the Left." *Truthout.* https://truthout.org/articles/ted-cruzs-antifa-are-terrorists-resolution-seeks-to-stifle-the-left/.

Sunshine, Spencer. 2019b. "Antifa Panic." *Battleground.Eu.* https://www.thebattleground.eu/articles/2019/08/05/antifa-panic/.

Taylor, Jodie. 2011. "The Intimate Insider: Negotiating the Ethics of Friendship When Doing Insider Research." *Qualitative Research* 11 (1): 3–22. doi:10.1177/1468794110384447.

Taylor, Verta. 1989. "Social Movement Continuity: The Women's Movement in Abeyance." *American Sociological Review* 54 (5): 761. doi:10.2307/2117752.

Templeton, Amelia. 2018. "Review Faults Portland Police for June 2017 Mass Detention of Protesters." https://www.opb.org/news/article/portland-police-protesters-detention-patriot-prayer-rally/.

Tenold, Vegas. 2018. *Everything You Love Will Burn: Inside the Rebirth of White Nationalism in America.* New York, NY: Nation Books.

Terry, Don. 1998. "Skinhead Split on Racism Is Seen in Killing of 2 Friends." *The New York Times*, August 29, sec. U.S. https://www.nytimes.com/1998/08/29/us/skinhead-split-on-racism-is-seen-in-killing-of-2-friends.html.

Testa, M. 2015. *Militant Anti-Fascism: A Hundred Years of Resistance.* Oakland, CA: AK Press.

Tester, Griff M. 2004. "Resources, Identity, and the Role of Threat: The Case of AIDS Mobilization, 1981–1986." *Research in Political Sociology* 13: 47–75.

Thomas-Peter, Hannah. 2018. "Fascist Fighters or Criminals? On the Streets with Portland's Antifa Group." *Sky News.* https://news.sky.com/story/fascist-fighters-or-criminals-on-the-streets-with-portlands-antifa-group-11217880.

Thornton, Sarah. 2013. *Club Cultures: Music, Media and Subcultural Capital.* Cambridge: Polity Press.

Tifft, Larry L. 1979. "The Coming Redefinitions of Crime: An Anarchist Perspective." *Social Problems* 26 (4): 392–402. doi:10.2307/800503.

Tifft, Larry, and Dennis Sullivan. 1980. *The Struggle to Be Human: Crime, Criminology, and Anarchism.* Sanday. UK: Cienfuegos Press.

Tilly, Charles. 1978. *From Mobilization to Revolution.* New York, NY: McGraw-Hill.

Tilly, Charles. 2000. "Spaces of Contention." *Mobilization: An International Quarterly* 5 (2): 135–159. doi:10.17813/maiq.5.2.j6321h02n200h764.

Tilly, Charles. 2003. "Contention over Space and Place." *Mobilization: An International Quarterly* 8 (2): 221–225. doi:10.17813/maiq.8.2.f1429714767152km.

Tilly, Charles. 2006. *Regimes and Repertoires.* Chicago, IL: University of Chicago Press.

Tilly, Charles, and Sidney G. Tarrow. 2006. *Contentious Politics.* Boulder, CO: Paradigm Publishers.

Torres, Phil. 2017. "How Did 'New Atheism' Slide so Far Toward the Alt-Right?" *Salon*. https://www.salon.com/2017/07/29/from-the-enlightenment-to-the-dark-ages-how-new-atheism-slid-into-the-alt-right/.

Travis, Tiffini A., and Perry Hardy. 2012. *Skinheads: A Guide to an American Subculture*. Santa Barbara, CA: Greenwood.

Unicorn Riot. 2017. "Charlottesville Violence Planned Over Discord Servers." *Unicorn Riot*. https://unicornriot.ninja/2017/charlottesville-violence-planned-discord-servers-unicorn-riot-reports/.

Unicorn Riot. 2018. "Georgia Police Used Fake News from Militia to Plan for Nazi Rally, Emails Show." *Unicorn Riot*. https://unicornriot.ninja/2018/georgia-police-used-fa ke-news-from-militia-to-plan-for-nazi-rally-emails-show/.

Valeri, Robin, and Kevin Borgeson. 2005. "Identifying the Face of Hate." *Journal of Applied Sociology* 22 (1): 91–104.

Van Dyke, Nella. 2003. "Crossing Movement Boundaries: Factors that Facilitate Coalition Protest by American College Students, 1930–1990." *Social Problems* 50 (2): 226–250. doi:10.1525/sp.2003.50.2.226.

Van Dyke, Nella, and Bryan Amos. 2017. "Social Movement Coalitions: Formation, Longevity, and Success." *Sociology Compass* 11 (7): 1–17. doi:10.1111/soc4.12489.

Van Dyke, Nella, and Sarah A. Soule. 2002. "Structural Social Change and the Mobilizing Effect of Threat: Explaining Levels of Patriot and Militia Organizing in the United States." *Social Problems* 49 (4): 497–520. doi:10.1525/sp.2002.49.4.497.

Varon, Jeremy. 2004. *Bringing the War Home: The Weather Underground, the Red Army Faction, and Revolutionary Violence in the Sixties and Seventies*. Berkeley, CA: University of California Press.

Vitale, Alex S.2017. *The End of Policing*. New York, NY: Verso.

Vysotsky, Stanislav. 2004. "*Understanding the Racist Right in the Twenty First Century: A Typology of Modern White Supremacist Organizations*." American Sociological Association Annual Meeting. San Francisco, CA.

Vysotsky, Stanislav. 2013. "The Influence of Threat on Tactical Choices of Militant Anti-Fascist Activists." *Interface: A Journal for and about Social Movements* 5 (2): 263–294.

Vysotsky, Stanislav. 2015. "The Anarchy Police: Militant Anti-Fascism as Alternative Poli-cing Practice." *Critical Criminology* 23 (3): 235–253.

Vysotsky, Stanislav. 2017. "Drawing Equivalencies Between Fascists and Anti-Fascists Is Not Just Wrong—It's Dangerous—in These Times." https://inthesetimes.com/article/20427/false-equivalency-white-supremacist-nazis-fascists-antifa-Charlottesville.

Vysotsky, Stanislav, and Dianne Dentice. 2008. "The Continuing Evolution of the White Supremacist Movement: A New Social Movement." In *Social Movements: Contemporary Perspectives*, edited by Dianne Dentice and James L. Williams, 86–97. Newcastle upon Tyne: Cambridge Scholars Publishing.

Vysotsky, Stanislav, and Eric Madfis. 2014. "Uniting the Right: Anti-Immigration, Orga-nizing, and the Legitimation of Extreme Racist Organizations." *Journal of Hate Studies* 12 (1): 129. doi:10.33972/jhs.106.

Vysotsky, Stanislav, and Adrienne L. McCarthy. 2017. "Normalizing Cyberracism: A Neu-tralization Theory Analysis." *Journal of Crime and Justice* 40 (4): 446–461. doi:10.1080/0735648X.2015.1133314.

Waldner, Lisa K., and Betty A. Dobratz. 2013. "Graffiti as a Form of Contentious Political Participation." *Sociology Compass* 7 (5): 377–389. doi:10.1111/soc4.12036.

Waller, Signe. 2002. *Love and Revolution: A Political Memoir*. Lanham, MD: Rowman & Littlefield.

Wamsley, Laurel. 2017. "White Supremacist Charged With Killing 2 in Portland, Ore., Knife Attack." *NPR.Org*. https://www.npr.org/sections/thetwo-way/2017/05/27/530351468/2-dead-1-injured-after-stabbing-in-portland-ore.

Ward, Eric K. 2017. "Skin in the Game: How Antisemitism Animates White Nationalism." *Public Eye*, June 29. https://www.politicalresearch.org/2017/06/29/skin-in-the-game-how-antisemitism-animates-white-nationalism/.

Ward, Justin. 2019. "Day of the Trope: White Nationalist Memes Thrive on Reddit's R/The_Donald." *Southern Poverty Law Center*. https://www.splcenter.org/hatewatch/2018/04/19/day-trope-white-nationalist-memes-thrive-reddits-rthedonald.

Ward, Matthew. 2013. "Mobilising 'Minutemen': Predicting Public Support for Anti-Immigration Activism in the United States." *Sociological Research Online* 18 (4): 1–18. doi:10.5153/sro.3141.

Ward, Matthew. 2017. "Opportunity, Resources, and Threat: Explaining Local Nativist Organizing in the United States." *Sociological Perspectives* 60 (3): 459–478. doi:10.1177/0731121416655994.

Weber, Max. 1949. "'Objectivity' in Social Science and Social Policy." In *Max Weber on the Methodology of the Social Sciences*, translated by Edward Albert Shils and Henry A. Finch. Glencoe, IL: Free Press.

Weber, Max. [1910] 1998. "Politics as a Vocation." In *From Max Weber: Essays in Sociology*, translated by H.H. Gerth and C. Wright Mills, 77–128. New York, NY: Routledge.

Weiß, Peter Ulrich. 2015. "Civil Society from the Underground: The Alternative Antifa Network in the GDR." *Journal of Urban History* 41 (4): 647–664. doi:10.1177/0096144215579354.

Wendling, Mark. 2018. *Alt-Right: From 4chan to the White House*. London: Pluto Press.

Wessinger, Catherine Lowman. 2000. "Introduction." In *Millennialism, Persecution, and Violence: Historical Cases*, edited by Catherine Lowman Wessinger, 3–39. Syracuse, NY: Syracuse University Press.

Williams, Dana M. 2018. "Contemporary Anarchist and Anarchistic Movements." *Sociology Compass* 12 (6): 1–17.

Williams, Dana M. 2019. "Tactics: Conceptions of Social Change, Revolution, and Anarchist Organisation." In *The Palgrave Handbook of Anarchism*, edited by Carl Levy and Matthew S. Adams, 107–123. New York, NY: Palgrave.

Williams, Dana M., and Matthew T. Lee. 2012. "Aiming to Overthrow the State (Without Using the State): Political Opportunities for Anarchist Movements." *Comparative Sociology* 11 (4): 558–593.

Williams, J. Patrick. 2006. "Authentic Identities: Straightedge Subculture, Music, and the Internet." *Journal of Contemporary Ethnography* 35 (2): 173–200. doi:10.1177/0891241605285100.

Williams, J. Patrick. 2011. *Subcultural Theory: Traditions & Concepts*. Chichester: Polity Press.

Williams, J. Patrick, and Heith Copes. 2011. "'How Edge Are You?' Constructing Authentic Identities and Subcultural Boundaries in a Straightedge Internet Forum." *Symbolic Interaction* 28 (1): 67–89. doi:10.1525/si.2005.28.1.67.

Williams, Kristian. 2015. *Our Enemies in Blue: Police and Power in America*. Oakland, CA: AK Press.

Williams, Rhys H. 2007. "The Cultural Contexts of Collective Action: Constraints, Opportunities, and the Symbolic Life of Social Movements." In *The Blackwell Companion to Social Movements*, 91–115. Malden: MA: Wiley-Blackwell. doi:10.1002/9780470999103.ch5.

Williams, Robert F. 1998. *Negroes with Guns*. Detroit, MI: Wayne State University Press.

Wilson, Jason. 2018. "Portland Far-Right Rally: Police Charge Counterprotesters with Batons Drawn." *The Guardian*, August 5, sec. US News. https://www.theguardian.com/us-news/2018/aug/04/patriot-prayer-to-carry-guns-at-portland-rally-as-fears-of-violence-rise.

Wood, Evan. 2017. "Marcus Pacheco and the Birth of Skinheads Against Racial Prejudice." *Frank151*. https://web.archive.org/web/20170501185813/http://frank151.com/marcus-pacheco-sharp.

Wood, Robert T. 1999. "The Indigenous, Nonracist Origins of the American Skinhead Subculture." *Youth & Society* 31 (2): 131–151. doi:10.1177/0044118X99031002001.

Worley, Matthew. 2017. *No Future: Punk, Politics and British Youth Culture, 1976–1984.* Cambridge: Cambridge University Press.

Yates, Luke. 2015. "Everyday Politics, Social Practices and Movement Networks: Daily Life in Barcelona's Social Centres." *British Journal of Sociology* 66 (2): 236–258. doi:10.1111/1468-4446.12101.

Yinger, J. Milton. 1960. "Contraculture and Subculture." *American Sociological Review* 25 (5): 625–635.

Young, Jock. 2011. *The Criminological Imagination.* Malden, MA: Polity.

Zald, Mayer N. 2000. "Ideologically Structured Action: An Enlarged Agenda for Social Movement Research." *Mobilization* 5 (1): 1–16.

Zald, Meyer N., and Bert Useem. 1987. "Movement and Countermovement Interaction: Mobilization, Tactics and State Involvement." In *Social Movements in an Organizational Society: Collected Essays,* edited by Meyer N. Zald and John D. McCarthy. New Brunswick, NJ: Transaction Books.

Zielinski, Alex. 2019. "Undercover in Patriot Prayer: Insights from a Vancouver Democrat Who's Been Working Against the Far-Right Group from the Inside." *Portland Mercury.* https://www.portlandmercury.com/blogtown/2019/08/26/27039560/undercover-in-patriot-prayer-insights-from-a-vancouver-democrat-whos-been-working-against-the-far-right-group-from-the-inside.

INDEX

4 chan 48, 132
8 chan 48, 63, 132

abolitionist movement 3–4
affinity group 13, 51, 58, 61, 96, 97, 152, 157, 171
alliance structures 21, 27, 58–60, 61, 134
alt-light 41, 79
alt-right 1, 39, 41, 46, 49, 76, 80, 82, 116, 120, 130
American Nazi Party 6
American Renaissance 46
anarchism 3, 17, 27, 55–6, 61, 73, 91–2, 96–97, 111, 136, 147, 154–8, 161–2, 169; anarchist criminology 17, 18–19, 147–9, 154–8, 161–2, 171; anarchist movement 3, 8, 55–7, 58–9, 90, 94, 115, 116, 120, 135, 137–8, 150, 153–4, 171
anarchist punk *also* anarcho-punk 107, 112, 123
Anti-Defamation League 87
Antifa: Chasseurs de Skins 116, 119
antifascism; definition of 1–2
Antifascist Action 110
The Antifascists (film) 119
Anti-Racist Action (ARA) 8–9, 51, 53, 55, 59, 110, 115, 133, 140, 146, 169, 176
anti-Semitism 30, 46, 48, 53, 78, 80, 128, 130, 135
apocalypticism 29, 30, 31, 33, 36, 44, 60
Aryan Brotherhood 48
Aryan Nations 44, 47; *see also* Christian Identity

Ásatrú 44, 45, 48
authoritarianism 3, 27, 29, 31–2, 33, 36, 41, 60–1, 155, 160,
autoethnography 20–1, 176, 177, 181

Battle of York 153
Berger, V. 132
Berkeley, CA 1, 60, 76, 153
bias crime 83–4, 85, 129
black bloc 118
Black Panther Party 5
Blood in the Face (film) 118
Boston, MA 9, 60
Buffy the Vampire Slayer 115
Burdi, G. 45

Cantwell, C. 117
Captain America 115
Care Bears 115
Charlottesville, VA 1, 49, 60, 76, 77, 133, 135
Christian Identity 40, 42, 44, 45, 83
Christian, J. 60, 159
Church of Satan 45
Cider Riot 154, 155
Civil Rights movement 4–5, 6,
coalitions *see* alliance structures
conspiracism 29–30, 31, 33, 35, 36, 42, 43, 44, 53, 60, 75, 80–1, 130, 135
communist movement 3, 5, 6–7, 55, 137
Communist Workers' Party 6–7, 55
countermovements 2, 10–11, 12–13, 21, 26, 49–50, 61, 71–2, 73–4, 89, 93, 97, 105,

117, 119, 122–3, 129, 136, 137, 146, 153, 158, 160, 168–9, 170, 172, 183
Creativity movement 9, 44–5, 153, 175
criminological verstehen 117, 179–80
culture jamming 115, 122

Daily Stormer 77, 95
dark web 77
Deacons for Defense 4–5
decentralization 11, 13, 28, 34, 36–7, 37, 45, 46–7, 51, 60–1, 78, 82, 97, 111, 156, 158, 161–2, 171–2, 183
decision-making process 13, 17, 20, 34, 96–7, 156–7, 162, 171–2
direct action 11, 18–19, 51, 55, 56–7, 73, 91, 92, 136, 146, 147, 154–5, 157–8
direct democracy 13, 22, 96–7, 147, 154–7, 162, 171
Discord 78
doing difference 85, 128
do-it-yourself also DIY 47, 111
doxing; by antifascists 88–9, 91, 132, 149, 169; by fascists 41, 82, 132, 150, 181
dualism 29, 30–3, 35, 37, 44, 60, 85

economic class 7–8, 9, 16, 31, 34, 35, 39, 47, 54–55, 61, 85, 110, 114, 137–8
edgework 17, 179–81, 183
emotions in social movements 2, 10–11, 19, 51, 72, 128, 130, 140, 141, 168, 170; see also threat
ethnic claims-making 29, 32, 33, 35, 48, 60, 76, 79
ethnography 17, 20–1, 117, 176–7, 179, 181, 182, 183
everyday antifascism 50, 152, 161, 171; see also informal antifascism

Facebook 79, 88, 98
fascism; creep into left-wing 35, 42, 137; definition of 27–8; master frames 29–33; movement structure 35, 36–7, 38 see also leaderless resistance
Fields, J.A. 133
formal antifascism 2, 8–10, 20–1, 27, 51, 55, 58, 60, 61, 63, 71, 88, 90, 94, 96, 113, 119, 120, 134, 139, 150, 152, 156–7, 161–2, 168, 171–2, 176–7
framing processes 18, 29–33, 88, 106, 120; criminalization frame 159–60, 162, 172, 183; protest paradigm 158–9, 162; victimization frame 80–1, 160, 162
Freedom Socialist Party 59
free space see prefigurative space

Gab 77
gamer 41, 48, 78
Gamergate 41, 82
General Defense Committee (GDC) 56, 58
gender identity; in antifascist movements 51–3, 61, 130, 134, 140, 170; in fascist movements 38–41
German American Bund 5–6
Gilley, B. 46
Golden State Skinheads 92
Greensboro massacre 6–7; see also Communist Workers' Party

Harris, D. 135
hate crime see bias crime
hatemonger 83, 129
Heimbach, M. 115
Heyer, H. 133
hipster 48
homophobia 39, 62, 130
horseshoe theory also fishhook theory 26, 137
Huntington Beach, CA 160

Identitarianism 32, 42, 80
Identity 13, 21, 22, 27, 34, 38, 61, 72–3, 74, 83, 119, 132, 134, 140, 141; construction of 16, 18, 32, 34, 38, 39–40, 85, 108–110, 119; identity politics 28, 34–5, 74; racial identity 28, 31–2, 34–5, 53, 74; social movement identity 13, 19, 28, 34–5, 61, 74, 81, 89, 90, 96, 106–7, 119; subcultural identity 16, 38, 48, 81, 90, 108–110, 114, 119, 123, 152, 169, 171
Ideology 11, 13, 15, 22, 57, 62, 72–3, 98, 106, 107, 108–109, 111–14, 123, 139–140, 170; of antifascist movement 53, 55–6, 58–60, 61, 73, 91–2, 96, 97, 111–14, 119–20, 123, 129, 131, 134, 136–8, 146, 148, 149, 154, 157, 158, 169–71, 172 see also anarchism; of fascist movement 26–7, 28, 29–49, 60–1, 82–4, 85–6, 117, 128–9, 134, 136–8, 140, 149, 154; ideologically structured action 56, 62, 85
Industrial Workers of the World also General Defense Committee (GDC) 56
informal antifascism 2, 7–8, 10, 17, 20–1, 50, 51, 61, 63, 71, 88, 90, 94, 111, 119, 124, 139, 150, 151–2, 156, 161–2, 168, 171, 176
Inglourious Basterds 115
insider research 177–9, 181, 183
Islamophobia 46, 83, 98
intellectual dark web 79; see also alt-light

intellectualization 29, 32–3, 46, 48, 60, 76
International Socialist Organization 59
internet *also* online 11, 177; antifascist use of
  87, 88–9, 115, 132; fascist use of 36–7,
  38, 41, 48, 60, 74, 75, 77–80, 81, 82,
  83, 132
Iron Front 55, 105, 112, 113

Jenkins, D.L. 54
Jewish resistance 6, 130–1, 140
John Brown 4, 7
John Brown Anti-Klan Committee
  (JBAKC) 7, 55
John Brown Gun Club 58

Ku Klux Klan 3–7, 40, 41, 42, 44, ; see also
  Christian Identity
Kuhn, F. 5–6

Las Vegas, NV 133
LaVey, A.S. 45 *see also* Church of Satan
leaderless resistance 28, 36–7, 41, 78, 82, 83
lifestyle movements 15, 81, 90, 108–9
Long, C. 135
Lynn, R. 46

mass shooting 63, 83, 85
May Day 154
McDonald, K. 46
McInnes, G. 48; *see also* Proud Boys
memes; antifascist use of 1, 115, 116–18,
  170; fascist use of 37, 46, 48, 80, 81, 98,
  129, 132
meta-politics 43, 75, 76–7, 79, 81
Metropolitan Anarchist Coordinating
  Council 56
Metzger, T. 47
Misogyny 38–9, 40–1, 48, 62, 76–77,
  80, 130
militant research 182–3
monopoly of force *also* monopoly on
  violence 17, 18, 19, 22, 91, 116, 147,
  155, 158, 160–162, 168, 172
moralistic violence 155, 158, 161

NAACP 5
National Alliance 9, 83, 153, 175
national anarchism 36, 42–3, 80
national Bolshevism 36, 43
nationalism *also* nationalist 3, 4, 27, 32, 42
National Policy Institute 46, 49
National Socialist Black Metal (NSBM) 45,
  47–8, 94,
neo-paganism 36, 42, 44, 45
new atheism 44, 45–6

Newborn, L. 133; *see also* Shersty, D.
New Century Foundation 46
New Left 6
New Orleans, LA 60
new social movements 11, 13–14, 28, 33–8,
  71–2, 80, 87, 96, 105, 107, 120
New York 5, 7–8, 160
non-militant antifascism 2, 61, 72, 86–90,
  153, 159, 168, 169, 176; as militant
  antifascism 91–2, 97, 149, 151
Northeast Antifascists 9, 114

Oi! (music) 20, 47, 112, 113, 128
One People's Project 54, 88, 89
opposing movements *see* countermovements
outing *see* doxing by antifascists

Party for Socialism and Liberation 59
paternalism 39–40, 41
Patriot Front 133; *see also* Vanguard America
Patriot Payer 60, 120, 154
Philly Antifa 114–15
Pikeville, KY 60
Populism 3, 6, 9, 28–9, 31, 32, 33, 35, 42,
  43, 55, 60, 62, 75, 135, 160
Portland, OR 1, 9, 47, 60, 76, 120, 133,
  152, 153, 154, 159, 160
prefigurative practice 15, 18–19, 22, 38, 43,
  47, 55, 61, 81, 90, 92, 96, 108–9, 119,
  140, 147, 148, 154, 155, 157, 158,
  161–2, 168, 171, 176; *see also* lifestyle
  activism
prefigurative space 15, 16, 38, 84, 109, 110,
  114, 139, 169, 171
proof of death *also* proof of life 116–118
punk 7–8, 16, 20, 26, 47, 55, 90, 94, 107,
  110–14, 119, 121–2, 123, 128, 137–8,
  139–40, 149, 150, 152, 156, 169–70

Querner, L. 133

racial holy war 45
radical social movements 10, 11–12, 22, 47,
  73, 74, 91–2
Radix Journal 77
Rahowa (band) 45
Raiders of the Lost Ark 115, 118
Reddit 79
repression 6, 18, 35, 129, 146, 155, 159; of
  antifascists 90, 146, 149, 155, 158–61,
  162, 172; of fascists 153, 161, 171
researcher bias 182–3
resistance; by social movements 4, 55, 105,
  115–16, 118, 154, 161–2, 170; by
  subcultures 7, 14–16, 81, 105–6, 107–110,

111–14, 122, 139, 140, 169–70; *see also* Jewish resistance
Resistance Records 45
riot porn 116
Rose City Antifa 9, 60, 114, 120
Rushton, J.P. 33

Sacramento, CA 59, 92
Sad But True: Ivan. In Memory of Our Friend 119
Satanism 44, 45; *see also* Church of Satan
scenes; in social movements 106–7, 119; in subcultures 16, 109, 119, 123, 171
sectors of the fascist movement 41–9, 61; criminal 48; intellectual 46; political 42–3; religious 43–46; subcultural 46–48
self-defense 3, 4–5, 6, 7, 10, 22, 131, 135, 136, 146, 151–2, 154–8, 160, 161–2, 168, 171, 172
self-management 55, 156; *see also* direct democracy
Shersty, D. 133; *see also* Newborn, L.
Skinhead 16, 26, 110, 121, 122, 123, 150, 152; anti-racist skinhead 63, 107, 110–14, 115, 122, 133, 141, 149, 150, 169; racist skinhead 7–8, 40, 42, 45, 47, 49, 83, 84, 92, 93, 128, 133, 134, 141, 149; red and anarchist skinheads 63, 107, 123, 141; Skinheads Against Racial Prejudice (SHARP) 7–8, 63, 110, 141
Snyder, G. 132
socialist movement 3, 5, 55, 59, 60, 137
Southern Poverty Law Center 41–2, 87, 91
Southside Chicago Anti-Racist Action 95
Spencer, R. 1, 46, 49, 71, 82, 115, 117, 118
spontaneous action 2, 19, 50, 61, 71, 147, 148, 150, 151–2, 154–5, 155–7, 158, 161–2, 171
stigmatized knowledge 30, 48; *see also* conspiracism
Stormfront 77, 79
Subculture; antifascism as unique 114–21, 122–3, 168; antifascist participation in 2, 7–8, 14, 19, 20, 22, 26, 50, 51, 90, 97, 110–14, 121–2, 123, 131, 138–40, 168; art 105, 111, 112, 114–18, 120–1, 122; authenticity 15–16, 63, 109–10, 169; events 20, 84, 94, 108, 111, 112, 118–19, 140, 150 151–2, 155–6; fascist participation in 26, 37–8, 41–2, 45, 46–8, 49, 63, 76, 78, 80–1, 83, 111, 129, 131,

138–40, 169, 170–1; music 8, 16, 37–8, 45, 47–8, 78, 80, 90, 94, 107, 110–14, 119, 122, 128, 150, 170; research 177–9; resistance in 14–15, 107–10, 169; self-defense 22, 149, 150, 151–2, 154, 155, 156, 157–8, 161–2, 171; in social movements 105–7; style 38, 50, 78, 80, 90, 112–14, 152, 170; subcultural space 22, 63, 128, 129, 131, 138–40, 150, 151–2, 154, 155, 156, 161–2, 170–1; theories of 14–16, 107–10; violence 84, 111, 149, 151–2, 154, 155, 170

tactics; antifascist tactics 86–97; decision-making; 13, 17, 96–7, 156–7; fascist tactics 74–86; repertoire 2, 3, 11, 21, 27, 72, 74, 86, 92, 95, 97, 168, 169, 171
Talk Radio (film) 118
Tattoos 94, 113–14, 122, 152
Taylor, J. 46
Telegram 77
threat; intensity 131–4; physical 134–6; political 136–8; spatial 138–40
three-way fight 5, 162, 169
third position 36, 42
Torch Antifa Network 9–10, 51, 53, 55, 59, 146, 169
Traditionalist Worker's Party 92
Transphobia 130
troll *also* trolling 41, 48, 76
Twitter 79, 88, 98

Unite the Right rally 49, 77, 117, 133; *see also* Charlottesville, VA

Vanguard America *see* Patriot Front
VDare 77

Weather Underground 7; *see also* New Left
White Aryan Resistance *see* Metzger, T.
white genocide 30
white supremacy 3–4, 29–33
Wonder Woman 115
Workers Viewpoint Organization *see* Communist Workers' Party
World Church of the Creator *see* Creativity movement

York, PA 153; *see also* Battle of York
YouTube 79, 98